Archaeological Ceramics

Editors
JACQUELINE S. OLIN
ALAN D. FRANKLIN

Papers presented at a seminar on Ceramics as
Archaeological Material held at the Smithsonian
Institution, Washington, D.C., and the National
Bureau of Standards, Gaithersburg, Maryland,
29 September – 1 October 1980, one of the
Smithsonian Institution / National Bureau of
Standards seminars on the Application of the
Materials and Measurement Sciences to
Archaeology and Museum Conservation organized
by Jacqueline S. Olin and Alan D. Franklin.

Smithsonian Institution Press
Washington, D.C.
1982

Cover: See Figures 1, 2, 3, 4, and 10 in Chapter 10, by M. S. Tite et al. The photomicrographs are courtesy of the Trustees of the British Museum.

This book was edited by Ruth W. Spiegel.

CONTENTS

Participants

Sergio Aburto
Universidad Nacional
  Autonoma de Mexico
Ciudad Universitaria, Mexico

Jane Adams
IIT Research Institute
10 W. 36th Street
Chicago, IL 60616

Virginia H. Adams
Brown University
Public Archaeology Laboratory
137 Waterman Street
Providence, RI 02912

Frank Asaro
Lawrence Berkeley Laboratory
1 Cyclotron Road
Berkeley, CA 94720

Michael Attas
McGill University
Chemistry Department
801 Sherbrooke Street West
Montreal, Quebec, Canada

Bradley K. Baker
Ohio Historical Society
Department of Archaeology
1982 Velma Avenue
Columbus, OH 43211

Robert Ballentine
Johns Hopkins University
Charles and 34th Street
Baltimore, MD 21218

Marilyn P. Beaudry
UCLA
Institute of Archaeology
Los Angeles, CA 90024

Philip P. Betancourt
Temple University
Department of Art History
Philadelphia, PA 19122

M. James Blackman
Smithsonian Institution
Conservation Analytical Laboratory
Washington, DC 20560

Gregory S. Byrne
N.P.S. Conservation Laboratory
Harpers Ferry Center, WVA 25425

J. W. Cahn
National Bureau of Standards
Building 223, Room A153
Washington, DC 20234

Ronald C. Carlisle
University of Pittsburgh
Department of Anthropology
31101 Forbes Quad.
Pittsburgh, PA 15260

Gary W. Carriveau
Metropolitan Museum of Art
Fifth Avenue at 82d Street
New York, NY 10028

W. T. Chase
Freer Gallery of Art
12th Street and Jefferson Drive, SW
Washington, DC 20560

S. Terry Childs
Boston University
232 Bay State Road
Boston, MA 02155

Meg Craft
Walters Art Gallery
Charles and Center Streets
Baltimore, MD 21201

Suzanne P. De Atley
Smithsonian Institution
Conservation Analytical Laboratory
Washington, DC 20560

R. David Drucker
Krueger Enterprises
24 Blackstone Street
Cambridge, MA 02139

Jonathan E. Ericson
Harvard University
Peabody Museum of Archaeology
and Ethnology
11 Divinity Avenue
Cambridge, MA 02138

Csilla Z. Felker
Smithsonian Institution
National Museum of Natural History
Washington, DC 20560

Sonja Fogle
George Washington University
7 Park Overlook Court
Bethesda, MD 20817

Alan D. Franklin
P.O. Box 39
Shepherdstown, WV 25443

Kit Franklin
American University
6510 Ridge Drive
Washington, DC 20016

Albert D. Frost
University of New Hampshire
Department of Electrical
and Computer Engineering
Kingsbury Hall
Durham, NH 03824

Martha Goodway
Smithsonian Institution
Washington, DC 20560

Barbara Hall
University of Chicago
Oriental Institute Museum
1155 East 58th Street
Chicago, IL 60637

Ron G. V. Hancock
University of Toronto
Toronto, Ontario, M5S 1A4
Canada

Garman Harbottle
Brookhaven National Laboratory
Department of Chemistry
Upton, NY 11973

Robert B. Heimann
Atomic Energy of Canada Ltd.
Whiteshell Nuclear Research Establishment
Fuel Waste Technology Branch
Pinawa, Manitoba, ROE 1LO, Canada

Ellen Herscher
3309 Cleveland Avenue, NW
Washington, DC 20008

Ellen Howe
Walters Art Gallery
Charles and Center Streets
Baltimore, MD 21201

Ann M. Johnson
HCRS-IAS
2400 South Irving
Denver, CO 80219

Paul F. Johnson
New York State College of Ceramics
Alfred University
Alfred, NY 14802

W. C. Johnson
University of Pittsburgh
Department of Anthropology
31101 Forbes Quad.
Pittsburgh, PA 15260

Robert H. Johnston
Rochester Institute of Technology
College of Fine and Applied Arts
One Lomb Memorial Drive
Rochester, NY 14623

W. D. Kingery
MIT
Room 13-4090
Cambridge, MA 02139

Carolyn G. Koehler
University of Maryland
Baltimore County
Department of Ancient Studies
5401 Wilkens Avenue
Baltimore, MD 21228

Charles C. Kolb
Pennsylvania State University
Behrend College
Department of Anthropology
Erie, PA 16563

Louana M. Lackey
American University
Department of Anthropology
Washington, DC 20016

Heather Lechtman
MIT
Room 16-401
Cambridge, MA 02139

Charlotte Lemoine
Laboratoire de Ceramologie Lyon
1 rue Raulin
Lyon 69365, France

Yannis Maniatis
Nuclear Research Center Demokritos
Aghia Paraskevi
Attiki, Greece

Marino Maggetti
Min. Petr. Institut
(Institute for Mineralogy
and Petrography)
University, Pérolles
1700 Fribourg, Switzerland

Frederick R. Matson
Pennsylvania State University
519 Carpenter Building
University Park, PA 16802

Bette Mehalko
3241 Faragut Court
Falls Church, VA 22044

George H. Myer
Temple University
Department of Geology
Philadelphia, PA 19122

Michael R. Notis
Lehigh University
Department of Metallurgy
and Materials Engineering
Bethlehem, PA 18015

Nancy Odegaard
Smithsonian Institution
Washington, DC 20560

Jacqueline S. Olin
Smithsonian Institution
Conservation Analytical Laboratory
Washington, DC 20560

Robert M. Organ
Smithsonian Institution
Conservation Analytical Laboratory
Washington, DC 20560

William O. Payne
365 E. 19th Street
Costa Mesa, CA 92627

Maurice Picon
Laboratoire de Ceramologie Lyon
1 rue Raulin
Lyon 69365, France

Prudence M. Rice
University of Florida
Department of Anthropology
1350 GPA Building
Gainesville, FL 32611

Carl R. Robbins
National Bureau of Standards
Division 565
Washington, DC 20234

Alfred Romer
St. Lawrence University
Canton, NY 13617

Carolyn L. Rose
Smithsonian Institution
NHB-361
Washington, DC 20560

Carol E. Snow
Walters Art Gallery
Charles and Center Streets
Baltimore, MD 21201

Robert L. Snyder
New York State College
of Ceramics
Alfred University
Alfred, NY 14802

Carole Stimmell
University of Toronto
Department of Anthropology
530 Brunswick Avenue
Toronto, Ontario
Canada

Donna K. Strahan
Smithsonian Institution
Anthropological Conservation Lab
4501 Oliver Street
Riverdale, MD 20840

Shelly Sturman
Walters Art Gallery
Charles and Center Streets
Baltimore, MD 21201

Charles P. Swann
Bartol Research Foundation of the Franklin Institute
University of Delaware
Newark, DE 19711

Robb Thomson
National Bureau of Standards
Washington, DC 20234

M. S. Tite
British Museum Research Laboratory
London WC1B 3DG, England

R. F. Tylecote
Institute of Archaeology, London
Yew Tree House
East Hanney, Near Wantage
Oxford OX120HT, England

Pamela Vandiver
MIT
Department of Materials Science and Engineering
Room 16–302
Cambridge, MA 02139

Terry Weisser
Walters Art Gallery
Charles and Center Streets
Baltimore, MD 21201

Elizabeth C. Wheeler
Brandeis University
294 Harvard Street
Cambridge, MA 02139

Donald S. Whitcomb
Field Museum of Natural History
Roosevelt Road at Lake Shore Drive
Chicago, IL 60605

F. Widemann
Groupe d'archéologie nucléaire
d'Orsay-Saclay (CNRS)
91406 Campus Orsay
Orsay, France

Wendell S. Williams
University of Illinois
Materials Research Laboratory
Urbana, IL 61801

Sara J. Wolf
Smithsonian Institution
Native American Training Program
Washington, DC 20560

Leo Yaffe
McGill University
Department of Chemistry
845 Sherbrooke Street West
Montreal, Quebec, Canada

John E. Yellen
National Science Foundation
Anthropology Program
Washington, DC 20550

Introduction and Summary

ALAN D. FRANKLIN
National Bureau of Standards

Introduction

The seminar on Ceramics as Archaeological Material, of which these are the proceedings, was held at the National Bureau of Standards and the Smithsonian Institution, 29 September through 1 October 1980. It was one of a continuing joint series by the Conservation Analytical Laboratory of the Smithsonian and the National Measurement Laboratory of the Bureau of Standards on the general subject of the Application of the Materials and Measurement Sciences to Archaeology and Museum Conservation.

The seminar was intended not only to develop and exemplify as much as possible the use of a materials science approach to archaeological problems, but also to show the connection between those problems and the way in which the technical studies are conducted. Although in the interest of clarity for a reading audience these proceedings are not arranged this way, the seminar was planned around, and the resulting papers do reflect, three areas of discussion: (1) physical science studies whose ultimate goal is to reveal information on ancient ceramic technologies and the organization of ceramic production or to cast light on the function of ancient ceramics; (2) studies of composition, both chemical and mineralogical, or other methods of "fingerprinting" the materials involved for the investigation of provenience, sources of raw materials, and trade or exchange patterns; and (3) standardization of the physical and chemical measurements involved.

In presenting these proceedings, the editors felt that a logical arrangement for the volume would be by material and by disciplinary approach; the table of contents reflects this. While the seminar by no means exhausted its subject matter, the editors hope that it did include some of the most significant work now going on, and that this volume will serve to stimulate and to act as a reference for interdisciplinary studies that combine the efforts of physical and archaeological scientists.

Summary

Archaeometric research involves the physical and biological sciences applied to problems in archaeology. The research must be centered around archaeologically defined questions and must produce information that advances archaeological understanding. In his paper, F. R. Matson states that "it is essential to ask the question, 'What is one trying to learn from the study of ancient pottery?'" W. D. Kingery records the need, in research on ceramics as archaeological material, to address the questions of When, Where, How, By Whom, and Why a particular ceramic was made. The Where, When, and How involve largely problems in characterization and material science study of the ceramic as a material. Study of these problems, once defined within an archaeological context, is an appropriate activity for a physical scientist or measurement specialist working closely with archaeologists. An example might be the work of a chemist who determines the elemental compositions of ceramics in an effort to define relations among them, relations that in turn might shed light on their origins or on mechanisms of trade and exchange. Another example is a materials scientist studying physical properties that in turn may give clues to the firing conditions under which the ceramic was formed.

Why and By Whom involve problems of process and function. Not only do these have a much more strongly anthropological character, but also they involve questions of ceramic technology, a familiarity with how and why ceramics have been prepared in general, and how the process interacts with the final properties. These proceedings deal mainly with the questions of When, Where, and How; however, the questions of Why and By Whom were to some extent considered in the discussions during the seminar. In a general way, it was recognized that the active participation in archaeometric research by ceramic technologists, people familiar with ceramic production processes and ceramic function, is relatively rare and should be encouraged.

Problems of Characterization and Materials Science Studies

The seminar was organized to concentrate on the physical problems of interpreting ceramics. The interpretation of material residues found at archaeological sites, however, requires the participation of other scientists, such as ethnoarchaeologists, as well. The archaeometric study of ceramic specimens involves characterizing the specimens with respect to chemical composition, physical properties, and microstructure, along with the examination of stylistic details, in order to discern with as much certainty as possible relations among the specimens. In this way it is hoped to determine the source clays from which a set of specimens was made, or determine that various sets of specimens are products of the same workshop or potter and therefore probably can be used to delineate exchange mechanisms. As Kingery's analysis suggests, the credibility of the relations deduced can be increased in a number of ways. One is to include data of very different sorts, such as chemical composition together with microstructure and stylistic detail. A second is to work with specimens of well-known provenience, thus bringing to bear as

much archaeological information as possible. A third is to quantify the observations and make the measurements as accurate as possible. This was the subject of the paper by De Atley, Blackman, and Olin, who investigated the problems involved in using electron microprobe analysis for quantitative bulk chemical analysis of ceramics. Finally, the base of the comparisons should be made as broad as possible. This last point was discussed in detail by Lemoine and Picon, who pointed out the need for a local network or data base on all the possible sources, or at least the most probable ones, when trying to locate the origins of a given ceramic. This in turn suggests the very great value of absolute measurements, or at least measurements made in all laboratories relative to the same standards, so that measurements from one laboratory are interchangeable with those of other laboratories. By this means the data base for one study by one laboratory may be expanded by using data from the others.

The paper of G. Harbottle addressed the question of standardization and interlaboratory comparison for chemical characterization by neutron activation analyses. The use of common standard reference materials by all laboratories would be ideal and may be necessary if precision levels of 5 percent or better in the concentrations of significant elements are required by the archaeological problems. In addition, joint studies by several laboratories of cases of particularly serious disagreement may be needed to achieve this level of agreement. The difficulty at the moment is that no fully certified common standards have been available. Several laboratories have created working standards, e.g., the Asaro-Perlman Pottery Standard and the six U.S. Geological Survey Rocks used by Harbottle et al. at Brookhaven, and agreement on their composition is gradually being reached. A great deal of work would be required to calibrate each laboratory's working standards with respect to a common certified standard, and the practical utility of doing so is still very much a matter of discussion. Adequate standards for other measurements are also lacking. Compendia of ceramic microstructures, especially for scanning electron microscopy, could be very valuable. An example might be the microstructure of calcite reformed by hydration and carbonation of primary calcite decomposed during the firing process. The range of useful patterns could be very large, but a trial collection of perhaps 50–100 was suggested as a test.

In a somewhat parallel vein, it is not always appreciated that all measurements contain a bit of uncertainty. Not only must the archaeologist recognize this uncertainty in the archaeometric data with which he is provided and temper his expectations and interpretations accordingly, but also the archaeometrist has a responsibility to ascertain the uncertainty and to report it with the data.

In addition to recognizing the limits of precision inherent in physical measurement, it is also necessary to recognize the limits to absolute knowledge of a given class of ceramics imposed by sampling. No given collection of pieces or sherds can ever be stated to "represent" a class of ceramics in the sense that a random sample properly selected from the total population of such sherds would. Every archaeological collection must be presumed to have some unknown bias. It is a perfectly valid procedure to compare properties of two archaeological collections using statistical tests — such as Student's t-test for means or the F-test for variances — and to conclude that at a certain confidence level the collections do not represent randomly drawn samples from the same normally distributed population. It must be kept in mind, however, that the reasons *why* they do not may always include, not that they are not drawn from the same population, but that they were not randomly drawn, owing to the uncontrollable accidents in the archaeological processes of assembling the collections. Furthermore, there is no guarantee that the population is normally distributed. Such problems were considered in the paper of Lemoine, Walker, and Picon and the ensuing discussion. The fact that the chemical analyses are usually made on only a very small specimen taken as inconspicuously as possible from the piece or sherd accentuates the problem, since ceramics are often not very homogeneous.

The firing processes used by the potter contribute to the ceramic's microstructure, but other variables as well have important effects. The role of calcium in the development of the microstructure received particular attention in this seminar, especially in the papers of Maniatis et al., Tite et al., and Stimmel et al. Tite et al. developed in detail the apparent control exercised in Greek Attic pottery and Roman terra sigillata over the porosity of both body and slip. The slip was rendered dense and impervious by the use of a noncalcareous clay, while the body was made porous and open in structure by use of a calcareous clay. Chemical analysis of the clay fractions using the electron microprobe showed some change in concentration of elements other than calcium in going from body to slip. Tite felt the calcium carbonate involved was an integral part of the clays rather than added in finely ground form, since he has found in separate experiments that finely ground calcium carbonate was ineffective in producing the open structure. The possibility was considered in the discussion that the difference in calcium content might have resulted from levigation of a single clay, with the slip being produced from the fine fraction and the body from the heavy. Harbottle and R. B. Heimann both report that this possibility is discussed in forthcoming publications.

Calcareous clays produce these open-structured high-fired ceramics even though carbon dioxide release is over before serious vitrification begins. Tite suggested that the carbon dioxide release separates the particles of the various minerals forming an open structure which is then captured by the cementing action of the vitrification.

Tite noted that the impervious nature of the slip on the Greek Attic pottery might account for the failure of the iron ions in the slips to reoxidize during the final, oxidative phase of the ancient firing schedule, whereas the iron in the porous body would reoxidize. This suggestion, which would account for the black slip on a light-colored body, first appeared as the explanation of how the black and red glazes were achieved on Attic painted vases in the book by Joseph Noble, *The Techniques of Painted Attic Pottery*, in 1965. Tite suggested that this might not be the whole story, however, since the red slip on Roman terra sigillata was observed to reduce readily, but to reoxidize only with difficulty. In noncalcareous clays, as in the slips, the iron oxides in the reduced state may form magnetite, which is difficult to oxidize, whereas in the presence of calcium, iron-bearing silicates are formed and these reoxidize readily.

Maniatis invoked exactly the same explanation to account for the difference in behavior of calcareous versus noncalcareous clays with firing in Mössbauer experiments. The noncalcareous clays appeared to form large particles of ferric oxides when fired in air, whereas the calcareous clays did not.

Stimmel et al. also use the notion of the open structure produced in fired ceramics by the presence of calcium to explain why the use of burnt shell temper in North American Indian pottery did not result in popping, even though the firing temperature apparently exceeded that at which calcium carbonate decomposes.

The determination of the firing conditions, especially temperature, was one of the major themes of the seminar. Matson pointed out that an international meeting was held in Berlin during 1977 on "Ceramic Firing Techniques and their Determination through Experimental Archaeology." Papers by Maniatis and Tite dealt with specific techniques for determining firing temperatures.

In general, two methods are used. The sherd may be examined and its properties compared to a series of similar materials fired at various temperatures. These standards form a sort of temperature scale, and the unknown's place is found along the series. Alternatively a structure-sensitive property or properties may be monitored while the sherd is reheated, and the firing temperature derived from the discontinuity observed when the original firing temperature is reached and the structure begins to change. In both cases, the firing atmosphere and firing time, or rate, can influence the results and since these conditions during the original firing are unknown, an undeterminable uncertainty is introduced. Also, changes occurring during burial can produce false estimations of the firing temperatures.

Problems of Functions and Process

A few problems involving archaeological inferences upon archaeometric data were very briefly considered in the discussion periods. These topics include the nature of firing chambers used and the variability of output from a given facility; the study of workshops in economic terms; and the historical study of the development of ceramic technology.

The uncertainty in a firing temperature as determined by either method described above appears to be at least $50°$ to $100°C$, about the same as the variation to be expected within a kiln or other firing chamber. For the purpose of distinguishing whether the pottery was fired in a bonfire or in a kiln, this present accuracy appears adequate. On the other hand, the variability within a given production facility may be of archaeological concern so that increased accuracy may be useful. At present the determination of a firing temperature is a fairly cumbersome process, and it may not be feasible to do enough specimens to make a study of variability possible.

The unfolding of the historical development of ceramic technology in a given cultural setting is of considerable archaeological interest. Development with both time and place should be amenable to study, given a broad enough area within which to work. Such studies involve familiarity with ceramic technology, its uses and functions, and its underlying science. Kingery gave as an example the fact that in the nineteenth century new refractories appeared, chemically basic in nature. It would be difficult to understand this development and how it came about without realizing that the rapidly developing steel industry needed refractories that would not decompose in contact with basic slags, as do silicate-rich, clay-based acidic refractories. Here there is an interaction of historical development with deliberate problem solving, and chemical as well as archaeological questions are involved.

Patterns of Research

A number of questions concerning the way archaeometric research is managed or done were considered. The work of Robert Snyder (*see* "The Rebirth of X-ray Powder Diffraction," *New York State College of Ceramics Technical Report*, no. 144, 1980) exemplifies the way computers are being used, or can be used, to improve vastly the quality and amount of data that can be obtained for archaeometric studies. Computers can take and process data more rapidly than the human hand, and so increase the quantity and reduce the time. Computers can make instrumental corrections and compare masses of data objectively to mathematical and statistical functions, and so increase the precision. Computers can make many repeat determinations, improving the ratio of signal strength to noise, and so improve the sensitivity. Relatively inexpensive desk-top minicomputers, with great program flexibility, are available and can often be dedicated to several experiments simultaneously, and many kinds of microprocessors exist which can be built into specific pieces of equipment. It is a reasonable guess that almost all physical measurement of any sophistication will be done in this way a very few years from now.

By its nature, archaeometry is an interdisciplinary activity. With regard to ceramics, there is need to combine the talents of archaeologists, ceramic technologists, and materials scientists drawing on chemistry, physics, and mathematics. Two sorts of collaborations can be envisaged. In one, the design and operation of the research program is carried out by a team involving such combinations, preferable always with the archaeologist at the center. In the other, because so many valuable measurements are now available that are possible only with large, expensive equipment, at least some of the research is done at large national facilities where the active collaboration of specialists in the use of the facility is necessary. The example that comes to mind is the use of chemical analysis by neutron activation. Very effective collaborative teams have been operating at a number of major research reactors. The same kind of pattern will probably have to develop around other large-scale facilities, such as various types of electron microscopes, sophisticated forms of elemental analyses using ion and electron-beam excitation, X-ray diffraction, particularly with high-intensity sources and perhaps a high-temperature capacity, and so forth.

In these interdisciplinary teams, two participants might always be necessary, one the archaeologist, whose expertise defines the problem, and the other a new specialist, expert in the interpretation of ceramic artifacts. This latter person will need a solid back-

Alan D. Franklin

ground in materials science and a good knowledge of ceramics and ceramic technology, and enough archaeology to connect the ceramic science to the archaeological problem. Training for such people scarcely exists now and clearly represents a challenge to the universities concerned with archaeological science.

The successful conduct of research of this kind, combining archaeology with materials science at an advanced level, will also require some adjustment on the part of agencies providing support for university research. It represents an application rather than a development of materials science and as such is difficult to consider as the responsibility of the materials science community. It is considerably more expensive than the archaeological community is used to, and is generally thought to be beyond the means of that community. If, however, the power of materials science is to be made available to archaeological science, some form of a *rapprochement* between these extremes will have to be made.

Methodology

1. Archaeological Ceramics and the Physical Sciences: Problem Definition and Results

FREDERICK R. MATSON
Pennsylvania State University

Ceramic archaeology has many facets, a few of which are being considered at our seminar. When I was asked to prepare a paper, it was suggested that the topic might be, "Have physical scientists been of much aid to archaeologists?" The answer today in this gathering would be a resounding *yes*. Not all archaeologists would share my enthusiastic affirmation of this position, but I hope you do. It is possible that some of you do not care whether or not we take the initiative toward increased interaction, but I suggest that single cells and ivory towers, to use two inappropriate similes, are not viable in the 1980s.

It would be appropriate to discuss the current archaeological research programs of physical scientists as evidenced by the papers presented at many meetings and in some journals within the past few years — but you are quite familiar with such materials and will contribute to them as this program proceeds. Instead, I should like to suggest some research problems that it might be interesting to consider, trace some of the steps toward our present international activities in ceramic technology, and offer suggestions for action.

Definitions

I view the term "ceramics" in the traditional way — pertaining to products of the clay and silicate industries. Therefore, not only pottery, but brick, tile, glazes, glasses, frits, enamels, pigments, plasters, and cements can and should be included in our roster of archaeological ceramic materials. The sampling and analytical techniques useful in the study of pottery are applicable to the other materials noted. Unfortunately, because of the time constraints, most of them must be ignored in this present paper.

Etymologically, the word "ceramics" pertains to "burnt stuff." Professor W. A. Oldfather, a classicist at the University of Illinois, traced the history of the word in two papers about sixty years ago. I mention this reference for the record (Oldfather 1920, 1924).

Everyone concerned with ceramic technology should have the privilege of working with clay — a temperamental but manageable material — and experiment with adding what archaeologists term "temper" to it, forming vessels and firing them, before drawing broad archaeological conclusions from analyses of ancient products. Such experience, even if very limited, would also help one do a better job in selecting samples for analysis. These statements, of course, are equally applicable to glass, glaze, cement, and other material aspects of ceramic studies. One should also be aware of regional variations in raw materials and in processing changes with time through man's ceramic history. These may be obvious statements, but they have not always been kept in mind when broad conclusions have been drawn.

Ceramic remains form a major part of many archaeological records, but do they tell us much about the people who made and used them? Could they tell us more? It is essential to ask the question, "What is one trying to learn from the study of ancient pottery?" It is not always obvious what questions should be asked when using the data provided by scientists, who should help formulate the archaeological questions. Too often, pottery and glass fragments, uncritically selected, have been studied because interesting analytical and descriptive problems were apparent and samples for study were available.

An archaeologist is trained to describe his materials accurately, in detailed records, whether these materials be architectural fragments, fallen frescoes, or potsherds. This helps explain, perhaps, the great desire to have precise descriptions in terms of physical properties as well as form and decoration. Such descriptions encourage close and accurate observations, but can be a bit misleading, resulting in over-classification. In practice, if one wishes to compare his sherds with others that have been published, he attempts to see and study the latter. When he notes the textural and color variations that can and frequently do appear on one vessel, he may become a bit skeptical at overprecise descriptions that do not include a discussion of the range observed. Decisions must of course be based on the nature of the materials being studied, and not on textbooks. When read carefully, Anna Shepard's classic volume, *Ceramics for the Archaeologist*, will make this clear with respect to the measurement and recording of physical properties of potsherds (Shepard 1956). One must be prepared to recognize the limited variability that can occur in pottery production conditioned by the available clays, aplastics, fuels, etc. Because of the conservative nature of village cultures, there is little room for innovative processes or design and form alteration as expressions of the individual potter's whims. Conformity with the norms is most important.

Early villagers in all parts of the world were dependent upon the local raw materials that were available when they produced pottery. The essential materials were clay, water, sand, and fuel. These basic materials are not unlike the ancient Chinese alchemical concept of the five elements: earth, water, wood, fire, and metal. At the village level the potter also had available ferruginous pigments and tempering materials that ranged from special sands to grog, fireplace ash, dung as a plasticizer, plant materials, asbestos, hair, even feathers, and salt water from saline springs or the sea. When making technological ceramic studies, it is well to keep in mind the possibility of local availability and variability of raw materials. Designations as foreign imports and traded items may provide too facile a solution with which to explain variants. There will also be changes with time as techniques of production improve, agricultural disturbance of the land increases, and erosion due to deforestation occurs.

Determination of Chemical and Physical Properties

Knowledge about many properties of clays, glasses, and glazes, well known to ceramic engineers, would help archaeologists and chemists understand better the pottery being studied. A few such properties might be mentioned: chemical and mineralogical composition, color development, firing temperatures, phase relationships and development, the roles of alkalies and lime in ceramic bodies, macro- and micro-porosity, thermal and impact fractures, moisture expansion, kiln heating rates, atmospheres, temperature variability, and so on.

As elemental analyses of ceramic materials continue to be published at an increasing rate, we must not only be concerned with the sampling and analytical techniques and avoid a trusting faith in what someone has termed "computer overkill," but also consider the geochemical significance of the relative proportions of the trace elements. It would indeed be helpful to solicit a geochemical input for the interpretive work. Perhaps this can come from those termed "geoarchaeologists." Now that the Geological Society of America regularly has at its annual meetings symposia devoted to Archaeological Geology, such collaboration should be possible.

Standards for use in analytical work continue to be discussed. Perhaps some action can be taken at this meeting. The term "standards" is subjectively used in a nonanalytical sense by archaeologists wishing to classify pottery in terms of color, surface finish, texture, etc. Alan Franklin of the National Bureau of Standards quite rightly objects to this use of the term, and suggests that "representational pattern" might be better; some of you may have other suggestions. Perhaps archaeologists can be encouraged not to use parochially the term "standards" as they have "faience" and "temper."

Ceramic petrography has been an important aspect of archaeological studies for many years. Anna Shepard's important studies of pottery from the southwestern United States and later from Guatemala are well known. Among the major studies in recent years have been those by D. P. S. Peacock. Recently, he and his colleagues have published a book on *Pottery*

Frederick R. Matson

and Early Commerce: Characterization and Trade in Roman and Later Ceramics (Peacock 1977). In the preface (p. viii) he comments:

> Since the appearance of Anna Shepard's classic works the potential of petrology has been widely appreciated but recently other methods, more readily automated, seem to be favoured, even though the results may not have the same range of archaeological implications.

The separation and identification of the heavy minerals in clay fabrics have been of particular importance in obtaining results of archaeological value. This approach, by no means new in petrological studies, has been significantly applied to archaeological materials from northern Europe. As Peacock points out in his useful essay, "The Scientific Analysis of Ancient Ceramics: A Review" (Peacock 1970, p. 379):

> In some parts of the world, such as Britain, a considerable amount of work has been done on the distribution of heavy minerals throughout the geological systems and in such cases it may be possible to refer to the geological literature to discover the system with which the mineral assemblage in the pot is most closely related.

Scott and Cazeau's study of pottery distribution in western Mexico showed that its place of origin could be suggested when the heavy mineral distributions in the river bed sands were determined (Scott and Cazeau 1976).

Professional ceramists, whether they be trained as chemists, physicists, engineers, or potters, can contribute and have contributed to archaeological studies. Their input should be actively sought by archaeologists concerned with the understanding of the analytical results being obtained in many laboratories. Several ceramists, for example, have studied classical Greek pottery. Joseph Noble has ably summarized and advanced this work through the publication of his book, The Techniques of Attic Painted Pottery (Noble 1965). Marie Farnsworth's studies of Corinthian and other wares have been important (Farnsworth et al. 1977). Adam Winter, a professional potter, in a recent book, Die antike Glanztonkeramik, shows empirically how the ancient Greeks could have selected and purified their clays and pigments and used them to produce the well-known black-figured and red-figured wares decorated with a black ferruginous vitrified slip (Winter 1978). Some scientists may have other suggestions that might modify these conclusions.

It would be impossible to cite much of the pertinent technical ceramic literature, but Harrell and Russell's monograph, Influence of Ambient Atmosphere in Maturation of Structural Clay Products, demonstrates effectively — with colored plates of their test pieces — the color changes that develop in five different clays fired under varying controlled conditions (Harrell and Russell 1967). Students of ancient pottery should be aware of these variables when they discuss ancient firing processes. The development and persistence of black or dark-colored cores in pottery has been discussed many times in the technical ceramic literature. Similarly, the white surface scum, so often termed a "white slip" by archaeologists, can better be understood by referring to the structural clay products publications (Brownell 1976, p. 121).

Many scientists have attempted to determine the original firing temperatures of potsherds by refined laboratory techniques. This continues to be a problem of current interest, particularly in tracing the history of ceramic technology and man's control of hearths and kilns. From an archaeological standpoint, the results may be a bit misleading unless the sherds sampled represent the probable range of temperatures for the ware as evidenced by color, hardness, scanning electron microscope photographs, etc. Even today the temperature range that can occur in one commercial firing is considerable. Certainly, in antiquity, it would have been significant, influenced by the structure and loading of the kiln, the types of fuel and the ways in which they were introduced, changes in the effective draft and combustion due to the rate at which the fuel was introduced, variable winds, sudden rains, and the like.

Two relevant papers might be mentioned. Eto determined the probable firing temperature of the prehistoric Japanese Jomon pottery to be about 550°C, based on the measurement of the thermal linear expansion and contraction (Eto 1963). Bouchez and his associates (1976) reported on the study of northeastern Iranian potsherds from Tureng Tepe and Tepe Hissar that had been assigned to period II, dating from the early third millennium B.C. They found different temperatures for different wares, ranging from below 750° to greater than 1100°C. It would be helpful if a physicist would critically examine the increasingly extensive data on firing temperatures. An archaeologist could helpfully comment on the representative nature of samples that were tested if the sherds have been sufficiently identified. The publication of the 1977 international symposium in Berlin on Ceramic Firing Techniques and Their Determination through Experimental Archaeology contains many excellent contributions to this field (Hoffmann and Goldmann 1979). Being aware that some of the participants in our symposium have an active interest in this subject, I will not infringe on their presentations.

Questions Worth Asking

Some of the broader problems that must be considered by ceramic technologists as they select materials for specialized study might be mentioned. This list of topics of course reflects my personal interests and experiences. A few pertinent references are appended to the following topics although they may not directly address the question posed.

a. How do tropical climates and laterized soils relate to the techniques used in making pottery? Are the availability of loess deposits or of water-stratified clay beds that vary in texture important factors when the potter selects clays? In northern regions, do the properties of glacial outwash clays and of podsols influence pottery production? Success in making very thin-walled vessels in Ecuador and Nepal, for example, is certainly related to the special working properties of the clays. Cornwall's *Soils for the Archaeologist* (1958) provides useful initial orientation.

b. The addition of aplastics, archaeological "temper," to clays helps potters in the forming of vessels, but not always in their firing or long life. Is there a degree of control in aplastics use with respect to the clay near the village site and the size and shape of the vessel being formed? Is there a cultural as well as a technical component in its use? (Rye 1976).

c. How do the firing techniques, particularly hearth and kiln design together with the fuels available, relate to the wares that are produced? Ethnoarchaeological studies of potters at work today may provide some helpful information (Cook 1961; Hampe and Winter 1962, 1965).

d. What are the technological origins of the vitrified black slip that appears on Neolithic and Early Bronze Age pottery in Greece and culminates in its sophisticated application to black-figured and red-figured ware?

e. Did a significant technological change occur in Mesopotamia in 'Ubaid times (fifth millennium B.C.) that is reflected in the properties of the pottery, or is this a selective phenomenon caused by the archaeologists' shipping back to their museums the more durable and interesting ceramics? 'Ubaid pottery, as seen in collections, is characteristically yellow, thin-walled, "well-fired," frequently deformed from overfiring, and quite vitrified. It is decorated with a black ferruginous slip. Yet visits to excavation site wasteheaps show that there was much lower-fired and more fragile detritus that at times had red painted decoration (Tite and Maniatis 1975).

f. During the period of the Roman Empire there was a great stimulus in trade induced by conquest and military occupation. This was a period of ceramic progress. In what ways? Terra sigillata ware, Roman cooking pots, Nabataean pottery, and specialized fabrics that were in use in Iran and other parts of the Near East must relate to the introduction of specific clay processing and kiln firing techniques.

g. The Nabataean ware of the first century B.C. and the first centuries A.D. found in Jordan and southern Palestine is unique in the thinness of the bowls and other shapes whose walls are often but two millimeters in thickness. Peter Parr has provided a most persuasive study of the limited distribution and cultural significance of Nabataean ware, but makes little comment on the texture of the fabric nor on the clays available for the production of such pottery (Parr 1978). Cut and ground edges of some Nabataean sherds from surface collections show significant variations in texture and possibly in degree of vitrification as well as core oxidation. On some pieces the painted decoration evidences vitrification. This would be an interesting ware to study.

h. What is the cultural significance of the introduction of lead into the compounding of glazes and glasses? Does this relate to the use of an engobe so that glazes would better fit the bodies on which they were used? Is the development of the several faience bodies and their glazes or the use of sand-lime brick at Susa part of this siliceous picture? (Bezborodov 1975; Brill 1968; Caley 1962; Hedges and Moorey 1975; Hetherington 1948; Sayre 1967; Sundius and Steger 1963; Tichane 1978).

i. Shell was used as an aplastic in some of the American Indian pottery made in the eastern and midwestern United States. Does shell use have cultural or purely technological implications? Mussel shells occurred at many Indian campfires as the residuum of meals. Such shells laminate readily when heated to the low temperatures needed to steam or bake the mussels because of the great difference in thermal expansion and contraction of $CaCO_3$ parallel to and perpendicular to the c-axis. After such heating, shells are easily crushed and could have been added with ash to the potter's clay. Is there a cementation process due to the hydration of the partially calcined shell in the fired pottery that strengthens the vessels used for cooking foods? (Rye 1976, p. 120).

Many other items could be mentioned, but these suggest the nature of questions that may be of interest to materials scientists. We have been at the What stage for the most part. I hope we can advance to the Why.

To make this advance we need interdisciplinary consultation, cooperation, and coordination. It is wryly interesting to note that statements made and hopes expressed over forty years ago can be reiterated today. Anna Shepard has written on aspects of the subject many times, and is always quotable. In what was perhaps her last paper, prepared for the

Frederick R. Matson

fourth symposium on Archaeological Chemistry in 1968, she said in her opening statement, "Pottery is a great challenge to the analyst because of its complexity." She concludes with comments on the relationship between the analyst and the archaeologist, based upon her own laboratory and field work in the American Southwest, Guatemala, and the Near East, arguing effectively the case for specialists' becoming involved in archaeological field experience (Shepard 1971).

One cannot think of interdisciplinary archaeological research without remembering the many contributions and characteristically great breadth of vision of Cyril Stanley Smith. Smith added a post-symposium note to his paper at the same 1968 symposium. In it he cogently argues the case for scientists to become more actively involved in the broader aspects of man's history with respect to the important role in it of the history of technology. "Let scientists therefore ask and answer their own historical questions as well as help to answer those presently posed by the archaeologist and general historian." As we all know, he is a fine exemplar of this approach (Smith 1971).

Perhaps we can measure our interdisciplinary progress as Ursula Franklin has done for archaeological metallurgy. In her paper on "The Science of Ancient Materials — A New Scholarly Field," she lists the criteria she recognizes for the emergence of such a field. They are "*1* — a body of autonomous knowledge is being assembled; *2* — there are identifiable practitioners of the craft and institutions for their study and training; *3* — specialized journals exist to serve the new field." She documents each of these criteria in her optimistic report (Franklin 1977). Ceramic archaeology as a subdiscipline would appear to meet her requirements.

Yesterday and Today

In an overview paper it is appropriate to indicate some of the steps in the progress of ceramic technological studies. Having been associated with ceramic technological work — industrial, academic, and archaeological — since the early 1930s, I have witnessed a bit of its progress and would like to cite some of the developments, with particular reference to the United States. Perhaps at another time a more detailed presentation of the subject, international in scope, would be in order. This would include early ceramic analyses by several of the great chemists and physicists of England, France, and Germany, some of which can be found in Partington's *Origins and Development of Applied Chemistry* (1935). Mention would of course be made of Linné's pioneer study of *The Techniques of South American Ceramics* (1925).

In this present paper no attempt will be made to include all relevant names, places, institutions, or meetings.

Cameron Creek Village, A Site in the Mimbres Area in Grant County, New Mexico, written by Wesley Bradfield in 1929, was published posthumously in 1931. This is perhaps the first archaeological report, at least in America, whose author places the site in its ecological context and presents a meticulous description of the pottery in terms of texture, color, and techniques of manufacture. It is still well worth reading. Bradfield's pioneer work in archaeological ceramic studies influenced A. V. Kidder (who credited him, when asked, with the example which led to the detailed ceramic studies carried on at Pecos and elsewhere). Kidder, in turn, encouraged Carl E. Guthe in his time-production studies of the potters at the pueblo of San Ildefonso (Guthe 1925) and Anna Shepard in her classical studies in the 1930s of the pottery of the Rio Grande sites. When asked in 1961 to evaluate critically her technological studies, Shepard wrote an excellent overview, "Rio Grande Glaze-Paint Pottery: A Test of Petrographic Analysis." The concluding section, General Inferences, is particularly valuable for students of ceramic areas other than the American Southwest (Shepard 1965).

The Bradfield impetus continued, for Guthe established the Ceramic Repository for the Eastern United States at the University of Michigan, where it has been well nurtured and used by James B. Griffin and his associates. Sherds from key sites repose there, available for examination. Guthe also encouraged the development of ceramic technological studies at Michigan. An early aspect of this was the publication of Benjamin March's little-known book, *Standards of Pottery Description* (March 1934).

Archaeological field work in the Near East and some of the Mediterranean lands was most actively undertaken in the 1920s by European and American universities and museums because political and financial considerations made this an opportune time for exploring the impressive remains of ancient cities. Large quantities of ceramic and other items were shipped back to the supporting institutions. These collections now provide much of the source material for technological studies at a time when field work is directed toward more modest and specific projects — or toward surveys before lands are inundated behind new dams being built for irrigation and hydroelectric projects. In the United States the current laws mandate the preparation of Environmental Impact Statements (EIS) before government-funded construction can begin. Archaeological field work, under contract, is often involved in preparing such statements.

It can provide further ceramic items for study. Most newly recovered ceramic materials must today remain in the countries in which they are excavated, so the museum storerooms are now being mined assiduously by technologists.

Funds became available to provide needed employment through the Works Progress Administration (the WPA) late in the decade of the 1930s, during the administration of President Roosevelt, for archaeological field and laboratory work. The classical archaeologists Clark Hopkins and Robert H. McDowell at the University of Michigan obtained a grant and established a laboratory in a firehouse in Detroit, Michigan. So-called white-collar workers who were unemployed were used to process materials and data primarily from Michigan's excavations during seven field seasons at Seleucia on the Tigris, just south of Baghdad. Chemists, nurses, secretaries learned to make thin sections of pottery from several parts of the world and also to determine the shell content and porosity of American Indian pottery of the Fort Ancient culture that was centered in Ohio.

A similar WPA project at the University Museum of the University of Pennsylvania was under the direction of Vladimir J. Fewkes and, later, Donald Horton. World War II terminated these activities, but extensive thin-section libraries produced as part of the Michigan and Pennsylvania projects are still in use at The Pennsylvania State University. Perhaps MASCA (Museum Applied Science Center for Archaeology) at the University Museum with its now-superseded *Newsletter* and current *MASCA Journal* is an outgrowth of the University of Pennsylvania's WPA project.

Staff members at many institutions are now actively engaged in some aspect of the analysis of ancient ceramics and often have funding support from governmental agencies. It would not be possible here to survey adequately these developments since World War II. However, it is satisfying to note that ancient ceramics continue to provide challenging study material.

Conferences, symposia, and seminars are a hallmark of respectability in the realm of science. It is not possible to include in these comments all of the important meetings primarily devoted to technological ceramic studies, especially those in Europe and other parts of the world, but some indication should be given of such gatherings. Perhaps the earliest devoted to ceramic technology was that at the University of Michigan's Museum of Anthropology in 1938. Carl Guthe, who served as chairman for this meeting of eleven invited conferees, obtained financial support for it from the National Research Council. At its conclusion, continuing committees

were organized. The objectives of ceramic technological research, as stated in the brief conference report (Shepard and Horton 1939), sound very familiar today. Following World War II, under the able and energetic leadership of Paul Fejos the Wenner-Gren Foundation for Anthropological Research, at that time named the Viking Fund, was a major supporter of archaeological efforts. It sponsored a conference in 1950 on the use of scientific techniques in archaeological work. Ceramic technology was represented among the papers (Griffin 1951), as it was at the 1959 conference on the Application of Quantitative Methods in Archaeology (Heizer and Cook 1960) and the 1961 meetings on Ceramics and Man (Matson 1965). Archaeological studies of many kinds owe their advancement to the support of the Wenner-Gren Foundation and Paul Fejos.

Neutron activation analyses of ceramic materials received a major impetus from a meeting organized at the Institute for Advanced Study in Princeton by Robert Oppenheimer in 1956. He served as host and blackboard secretary for the meeting. During the preceding year E. V. Sayre and R. W. Dodson had initiated preliminary activation studies of Greek and Asia Minor sherds provided by Institute staff member Homer A. Thompson, for many years director of the Agora excavations in Athens. About half of the fourteen participants in this conference are actively engaged in archaeological and ceramic studies today (Sayre and Dodson 1957).

Archaeological Chemistry has been the subject of a symposium approximately every five years sponsored by the History of Chemistry Section of the American Chemical Society. The proceedings of four of these symposia, edited by Caley (1951), Levey (1967), Brill (1971), Beck (1974), and Carter (1978), contain many major papers on ceramics. At the 1977 meeting it was recommended that task forces be assembled to consider five major topics: data storage, retrieval, and reporting; specimen handling and sampling; standards, interlaboratory test programs to ensure agreement in the analysis of archaeological objects; and funding sources for research. This is an effort that we should energetically support.

A meeting to consider the problems related to standards for archaeological chemical work was held in 1978 at the Brookhaven National Laboratory. The thirty chemists and archaeologists present agreed to institute an international program for the sharing of analytical standards and to establish procedures for the standardization of data handling.

At the Materials Research Society's meeting in Boston in 1978, a symposium was organized to discuss Materials Characterization in Archaeology, Historic Preservation, and the Fine Arts. Again, ceram-

Frederick R. Matson

ics was an important material considered.

As an indication of the nature of the many European conferences pertinent to our interests, for excellent technical papers on ceramic studies are presented at them, let me cite one in 1975 at the Free University in Berlin, organized by the Archaeometry Section of the Institute for Inorganic Chemistry (Arnold, Busch, and Hoika 1976). In 1977 the Analytical Chemistry Section of the Gesellschaft Deutscher Chemiker had a symposium devoted to Archaeometry, specifically mineralogical raw materials as sources of culture-historical information (Hennicke 1978). I am indebted to Professor R. Heimann for these references. I should appreciate learning of similar meetings taking place in other countries.

No attempt will be made in this paper to list or critically discuss the many chemical and physical analytical techniques that are being used, at times in an exploratory sense, in the study and characterization of ancient ceramics. The reports appearing in *Archaeometry* and in *Art and Archaeology Technical Abstracts* make it possible for one to survey this field.

The Research Laboratory for Archaeology and the History of Art at Oxford University has, in addition to publishing our indispensable journal, *Archaeometry*, organized what have become annual international symposia on Archaeometry and Archaeological Prospection. Recent meetings have been held at Oxford, Philadelphia, Bonn, London, and Paris. Next May the twentieth symposium will take place at the Brookhaven National Laboratory, Long Island, New York. As we all know, these sessions provide the participants with a splendid opportunity for learning of and participating in the advancement of ceramic studies. At the Bonn meetings in 1978, for example, twelve of the forty-three papers presented in the general sessions were concerned with scientific aspects of ceramic studies (Scollar 1979).

When the Royal Society and the British Academy decided "to work together in the many fields of learning where their interests overlap," they selected archaeology as the subject for their first symposium, held in 1969, thus "linking science with the humanities." The ceramic aspects were well represented by R. H. Brill's discussion of "Lead and Oxygen Isotope Ratios in Ancient Objects," and H. W. Catling's brief summary to that time of the "Analysis of Pottery from the Mycenaean Period" by optical spectroscopy. These papers and the rest of the proceedings were published as *The Impact of the Natural Sciences on Archaeology* (Allibone 1970).

In 1973 a symposium was organized around the subject "Technologie der altägyptischen Keramik"

with twenty-five participants. It met at Höhr-Grenzhausen, the regional center of the salt-glazed stoneware industry in Germany. Some members of this group are part of an international study group concerned with the better use of Egyptian pottery, a material occurring in large and at times almost uncontrollable quantities in excavations. A "Manual on Ancient Egyptian Pottery" is being prepared.

The University of California at its Los Angeles campus and at its Lawrence Radiation Laboratory in Berkeley sponsored a conference in 1975 on Applications of the Physical Sciences to Medieval Ceramics. Several of its participants are present today.

Tomorrow

In concluding this personal overview of archaeological ceramics and the physical sciences, I believe a few suggestions to be in order. I shall state them briefly in the hope that some of them will be considered during the discussion periods, for it is more interesting to plan where we are going in our studies than to record where we have been.

1. Greater use should be made of the resources available in the *Art and Archaeology Technical Abstracts*. It is difficult to remain informed of the recently published articles and books of interest to ceramic technologists concerned with archaeological materials, for papers may appear in the proceedings of many symposia in many countries and in unexpected places. It was suggested at the meeting of the Society for Archaeological Sciences this spring that an abstract journal might be a desirable project to investigate. There is certainly a need for such a service, but it already exists: *Art and Archaeology Technical Abstracts* (*AATA*), now in its seventeenth year of publication, contains a section on Glass and Ceramics, together with an excellent annual *subject* and *author* index. These materials are registered in the British Museum computer-generated bibliography. This excellent abstract journal, published at the Institute of Fine Arts, New York University, for the International Institute for Conservation of Historic and Artistic Works (London) should be more widely known and used.

2. There should be planned constructive evaluation of published data. The McArthur paper on the Cretan provenance of the inscribed jars found at Thebes (McArthur 1978), and Wilson's detailed review of elemental analyses reports (Wilson 1978) point in the right direction, but it would be helpful to have responses from the initial authors printed at the same time. Laboratory scientists wish to select their own problems and ways of analysis, but an overview of a specific subject could suggest interesting black holes worthy of study.

3. As data banks are developed, should questionable items be eliminated, preferably on the initiative of those who first reported them in past years?

4. Critical reviews such as those advocated above are excellent and can lead to productive disagreement, but further experimental work is also desirable. Replication of ancient products is one approach. To cite an example — Maya Blue, a decorative pigment used in Mesoamerica from about 300 to 1500 A.D., has been shown to be reproducible using the clay mineral attapulgite and the natural dye indigo. Recently E. R. Littmann (1980) has broadened the scope, testing blue montmorillonite from Palenque in Yucatan by X-ray diffraction and suggesting that "any clay containing palygorskite, sepiolite, montmorillonite, or possibly other minerals free of plate-like crystal structures can be converted to a Maya Blue pigment." This would seem to be an interesting subject to investigate further.

5. Philip Betancourt's cooperative studies with laboratory scientists in the study of ancient Cretan pottery from Vasiliki and Gournia offer one of the encouraging cooperative developments at the present time.

6. There should be more funding provided for the interdisciplinary training of students so that continuity in archaeological ceramic studies will be ensured. Can more constructive support be given to the several archaeometric programs now in operation? Can help be given in attracting good students and in providing employment opportunities?

7. A repository for archaeological technology is being established so that record of a scientist's individual efforts and his data and materials do not disappear when his professional interests in the subject terminate. If you are interested, we can discuss the merits of this development.

8. Should there be a simple newsletter circulated among those interested in archaeological ceramic technology? Should use be made of the columns of the *Archaeometric Clearinghouse* that appear in the *Journal of Field Archaeology* or of the *Newsletter* of the Society for Archaeological Sciences?

I look forward to our discussion periods throughout these meetings. I hope that some actions will be taken during our last session so that this seminar does not become remembered as just another fine meeting at which we listened to papers.

We have a lot to do.

References

Allibone, T. E. 1970. *The impact of the natural sciences on archaeology.* London: Oxford University Press.

Arnold, Volker; Busch, Ralf; and Hoika, Jürgen, eds. 1976. Untersuchungsmethoden für Keramik. *Informationsblätter zu Nachbarwissenschaften der Ur- und Frühgeschichte* 7.

Beck, Curt W. 1974. *Archaeological chemistry.* Advances in Chemistry Series, no. 138. Washington, D.C.: American Chemical Society.

Bezborodov, M. A. 1975. *Chemie und Technologie der antiken und mittelalterlichen Gläser.* Mainz: Verlag Philipp von Zabern.

Bouchez, R. et al. 1976. Détermination des modes de cuisson de céramiques dê l'Iran protohistorique, d'après leurs propriétés magnétiques et leurs spectres Mössbauer. *IXᵉ Congres Union Internationale des Sciences Préhistoriques et Protohistoriques*, p. 1-33. Grenoble: Laboratoire de Recherche Archéologique.

Bradfield, Wesley. 1931. *Cameron Creek Village, a site in the Mimbres Area in Grant County, New Mexico.* Sante Fe, New Mexico: School of American Research.

Brill, Robert H. 1968. The scientific investigation of ancient glasses. *Proceedings of the 8th International Congress on Glass*, pp. 47-68.

———. 1970. Lead and oxygen isotope ratios in ancient objects. In Allibone, T. E., *The impact of the natural sciences on archaeology,* pp. 143-64. London: Oxford University Press.

———, ed. 1971. *Science and archaeology.* Cambridge, Massachusetts: Massachusetts Institute of Technology.

Brownell, W. E. 1976. *Structural clay products.* Vienna and New York: Springer-Verlag.

Caley, Earle R. 1951. Symposium on archaeological chemistry. *Journal of Chemical Education* 28:63-96.

———. 1962. *Analyses of ancient glasses 1790-1957: A comprehensive and critical survey.* Corning, New York: Corning Museum of Glass.

Carter, Giles F. 1978. *Archaeological chemistry II.* Advances in Chemistry Series, no. 171. Washington, D.C.: American Chemical Society.

Catling, H. W. 1970. Analysis of pottery from the Mycenaean period. In Allibone, T. E., *The impact of the natural sciences on archaeology,* pp. 175-78. London: Oxford University Press.

Cook, R. M. 1961. The "double stoking tunnel" of Greek kilns. (Appendix: Ancient kilns in Greece). *Annual of the British School at Athens* 56:64-67.

Cornwall, I. W. 1958. *Soils for the archaeologist.* London: Phoenix House.

Eto, Moriharu. 1963. Firing temperature of Jomon pottery. (*Zinruigaku Zassi.*) *Journal of the Anthropological Society of Nippon* 71:23-51.

Frederick R. Matson

Farnsworth, Marie; Perlman, I.; and Asaro, Frank. 1977. Corinth and Corfu: A neutron activation study of their pottery. *American Journal of Archaeology* 81:455–68.

Franklin, Ursula. 1977. The science of ancient materials — a new scholarly field. *Canadian Mining and Metallurgy Bulletin* 70:207–210.

Griffin, James B. 1951. *Essays on archaeological methods, proceedings of a conference held under auspices of the Viking Fund.* Anthropological Papers of the Museum of Anthropology, University of Michigan, no. 8. Ann Arbor, Michigan: University of Michigan Press.

Guthe, Carl E. 1925. *Pueblo pottery making: A study of the village of San Ildefonso.* New Haven, Connecticut: Yale University Press.

Hampe, Roland, and Winter, Adam. 1962. *Bei Töpfern und Töpferinnen in Kreta Messenien und Zypern.* Mainz: Verlag des Römisch-Germanischen Zentralmuseums Mainz.

_____. 1965. *Bei Töpfern und Zieglern in Süditalien Sizilien und Griechenland.* Mainz: Verlag des Römisch-Germanischen Zentralmuseums Mainz.

Harrell, George O., and Russell, Ralston Jr. 1967. *Influence of ambient atmosphere in maturation of structural clay products.* Engineering Experiment Station, Ohio State University, Bulletin, no. 204.

Hedges, R. E. M., and Moorey, P. R. S. 1975. Pre-Islamic glazes at Kish and Nineveh in Iraq. *Archaeometry* 17:25–43.

Heizer, R. F., and Cook, S. F. 1960. *The application of quantitative methods in archaeology.* Viking Fund Publications in Anthropology, no. 28. New York: Wenner-Gren Foundation for Anthropological Research, Inc.

Hennicke, H. W., ed. 1978. *Mineralische Rohstoffe als kulturhistorische Informationsquelle.* Hagen: Verlag des Vereins Deutscher Emailfachleute.

Hetherington, A. L. 1948. *Chinese ceramic glazes.* 2d rev. ed. South Pasadena, California: P. D. and Ione Perkins.

Hoffmann, Bettina, and Goldmann, Klaus, eds. 1979. *Brenntechniken von Keramik und ihre Wiedergewinnung durch experimentelle Archäologie.* Acta praehistorica et archaeologica 9/10. Berlin: Verlag Volker Spiess.

Levey, Martin. 1967. *Archaeological chemistry, a symposium.* Philadelphia: University of Pennsylvania Press.

Linné, S. 1925. *The technique of South American ceramics.* Göteborg.

Littmann, Edwin R. 1980. Maya Blue — a new perspective. *American Antiquity* 45:87–100.

March, Benjamin. 1934. *Standards of pottery description. With an introductory essay by Carl E. Guthe.* Occasional Contributions from the Museum of Anthropology, University of Michigan, no. 3. Ann Arbor, Michigan: University of Michigan Press.

Matson, Frederick R. 1965. *Ceramics and man.* Viking Fund Publications in Anthropology, no. 41. New York: Wenner-Gren Foundation for Anthropological Research, Inc.

McArthur, J. T. 1978. Inconsistencies in the composition and provenance studies of the inscribed jars found at Thebes. *Archaeometry* 20:177–82.

Noble, Joseph Veach. 1965. *The techniques of Attic painted pottery.* New York: Watson-Guptill Publications.

Oldfather, William A. 1920. A note on the etymology of the word "ceramic." *Journal of the American Ceramic Society* 3:537–42.

_____. 1924. The meaning of "Keramos" once more. *Bulletin of the American Ceramic Society* 7:114–16.

Parr, Peter J. 1978. Pottery, people and politics. In Moorey, Roger, and Parr, Peter, eds., *Archaeology in the Levant. Essays for Kathleen Kenyon,* pp. 203–209. Warminster, England: Aris and Phillips Ltd.

Partington, J. R. 1935. *Origins and development of applied chemistry.* London: Longmans, Green and Co.

Peacock, D. P. S. 1970. The scientific analysis of ancient ceramics: A review. *World Archaeology* 1:375–89.

_____, ed. 1977. *Pottery and early commerce: Characterization and trade in Roman and later ceramics.* London: Academic Press.

Rye, O. S. 1976. Keeping your temper under control: Materials and the manufacture of Papuan pottery. *Archaeology and Physical Anthropology in Oceania* 11:106–37.

Sayre, E. V. 1967. Summary of the Brookhaven program of analysis of ancient glass. In Young, W. J., ed., *Application of science in examination of works of art,* pp. 145–54. Boston: Museum of Fine Arts.

Sayre, E. V., and Dodson, R. W. 1957. Neutron activation study of Mediterranean potsherds. *American Journal of Archaeology* 61:35–41.

Scollar, Irwin. 1979. *Proceedings of the 18th International Symposium on Archaeometry and Archaeological Prospection, Bonn, 14–17 March 1978.* Archaeo-Physika, no. 10.

Scott, Stuart D., and Cazeau, Charles J. 1976. Interdisciplinary approach to west Mexican ceramic history: Cultural and mineralogic sherd analysis. *American Ceramic Society Bulletin* 55:213–14.

Shepard, Anna O. 1956. *Ceramics for the archaeologist*. (New foreword to 5th printing, 1965: Ceramic studies 1954 to 1964). Washington, D.C.: Carnegie Institution of Washington. Publication no. 609.

_____. 1965. Rio Grande glaze-paint pottery: A test of petrographic analysis. In Matson, Frederick R., ed., *Ceramics and man*. Chicago: Aldine Publishing Company.

_____. 1971. Ceramic analysis: The interrelations of methods; the relations of analysts and archaeologists. In Brill, Robert H., *Science and archaeology*, pp. 55–63. Cambridge, Massachusetts: Massachusetts Institute of Technology.

Shepard, Anna O., and Horton, Donald. 1939. Conference on archaeological technology in ceramics. *American Antiquity* 4:358–59.

Smith, Cyril Stanley. 1971. A post-symposium note: Science in the service of history. In Brill, Robert H., *Science and archaeology*, pp. 53–54. Cambridge, Massachusetts: Massachusetts Institute of Technology.

Sundius, Nils, and Steger, Walter. 1963. The constitution and manufacture of Chinese ceramics from Sung and earlier times. In Palmgren, Nils, *Sung Sherds*, pp. 373–505. Stockholm: Almquist and Wiksell.

Tichane, Robert. 1978. *Those celadon blues*. Painted Post, New York: New York State Institute for Glaze Research.

Tite, M. S., and Maniatis, Y. 1975. Examination of ancient pottery using the scanning electron microscope. *Nature* 257:122–23.

Wilson, A. L. 1978. Elemental analysis of pottery in the study of its provenance: A review. *Journal of Archaeological Science* 5:219–36.

Winter, Adam. 1978. *Die antike Glanztonkeramik: Praktische Versuche*. Mainz–am–Rhein: P. von Zabern.

2. Why Is Archaeometry So Boring for Archaeologists?

F. WIDEMANN
Groupe d'archéologie nucléaire d'Orsay-Saclay

The title of this meeting, "ceramics as archaeological material," is a welcome reminder in a meeting dedicated to a branch of archaeometry. It is a common observation that the archaeometry international symposia, just as some more limited meetings of the same kind, are more and more successful in the sense they attract more specialists of the natural sciences, and in a certain way a failure because a very small proportion of field archaeologists and practically no historians feel enough concern to attend them. This is quite paradoxical, and I would like to try some sort of study of this phenomenon, and its relation to the current development of methods of natural sciences for archaeology, in particular for analytical origin studies in ceramics. I will try to analyze advantages and disadvantages of this situation, not particularly for the archaeologists, but for a rational handling of origin studies and a complete exploitation of their possibilities. Then I will present, more in a methodological way than to expose detailed results, our work on Gallo-Roman amphorae as a contribution to solving the historical problem of food supply in the western Roman Empire.

The Place of Archaeologists at Archaeometry Symposia

The scarcity of archaeologists at archaeometry symposia, less than 10 percent of the participants in the last published symposium in Bonn (Scollar 1978), certainly measures the cultural fence standing between scholars of a classical education and scientists nurtured on mathematics, physics, or chemistry. Some old-fashioned archaeologists feel their *carrière* was going well without all of those new methods and just want to go on. For example, Schachermeyr who has made important contributions in his field did not hesitate recently to write against the introduction of natural sciences into archaeology and even against the use of carbon 14 for absolute chronology (Schachermeyr 1978).

We could just smile at these positions if they were those only of a few closed minds, but such lack of understanding is still shared by numerous archaeologists. However, an increasing number of their colleagues are ready for an effort of adaptation, and I wonder if we offer them an encouraging environment. Discussing this problem with various leaders of archaeometry laboratories, I met people perfectly aware of this lack of contact, but their reactions went from resignation (to a phenomenon going to disappear slowly) to frank gladness (thank God archaeologists are not coming!).

I did not feel philosophically satisfied with those responses, simply because in a given problem, I feel the method may adjust to the aim, but the contrary is

Figure 1. Amphora of type Gauloise 1 from Saint-Just drain in Lyon. Musée de la civilisation gallo-romaine (Lyon). Photo GANOS 10 648.

Figure 2. Magnetic prospection in Salleles d'Aude workshop (Aude) by Daigneres et al. The location of kilns is shown to be exactly where maxima of field anomaly occur.

difficult to imagine. So, research in methods cut off from their field of applications can lead to all sorts of nonsense. And it is interesting to revisit the programs of the last international Symposia for Archaeometry from this point of view. I may not be capable of understanding all the hidden wonders in some of the papers presented, but I could not help asking myself a few questions, without any personal acrimony to anyone: there are methods applied, for instance, to ceramics that just do not bring the answer searched for; what is the meaning of a "characterization" of ceramics through the Mössbauer effect? No serious provenance study can be done through this method. It certainly can help recognizing black ware from red ware, but do we need Mössbauer for that? It is not the only case of methods just not fitting the pursued aim. There is still qualitative or semiquantitative analysis for characterization of ceramics; but for analytical origin studies, the most careful calibration and hunt for causes of error cannot be avoided to detect significant but small differences in clay compositions.

Another illusion that archaeologists may be able to take to pieces even better than we do is the abusive conclusion(s) taken from an irrelevant or insufficient sampling. Dusty drawers of museums are easier to reach than remote archaeological fields, but in recent publications available, we do not avoid completely large economical schemes based on isolated artifacts from old crumb-trays. Poverty of measurements is sometimes hidden behind sophisticated data processing displays. I will not give precise examples, not because of any fear of murder, but in order to stay on the philosophical level.

This leads to the idea that people doing analysis cannot say they do not understand the choice of the samples they run. Sooner or later they will face a wrong choice, or difficulties in the interpretation of results obtained even in the most careful way. To finish with criticism of the archaeometry symposia is not our main purpose; mention may be made of the bad habit of papers on technical details, given in large sessions, which only a few persons will follow. It is simply the difficulties of organizing large congresses with the respectable will of letting people freely express their ideas and results, or something more peculiar to the situation of a discipline when the development of methods is taken too often independently of the scientific needs?

Rather than begin a sad enumeration of the ways ceramics studies should not be done, I would like to present the last five years' development of the Orsay-Saclay laboratory especially for the ceramics studies.

The Gallo-Roman Amphorae Study

Our main program in ceramics is on Gallo-Roman amphorae. The study of this problem started four years ago with the first evidence for a type of amphora peculiar to Roman Gaul (Laubenheimer 1977)

F. Widemann

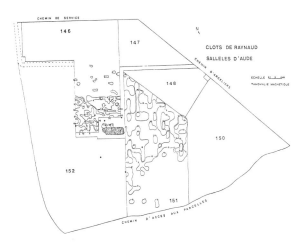

Figure 3a. Spatial distribution of tile and brick sherds in the Salleles d'Aude workshop. The curves mark equal density for this type of object. Maximum density has been shown to be always on the top of potter's dumps. Ploughing, even rather deep as it is used for vine clearing from time to time (80 cm), does not completely destroy the original location of the sherds.

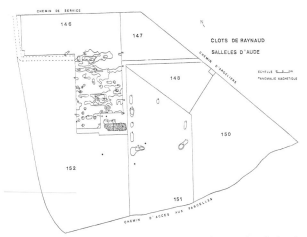

Figure 3b. Spatial distribution of amphorae sherds in the Salleles d'Aude workshop. Comparison with the previous map brings evidence for a specialization of kilns. The position of the center of the magnetic anomalies is indicated with a star. Before any excavation it is possible to foresee the number of kilns, the spatial extension of the workshop, and the type of production of each kiln. Excavation remains necessary for quantitative studies, and of course for the chronological study of successive levels.

(Fig. 1). To imagine the state of the question a few years ago, H. Callender in 1965 could write with good reason: "within the writer's experience, it is impossible to assign with certainty any particular type of vessel to Gaul, although there is some evidence that one or two forms were Gaulish in origin" (Callender 1965). No workshop was known yet. Later on, E. Ettlinger reported finding in Vindonissa some amphorae without clear origin: "as I have not found any parallels in literature till now, I guess an origin in Southern France" (Ettlinger 1977).

In fact several workshops were discovered — before we started — in southern Gaul (Tchernia and Villa 1977), and C. Panella in the work on Ostia's imports suspected, without real evidence, that an important proportion of amphorae were coming from Gaul (Panella 1973).

The problem was not just to analyze objects and give them the right origin. We had no idea of the shapes of the amphorae, practically no sites of production, and a general neglect on the part of most archaeologists for those big ugly things. Practically all the complete amphorae were coming from the sea, and were no help for building up reference groups. The most frequent practice of field archaeologists was to keep stamps, lips, handles, and bottoms and throw away the rest. The few workshops discovered were fast and haphazardly excavated, and no care was given to the protection of the sites.

Those details are just to show how the feeling developed that we could not solve the origin question without handling the whole problem: definition of the shape of the amphorae, a survey for discovering the workshops, and the building up of chemical reference groups. We naturally came to the necessity of magnetic prospections done first by an associated team of Montpellier (Bouisset et al. 1979) (Fig. 2), and then by ourselves when we could get our own proton magnetometer, particularly adapted to kiln detection. We also used spatial density studies for detection of potter's dumps (Figs. 3a and 3b).

Excavation of workshops was undertaken in four of these, chosen to present a large variety of productions and situations: Salleles d'Aude (Aude) (Fig. 4), Corneilhan (Hérault), Tresques (Gard), and Frejus (Var).

Our first analytical and typological results on the Corneilhan workshop (near Béziers in southern France) showed a complicating aspect of the question. This first century A.D. workshop was producing amphorae with shapes generally attributed to Spain or Italy (Laubenheimer and Widemann 1977). It can be likely interpreted as a tendency among the early Roman colonists for imitating shapes carrying successful wines. A further step in this study showed a later general tendency in Gaul for standardization in shape and size of amphorae, most workshops producing only the type Gauloise 4 (Widemann et al. 1978) (Fig. 5) after the second century.

After a three-year survey we have found about forty workshops in France where amphorae were produced during the Roman era (Fig. 6) — without counting those we saw that produced something else.

Figure 4. General view of excavations in the workshop of Salleles d'Aude (Summer 1980) towards the south. Kilns of different shapes and sizes, as well as walls from other buildings of the workshop, are distinct. The little square kiln was found with its last loading still on the sole. There is stratigraphic evidence showing it was given up and filled up before the amphorae production started in the workshop around the middle of the first century A.D.

Material from about half of the workshops has been analyzed by neutron activation analysis, and we started provenance searches for exported amphorae (Laubenheimer et al. 1980) during completion of the reference collection (Fontes et al. 1980). We distinguished seven principal shapes of flat-bottom amphorae particular to Gaul, out of which the Gauloise 4 and Gauloise 1 remain the most frequent. Also, four shapes in common with other provinces were observed (Figs. 7, 8, 9).

Interdisciplinary Understandings

We feel this work could not have been possible in this relatively brief period of time without a close association between classical archaeologists, physicists, and computer specialists sharing all of the different parts of the work. Coming to our laboratory, people are sometimes surprised to see a classical archaeologist doing very well at practicing activation analysis or a physicist at working in the field. This work is good for both, and gives a very useful mutual understanding.

The contribution of people of apparently very "disadapted" training reveals itself to be often original and worthy, such as the contribution of archaeologists to the organization of sampling and measurements, or the contributions of natural science people to prospections and excavations and the computer recording of ceramics. Our main problem in working on sites with numerous potter's dumps is to

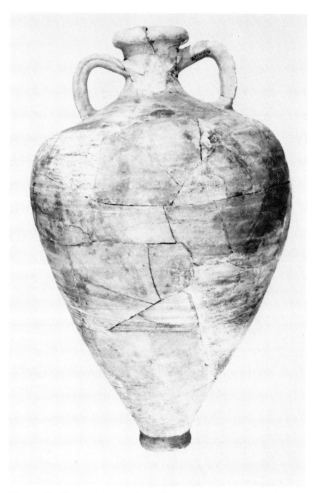

Figure 5. Type G.4 amphora from a potter's dump in the Salleles d'Aude workshop. This type, the standard Gaulish type after the second century A.D., was produced in many workshops distributed in all Gaul with little shape variations. Analyses are necessary in this case for the reconstruction of food production and trade. This type was produced at least until the fourth century A.D.

build up sampling methods in the field and really understand what is representative in the limited number of objects we work on. The use of such sampling methods is an essential condition for considering any quantitative studies with economy through origin results (Evans 1973).

We cannot escape facing the problem of the conservation of workshop sites. Wine producers sometimes like to drink an amphora of foreign wine and we frequently find in given workshops ceramics of a different origin (Widemann et al. 1978). Gathering sherds on the surface of a workshop is often misleading for the making of reference groups. However, we are forced to do this in many occurrences because we cannot dig everywhere. We know that reference groups made in this way can be taken only as tentative, both for uncertainty of real local origin and for lack of information on the representativeness of the

F. Widemann

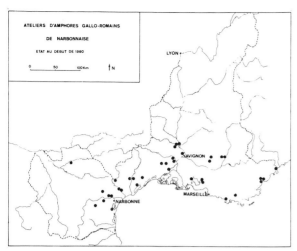

Figure 6. Map of the workshops that produced amphorae in Roman Gaul. Locations shown are inclusive as of March 1980; some other workshops have been located since.

Figure 7. Amphora found in Wiesbaden (W. Germany) and shown by neutron activation analysis to come from the Salleles d'Aude workshop. Size parameters agree with this attribution.

sampling. People dealing with origin studies of ceramics cannot be indifferent to the future of the workshop sites. These are the only places containing information for a rational definition of the shapes as well as the composition ranges associated with an origin. Progress in intensity measurement of magnetic thermoremanent field and thermoluminescence dating are soon going to give workshops a very important place in dating (Aitken 1979).

All these reasons led us to be perhaps the first nuclear physics laboratory to get money from administration to buy a 20,000 m² vineyard and find legal tricks for the protection of some others against building constructions.

The point I have tried to make is that if archaeology needs the introduction of physical and other methods, correct application of those methods to historical problems equally requires close cooperation of archaeologists with classical training. This is why we have organized an interdisciplinary team in Orsay. Our archaeologists do not work the same way as their colleagues who are indifferent to or only occasionally deal with natural sciences. The choice of excavation sites, for instance, or the strategy of excavations, and the definition of series of artifacts are not at all classical. The attitude concerning conservation of sites is also conditioned by the needs of this integrated work.

It is not a question of developing archaeometry as a separate discipline, but we have the feeling of interfering in archaeology that gives way to all sorts of accusations of usurpation of competence. It would be true for a single man trying to go out of his specialty, but not for an interdisciplinary team. I believe this organization is very stimulating and well adapted to our frontier.

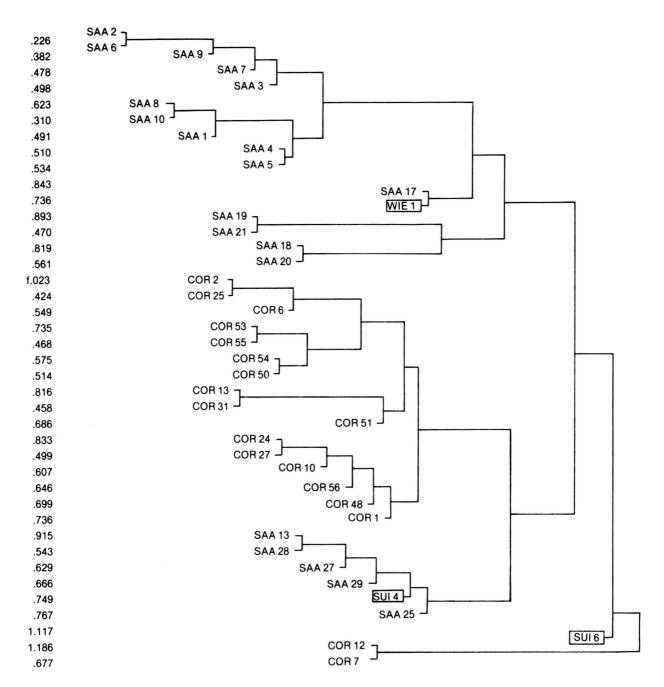

.226	SAA 2
.382	SAA 6
.478	SAA 9
.498	SAA 7
.623	SAA 3
.310	SAA 8
.491	SAA 10
.510	SAA 1
.534	SAA 4
.843	SAA 5
.736	
.893	SAA 17
.470	WIE 1
.819	SAA 19
.561	SAA 21
f.023	SAA 18
.424	SAA 20
.549	COR 2
.735	COR 25
.468	COR 6
.575	COR 53
.514	COR 55
.816	COR 54
.458	COR 50
.686	COR 13
.833	COR 31
.499	COR 51
.607	COR 24
.646	COR 27
.699	COR 10
.736	COR 56
.915	COR 48
.543	COR 1
.629	SAA 13
.666	SAA 28
.749	SAA 27
.767	SAA 29
1.117	SUI 4
1.186	SAA 25
.677	COR 12 / COR 7 / SUI 6

Figure 8. Cluster analysis of neutron activation analysis of Salleles and Corneilhan workshops showing several attributions of amphorae exported during the first and second centuries to the northern military frontier of the Empire and Rhaetia (Switzerland). The program Bacchus (for CDC 6600) was derived by Joseph Lleres (GANOS) from the one used in Brookhaven thanks to its friendly communication by Garman Harbottle and Dominique Fillieres.

Figure 9. Cluster analysis of the chemical composition of productions of three workshops in southern France: Aspiran, Tressan, and Frejus. Notice the clear separation of composition subgroups of different shapes within the Aspiran workshop, a rather important one in the Hérault basin: Pascual 1 are amphorae of a shape produced in the Tarraconnensis region (Spain). Their group is distinct from the Gauloise 4. The terra sigillata group, although local, shows more differences than the Tressan Gauloise 4 amphorae produced in another workshop of the neighborhood.

F. Widemann

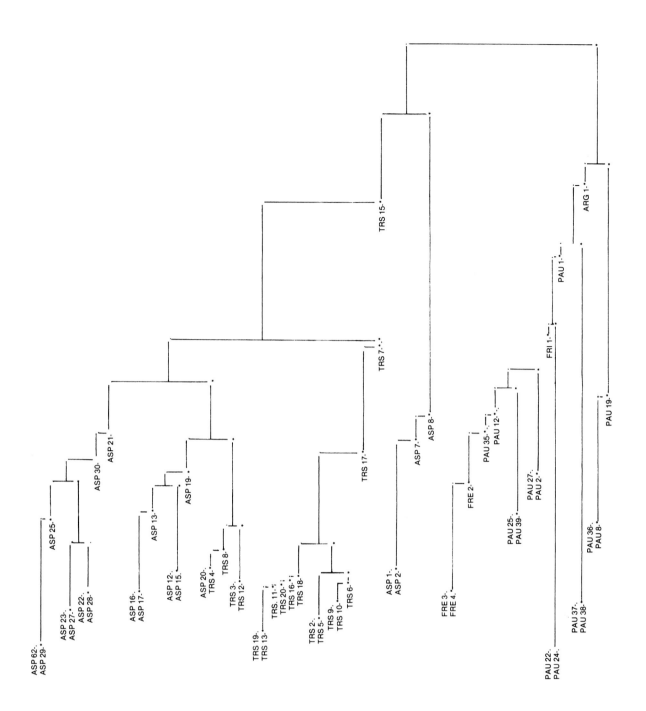

References

Aitken, M. 1979. Communication at the XIXth Symposium for Archaeometry, London. Forthcoming.

Bouisset, P.; Daigneres, M.; Gruel, K.; Laubenheimer, F.; Leblanc, J.; and Widemann, F. 1979. Prospections sur l'atelier de potiers gallo-romains de Salleles d'Aude. *Revue d'archéometrie* 3:23–44.

Callender, H. 1965. *Roman amphorae.* London.

Ettlinger, E. 1977. Aspects of amphora typology seen from the North. In *Méthodes classiques et méthodes formelles dans l'étude des amphores*, pp. 9–16. Paris and Rome.

Evans, J. D. 1973. Sherd weights and sherd counts: A contribution to the problem of quantifying potters studies. In *Archaeological theory and practice*, pp. 131–49. London.

Fontes, P.; Laubenheimer, F.; Leblanc, J.; Bonnefoy, F.; Gruel, K.; and Widemann, F. 1980. Nouvelles données analytiques et typologiques sur les ateliers de production d'amphores en Gaule du Sud. XXth International Symposium of Archaeometry, Paris. *Revue d'archéometrie*, suppt. 1981:95–110.

Laubenheimer, F. 1977. Amphores gauloises de la région de Nimes. Proceedings of the meeting on Géographie commerciale de la Gaule, Paris, June 1976. *Caesarodunum* 12:197–226.

Laubenheimer, F., and Widemann, F. 1977. L'atelier d'amphores de Corneilhan (Hérault): Typologie et analyse. *Revue d'archéometrie* 1:59–82.

Laubenheimer, F.; Fontes, P.; Leblanc, J.; Dodinet, M.; Lacharme, Y.; Lleres, J.; and Widemann, F. 1980. Analyse par activation neutronique d'amphores gallo-romaines. Mise en évidence d'exportations aux frontières de l'Empire. XXth International Symposium of Archaeometry, Paris. *Revue d'archéometrie*, suppt. 1981:155–175.

Panella, C. 1973. *Ostia III*, parte seconda, Anfore, pp. 463–643. Rome.

Schachermeyr, F. 1978. Die agäische Frühzeit I. Die vormykenischen Perioden des griechischen Festlandes und der Kykladen, pp. 20, 35. *See* review by René Treuil in *Revue archéologique* 2:323.

Scollar I., ed. 1978. *Proceedings of the 18th International Symposium on Archaeometry and Archaeological Prospection.* Bonn, 14–17 March 1978. *Archaeophysika* 10.

Tchernia, A., and Villa, J. P. 1977. Note sur le matériel recueilli dans la fouille d'un atelier d'amphores à Velaux (B.d.R). In *Méthodes classiques et méthodes formelles dans l'étude des amphores*, pp. 231–39. Paris and Rome.

Widemann, F.; Laubenheimer, F.; Attas, M.; Fontes, P.; Gruel, K.; Leblanc, J.; and Lleres, J. 1978. Analytical and typological study of Gallo-Roman workshops producing amphorae in the area of Narbonne. *Archaeophysika* 10: 317–41.

3. Plausible Inferences From Ceramic Artifacts

W. D. Kingery
Massachusetts Institute of Technology

Abstract

Ceramic artifact examination requires evaluation, either implicitly or explicitly, of conjectures (hypotheses, postulates) from which more or less credible inferences can be deduced and tested. The nature of the induction process and the nature of artifact data are discussed in order to evaluate the sorts of inferences with which we are concerned, and how we may hope to achieve a higher degree of credibility for the plausible inferences which we derive from ceramic artifact examination. These inferences lead directly to statements about the history and prehistory of ceramic technology, which is a worthy goal in itself, but also a requirement for subsequent archaeological, anthropological, and historical inferences. Essential requirements for more rapid advancement of the field are discussed.

Introduction

We have a heritage of trial by combat, an adversary legal system and debating procedures, and in general tend to anticipate confrontations of the good and the bad. Perhaps it is not strange that in this environment, stylistic analysis is occasionally pictured as somehow opposed to and ''less scientific'' than chemical analysis. In my view, nothing could be further from the truth.

I should like to attempt starting with an empty plate, so to speak, going on to consider the nature of plausible inferences, the nature of data extractable from ceramic artifacts and how these, in tandem, can lead to credible ceramic artifact interpretations. These interpretations are directly related to the history and prehistory of ceramic technology and form a basis for subsequent inferences about many other things.

I shall not discuss experimental methods in any detail; that decision is made easy by the fact that after eight years Michael Tite's book *Methods of Physical Examination in Archaeology* (Tite 1972) continues to provide superb general coverage of that subject, and more recent descriptions of rapidly developing techniques are easily accessible.

Time limitations have led me to organize a conceptual and incomplete rather than an analytical and fully documented presentation, and to provide rather less anecdotal evidence than might be usual.

Plausible Inference

Philosophic discussions of science often focus on the negative concept of demonstrative falsification; historical discussions more often focus on the positive aspects of credible discoveries. There have been many analyses of induction and the development of plausible inferences, but by far the best is the one by

G. Polya, who has rationalized these positive inductive approaches in a unified treatment on which we shall rely (Polya 1954). It illuminates some of the common ground between natural science, archaeology, and history (Bloch 1953). While there are several patterns of plausible reasoning, we shall for illustrative purposes consider only one: examining a consequence implied by and deduced from a conjecture. If the deduced consequence is true, then we can have more confidence in the credibility of our conjecture, but it is not in any logical sense proved "true." If the deduced consequence is false, logic requires that the hypothesis is also false. However, the history of the hardest of our hard sciences shows that the truth or falsity of an experimental result or observation is never absolute (Polanyi 1958). As a result, outside of pure mathematics, we are always operating in a gray region of shaded inference such as illustrated in Table 1.

One way of differentiating the series *mathematics-physics-materials science-archaeology* is that mathematics deals with defined systems in which consequences can be quite definitely true or false; physics deals with defined systems in which near certainty can sometimes be approached; artifact interpretation operates in the central region of shaded, relatively uncertain inference. Clearly one way in which we can aim to achieve more credible conclusions is by dealing with more certain "consequences," and that is a very strong reason why some tests and measurements are preferable to others.

Working in an area where any one test is unlikely standing alone to be fully conclusive, or even highly convincing, we must ask: How can we make our inferences more credible, indeed even highly credible? Various possibilities exist; the patterns of a few are illustrated in Table 2. If a consequence is verified so that a conjecture becomes more credible, subsequent successive verifications can only increase its credibility. However, by analogy we might well *expect* that these successive verifications would occur, so the strength of additional confidence generated by cumulative verifications increases when the new consequences verified are very *different* from the previous ones. This is a point where statistics can get us into trouble. While achieving credibility for a "statistical conjecture" is possible, statistics can never tell us how "different" are different "statistical conjectures"!

Even more important than successive verifications, the degree of confidence generated by a verification of a consequence is related to the likelihood of the consequence's occurring or being observed independent of the conjecture being tested. For that reason,

quantitative and mathematical consequences that are inherently unlikely and improbable standing by themselves lead to a much stronger degree of credibility than qualitative tests, which do not seem necessarily unlikely with or without a precedent hypothesis. Statistics can help here, but also can be dangerous (see Polya).

But, we may ask, how does all this affect the study of ceramic artifacts as archaeological material? Well, first it suggests posing the question as to whether the traditional sorts of stylistic analysis or the kinds of measurements sometimes described as "physics applied to archaeology" can, by themselves, lead to strong conclusive statements. Without arguing the point, I shall assert that the historical evidence says no (e.g., Bonn Symposium 1978); we are most commonly, but not always, in the region of shaded inference (Table 1). Therefore, it behooves us to consider seriously ways in which *successive verifications of very different sorts* and even *quantitative mathematical verifications* (Table 2) may be attempted in an effort to achieve strong, highly credible support for our conjectures.

Artifact Data

The sorts of information available from careful examination of a ceramic artifact are not unlimited, but they are also seldom fully utilized.

Provenance For artifact interpretation it is an enormous advantage to know precisely from where an artifact has come. I have a so-called "T'ang" horse I believe was manufactured in China early in this century, as is true of some museum samples (Fleming 1974), but all I really know is that it was purchased from a dealer in China about forty years ago; it is not an appropriate object for research. I am currently interested in the preparation of prehistoric Azilian pigment materials, which is a bit complicated because some fraction of museum samples were made in the late nineteenth century. Studies of artifacts having doubtful provenance are to be avoided, if possible.

In provenance we often need to have a description of the entire sample environment, not merely its archaeological stratification and site location, associated artifacts and features, important as those are. Is the environment one subjected to ground water? What is the radioactivity of the surrounding soil? What is the geology of the area? What are the characteristics of the local mineral deposits? These sorts of environment data are extremely important but seldom available.

Style A principal and powerful tool of museum curators and classical archaeologists has been style (Amiran 1965, 1970; Lane 1947, 1971; Jenyns 1971).

W. D. Kingery

Table 1. *Examining a Consequence*[1]

Demonstrative:	1.	Conjecture implies consequence	Mathematics
	2.	Consequence false	
	3.	Therefore conjecture false	
Shaded Demonstrative:	1.	Conjecture implies consequence	
	2.	Consequence *probably* false	ARTIFACT INFERENCES
	3.	Therefore conjecture less credible	
Uncertain:	1.	Conjecture implies consequence	
	2.	Consequence uncertain	
	3.	Therefore conjecture credibility unchanged	
Shaded Inductive:	1.	Conjecture implies consequence	
	2.	Consequence *probably* true	
	3.	Therefore consequence somewhat more credible	
Inductive:	1.	Conjecture implies consequence	
	2.	Consequence true	
	3.	Therefore consequence more credible	Mathematics

[1]Adapted from Polya (1954), p. 26.

Recognizable motifs, patterns, sizes, and shapes characterize particular artifact assemblages, artists, periods, and localities. However, well-known controversies such as the New York Metropolitan Museum of Art's "Bronze Horse" (Zimmerman, Yuhas, and Meyers 1974), and many less famous examples argue

Table 2. *Different Sorts of Consequences*

Successive Verification:

A. 1. Conjecture implies several similar consequences
   2. All these similar consequences true
   3. Therefore conjecture more credible

B. 1. Conjecture implies several *very different* consequences
   2. All these *very different* consequences true
   3. Therefore conjecture *much more credible*

"Incredible" Verifications:

A. 1. Conjecture implies a consequence which is quite likely in any event
   2. Consequence true
   3. Therefore conjecture only slightly more credible

B. 1. Conjecture implies a consequence which is *almost incredible* standing by itself
   2. Consequence true
   3. Therefore conjecture is much more *credible, even almost certain*

that conclusions based on style alone may be in the region of relatively weak inference. There is on display at the Musée de Saint-Germain-en-Laye in Paris an Azilian pebble with an animal representation, but stylistic argument indicates that animal representations are not Azilian. What are we to conclude?

External Characteristics Falling into the gap between the work of a physicist and that of an archaeologist, careful and thoughtful examination of a ceramic artifact with the naked eye, magnifying glass, or low-power binocular microscope can often lead to useful data (Richter 1923; Medley 1976; Gettens 1969; Palmgren et al. 1963). For example, there is some difference of opinion about the time of appearance of wheel-thrown ware. A ceramist looking at the cross section and foot of a 3500 B.C. sample from Tepe Yahya (Kingery 1980) can be most confident that it was thrown on a fast wheel. Articulating the reasons for this conclusion may be somewhat more difficult as it is a conclusion based on ceramic experience as well as either physics or archaeology; other wheel-thrown ware may be very difficult to identify. We recently examined a sample for which wildly different chemical analyses had been reported to the archaeologist in charge. Observation with a binocular microscope indicated that the sample was a mixture on a scale such that sampling technique was responsible for the variable chemical analyses, rather than any archaeological factor. In another case, we have examined a sample of sandstone refractory used for copper smelting and been able to establish with subsequent microscopy that structural changes of the heat-altered region are related to the time-temperature history of the smelting process (Kingery and Gourdin 1976). Many other examples can be cited in which thoughtful, careful sample examination is most fruitful.

Laboratory Replication A proposed ancient process can only become more credible if laboratory replication shows that it is indeed a possible and practical method. Thus, it has been an important constituent in many classic and important studies (Franchet 1911; Wu 1938; Kieffer and Allibert 1971; Noble 1965; Coles 1973; Weiss 1979).

Ethnographic Observations Direct observation of traditional techniques for making or using ceramic articles can provide detailed information about ways of working which experience has shown to be successful, and also provides insight into ways of looking at phenomena and operations that influence production methods in a way very different from our own cultural environment (Franchet 1911; Wulff 1966; Matson 1980; David and Hennig 1972; Rye and Evans 1976).

Dating The principal and most important laboratory development of the last thirty years has been the new capability offered by carbon 14, magnetic, thermoluminescence, fission tract, and surface hydration dating (Michael and Ralph 1971; Young 1973).

Chemical Composition Artifact chemistry can be done on several levels, often complicated by the fact that minimal sample destruction is allowed and that sampling problems can be substantial. In addition to the question of obtaining a representative sample from any one artifact, there is the associated problem of how to treat the artifact population. Over-all analyses can consist of the major constituents, or of trace elements, or of particular isotopes (Perlman and Asaro 1971; Brill et al. 1967, 1970, 1979; Sayre 1967, 1974; Brill and Wampler 1967; Brill et al. 1973; Yellin et al. 1978; Lambert and McLaughlin 1978) — or any of these can be applied to particular constituents in the artifact; for example, feldspar or quartz grains added as tempering or present as impurities (Kamilli and Lamberg-Karlovsky 1979; Oates et al. 1977). One or more of these measurements may or may not be useful in leading to plausible interpretations and inferences about the artifact and the artifact population. Without some clear inferential objective, it would seem that a lot of time and effort and money could be expended with but little advantage. Fortunately, modern instrumental methods make such efforts substantially less time- and fund-consuming than was formerly the case.

Physical Properties Artifact properties can be determined in an almost unlimited number of ways depending on the apparatus, samples, and skills available (Palmgren et al. 1963; Matson 1965, 1974; Beck 1934; Coey, Bouchez, and Dang 1980). Strength, hardness, color, density, porosity, Mössbauer spectra, magnetic properties, electrical properties, thermal properties, and many others are susceptible to measurement and have been measured. As is true of chemical determinations, these measurements are only likely to have significance when coupled with a clear inferential objective.

Phase Composition The individual crystalline and amorphous phases present and their relative amounts can often be determined (Bimson 1969; Rooksby 1964; Noll et al. 1978, 1979) by optical, electron and X-ray diffraction techniques aided by chemical analysis of the individual phases which can be done without too much difficulty using modern instrumental methods. The nature and amount of different phases present characterize a particular artifact in a way that strengthens and complements chemical analyses. However, ceramic artifacts are seldom equilibrium-phase assemblages, so it is rare for process inferences to be strongly supported by phase data alone.

Microstructure By microstructure, we mean the size, composition, shape, and relative amounts and arrangement of the different phases present, including porosity, as well as the observation of partially complete reactions at the boundaries between phases (Shepard 1942, 1948; Farnsworth 1964, 1970; Kingery 1974; Tite et al. 1981). Microstructure can be determined optically in polished or thin sections and with the much higher magnification appropriate to fine particle size clay constituents by scanning electron microscopy, or in a few rare cases, by transmission electron microscopy. Because the microstructure tends to be characteristic of particular mineral assemblages and reaction processes, it is a much stronger tool than chemical analysis or phase analysis standing alone, but it also requires more ceramic and physical chemical background to properly interpret (Kingery and Frierman 1974; Gourdin and Kingery 1975; Kingery, Bowen, and Uhlmann 1976). It should be used more often.

Summary

It seems that, in principle, these are the different sorts of artifactual data with which we can test our conjectures and from which we can draw inferences: provenance, style, external characteristics, laboratory replication, ethnographic observations, dating, chemical composition, physical properties, phase composition, microstructure. These possibilities, with the exception of laboratory dating and electron microscopy, have been available for fifty years and more, and all of these methods have been long employed in studies of ceramic artifacts. However, there has been a dramatic change in the power of these methods with the electronic, computation, and instrumentation revolutions of the last twenty years. More, and more precise measurements are possible; this increased capability puts a greater burden of *choice* on artifact examiners.

In passing we may note that it is implicit in the greater observational possibilities that requirements of artifact evaluators to maximize their results with what are increasingly effective laboratory examinations sooner or later will force substantial changes on the over-all budgetary patterns appropriate to serious archaeological studies.

Inferences

According to the patterns of the inductive reasoning which we have briefly discussed, it is *first of all necessary to have a conjecture* (hypothesis, postulate) *that can be made more or less plausible, perhaps even highly credible, by examining its consequences.* Without some sort of conjecture to direct the research effort, the most expert artifact examination may become merely an exercise in technique. Whenever possible, it is desirable to have clearly articulated conjectures. Of course, having a conjecture and deducing consequences from it which can be tested presupposes some knowledge — specifically some knowledge about ceramics.

While the *direction* of the change in plausibility of our inferences usually can be categorically stated, *the strength of these conclusions is always a matter of judgment.* Examination of the historical level of acceptance of inferences in a field is the best guide to the degree in which a high degree of credibility has been achieved. Judged by this standard, it is fair to say that we are often dealing with weak or moderately weak inferences when we interpret ceramic artifacts (e.g., Bonn Symposium 1978) and that a good deal of advance thought aimed at strengthening our inferences is warranted. For example, a great advantage of carbon-14 and thermoluminescent dating is that they yield quantitative numerical data. However, when results of these methods conflict with conclusions based on stratification data, archaeologists normally assume that "something went wrong" with the laboratory measurements — often rightly so. Precisely because these methods lead to quantitative data, strong efforts aimed at improving and refining them, applying them to larger classes of artifacts,

and eliminating factors leading to erroneous results are of the greatest importance.

In the same way that the classes of artifact data are limited, the classes of artifact inference are but few. We may hope to infer: when an artifact was made; where an artifact was made; how an artifact was made; by whom an artifact was made; and why an artifact was made. There are also questions of where, when, how, by whom, and why an artifact was used and discarded, but we shall focus on manufacture. From these inferences, anthropologists and archaeologists and art historians and even TV producers may go on to other sorts of inferences, but that need not concern us here.

When an Artifact Was Made
This formerly difficult and vexing problem is fascinating history and has now become our most solid knowledge. The quite different evidences of provenance, style, carbon-14, thermoluminescence and other dating techniques, when in accord, lead to highly credible statements about the age of artifacts. Extension of both the range of materials and time periods covered, as well as of the reliability, availability, and use of laboratory dating techniques, remains a continuing serious need.

Where an Artifact Was Made
Depending on the precision aimed at and the conjecture proposed, nontrivial strong inferences about exactly where an artifact was made have seldom been possible by provenance and style alone, even when "style" is interpreted to mean measurement of several different attributes. However, when combined with laboratory tests, particularly tests that are of quite a different kind, highly credible conclusions that a body of ware forms a self-coherent group are entirely feasible. A criticism that might be leveled at some particular researches is that they used only *one* laboratory test, and therefore did not achieve the degree of credibility that could have been possible, or that they did not quantify measurements to the extent possible. A recent combination of exhaustive stylistic and geographical distribution analysis *plus* neutron activation analysis of several elements on the same group of samples much more than doubled the credibility of either analysis standing alone (Kaplan, Harbottle, and Sayre 1979).

Now "self-coherent group" and "where an artifact was made" are not identical statements, and a severe deficiency with regard to ceramic artifact interpretation is the paucity of data and standards with regard to raw materials used for ceramics, variations in raw materials, and our meager collections and tests of raw materials. There has been but little support for developing the level of characterization of raw material standards that is an absolute prerequisite to develop highly credible inferences about where an artifact was made.

How an Artifact Was Made

There are many levels of the question "how an artifact was made," and inferences about "how" are often ones from which the most interesting further inferences can be anticipated. We can pose questions as to how and from where raw material was collected, how the raw material was treated before forming, how the ceramic ware was shaped, how it was finished, how it was decorated or treated before firing, how it was fired, how it was decorated or treated after firing, and so forth. By and large these questions are not absolute, as is age or a geographical location, but are relative and require a comparison which again implies standards, implicit or explicit.

Consider the question, How was it fired? The temperature of firing can be estimated in various ways — thermal expansion, porosity, magnetic properties, changes in microstructure — compared to standards, which are most often refiring tests of the piece itself, and most often lead to inferences only about the maximum temperature to which the particular sherd could have been exposed. Inferences about general production techniques from one sherd are obviously very weak. Experienced potters know that obtaining a uniform kiln temperature in a well-designed, well-instrumented kiln is quite difficult, and that interpreting the temperature of one sample as the average kiln temperature is absurd. An interpretation that a range of apparent "firing temperatures" at a single "kiln site" signify a "misfiring" is clearly an inference involving much judgment. Oxidizing and reducing conditions can affect phase equilibria, the formation of a liquid phase, the degree of vitrification achieved, and therefore the apparent firing temperature. A mostly oxidizing fire with a final reduction, or a mostly reducing fire with a final oxidation, can obscure interpretations.

From this simplest and most quoted production characteristic, it is clear that both excellent comparison standards and trained judgments based on a good knowledge of physical chemistry, the potter's art, and ceramic structure and properties are essential for the development of strong inferences and proper interpretations.

Other aspects of the question as to how a particular artifact was made show different variations on the theme, but in each case we find that *(a)* adequate standards and *(b)* professional judgments are required. The training of professional ceramists is adequate, but demands of the current marketplace force almost all into a sort of specialization that does not develop the broad experience necessary for evaluation of a wide range of artifact properties and types. A superficial papering of pottery onto an archaeologist or anthropologist, without the requisite physics, chemistry, and thermodynamics, is more often harmful than helpful. I see no ready solution other than that agencies and foundations give their maximum support to promising opportunities for the development of specialists in the field of artifact interpretation.

With regard to standards, we must again admit that our field is in its infancy, and that the level of current assets is completely inadequate. The potentially most useful techniques are our new capacity for supermagnification with transmission and scanning electron microscopes (discussed in this symposium by Michael Tite [*see* Sec. II, chap. 10]), for trace element analyses by neutron activation and other methods, and for the chemical analysis of tiny mineral fragments of a ceramic with Auger spectroscopy and other instrumental methods. Alas, there is but little with which to compare these data. (This is in contrast to our hundred years' experience with metallurgical and geological optical microscopy which, unfortunately, does not have the resolution necessary for many aspects of examination required for clay-based ware.) Supporting agencies should give high priority to the development of appropriate standards.

By Whom an Artifact Was Made

In combination with provenance, style is the predominant tool of identifying authorship, and the use of different aspects of style is required. But styles can be cleverly forged, and other tests — chemical analyses, physical properties, microscopic and electron microscopic characterizations, thermoluminescence, among others — can provide independent confirmations that render a stylistic interpretation very credible.

Why an Artifact Was Made

Provenance, style, external examination, laboratory replications, and ethnographic observations lead to inferences about why an artifact was made. Obviously, a funerary urn is quite different from a pitcher, but the intended function of an artifact may be questioned from many levels and points of view. The number of similar artifacts and their uniformity or perhaps their scarcity may be pertinent. But additional support for such inferences may be derived from measurable characteristics having an influence on utility. As an example, crucibles which melt at 950° C cannot possibly have been used as containers for molten copper melting at 1050° C, as has sometimes been suggested. Ovens that have never been hotter than a few hundred degrees centigrade cannot have

W. D. Kingery

been used for firing higher-temperature ceramics. Permeable jars cannot have been used for transporting wine, at least without some sort of lining. An abrasive must be harder than the material being abraded.

In general, laboratory measurements have not been much aimed at supporting or contradicting inferences about functional utility and why artifacts were made. This may well be an area of fruitful research which should be pursued.

Selection of Procedures

It is tempting to prepare a table of macroscopic and microscopic, physical and chemical, field and laboratory procedures to be recommended. And we cannot avoid the temptation to urge that provenance, style, and careful, thoughtful, repeated hand lens and binocular microscope examination of external characteristics be a part of every artifact examination. Further procedures should be decided only after the formulation of conjectures to be tested.

Discussion

While the number of different classes of artifact data is limited, there are an enormous number of quite different specific measurement techniques which may be used. Similarly, while there are only a limited number of different types of inferences which may be conjectured about artifacts, there are numberless specific ones we might imagine. The essential task in interpreting artifacts is to find a conjecture that can be tested, and then to select and obtain measurements and data leading to highly credible inferences.

Among the most important of such data are provenance and style, whose characteristics can lead to surer inferences as they become more precisely articulated — in some cases, even mathematical and quantitative. Style of ceramics should often be extended to include the idea of technological style of materials preparation, shaping, and finishing, as well as size, shape, and decoration.

The principal technological advance toward credible artifact interpretations has been the development of dating techniques — and technique improvement is a continuing need. The principal deficiencies preventing highly credible interpretations of artifacts have been (1) a lack of sufficiently different sorts of tested consequences (i.e., dependence on only one kind of test or several very similar tests); (2) a lack of interpretations based on a combined knowledge of measurement techniques, physical chemistry, and ceramic technology; and (3) an almost complete lack of satisfactory comparison reference standards, most particularly in the areas of raw materials (including their chemical and trace element variability), fine-scale microstructure and fine-scale chemical analyses on which to base interpretations.

High credibility requires confirmations that are as sure as possible, as many as possible, as different as possible, and as many as can be found which verge on being incredible unless our conjecture is true (which usually means being as mathematical and quantitative as possible). In this inductive process there are no automatic procedures; judgments are necessary. It is because of this judgmental aspect that we should separate out the process of artifact interpretation from the quite different and equally creative roles of the archaeologist, design engineer, tort lawyer, anthropologist, and TV producer.

I've recently asked a student to review published studies of the influence of heat treatment on flint flaking. This requires study of the appropriate phase equilibrium diagrams (physical chemistry), the nature of flint microstructure and microstructure changes (physical ceramics), the structures of natural flint (petrography), and the fracture process (fracture mechanics). He has much to learn. I mention this because I believe that the relatively weak inferences possible from only one measurement similarly require that effective artifact interpretation must utilize multiple and different tools.

Information as to when, where, how, by whom, and why an artifact was made leads very naturally to important ideas about the whole process of technological development. Whether an artifact was wholly decorative or also useful tells us much about why the technology was attempted as well as where, when, and by whom. It is both appropriate and desirable for us to forge ahead in the direction of synthesizing, building, and developing an identity for the specialist field of artifact interpretation. It leads to immediate inferences about the history and prehistory of ceramics, and is an essential component of every approach toward more all-encompassing historical, archaeological, and anthropological interpretations.

Artifact interpretation deserves being a discipline itself, one able and willing to utilize multidisciplinary tools.

Acknowledgments: The helpful comments and assistance of P. Vandiver and H. Averback are much appreciated.

References

Note: Included in this list are a few pertinent references not explicitly cited in text.

Amiran, Ruth. 1965. The beginnings of pottery making in the Near East. In Matson, F., *Ceramics and man.* Chicago: Aldine Publishing Co.

_____. 1970. *Ancient pottery of the Holy Land.* New Brunswick, N.J.: Rutgers University Press.

Bannister, F. A., and Plenderleith, H. J. 1936. Physico-chemical examination of a scarab of Tuthomosis IV bearing the name of the god Aton. *Journal of Egyptian Archaeology* 22: 3-6.

Beck, Horace C. 1934. Notes on glazed stones, part I, glazed steatite. *Ancient Egypt and the East.* 19-37.

Bimson, M. 1969. The examination of ceramics by X-ray powder diffraction. *Studies in Conservation* 14: 83-89.

Bloch, Marc. 1953. *The historian's craft.* New York: Alfred A. Knopf, Inc.

Bonn Symposium. 1978. *Proceedings of the 18th International Symposium on Archaeometry and Archaeological Prospection.* Bonn: Rudolf Habelt Verlag.

Brill, Robert H.; Yamasaki, Kazuo; Barnes, I. Lynus; Rosman, K. J. R.; and Diaz, Migdalia. 1979. Lead isotopes in some Japanese and Chinese glasses. *Ars Orientalis* 11: 87-109. Washington, D.C.: Freer Gallery of Art.

Brill, Robert H., and Wampler, J. M. 1967. Isotope ratios in archaeological objects of lead. In *Applications of science in the examination of works of art.* Boston: Museum of Fine Arts.

Brill, Robert H.; Shields, W. R.: and Wampler, J. M. 1973. New directions in lead isotope work. In *Applications of science in the examination of works of art.* Boston: Museum of Fine Arts.

Coey, J. D. M.; Bouchez, R.; and Dang, N. V. 1980. Ancient techniques. *Journal of applied physics,* in press.

Coles, John. 1973. *Archaeology by experiment.* London: Hutchinson University Library.

David, N., and Hennig, H. 1972. *The ethnography of pottery: A Fulani case seen in archaeological perspective.* Addison-Wesley Modular Publications, no. 21.

Dobel, Alan; Asaro, Frank; and Michel, H. V. 1977. Neutron activation analysis and the location of Wassukanni. *Orientalia* 46: 375-82.

Farnsworth, Marie. 1964. Greek pottery: a mineralogical study. *American Journal of Archaeology* 68: 221-28.

_____. 1970. Corinthian pottery: technical studies. *American Journal of Archaeology* 74: 9-20.

Fleming, S. J. 1974. Thermoluminescent authenticity studies of unglazed T'ang dynasty ceramic tomb goods. *Archaeometry* 16: 91-95.

Franchet, L. 1911. *Ceramique primitive.* Paris: Geuthner.

Franken, H. J. 1974. *In search of the Jericho potters.* New York: Elsevier Pub. Co.

_____, and Kalsbeek, J. 1975. *Potters of a medieval village in the Jordan Valley.* New York: Elsevier Pub. Co.

Gettens, Rutherford John. 1969. *The Freer Chinese bronzes. Vol. II, Technical Studies.* Washington, D.C.: Smithsonian Institution.

Gourdin, W. H., and Kingery, W. D. 1975. The beginnings of pyrotechnology: Neolithic and Egyptian lime plaster. *Journal of Field Archaeology* 2: 133-50.

Jenyns, Soame. 1971. *Japanese pottery.* London: Farber and Farber.

Kamilli, Diana C., and Lamberg-Karlovsky, C. C. 1979. Petrographic and electronic microprobe analysis of ceramics from Tepe Yahya, Iran. *Archaeometry* 21, pt. 2.

Kaplan, M. F.; Harbottle, G.; and Sayre, E. V. 1979. An archaeological and chemical analysis of Tell el Yahudiyeh ware. *Brookhaven National Laboratory Report.* BNL C-2203.

Kieffer, Charles, and Allibert, A. 1971. Pharoanic blue ceramics: The process of self glazing. *Archaeology* 24: 107-117.

Kingery, W. D. 1974. A technological characterization of two Cypriot ceramics. In Bishay, A., *Recent advances in the science and technology of materials.* New York: Plenum Press.

_____. 1980. Edward Orton, Jr., Memorial lecture: Social needs and ceramic technology. *Bulletin of the American Ceramic Society* 59, no. 6: 598-600.

_____, and Frierman, J. D. 1974. The firing temperature of a Karanova sherd and inferences about south-east European Chalcolithic refractory technology. *Proceedings of the Prehistoric Society* 40: 204-205.

_____, and Gourdin, W. H. 1976. Examination of furnace linings from Rothenberg site #590 in Wadi Zagha. *Journal of Field Archaeology* 3: 351-53.

_____, Bowen, H. K.; and Uhlmann, D. R. 1976. *Introduction to ceramics.* 2d ed. New York: Wiley.

Lambert, J. B., and McLaughlin, C. D. 1978. Analysis of early Egyptian glass by atomic absorption and X-ray photoelectron spectroscopy. In Carter, G. F., *Archaeological chemistry II.* Washington, D.C.: American Chemical Society.

Lane, Arthur. 1947. *Early Islamic pottery.* London: Faber.

_____. 1971. *Later Islamic pottery.* London: Faber.

Matson, Frederick. 1965. Ceramic ecology: an approach to the study of the early cultures of the Near East. In Matson, F., *Ceramics and man.* Chicago: Aldine Publishing Co.

_____. 1971. A study of temperatures used in firing ancient Mesopotamian pottery. In Brill, R. H., *Science and archaeology.* Cambridge: M.I.T. Press.

_____. 1974. Archaeological ceramic study possibilities with a thermal gradient furnace. In Beck, C. W., *Archaeological chemistry.* Washington, D.C.: American Chemical Society.

W. D. Kingery

_____. 1980. Archaeological ceramics and the physical sciences: Problem definition and results. In Olin, Jacqueline S., and Franklin, Alan D., eds., *Archaeological ceramics*, Sec. I, chap. 1. Washington, D.C.: Smithsonian Institution Press, forthcoming [1982].

Medley, Margaret. 1976. *The Chinese potter.* New York: Charles Scribner's Sons.

Michael, Henry N., and Ralph, Elizabeth K. 1971. *Dating techniques for the archaeologist.* Cambridge: M.I.T. Press.

Noble, Joseph V. 1965. *The techniques of painted Attic pottery.* London: Farber and Farber.

Noll, Walter. 1978. Mineralogie und Technik der bemalten Keramiken Altägyptens, *N. Jb. Miner. Abh.* 133: 227–90.

_____. 1979. Anorganische Pigmente in Vorgeschichte und Antike. *Fortschr. Miner.* 57: 203–263.

_____; Holm, R.; and Born, L. 1975. Bemalung antiker Keramik. *Angewandte Chemie* 87: 639–51.

Oates, J.; Davidson, T. E.; Kamilli, D.; and McKerrell, H. 1977. Seafaring merchants of Ur? *Antiquity* 51: 221–34.

Palmgren, Nils; Steger, Walter; and Sundius, Nils. 1963. *Sung sherds.* Stockholm: Almquist and Wiksell.

Peacock, D. P. S. 1967. The heavy mineral analysis of pottery. A preliminary report. *Archaeometry* 10: 97–100.

_____. 1970. The scientific analysis of ancient ceramics: A review. *World Archaeology* 1: 375–89.

Perlman, I., and Asaro, F. 1971. Pottery analysis by neutron activation. *Archaeometry* 13: 21–52; 1971. [Pottery analysis by neutron activation. In Brill, R. H., *Science and Archaeology.* Cambridge: M.I.T. Press, 1974.]

Pike, H. H. M. 1976. Pottery firing temperatures. *Archaeometry* 18: 111–14.

Polanyi, M. 1958. *Personal knowledge.* Chicago: University of Chicago Press.

Polya, George. 1954. *Patterns of plausible inference.* Vol. II, *Mathematics and plausible reasoning.* Princeton, N.J.: Princeton University Press.

Richter, Gisela. 1923. *The craft of Athenian pottery.* New Haven: Yale University Press.

Rooksby, H. P. 1964. A yellow cubic lead tin oxide opacifier in ancient glasses. *Physics and Chemistry of Glasses* 5, no. 1: 20–25.

Rye, Owen S., and Evans, Clifford. 1976. *Traditional pottery techniques of Pakistan.* Smithsonian Contributions to Anthropology, no. 21. Washington, D.C.: Smithsonian Institution Press.

Saleh, S. A. 1972. Study of glass and glass-making processes at Wadi el-Natrun, Egypt, in the Roman period 30 B.C. to 359 A.D. In *Studies in Conservation* 17: 143–72.

Sayre, Edward V. 1967. Summary of the Brookhaven program of analysis of ancient glass. In *Applications of science in the examination of works of art.* Boston: Museum of Fine Arts.

_____, and Smith, R. W. 1974. Analytical studies of ancient Egyptian glass. In Bishay, A., *Recent advances in the science and technology of materials,* no. 3. New York: Plenum Press.

Shepard, Anna O. 1942. *Rio Grande glaze paintware.* Publication 528. Washington, D.C.: Carnegie Institute.

_____. 1948. *Plumbate, a Meso-american trade ware.* Publication 573. Washington, D.C.: Carnegie Institute.

Tite, M. S. 1969. Determination of the firing temperature of ancient ceramics by measurement of thermal expansion: A reassessment. *Archaeometry* 11: 131–43.

_____. 1972. *Methods of physical examination in archaeology.* New York: Seminar Press.

_____, et al. 1979. Technological studies of ancient ceramics. In Wertime, T. A., and Wertime, S. F., eds., *Early pyrotechnology.* Washington, D.C.: Smithsonian Institution Press, forthcoming [1982].

Weiss, Gustav. 1979. *Alte Keramik neu entdekt.* Frankfurt/Main: Ullstein.

Wu, G. P. 1938. *Prehistoric pottery in China.* London: University of London.

Wulff, H. E. 1966. *The traditional crafts of Persia.* Cambridge: M.I.T. Press.

Yellin, J.; Perlman, I.; Asaro, F.; Michel, H. V.; and Mosier, D. F. 1978. Comparison of neutron activation analysis from the Lawrence Berkeley Laboratory and Hebrew University. *Archaeometry* 20, no. 1: 95–100.

Young, William J. 1949. Some notes on Shōsō-in T'ang and Ming pottery. *Far Eastern Ceramic Bulletin* 6: 55–61.

_____. 1949. Discussion of some analyses of Chinese underglaze blue and underglaze red. *Far Eastern Ceramic Bulletin* 8: 20–26.

_____. 1973. *Application of science to the dating of works of art.* Boston: Museum of Fine Arts.

_____. 1978 and 1979. A specialist seminar on thermoluminescence dating. PACT Vol. 2 (1978) and PACT Vol. 3 (1979). Strasbourg: Conseil de l'Europe.

Zimmerman, D. W.; Yuhas, M. P.; and Meyers, P. 1974. Thermoluminescence authenticity measurements on core material from the Bronze Horse of the New York Metropolitan Museum of Art. *Archaeometry* 16: 19–30.

4. Pottery Production, Pottery Classification, and the Role of Physicochemical Analyses

PRUDENCE M. RICE
Department of Anthropology
University of Florida

Archaeological ceramic technology, having grown haphazardly, has reached a period of ferment. New analytical procedures are at our disposal. To use them effectively, we must focus our efforts on problems of broad significance, define them clearly, and choose analytical methods critically.

A. O. Shepard, *Ceramics for the Archaeologist* (1976, p. xix)

Shepard's challenge, originally issued in 1965 in closing the Foreword to the fifth printing of her manual on ceramic analysis, has been met with equivocal success. Technical analyses of ceramics have been employed toward the solution of interesting research problems and the methods have undergone a great deal of refinement in the last twenty years. Archaeologists have lagged, however, in developing the concepts to deal with these newfound capabilities. The difficulties rest, in Shepard's words, in focusing our efforts on clearly defined problems of broad significance.

That such limitations still exist in 1980 is surprising in some respects, yet understandable in others. It is perhaps even more true today than in 1965 that archaeological ceramic studies are in a "ferment." A great diversity of approaches has developed, from the ethnoarchaeological to the technical, with the latter marked by a striking sophistication of analytical instrumentation. The objectives of these studies have similarly broadened, as have the goals of archaeological science in general. Although there is by no means agreement among archaeologists as to a primary goal of their discipline, an early concern with chronology has been largely replaced by questions involving more social, behavioral, or, in the currently fashionable jargon, "processual" issues. Among these, to name a few of specific interest to ceramic researchers, we might include such matters as technological development, and the socioeconomic organization of production and trade.

The equivocal success of ceramic studies may be partially explicated in terms of a failure to examine and evaluate the appropriateness for technological research of traditional basic procedures, one of which is pottery classification. The sorting and labeling of pottery sherds into chronologically sensitive types is a time-honored duty for archaeologists during and after the excavation of a site, a necessary step for dating structures, burials, middens, storage pits, and all manner of human activity. Yet this fundamental procedure has not been subject to the same sort of critical review as was undertaken nearly two decades ago in the general field of archaeology method and theory. This is not an appropriate place to attempt a complete review of archaeological classification studies (one of the best to date is Hill and

Evans 1972), but I would like to take the opportunity in this paper to examine the role of archaeological ceramic classification as it relates to broader and more complex kinds of pottery analyses, particularly physicochemical or technological studies and their interpretation.

In so doing, I will be dealing with three kinds or levels of ceramic study. The first and most elementary level is that of classification or categorization, which involves the observation and description of gross characteristics of a pottery collection, and its organization into similarity groups. It is, in fact, where the archaeologist begins his or her work with pottery. The second level is that of analysis, the study of attributes of the pottery and their co-occurrence, often, if not usually, as these traits cross-cut classificatory units. In this paper I shall concentrate, for very specific reasons, on technological and physicochemical analyses, but there are a multitude of different kinds of analyses performed on pottery — functional, stylistic, and so forth. The third kind or level of ceramic study is that of interpretation of a ceramic collection, or interpretation of some part or whole of a site or region's cultural development in terms of the pottery recovered from that site or region. At this interpretational level I intend to confine my discussion specifically to inferences of organization of production and trade. It is recognized, however, that there are many other kinds of interpretations that occupy ceramicists' interests.

My purpose in focusing on these three aspects of ceramic study — categorization, analysis, and interpretation — is to reflect on what I see as a lag between the logic and practice of ceramic research in the current state of the art. The three levels are obviously interrelated, but I think it can legitimately be asked whether they are well integrated. That is, is the direction of information flow simply one way, from classification to analysis to interpretation? Or has there been an exchange of information — feedback, if you will — between these levels, so that analyses and interpretation are having some reciprocal impact on classifications?

Pottery Classification

Archaeologists derive scant comfort from the fact that over and above the certitudes of death and taxes, they are blessed with the additional constant of a seemingly limitless quantity of sherds to classify. Ceramic typological description is a very basic, if tedious, procedure at virtually all Neolithic and post-Neolithic period archaeological sites, and has been since the early days of archaeological exploration. The writing of the ceramic type descriptions for a site has often been considered not only necessary but suf-

ficient for a site's ceramic analysis; and for purposes of outlining a site's history and interrelationships with other sites, it is clearly essential. Classifications are, after all, basic to all sciences, and serve a multitude of purposes: (1) to facilitate communication within a science; (2) to provide a system for description of objects of study of the science; (3) to permit predictions about relationships of the objects with respect to other objects in the science; (4) to serve as extensions of and empirical justification for concepts used within the theory of that science (Blashfield and Draguns 1976, p. 574). With respect to classification of pottery in particular, its chronological value has been undisputed for over half a century. However, pottery classification schemes that are useful for one purpose — assessing time and space relationships — are not necessarily "best" for all other purposes, and herein lies the problem. Because classifications organize and structure data, they inevitably also organize and structure the formulation of research problems. However, classifications are only tools: they are a means to an end, not ends themselves. Thus it is necessary to ask continually if the goals and the procedures of ceramic research are existing in optimal relationships, or if classificatory systems, which are always conservative and resistant to innovation, may be impeding rather than enhancing ceramic research.

If the history of ceramic classification is reviewed, it can be seen that objectives have changed little over the last fifty years or more, although the procedures have become more formalized. The grouping of sherds and vessels into similarity classes began as an exercise in stylistic affinity for descriptive purposes, but quickly acquired the primary objective of delineating spatial and especially temporal relations within and between sites. Procedures of classification were developed that spelled out the criteria for selecting the attributes by which one class of pottery was distinguished from another (e.g., Spaulding 1953; Wheat, Gifford, and Wasley 1958). Because the goal of the grouping was usually to develop intrasite or intraregional chronology, the variables selected for primary differentiation of ceramic categories were those thought to be time sensitive — principally surface treatment or decoration and, less commonly, form.

The real "use-meaning" of a pottery type has not changed in half a century. The growing subdisciplines of ceramic technology and ceramic ethnoarchaeology have had little impact in the field at the level of excavation and descriptive synthesis, although a number of ethnographic studies (e.g., Hardin 1979; Hill 1977; Stanislawski 1975; Kirkpatrick 1978) have attempted to apply the classifica-

Prudence M. Rice

tory procedures used by archaeologists, or improve upon them. In American archaeology, increasing emphasis on regional as distinct from site-specific studies in the last two decades has led to greater recognition of the spatial distribution of classificatory units as a means of understanding synchronic inter-site dynamics (Gifford 1960). Nonetheless, typologies are still largely static and descriptive, focused on elucidating spatiotemporal relationships through ceramic index types. There has been little effort to implement the idea that different "kinds of types" may be necessary both to accommodate the processual explanatory goals of archaeology today, and to take effective advantage of the techniques of physicochemical analysis available almost routinely that were not available twenty-five or fifty years ago. J. O. Brew said it in 1946: "We need more rather than fewer classifications, different classifications, always new classifications, to meet new needs" (Brew 1946, p. 65).

Why does such a lag exist? Part of the problem is that archaeologists have not entirely agreed among themselves what a type is, how to obtain types, or even if a type is a meaningful unit with which to work. There are a number of major conflicts in archaeological systematics, the process of forming units for scientific study. Among these are: (1) whether types are inherent in the data set and *discovered* by the archaeologist, or are *created* by the archaeologist; i.e., are types "real" or "artificial"; (2) what are the limits to the type; i.e., is it better to "lump" or "split," better to emphasize general similarities or minor differences; (3) what and how many attributes should be used in classifications; (4) what "kinds of types" are there, i.e., historical, analytical, cultural; and (5) on the level of method and theory, what are the differences between a grouping, a classification, and a taxonomy. These issues have been argued at length, and there are of course no easy answers to the questions. Hill and Evans (1972) provide an excellent review of the debates on archaeological taxonomy that began in the 1940s, but *see also* Spaulding (1953) and Ford's reply (1954), Rouse (1960), Clarke (1968), Dunnell (1971a), and Whallon (1972).

Probably the best general treatment of the field of systematics with specific reference to archaeology is that of Dunnell (1971b), which provided a number of ideas for the present paper. Dunnell's fundamental distinction between the phenomenological (objectively "real") and the ideational (concepts, ideas) realms is extended to the general practice of "arrangement" or ordering of objects and events, for the purpose of distinguishing between "grouping" procedures and "classification" procedures. Grouping takes place in the phenomenological realm and refers to the ordering of actual objects or events. Classification, however, takes place in the ideational realm and is an ordering of attributes or features. Groups consist of things; they are historical or localized in that they are defined by a finite number of members, the particular things that were described to form the group. Classes are "ahistorical," consisting of their criteria for membership, and are infinite in their application. They function to organize the phenomenological realm, once entities are placed in the classes, through a process called "identification."

Two kinds of classification and grouping emerge from a further distinction: the relationship between the constituent features or criteria used in making the differentiation between entities (Fig. 1). The features may be equivalent and of equal weight, thereby creating equivalent unordered classes or groups; or they may be nonequivalent, ordered, or weighted, thereby creating hierarchical classifications or groupings. In the ideational realm, Dunnell refers to the creation of equivalent units (upper right cell in Fig. 1) as "paradigmatic classification" (an example would be classifying vessels on the basis of form: bowl, jar, plate, and cup are equivalent unordered "dimensions" of form), while the creation of hierarchical units (lower right cell) is "taxonomic classification" (exemplified by the type-variety system for pottery, or the familiar Linnean system of biological taxonomy). Groups, formed from discrete data sets by measuring association or similarity, may be of equivalent units (upper left cell), which Dunnell calls statistical clusters (e.g., groups formed by chi square operations), or hierarchical groups (lower left cell), exemplified by many of the procedures of numerical taxonomy and hierarchical cluster analyses. The boundaries between these four cells in Fig. 1 are somewhat artificial, particularly with respect to the varying procedures of numerical taxonomy. Other problems with the scheme are that polythetic classifications are not considered at all, and divisive versus agglomerative techniques are not explicitly distinguished.

What is clear from Dunnell's treatment, however, is that systematics is the first step in scientific explanation, the step that operates to link data and theory. Neither groups nor classes are explanations themselves: they are organizations of data and concepts which are then used as a basis for inference and explanation. Importantly, classification must always be carried out with respect to a particular problem and must be capable of testing and evaluation. That is, selection of the attributes in a classification, and therefore the creation of the classification itself, is predicated on a given problem. Evaluation of the

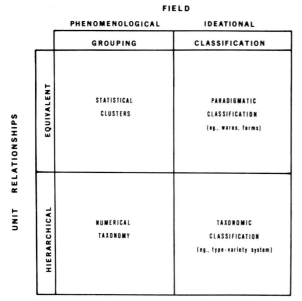

	FIELD	
	PHENOMENOLOGICAL	IDEATIONAL
	GROUPING	CLASSIFICATION
EQUIVALENT	STATISTICAL CLUSTERS	PARADIGMATIC CLASSIFICATION (eg., wares, forms)
HIERARCHICAL	NUMERICAL TAXONOMY	TAXONOMIC CLASSIFICATION (eg., type-variety system)

Figure 1. Representation of methods of forming units by classification and by grouping (after Dunnell 1971b, fig. 9, p. 94).

classificatory unit can be undertaken only in terms of the relevance of those criteria structuring the classification toward the problem. Groupings (statistical clusters and numerical taxonomy) are not seen by Dunnell as an appropriate means of constructing classes because they cannot be tested; they are derived from a localized or historical set of data and cannot be tested on the same data set, nor can they strictly speaking be tested on a different data set. The principal role of groupings is to generate and test hypotheses about classes.

Taxonomic classifications have the advantage over other kinds of arrangements because of their elegance and flexibility in showing complex relationships between entities and attributes, and because they can be tested. Taxonomy cannot, however, be used to order an unknown field in which the classes and their criteria are not specified. In Dunnell's view, taxonomic classification is most appropriately used at an intermediate stage, a bridge between raw data and inference, for purposes of explicating particular kinds of relationships between entities. The other techniques of arrangement — statistical clustering, numerical taxonomy, and paradigmatic classification — are suitable initial procedures, heuristic devices for exploring and categorizing unknown fields, and/or for formulating and testing categories formed by other means.

It is of some utility to review, as a background to discussion of physicochemical analyses and proces-

sual interpretations, some of the classificatory units or concepts that are in use today, particularly the "ware," the "type," and the "variety." Ware, a unit of paradigmatic classification in Dunnell's (1971b) terms, is particularly interesting and useful. The ware appears to be the primary ceramic category used in European and classical archaeology, and is formulated on a number of different dimensions. Among these are geographic location (e.g., French wares, Derbyshire wares), time period (Iron Age wares), form (beaker ware), technological characteristics of surface or fabric composition (black-burnished ware, coarse wares), decoration (black-figured ware), and function (kitchen wares, table wares). The members of the ware class share common characteristics of color, firing, method of construction, temper, surface treatment, form, age, or location as indicated by the ware name, but their fundamental distinction is in some aspect of technique or composition. In its interpretation, ware is employed in much the same way as are types in America, but as a broader and more informal category, presumably accommodating a somewhat greater amount of variability within the class.

A similar usage of the term *ware* characterized the early years of archaeology in North America and Mesoamerica, but gradually such informality has given way to the more rigorous terminology mandated by the dictates of the type-variety system of ceramic classification. In this hierarchical taxonomic classificatory procedure, ware is the broad, higher-order level of synthesis and comparison defined by commonalities of paste composition and surface treatment. Wares are composed of ceramic groups, which are identified by similar surface treatment (for example, the red-slipped Tinaja Group), and in turn groups are composed of types (Wheat, Gifford, and Wasley 1958; Smith, Willey, and Gifford 1960). American "types," the basic unit of ceramic description and comparison, are used like the Europeans' "wares" for dating or discussions of intersite contact. However, probably because of the historical link with anthropology in American archaeology, there is frequently an implicit or explicit "meaning" ascribed to types as the "material outcome of a set of fundamental attributes that coalesced, consciously or unconsciously, as a ceramic idea" or standard shared by members of a society at any given time (Gifford 1960, p. 343; *see also* Dunnell 1971b, pp. 132–38). Types are formed by combining varieties, the initial pottery sorting units, which are identified by minor variations (e.g., an incised type in a red-slipped group may have a fine-incised variety and a groove-incised variety). It is interesting (but at the same time confusing from the standpoint of systematics) that a

Prudence M. Rice

parallel to this hierarchic aspect of combining named variants or varieties into inclusive types is occurring in European ware nomenclature as well. An example is the identification of shell-tempered hand-built Dales *ware* jars and the wheel-thrown sandy imitations of this ware, which Loughlin (1977) calls Dales *types*.

Physicochemical Analysis

Physicochemical and technological analyses of pottery have the potential to allow investigation of meaningful problems within which the classificatory and the interpretational levels of archaeology method may be linked. In order to make such potential an actuality, either more consistent usage of technological attributes is needed within existing classificatory units and methods, or new units might be created. I do not pretend that this is an original observation on my part; in his review of analytical methods a decade ago, Peacock (1970, p. 375) observed that the results of technological studies "deserve to be more fully integrated with the findings of conventional typological examination, since technological data can contribute to the interpretation of ceramic evidence." Even earlier, Shepard (1976, pp. 310–14) summarized the advantages and disadvantages of employing technological criteria in ceramic classifications. But little has been done in the subsequent years to indicate that these scholars' suggestions have been heeded. Developments in both theory and analysis over the last twenty years make it clear that archaeologists must move beyond categorizations that are strictly similarity groupings for ordering data or for establishing spatiotemporal relationships. Classificatory units should have interpretational significance within today's processual research concerns (Dunnell 1971a): they should be units that are culturally "real" not in a mentalistic sense of existing in the ancient potters' minds, but that are scientifically, testably "real" in their functioning within archaeologists' explanatory frameworks.

From the viewpoint of physicochemical analyses, the significance of "ware," "type," and "variety" rests not in the terms themselves but as they are keys to the means by which the units were formulated and what can be done with them. To return to Dunnell's (1971b) distinctions, types and varieties are taxonomic classes — while wares, which are the units that most often explicitly treat technological dimensions, may be paradigmatic or taxonomic classes. Unfortunately, too frequently the sherds being studied represent in reality not classes but groups, mistakenly used as classes. Groups are bounded by the finite number of entities used to define them; they change when new entities are added, and are generally formulated without regard to a specific problem. When they are employed as classes to try to accommodate new data sets, difficulties arise because their characteristics are specific to the single original data set.

A recently completed study of Georgia coastal pottery by Marian Saffer (1979), University of Florida, illustrates the problems of working with poorly defined types, and highlights the advantages and contributions of technological analyses to classificatory and processual studies. Saffer oriented her study not around taxonomic classes (types) but toward paradigmatic classes (decorative categories) in an effort to relate variability in the pottery to local resources. On the Georgia coast, as elsewhere, the prehistoric chronology is based on changes in pottery inventories. The original type descriptions, published in 1939 (Caldwell and Waring 1939), were intended to cover one small area of the coastal mainland, but in the ensuing years have been extended up and down the mainland as well as to the offshore barrier islands, with unsatisfactory results. This is because the Georgia "types" were really "groups"; as discussed earlier, groups are historical, bounded by the time and space of their original defining members, and the inclusion of other entities is not appropriate. Nevertheless, from about 500 B.C. up to historic times, coastal pottery consisted of "sand," "grit," and "grog" tempered vessels with plain, cordmarked, or stamped surfaces. In some respects there appears to be little variability in Georgia coastal pottery for 2000 years, particularly in decoration: there are no slipped or painted pottery classes, for example, and no "fine wares." As a result, archaeologists emphasized variability in "temper" as a basis for conclusions as to spatial and temporal cultural differences. Temper practices that appeared to vary from published type descriptions were used by archaeologists to define many "new" cultures and historical phases.

Saffer opted to study two decorative categories, check stamped and complicated stamped pottery, and selected a sample of each group from two coastal islands (total N = 200). Comparisons were made with twenty-five clays collected from the islands and the adjacent mainland. A computerized cluster analysis was performed with the Clustan IC package (Wishart 1978), using an input similarity matrix calculated from Gower's Coefficient (which accommodates dichotomous, multistate qualitative, and multistate quantitative data). The cluster analysis was used to intercompare the sherds on twenty-five technological (including petrographic) variables, and the clays on thirty-four variables. The results of Saffer's study indicated that the considerable variability in aplastic "temper" in the sherds was paralleled by equal variability in aplastics in local clays: in kinds, in sizes, and in amounts of aplastics. In fact, one group of mainland clays was sufficiently similar to the pottery not only in aplastic characteristics but in porosity, coring, and color that Saffer tentatively hypothesized the use of similar sorts of mainland clays in the manufacture of the island pottery.

While most of Saffer's conclusions are specific to questions of Georgia coastal prehistory, one of the significant points of her study is to emphasize again that "temper," the favorite cornerstone of many archaeologists' typological castles, can be fickle (Shepard 1964). Small differences in pottery pastes, particularly in areas with homogeneous natural inclusions in clays, such as quartz sand, continue to be problematical for archaeologists. They cannot always be assumed to be a product of cultural (i.e., spatial, temporal, ethnic) differences, and therefore a valid basis for typological distinctions, until environmental factors are investigated.

Traditional classificatory frameworks are not designed to pursue such questions, however, and for the most part are not sufficiently flexible to provide units for analysis that can be interpreted in processual terms. Expanded usage of the ware concept, particularly in American archaeology, is one possibility for broadening the capability of ceramic classifications to absorb the needs and objectives of physicochemical analyses. Wares, as they are used both in Europe and in the type-variety system in the United States and Mesoamerica, are units based implicitly or explicitly on primarily technological features of paste or fabric, surface finish, and manufacture. As such, they are oriented toward the needs of physicochemical analyses, in which the objective is usually to characterize the composition of the ceramic in order to determine its probable geographical origin(s) of manufacture.

For archaeologists and physicochemical analysts, the advantages of a focus on paste or fabric units are: (1) These categories relate pottery to local resources, clays, and tempers, thereby permitting characterization of local versus nonlocal ceramics and integration into theoretical structures involving socioeconomic processes of manufacture and trade. (2) Study of technologically defined units can allow an understanding of the history of technological development at a site or region. (3) Such units permit measurement of properties common to archaeological pottery, contemporary pottery, and raw resources, allowing study of temporal and spatial continuities or changes not otherwise possible. (4) The variables used in physicochemical analyses of paste or fabric classes permit not only qualitative but quantitative measure-ment, thereby facilitating statistical manipulation and computerized data reduction to test the validity of interpretations. (5) Paste categories provide a useful base within which to interpret variability, either in fabric characteristics, or in characteristics of surface treatment, decoration, form, and so on.

A few years ago I suggested (1976) that within the type-variety system the unit "ware" should have its definition based principally on variables of paste or fabric composition, rather than in combination with surface treatment. Further, I indicated that a formalized hierarchy of units based on paste (e.g., paste wares, paste groups, paste types, paste varieties) could be useful in the context of growing applications of physicochemical analyses. Such a procedure would convert into taxonomic classes what are now groupings formed by primarily numerical taxonomy or paradigmatic (largely intuitive) classes. These taxonomic classes would then be capable of integration into broader problem-oriented research and continued testing and modification through statistical procedures.

Although "paste wares" are used, at least in Mesoamerica, such a technologically based taxonomy might best be considered a possible goal for the future rather than an immediate necessity. Other possibilities for technological units are Shepard's concept of a "technological counterpart of a style, a cluster of associated or of interdependent techniques," or her suggestion of a "technological tradition" (Shepard 1976, p. 320). Regardless of what such a unit may be called, there is a clear need for a more formal means of conceptually merging physicochemical analyses, and the problems to which they are addressed, into ceramic classifications.

Interpretations of Production and Trade

As a consequence of a number of developments in the field of archaeology, among them the concern with process-oriented regional problems in America and the application of concepts and methods of economic geography in Europe, socioeconomic interactions have become major interests of archaeologists in recent years. Trade and production of all classes of artifacts, with pottery at the forefront, have been the focus of numerous conference symposia, articles, and books (e.g., Peacock 1977; Earle and Ericson 1977; Fry 1980a). It is interesting that the emergence of these topics in economic archaeology has paralleled the earlier development of economic anthropology, in that first interregional or long-distance trade, then local exchange, and finally the organization of production have come under the scrutiny of researchers. These new archaeological concerns reflect the significant roles of ecological and evolutionary paradigms, Marxist theory, multivariate causality, and quantitative approaches to model building and testing in today's archaeology. They are manifestations of method and theory as applied to analysis and explanation of material cultural remains. Physicochemical analyses have gained wide acceptance as the appropriate means of investigating these socioeconomic problems. A multiplicity of available techniques provides the ceramic researcher with precise quantitative characterization of both the ceramic product and the local resources, thus making the results attractive from virtually all viewpoints within the new directions in archaeology.

A further advantage exists in that these analyses allow some resolution of the eternally thorny issue of variability and its interpretation in ceramic classifications. Theoretically, at least, classifications and groupings of any sort exist for the primary purpose of creating order out of chaotic variability, but in practice it is not so clear cut. Ceramic classificatory units are generally agreed to be polythetic abstractions (*cf.* Dunnell 1971b, pp. 139–40); that is, they are idealized constructs drawn from a collection of sherds, and no single sherd has all the attributes of the class. Inevitably, there appears a sherd that is a borderline member of a given category, and the fateful decision to "lump" or to "split" must be made. Lumping can obscure valid cultural distinction; splitting and the creation of new types can create meaningless categories (as in the Georgia coastal example). At this point in the development of the discipline, types as summaries of a series of attributes or traits may be too gross to permit meaningful interpretation of variability, particularly technological. Groups, on the other hand, as historical "points" of occurrence of traits, initially permit more fine-grained "real-world" analyses of how the attributes co-vary. Paradigmatic classes, such as ware or form, have the potential to accomplish the same thing, because they focus on attributes correlating with a single dimension of variability. In any case, the dimensions chosen, and the distinctions used to create or divide units, must be made in the context of a meaningful interpretational framework.

Creation of a "meaningful interpretational framework" is not a simple matter, obviously. It should be grounded in clear articulation of theory (goals) and methods (units of analysis). Production and trade constitute two such goals or "problems of broad significance" to which physicochemical and technological analyses of ceramics are increasingly being applied. For example, interpretations of production and/or trade were based on petrographic, geochemical, and technological studies in the recent edited volumes of Peacock (1977) on European pottery and Fry

(1980a) on American pottery analyses. Another interpretation of physicochemical variability within a pottery class is that of imitations and/or multiple production centers. Loughlin's (1977) study of Dales ware and imitation Dales types is an example of such an interpretation. The explanation of multiple production sites of course involves implicit temporal and spatial aspects, but these do not constitute the explanation itself. Rather, they establish the parameters within which archaeologists can begin to explore when and where competitors began to produce, why they might have done so, and how successful they were in the marketplace. A further interpretation of technological variability appears in an ethnographic survey of indigenous pottery produced in Guatemala (Reina and Hill 1978). The authors found a correlation between the distribution of two major pottery forming techniques, "orbiting" and convex basal molds, and language groups in the highlands. This reinforces the findings of other researchers (e.g., Foster 1965) that even in the face of severe pressures of acculturation and modernization, motor patterns are very slow to change, particularly in tradition-oriented closed corporate communities. Finally, one obvious interpretation of physicochemical variability in pottery was mentioned in connection with the example of Georgia coastal pottery: the variation may be essentially stochastic (from a human behavioral standpoint) variation in source materials. Such source variations in clays from several regions, as they affect assumptions in provenience studies, have been or are currently being tested geochemically and petrographically (e.g., Bishop 1980; Rands and Bishop 1980).

These examples of interpretation of physicochemical analyses and technological studies suggest that there are a number of productive approaches toward construction of a body of ceramic theory. However, a coherent, developed theoretical structure for explanation of variability within a ceramic system is currently lacking in the field. One constructive preliminary step toward development of such a model should begin with the modification of traditional classifications to incorporate technological data consistently. Any classification allows identification of variability on some level. The incorporation of physicochemical and technological data also allows identification of variability, specifically with respect to composition and technique of manufacture, but these analyses have the additional potential advantage of permitting interpretation of the significance of the variability in the solution of processually meaningful research questions of production and trade.

Recently I attempted to incorporate standard ceramic classificatory data into the interpretation of craft production through a model of the evolution of specialized pottery manufacture (Rice, 1981). The model, its theoretical underpinnings, and the exact details of its usage are too lengthy to cover here; suffice it to say that it focuses on the interpretation of differing degrees of variability in technological, decorative, and formal characteristics of pottery as indicators of differing degrees of standardization or elaboration in manufacture. Standardization, in turn, is interpreted as specialized manufacture. The ceramics of Barton Ramie, Belize (Gifford 1976), classified through the type-variety system, were utilized in the model. From the published descriptions of each classificatory unit (potential variety, variety, type, group) in each phase of the history of occupation of Barton Ramie, I counted the listed instances of technological, decorative, and formal variants, elaborations, or alternative attributes. These included variations in temper or firing, rim form, addition of vessel supports or appendages, kinds of decoration, and so forth. The counts were used in an ecological diversity index formula (Pielou 1974) to compare variability in different units within each temporal phase. The results suggested a general trend of reduction of variability through time, while standardization increased. The decline in variability was apparent first in unslipped vessel categories and later in slipped vessels.

The results were intriguing both in terms of the specifics of the model and in terms of Maya culture history, but with respect to the appropriateness of the classificatory system itself for studies of ceramic production, two observations can be made. First, the amount of technological detail on paste composition, firing, and manufacture was sparse and inconsistent, making that aspect of the study, which had the greatest emphasis in the model, the weakest point of its application. This is due in part to the ambiguity of the ware concept in the type-variety system, and to traditional inattention to (or unfamiliarity with) paste variables in favor of formal and decorative attributes.

Second, although the technological, formal, and decorative variants were tabulated within varieties and types, the effective working unit of comparison was the ceramic group (a higher and more inclusive unit in type-variety system nomenclature). This suggests that the study of production may be better served by broader organizational units than by finer discriminations.

A similar phenomenon can be seen in a recent edited volume on exchange (Fry 1980a). In this volume, the papers dealing with production employed not taxonomic units (types) but cross-cutting or modal vessel categories (paradigmatic classes) based on ware or form in their analyses (e.g., Fry 1980b; Rands and Bishop 1980; my own paper [Rice 1980] used "group," which in this particular instance is really more akin to a ware unit), whereas those papers giving more emphasis to exchange seemed to find ceramic types equally useful as were wares. Future researchers may find that classificatory needs or constraints in studies of exchange are different from those in studies of production. "Groups," in Dunnell's (1971b) sense, and paradigmatic classes as well, may prove to be more flexible or useful than taxonomic units in the study of production specifically. Groups, because they are particular to a time and place, permit more localized characterizations and comparisons. Paradigmatic classes such as wares, that are closely related to resources, should give a similar advantage in production studies.

Conclusions

Ceramic classifications and groups have traditionally been oriented toward the goal of delineating spatio-temporal relationships. This continues to be their major function, despite the fact that the larger field of archaeology is increasingly involved with new concerns, problems, and interests. Technological ceramic analyses can make significant contributions in the context of these new goals, but in order to do so researchers must be prepared to modify traditional classifications and procedures, or create new ones. Theory and classification must coexist productively for the advancement of the discipline.

Classifications are by nature conservative, not only slow to change but difficult to change. A new classification is "likely to evolve as an initially informal jargon within a small group of scientists. As the political power and social influence of this group increases, its terminology experiences wider and more general acceptance" (Blashfield and Draguns 1976, p. 575, citing Deutsch 1966). Thus, it is plain that the movement to modify ceramic classifications will come from those who feel the need the most, ceramic technologists and archaeologists working closely with materials scientists. It is possible, perhaps, to detect the beginnings of such jargon: for example, the trace elemental "reference groups" and "compositional groups" could eventually be given taxonomic significance. It was pointed out earlier in this paper that any classification serves at least four functions. Existing ceramic taxonomies serve two of these functions, communication and description, in acceptable fashion. However, the other functions, prediction and theory-building, are not served well. Because classifications must be constructed with relation to particular problems, an interrelationship between theory and prediction, research problems, and classificatory structure is clearly dictated. Yet little has been done at the prosaic level of ceramic classification to make the units relevant to new needs.

It could be argued that the significant problems in ceramic research have not yet been defined with sufficient precision either theoretically or operationally that the classificatory needs are readily apparent. Toward this end, a synthesis of the achievements of physicochemical and technological analyses to date might help identify areas in which such contributions could be made. In addition, it should be remembered that hierarchically ordered taxonomic classifications are logically the practical and theoretical end point of systematics. As Dunnell (1971b) pointed out, it is the other kinds of arrangement — groups and paradigmatic classes — that serve as heuristic devices in the initial exploration and probing of attribute covariation. The existence of a variety of quantitative techniques for creating and testing a variety of units makes this a relatively open and fruitful area for future work, and one that clearly needs to be addressed in order to maximize the potential of physicochemical analyses.

References

Bishop, R. K. 1980. Aspects of ceramic compositional modeling. In Fry, R. E., ed., *Models and methods in regional exchange*. SAA Papers, no. 1: 47–65. Washington, D.C.: Society for American Archaeology.

Blashfield, R. K., and Draguns, J. G. 1976. Toward a taxonomy of psychopathology: the purpose of psychiatric classification. *British Journal of Psychiatry* 129:574–83.

Brew, J. O. 1946. The use and abuse of taxonomy. In *Archaeology of Alkali Ridge*, pp. 44–66. Papers of the Peabody Museum of Archaeology and Ethnology, Harvard University, no. 24.

Caldwell, J. R. and Waring, A. J. 1939. Some Chatham County pottery types and their sequence. *Southeastern Archaeological Conference Newsletter* 1:1–12. Reprinted in Williams, S., ed., *The Waring Papers*, pp. 110–34. Cambridge, Mass.: Peabody Museum.

Clarke, D. L. 1968. *Analytical archaeology*. London: Methuen.

Deutsch, K. W. 1966. On theories, taxonomies and models as communication codes for organizing information. *Behavioural Science* 11:1–17.

Dunnell, R. C. 1971a. Comment on Sabloff and Smith's "The importance of both analytic and taxonomic classification in the type-variety system." *American Antiquity* 36:115–18.

_____. 1971b. *Systematics in Prehistory*. New York: The Free Press.

Earle, T. K. and Ericson, J. E., eds. 1977. *Exchange systems in prehistory*. New York: Academic Press.

Ford, J. A. 1954. The type concept revisited. *American Anthropologist* 56:42–53.

Foster, G. M. 1965. The sociology of pottery: questions and hypotheses arising from contemporary Mexican work. In Matson, F. R., ed., *Ceramics and Man*, pp. 43–61. Chicago: Aldine.

Fry, R. E., ed. 1980a. *Models and methods in regional exchange*. SAA Papers, no. 1. Washington D.C.: Society for American Archaeology.

_____. 1980b. Models of exchange for major shape classes of Lowland Maya pottery. In Fry, R. E., ed. *Models and methods in regional exchange*. SAA Papers, no. 1:3–18. Washington D.C.: Society for American Archaeology.

Gifford, J. C. 1960. The type-variety method of ceramic classification as an indicator of cultural phenomena. *American Antiquity* 25:341–47.

_____. 1976. *Prehistoric pottery analysis and the ceramics of Barton Ramie in the Belize Valley*. Memoirs of the Peabody Museum of Archaeology and Ethnology, Harvard University, vol. 18. Cambridge, Mass.

Hardin, M. A. 1979. The cognitive basis of productivity in a decorative art style: implications of an ethnographic study for archaeologists' taxonomies. In Kramer, C., ed., *Ethnoarchaeology, implications of ethnography for archaeology*, pp. 75–101. New York: Columbia University Press.

Hill, J. N. 1977. Individual variability in ceramics and the study of prehistoric social organization. In Hill, J. N. and Gunn, J., eds., *The individual in prehistory*, pp. 55–108. New York: Academic Press.

_____, and Evans, R. K. 1972. A model for classification and typology. In Clarke, D. L., ed., *Models in archaeology*, pp. 231–73. London: Methuen.

Kirkpatrick, M. 1978. The application of the type-variety method of ceramic analysis to a collection of contemporary pottery from Metepec, Mexico. Manuscript, Department of Anthropology, Temple University, Philadelphia.

Loughlin, N. 1977. Dales ware: a contribution to the study of Roman coarse pottery. In Peacock, D. P. S., ed., *Pottery and early commerce*, pp. 85–146. London: Academic Press.

Peacock, D. P. S. 1970. The scientific analysis of ancient ceramics: a review. *World Archaeology* 1:375–89.

_____. 1977. Pottery and early commerce. London: Academic Press.

Pielou, E. C. 1974. *Ecological diversity*. Halifax: Dalhousie University.

Rands, R. L., and Bishop, R. K. 1980. Resource procurement zones and patterns of exchange in the Palenque region, Mexico. In Fry, R. E., ed., *Models and methods in regional exchange*. SAA Papers, no. 1:19–46. Washington D.C.: Society for American Archaeology.

Reina, R. E. and Hill, R. M., II. 1978. *The traditional pottery of Guatemala*. Austin: University of Texas Press.

Rice, P. M. 1976. Rethinking the ware concept. *American Antiquity* 41:538-43.

————. 1980. Peten Postclassic pottery production and exchange: a view from Macanche. In Fry, R. E., ed., *Models and methods in regional exchange*. SAA Papers, no. 1:67-82. Washington D.C.: Society for American Archaeology.

————. Evolution of specialized pottery production: a trial model. *Current Anthropology* 22: 219-40 [June 1981].

Rouse, I. 1960. The classification of artifacts in archaeology. *American Antiquity* 25:313-23.

Saffer, M. E. 1979. Aboriginal clay resource utilization on the Georgia coast. M.A. thesis, Department of Anthropology, University of Florida, Gainesville, Florida.

Shepard, A. O. 1964. Temper identification: "technological sherd-splitting" or unanswered challenge. *American Antiquity* 29:518-20.

————. 1976. *Ceramics for the archaeologist*. Publication 609. Washington, D.C.: Carnegie Institute of Washington.

Smith, R. E.; Willey, G. R.; and Gifford, J. C. 1960. The type-variety concept as a basis for the analysis of Maya pottery. *American Antiquity* 25:330-40.

Spaulding, A. C. 1953. Statistical techniques for the discovery of artifact types. *American Antiquity* 18:305-313.

Stanislawski, M. B. 1975. What you see is what you get: ethnoarchaeology and scientific model-building. Paper presented at the annual meeting of the Society for American Archaeology, Dallas.

Whallon, R. Jr. 1972. A new approach to pottery typology. *American Antiquity* 37:13-33.

Wheat, J. B.; Gifford, J. C.; and Wasley, W. W. 1958. Ceramic variety, type cluster, and ceramic system in Southwestern pottery analysis. *American Antiquity* 24:34-47.

Wishart, D. L. 1978. Clustan IC, release 2. Edinburgh: Edinburgh University.

5. Archaeological, Geochemical, and Statistical Methods in Ceramic Provenance Studies

C. Lemoine, S. Walker, and M. Picon
Centre National de la Recherche Scientifique

Introduction

This study concerns pottery found on excavated medieval sites in the south of France: in Provence, Comtat Venaissin, Languedoc, and Roussillon (Fig. 1). The ceramic material found on these excavations includes, for the period of the thirteenth to the fifteenth centuries, many imports of tin-glazed pottery from Italy and Spain.

We have decided to discuss here the problems involved in the attribution to the workshop of Malaga in southern Spain of a small group of imported pottery found in France. The pottery in question is tin glazed and decorated either with a luster or with a luster and blue lines.

The best-represented categories of Spanish imports found in France are the Catalonian and above all the Valencian productions. These are both characterized by a green and a brown decoration, but amongst the Valencian productions we also frequently find a luster painted ware with additional blue lines. Some of the earliest productions of the workshops of the region of Valencia resemble the latest productions of Malaga, to such an extent that the identification can be carried out only in the laboratory. It is obvious that this identification is crucial to our understanding of trade in the western Mediterranean, particularly that of the fourteenth century which was a period of important historical transformation. For our purposes here, the imported pottery from Malaga will serve above all as an example of the difficulties encountered in the determination of ceramic provenance.

The first stage of our research consisted in sorting out the medieval Spanish ceramics found in France which concern this present study. We have determined for each ceramic sample eight principal chemical elements: potassium, magnesium, calcium, aluminium, iron, manganese, titanium, and silicon. The analytical method chosen was the X-ray fluorescence method using a fusion technique. The classification of the results of the analysis was carried out according to the standardized variables using the clustering by average linkage method. We have thus been able to distinguish different groups amongst the imported medieval pottery. The provenance of several of these groups was easily determined by comparing them with reference samples from the Spanish production centers. In this way we have been able to identify ceramics from Catalonia, Aragona, Valencia, and Malaga. On analysis we distinguish these different groups as easily as we distinguish those of Valencia and Malaga on the dendrogram (Fig. 2).

Comparison of the Results

We now come to the problems of the attribution to the production center of Malaga of the small group

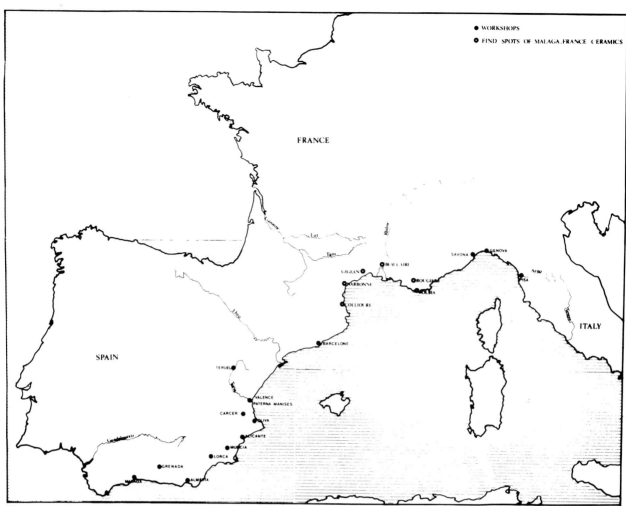

Figure 1. Map of principal exporting ceramic workshops in Spain and in Italy (black circles), and find spots of Ma-laga-France ceramics (stars).

POTTERY FROM VALENCIA AND

MALAGA FOUND IN FRANCE

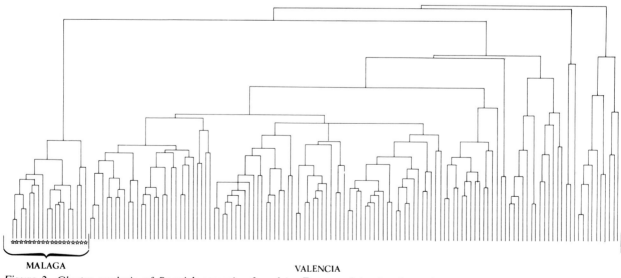

MALAGA   VALENCIA

Figure 2. Cluster analysis of Spanish ceramics found in France originating from the region of Valencia and Malaga.

C. Lemoine, S. Walker, M. Picon

	CaO	Fe_2O_3	TiO_2	K_2O	SiO_2	Al_2O_3	MgO	MnO
Malaga-Spain group								
average	15.1	6.11	0.79	2.44	56.5	15.6	3.35	0.089
standard deviation	1.1	0.17	0.05	0.34	1.1	0.4	0.24	0.009
Malaga-France group								
average	15.1	6.10	0.83	2.10	56.1	16.3	3.41	0.089
standard deviation	1.3	0.16	0.02	0.48	1.2	0.4	0.14	0.008

of imported pottery situated on the left of the diagram in Figure 2. We shall therefore compare the eighteen sherds of this group with a selection of forty-six sherds from the excavations of Malaga, the purpose being to distinguish if both sample groups come from the same production center.

The forty-six sherds from Malaga come in fact from excavations of domestic structures, but in order to simplify matters we shall exploit them as if they came from the workshop of Malaga itself. For the same reason we shall give the name Malaga-Spain to the forty-six sherds from the excavations of Malaga, and the name Malaga-France to the eighteen sherds found in the south of France. We now propose to discuss the relationship of the Malaga-France group to the Malaga-Spain group.

The average composition of these two groups and the standard deviations of their distributions are shown in the table above.

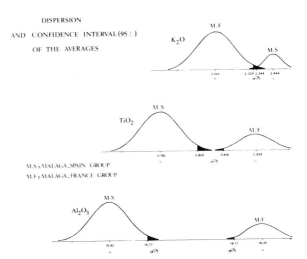

Figure 3. Dispersion and confidence interval (95%) of the averages of the Malaga-Spain and Malaga-France groups.

Use of the Average Compositions of Groups

Although the average compositions of the groups are closely related, there are important differences for aluminium, titanium, and potassium. One can say from a statistical point of view that the differences are significant, and are even highly significant (Fig. 3). This result does not permit us, however, to conclude that the two groups, Malaga-Spain and Malaga-France, do not come from the same production center. Indeed, these highly significant differences have little probability of being the result of a random sampling procedure carried out on the total production of a unique workshop. It is evident that we cannot consider a group made up solely of pottery from the workshop of Malaga and exported to France as being a representative result of a random sampling of the entirety of the Malaga production. Such a procedure does not take into account: *first*, the spatial and chronological evolution of the characteristics of clays supply to an important workshop; and *second*, the spatial and chronological evolution of the distribution circuits of this workshop, and more particularly of its long-distance trade. The group of exported pottery has a high probability of having characteristics which differ notably from the average characteristics of the entirety of the Malaga productions. In fact it is not rare to observe that between samplings carried out on ceramic production sites and those on domestic sites, there are differences which are often superior to those we have distinguished here. These differences can be further magnified by the sampling conditions on the workshop itself.

Thus, the difference in the averages of the two groups, Malaga-Spain and Malaga-France, does not justify on its own the conclusion that we are dealing with the productions either of different workshops or of a single workshop.

But if we had observed no significant difference between the average composition of the two groups, would we have been right in deciding that the two groups were identical? We would first of all point out that if the sampling conditions can separate the average compositions of the two groups, they can also bring them closer, thus perhaps hiding substantial differences. However, the probability that this would happen is very low. In any case, whether or not the average compositions of the groups present a significant difference, the risks of going wrong by accepting the hypothesis of a unique workshop are about the same. This is true insofar as the difference is moderate, as it is between the Malaga-Spain and the Malaga-France groups. The risks of going wrong result from the possible existence of two or several workshops presenting very similar compositional characteristics. Now, the study in our laboratory of more than a hundred workshops has shown that such risks do exist, but that eventual confusion between either distant workshops or workshops installed in different geological contexts is very rare. On the other hand, when we are dealing with workshops of a similar geological environment the risks of confusion become important.

In conclusion, the comparison of the average compositions of the two groups Malaga-Spain and Malaga-France does not allow one to exclude the hypothesis according to which the ceramics of the second group could come (totally or partly) from a workshop other than that of Malaga in southern Spain. On the contrary, this comparison permits one to consider that the hypothesis of a production center far from southern Spain — for example, in Italy or in Tunisia — is unlikely. The archaeological data relative to the two groups renders such a hypothesis even more improbable. It would indeed be necessary to imagine, for example, an Italian or a Tunisian workshop which would have produced pottery typologically and chronologically similar to that produced at Malaga and which, by an incredible chance, would have been composed of clays having for their eight principal constituents average characteristics as close as those of the Malaga-Spain group.

One must remember, as we have already said, that besides this, the differences observed between the averages of the two groups do not exclude the hypothesis of a unique workshop.

Use of Distances between Groups

One can seek to quantify the dissimilarity which exists between two groups by using either Euclidean distance or the generalized Mahalanobis distance. But it is very much evident that whatever the methods of calculation used, and the conventions required for their application, the quantification of resemblances does not resolve any of the previous difficulties. The quantification will rid one of the imprecisions that are the result of a sampling procedure which in the majority of cases is not random. Nor does it resolve the unreliability resulting from the necessarily limited nature of the sampling. Above all, such a quantification does not reduce the risks of confusion which result from the possible existence of several workshops possessing largely identical compositional charac-

teristics due to a similar geological environment. It is thus absolutely impossible to fix a limit below which one would be justified in considering that the two groups come well and truly from the same workshop.

Use of Individual Distances

Instead of comparing two groups, as has been done up until now, one can study the comparisons between the individual members of these two groups, or those between a group and the individual members of the other group. In the first case we will use a simple cluster analysis (Fig. 4). In the second case we can measure the Mahalanobis distances of all the individual members of the unidentified group with regard to the reference group; one can thus better visualize the interlocking of the two groups. If we examine our two groups, Malaga-Spain and Malaga-France (Fig. 5), we find that these comparisons (worked out using the Mahalanobis distance in relation to the Malaga-Spain group) contribute little that is new to permit us to remove the difficulties in the interpretation of averages. Obviously the possibility of observing resemblances between individual members belonging to different groups can lead us, in a certain number of limited cases, to consider as highly probable the likelihood of there being a single workshop. But in the majority of cases one cannot rid oneself of the imprecisions observed during the comparison of the averages.

Absolute Comparisons

If one wished to summarize the difficulties which have been pointed out concerning the attempt to attribute the Malaga-France group to the Malaga-Spain group, it would suffice to say that one always comes up against the same problem. This problem is the impossibility of deciding in an absolute way if the two groups correspond either to the productions of one (and the same) workshop, or to those of several workshops, the problem being the same whatever way one carries out the comparison between the two groups. In other words, it is impossible to determine in an absolute way the resemblance between two groups. This resemblance can in fact be interpreted only in relation to differences existing elsewhere. The important thing is (and that we shall discuss later on in connection with relative comparisons) that the characteristics of the Malaga-France group be closer to those of the Malaga-Spain group than to those of all the productions of the south of Spain, or that they be closer to those of clays found in the region of Malaga than to others found in the area under study.

The theoretical and practical consequences of such an attitude will be discussed later on, but it is already clear that such results will not lead to a lightening of

C. Lemoine, S. Walker, M. Picon

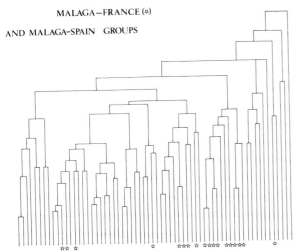

MALAGA–FRANCE (☆)

AND MALAGA-SPAIN GROUPS

Figure 4. Cluster analysis of Malaga-France (stars) and Malaga-Spain ceramics.

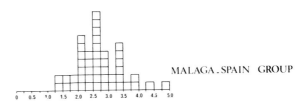

DISTRIBUTION OF THE MAHALANOBIS DISTANCES

MALAGA–SPAIN GROUP

MALAGA–FRANCE GROUP

Figure 5. Histogram of the Mahalanobis distances in relation to the Malaga-Spain group of the two groups.

the workload. It can be understood under such circumstances that one is led to ask oneself if there exist other techniques capable of distinguishing the characteristics of ceramics in such a way that one could be sure, except under very exceptional circumstances, of not running the risk of confusing productions which don't belong to the same workshop. If such a method existed, nothing, or nearly nothing, would stop one's being able to decide that the two groups, Malaga-France and Malaga-Spain, came from the same workshop, if indeed this be the case here. Such a decision would take into account only the laboratory measured characteristics of these two groups. This is why we shall now examine what an increase in the number of elements to be analyzed (fingerprint theory), and the introduction of qualitative characteristics (mineralogical and petrographic analyses), can bring us in the way of results.

Increase in the Number of Analyzed Elements

The assumption at the origin of the fingerprint theory is that on increasing the number of chemical elements to be measured one considerably reduces the risks of confusion. The problem is that of the definition of the potential risks of confusion that can be minimized, or even ignored. If it's a question of the accidental confusion of two workshops whose geological environment is not the same, but whose ceramics show the same compositions for the principal elements analyzed, it is certain that on increasing the number of elements to be analyzed one will likewise increase the chances of finding some differences between the productions of the two workshops. This of course results from the fact that no reason,

other than that of luck, is in any way responsible for the accidental correspondence noticed between the principal constituents. However, such cases are in fact extremely rare, as we suggested earlier on when advancing the hypothesis that the Malaga-France group could come from Tunisia or Italy. The most frequently encountered risks correspond to those cases where the possible confusion is not due to chance, but due to the fact that the workshops have the same geological environment. It is in such cases that it would be necessary to know whether on increasing the number of elements to be analyzed one could succeed, or not, in avoiding such confusion. It is clear that such a success would constitute a most definite advantage.

Unfortunately, it does not seem that one has taken sufficient care to demonstrate the validity of the assumption behind the fingerprint theory using well-chosen and sufficiently numerous examples. The comparisons that have been carried out for us, and the information that can be gleaned from different publications, seem indeed to contradict this basic assumption. We in fact encounter more or less the same difficulties when distinguishing different workshops whatever the number of elements analyzed (provided, of course, that one uses a minimum of about ten), especially when dealing with workshops whose geological environment is similar — and this we stress is a particularly frequent case. It is absolutely necessary for the integrity of our discipline that we get together and agree to study, using different and complementary analytical techniques, a certain number of cases where the risks of confusion seem evident when using one technique or another. In the meantime we must assume a very prudent position and adopt a suitable attitude which takes into account the potential sources of error. In conclusion, one can say that if an increase in the number of chemical elements to be analyzed is of use in the case of certain well-defined comparisons, it does not seem to be so in every case, and in particular when comparing workshops of a similar geological environment.

Introduction of Qualitative Characteristics

The important thing here is not that the characteristics one is dealing with be qualitatives, but that their variety be very wide. One could be tempted to consider petrographic and mineralogical characteristics as being inferior to chemical characteristics because they are most often used only on a presence and absence basis. Such an approach would present a serious handicap in comparison with the numerical possibilities of chemical analysis, if the variety of the petrographic and mineralogical observations did not largely compensate for this disadvantage.

In the case of the ceramics of the Malaga-Spain group, the examination of a thin section reveals the presence in the paste of different varieties of schist, often closely associated with some finely granulated quartzites. Many larger grains of quartz, associated sometimes with schists and quartzites as well as with ferruginous elements, present a marked cataclastic structure. These characteristics, as well as a few others (e.g., dimensions of the grains, appearance of the clay matrix), might not be the same over a large geographic area. One can also consider that the probability of finding the same characteristics in regions far from Malaga is virtually nonexistent. As we observe these characteristics in the ceramics of the Malaga-France group we can be sure that the two groups come from the same region. But we cannot affirm, on the sole basis of laboratory data, that we are dealing with the same workshop.

Thus, the study of the petrographic characteristics leaves us confronted with the same sort of situation encountered earlier on with that of the chemical characteristics. There can without doubt be risks of confusion, serious or not, depending on which characteristics one studies, but here also there is a lack of comparative studies. In the case of the Malaga productions we would be tempted, taking into account the local geology, to believe in the superiority of petrographic characteristics. Unfortunately, too many categories of pottery have a fine paste which presents an obstacle only overcome with great difficulty when one wishes to distinguish the petrographic characteristics of the ware in question. What is more, the fine wares are most often those that were most widely exported, and they must therefore be studied in the lab-

oratory. Besides, the sorting of a complicated material is often more supple and quicker using chemical data than when using mineralogical and petrographic data. However one must not ignore the value of mineralogical and petrographic data which often provide us with precise and irreplaceable geological information.

Relative Comparisons

We now propose to go back to the original problem we presented, namely, that of the localization of workshops. We have at our disposal a reference group, the Malaga-Spain group, which we take for granted as originating from Malaga. The determination of the provenance of the Malaga-France group ought to consist, if the group in question does really come from Malaga, in showing that the two groups have certain characteristics which could assure us as to their having a common origin. However we have already seen that if we take into account only these two groups there exists no laboratory study of ceramics, however complicated, that could permit us with our present knowledge to state positively the common origin of the two groups. Indeed, nothing indicates that there might not exist in southern Spain another workshop using clays of the same characteristics as those of Malaga. We know that such cases do exist, and that they are even frequent and can be found at a considerable distance, but unfortunately such cases have rarely been studied. Likewise, we have seen that as long as one limits investigations to the reference group and to the group of undetermined origin, nothing allows one to conclude as to the likelihood of a separate origin when faced with the differences between the two groups.

We must therefore accept the idea that the laboratory methods for the study of ceramics are imperfect, this in itself a banal statement for all experimental research. Nonetheless, the fact that these methods are generally less imperfect than the traditional approach to pottery studies in no way justifies their use without taking into account their imperfections.

If we wish to consider the flaws in these methods in order to minimize their drawbacks, the only logical procedure which would allow one to assert that the Malaga-France pottery was produced at Malaga would be to stop estimating the degree of resemblance between the two groups in an absolute way, and henceforth to estimate in a relative way. We intend to show, as has already been pointed out, either that the characteristics of the Malaga-France group are closer to those of the Malaga-Spain group than to those of any other productions in southern Spain, or that they are closer to clays existing in the region of Malaga than to any other clays existing in the area

62

C. Lemoine, S. Walker, M. Picon

under study. If it turned out that the characteristics of the Malaga-France group were found virtually unchanged over a long distance, the determination of the provenance would be relatively imprecise, but the knowledge of this imprecision would prevent the mistaken attribution of workshops.

The putting into practice of such a procedure necessitates the setting up for the region under study of what we shall call a network of localized data, which also brings us to the idea of an a priori probability. We now propose to discuss in greater detail the role of these two complementary themes.

The Network of Localized Data

Taking into account all we have said so far, it is easy to understand that generally the value of the determinations of ceramic provenance carried out in a laboratory depends above all on the density of the information that one has been able to gather concerning the clays of the region under consideration. It is the assemblage of this information that constitutes the network of localized data. The problems of localization being above all geological, one can make do with a loosely structured network where one is sure that certain geological formations would not have been the source of the raw material used by the potters. On the other hand, the network ought to be relatively tightly structured in zones where the formations might have been exploited for ceramic production. The construction of the network will involve the use of results obtained from the study of clay samples, as well as those from the study of regional ceramic workshops of all periods. The importance of the latter will be seen later on. Sometimes the assemblage of the network of localized data cannot be easily carried out, notably because the location of certain references is not the result of direct, incontestable observations. One is indeed often obliged to resort to information provided by ceramic comparison material whose localization is based on archaeological or other such methods of cross-checking. Such a procedure can be at the origin of many mistakes. We shall therefore point out that the procedure followed for the determination of ceramic provenance does not generally call directly on the nature of the observed or measured characteristics of the ceramics and the clays. In fact, we can use any method of characterization. This is all the more valid if certain methods are seen in practice to be of little discriminatory value and thus difficult to use. This deficiency would not lead one into error but only lead to a greater imprecision as to the localization of the ceramic source. The essential concern is to recognize and define the imprecision.

A Priori Probabilities

When one reads publications, including our own, that deal with the determination of ceramic provenance, it is clear that the procedure we have just described is rarely used. One can say that if the tightly structured network of localized data is rarely encountered, this is because laboratories nearly always accept that the data relevant to the problem of provenance includes a certain number of limitations which are more or less explicit. Indeed, certain possible locations can be considered a priori as being more probable than others. The existence of these a priori probabilities allows us, if not to get by without the network of localized data, at least to use a highly simplified version of the network. Such a simplified network can be used wherever we consider that a problem of provenance can be limited to a certain number of possible localizations. In using such a method, we accept that the sites proposed at the beginning as being the only likely ones present a certain probability of being the location one is looking for, whereas all other sites are of a zero probability. However, in the majority of cases it is not possible to be so categorical. Nevertheless it is evident, when one seeks to identify the origin of a group of pottery from a given region, that the workshop one is looking for has more chances of being situated at certain places and sites than at others. Bearing this statement in mind, we can construct a simplified network where all points have a high probability of being the location in question. Such a network necessitates the bringing together of the evidence of archaeology (workshops, domestic sites, markets, communication networks), ethnography (the study of modern production sites whose interest resides in the often noticed chronological continuity of artisanal production, technical traditions, and so on), and geology (clay sources and their suitability for certain ceramic productions). This simplified situation is represented on the map of southern Spain (Fig. 6).

If, in our search for the production site of a group of ceramics, we can show not only that their composition very closely resembles that of one of the high probability points on our network of localized data, but also that all the other high probability points have radically different compositions, we would be right in considering this first point as being that of the ceramic production source. One can above all accept that the probability of another production site's existing would be low, all the more so as greater care will have been taken in the inventory of the high probability points in the region under consideration.

It is clear that the principal difficulty encountered in the determination of ceramic provenance results

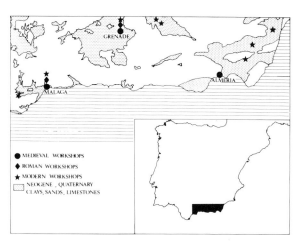

Figure 6. Simplified map of clay deposits and ceramic workshops, ancient and modern, in southern Spain.

We hope that this reflection will contribute to the discussion which enlivens present-day research in ceramology.

from the fact that an accurate distinction of the role of the laboratory and that of the different a priori probabilities is rarely carried out. The a priori probabilities which justify the use of a very simplified network are often not very clear, often implicit, and when they are explicit they are badly assessed, underestimated, and even more often overestimated.

Even in the relatively simple case of the Malaga-France group where we conclude, as indeed is the case, that the group does originate from Malaga, it must not be forgotten that though the laboratory has well and truly confirmed the attribution of the pottery to the Malaga region, the attribution to Malaga itself is more the result of historical evidence and therefore of certain a priori probabilities.

This reinstatement of geological, historical, archaeological, and ethnographic evidence in the conclusions reached by the laboratory ought to provide us all with food for thought. We are agreed that it is not so much a true reinstatement, as the realization of the exact role played by historical evidence (using the idea of a priori probabilities) in the general conclusions reached by work in the laboratory.

One can finally ask oneself if the construction of the network of localized data is not too long and costly an enterprise. But, apart from the fact that it seems difficult to dispense with such a network without running the risk of coming to false conclusions, it should be emphasized that it is not possible to count on luck alone in the localization of ceramic production sites. The surest, and in the long run the most economic, procedure for discovering these points is the use of the simplified network where, in priority, one takes into account the zones of high probability.

SECTION II.

Physical and Chemical Methods

6. Provenience Studies Using Neutron Activation Analysis: The Role of Standardization

GARMAN HARBOTTLE
Department of Chemistry
Brookhaven National Laboratory

In several laboratories ceramics of archaeological origin are currently being chemically analyzed — one can guess at a total yearly production rate running into the thousands. Since the present commercial price for multielement analyses by neutron activation is $500/sample or more, it is clear that a great deal of money is involved. I do not think it is necessary today to justify the method or expenditure: the steady stream of publications, theses, and privately circulated reports amply reward the archaeologist and his collaborator-analyst for their efforts by giving new answers and insights into ancient ceramic production and trade, insights that would not, in most cases, have been provided by stylistic analysis alone.

Development of Chemical Analysis of Archaeological Ceramics

The first chemical analysis of an archaeological artifact took place in 1790 (Caley 1962); I thought at one time that the first analysis of an archaeological ceramic dated to Fouque's investigations at Santorin in the 1860s (Murray 1900) but this is not so certain if one reads Fouque's report itself (Fouque 1869). In any case, T. W. Richards at Harvard in 1895 analyzed ancient Athenian pottery "at the request of Mr. Edward Robinson, of the Boston Museum of Fine Arts" and reported the results fully in the *Journal of the American Chemical Society* (Richards 1895). Two significant points emerge. The first is this collaboration between the humanities and the sciences. The second is Richards's observation that the "variations in the relative amounts [of the different chemical elements] are singularly small, the range being not nearly so large as that given by Brougniart (1854) in his *Traité des arts céramiques*. Hence it is possible that all of these specimens, which were picked up in the city of Athens itself, were the product of a local pottery." This observation carries the germ of what has been called the Provenience Postulate, which will be further mentioned below.

After the Harvard work, although there were analyses of archaeological metals (Caley 1964) little was done with ceramics for a long time. The reason is simple: anyone who was, like myself, trained in the classic school of wet quantitative analysis, which had in its curriculum the horror of an experiment in rock analysis, with peroxide and carbonate fusion for openers (Swift 1940), can easily see that the processing of the hundreds of archaeological specimens, which are very much like rocks, in a typical investigation, would be daunting to say the least. Emission spectroscopy has been used to shortcut the work (Richards 1959) but its precision is strongly concentration- and to some extent matrix-dependent. Although the method is still used, it produces results that are, in my opinion, of limited value in the resolution of ceramic groups, especially similar ones.

The history of the first application of neutron activation to archaeological ceramics has been told in detail elsewhere (Harbottle 1976): suffice it to say that twenty or more elements can be simultaneously measured in a single specimen and, as we shall see, the results are quite precise and may even be or become accurate as well.

The distinction between precision and accuracy of chemical analysis is an important one. Although in principle one could calculate the concentrations of elements in a neutron-activated specimen from an exact knowledge of neutron flux, its intensity, duration and spectral (energy) distribution, plus an exact gamma ray count calibrated for efficiency, corrected for branching ratio and so on, in practice it is far easier to compare one's unknown to a "standard" of known or assumed composition. Different laboratories have used different standards, but within one laboratory's work with its own archaeological problems, what is important is the precision: the ability to relate the concentrations of elements in one's samples reliably, in terms of ratios, to the assumed concentrations in the standard. Obviously, all the data generated in a given laboratory is intercomparable, provided only that the standard employed is homogeneous, and the level of intralaboratory precision is sufficiently good. Some laboratories and their standards are given in Table 1.

For a long time, probably extending from the beginning up to about the mid-1970s, the archaeological ceramic analysis projects were isolated, "self-contained" usually even within the laboratory concerned. That is, the data generated were useful to the archaeologist concerned, but did not overlap, in the universe of all conceivable data, the spheres of interest of any other archaeologists. But that situation has changed dramatically, and at Brookhaven in current archaeological studies extensive use is being made of our own past work, and of the "data bank." A few recent examples will suffice:

1) Sherds of a Mycenaean appearance are found in certain levels in the excavation of a cave in Jordan. They are analyzed and the computer search picks out Mycenaean sherds from Mycenae in Greece as the very closest match (McGovern 1979).

2) Sherds of a supposed "imitation" Crema ware are found in preclassic levels in a site called La Cañada that was thought to have only faint connections with Monte Alban. This great site in Oaxaca, Mexico, is the home of Crema ware. Analysis shows that some of the Crema *is* imitation, but some of the sherds are authentic, intrusive trade pieces (Redmond 1981): this is shown by reference to authentic Crema

Table 1. A partial list of laboratories engaged in archaeological ceramic neutron activation analysis, and the standards of these laboratories

Laboratory	Standard	Reference
GANOS (Groupe d'Archeologie Nucleaire d'Orsay-Saclay)	Asaro-Perlman	(Attas et al. 1979)
Brookhaven National Laboratory	6 USGS Rocks Ohio Red (in-house)	(Bieber et al. 1976a)
RISO	Danish Clay (in-house)[a]	(Hansen et al. 1979)
Berkeley	Asaro-Perlman	(Perlman and Asaro 1969)
Jerusalem	Asaro-Perlman	(Yellin et al. 1978)
Manchester	Podmore P1033 Red Plastic Clay (in-house)	(Newton and Krywonos 1974–75)
Smithsonian (Conservation Analytical Laboratory)	USGS Rocks and NBS Fly Ash	(De Atley et al. 1980)
McGill	Asaro-Perlman	(Attas et al. 1977)

[a] Analyzed by comparison with USGS–BNL 6 rocks, and Bradford Standard.

analyses in the data bank.

3) Examples of Tell-el-Yahudiyeh ware (small jugs) from along the Nile are thought possibly to have been fabricated in Palestine where the ware is also found. Analyses are compared with an extensive, already existing data bank of Nile and Palestinian clays of different types. Result: almost all the Tell-el-Yahudiyeh pieces are locally made, and the hypothetical "extensive trade" in these objects (and in whatever valuable commodity they contained) evaporates. This constitutes important information about the Hyksos (Kaplan 1978).

Numerous other examples of the "overlap" and reuse of data, within our own laboratory and, we are sure, within others, could be cited. It is also becoming increasingly clear that the fields of archaeological interest investigated by different groups are overlapping. For example:

1) Both the Berkeley and Brookhaven groups have

carried out extensive analyses of "Nile Mud" wares (Perlman and Asaro 1969; Kaplan 1978).

2) At Berkeley an archaeologist analyzed wares from the postclassic Valley of Mexico that are typologically related to similar wares analyzed at Brookhaven (Branstetter 1979).

3) Greek ceramics are being analyzed both at GANOS by Attas from McGill and at Brookhaven (Attas 1980; Fillieres 1980).

At a wild guess, there must exist worldwide some 40–50,000 analyses. It is obvious that there would be a great benefit if analyses could be exchanged among all users and/or generators of data. This benefit would increase constantly, with increase in the data. The main thrust of this paper will be: (1) how far are we from interlaboratory comparability of ceramic data; (2) what has been proposed in the past to achieve this goal; and (3) a new proposal. All of this may be subsumed under the general heading of "Analytical Quality Control" — i.e., how to achieve precise and accurate analysis, in the neutron activation sense. Then, (4) the relationship of analytical quality control to provenience location will be examined.

Precision, Accuracy, and Probability of Group Assignments

Some time ago, I attempted to indicate the rough ranges of concentrations of different elements encountered in "homogeneous" "natural" archaeological ceramic groups (Harbottle 1976). If an archaeological ceramic group — let us say a particular ware or group of wares made from a particular clay source, disregarding for a moment the possible deliberate addition of temper — is thought of as occupying an ellipsoid of 95% probability in the multivariate space whose n coordinate axes represent the (usually log-transformed) concentrations of the n analyzed elements, then it will be easier to discuss questions related to precision, accuracy, and the probability of group assignments. We may ask, for example:

(a) How large are the axial extensions of the group, expressed as standard deviation divided by the mean value, in percent? This is the "natural" size of the group, before sampling and measurement error have been folded in, and gives one the feeling of multivariate volume of the group.

(b) Does the inevitable analytical precision error, within a given laboratory, in the analyses that constitute the group enlarge the "natural" variation, or volume, appreciably?

(c) Could a second laboratory, using the same standard but a different reactor, counter, etc., place the same samples in the same multivariate volume?

(d) Could a second laboratory, but using a different standard, also do this?

If (d) is possible, then at one stroke we have greatly increased the mass of data available to the archaeometrist.

Before proceeding, let us answer the easy question first, that is, (c), and the answer is yes. If two laboratories use the same standard, they get the same answers (Yellin et al. 1978). What this study says is, that between two laboratories using the same standard, the precision is no worse than within either one of the laboratories alone. Which brings us back to (b), the question of the analytical precision within one laboratory, and the effect of this in enlarging the multivariate volume of the "natural" group. The Berkeley group early on studied and reported their precision: the small numbers which they obtained are a tribute to the care they have taken in their methodology (Perlman and Asaro 1969).

I would like to report a new set of data from the Brookhaven National Laboratory (BNL) group, which will also bear on the question of in-house analytical precision. The data derives from the way in which we standardize: namely, we always bombard weighed samples of all six USGS standard rocks, PCCl, DTSl, GSPl, AGVl, BCRl, and G2, together with our unknown ceramic samples. Then, using the "Master Table" of "best value" concentrations which we derived from data in Flanagan's report (Abascal et al. 1974; Flanagan 1976) we calculate for each element, in each standard in which it occurs (for example PCCl and DTSl have almost no rare earths, alkalis, alkaline earths, etc.) a constant that is essentially the corrected number of characteristic gamma counts recorded, per unit weight of the element present, per unit time. The unit weight is calculated from the weight of standard rock taken, times the "Master Table" concentration. If our "Master Table" concentrations were either (a) correct or (b) all different from the correct values by a constant factor, then the constants for a given element would all be the same. Some typical examples, from a neutron bombardment which took place on 20 September 1978 are given in Table 2: for simplicity the exponential factors, which are the same for all the constants reported for a given element, have been eliminated. In some cases, six independent values of this constant are reported (Fe, Co), in other cases four or fewer (Ba, Rb, Cr, etc.) since, as mentioned above, some of the rocks are so deficient in some of the elements that they cannot be used as standards for those elements (Bieber et al. 1976a). For these six or four independent constant values, the geometric mean, the standard deviation, and the standard error (standard deviation of the mean) are also listed (Table 2).

Table 2. Intensities of characteristic gamma rays, in counts per unit time, per unit weight of element activated, of the six USGS rocks, for a bombardment on 9/20/78

	PCCl	GSPl	DTSl	BCRl	AGVl	G2	Geo. Mean	Std. Deviation %	Std. Error %
Eu		2.75		2.85	3.05	2.93	2.89	4.4	2.2
Lu		12.56		7.11	5.96	5.58	7.38	44.	22.
Hf		5.88		5.55	4.85	5.83	5.51	8.6	4.3
Th		6.11		5.84	5.91	5.95	5.95	1.9	1.
Cr	5.00		4.86				4.93	9.9	7.
Fe	5.00	4.86	5.14	4.90	4.93	5.01	4.97	2.0	0.8
Co	3.08	2.68	3.00	2.87	2.89	2.69	2.86	5.6	2.3
Sc	5.65	4.15	5.10	5.53	5.63	4.88	5.13	11.4	4.6
Ba		1.55		1.54	1.64	1.64	1.59	3.5	1.7
Rb		8.51		7.85	7.86	7.89	8.03	4.0	2.0
Cs		2.28		1.84	2.14	2.31	2.13	10.	5.

It will be seen that some elements (Fe, Th) agree across the board very well. Others (Eu, Sc, Hf) are less consistent, while Lu is downright terrible, with a group standard deviation of 44%. The inconsistent constant values like Lu and Sc (large standard deviations) could be due to errors in recording the gamma counts (geometry errors, spectrum processing, etc.), inhomogeneous standards, weighing errors, or simply, incorrect, or at least noninternally consistent, values of the concentrations of the elements in our "Master Table." To investigate this we standardized the constants in Table 2 by dividing each constant by the corresponding geometric mean. For example, the six values for Fe become 1.006, 0.978, 1.034, 0.986, 0.992, and 1.008 when standardized, while the four values for Lu become 1.70, 0.96, 0.81, and 0.76. Then we similarly standardized all the elementary constants, in tables similar to Table 2, resulting from a whole series of bombardments in each of which the six USGS rocks were included. Altogether, about fifty data sets, one from each bombardment, were processed. We felt that this unique data set probably would furnish the best possible self-consistent sets of elementary concentration ratios in the six USGS rocks that could be obtained.

In the final step, for each element and for each rock the standardized constants were arithmetically averaged, and the standard deviation and standard error in *this* quantity calculated, across the whole set of ∿50 bombardments. The results of this exercise are presented in Table 3, where the "mean ratios" are the means of the fifty or so values of the ratio of the calibration coefficient for each standard to the geometric mean for six (or four) standards, as given for Fe and Lu in the example just above.

Our choices of values for the concentrations of elements in the "Master Table" are very directly reflected in the closeness with which the "mean ratio" entries in Table 3 approach each other, and unity. For example, the six values for Fe are 0.995, 0.995, 1.013, 1.006, 0.998, and 0.995, each with an error of ca ± .004 (Table 3). Obviously we have chosen for our "Master Table" a set of iron concentrations that are internally highly self-consistent. But each of those six concentration choices was made independently, by statistically treating some 30–40 independent iron values reported by Flanagan (1976) from nearly that number of laboratories, using methods as diverse as emission spectroscopy, atomic absorption, titration, neutron activation, and XRF to establish their absolute iron concentrations. Is it too much to think that we have here a very close approach to the true concentration values?

Looking through Table 3 we can see that there are, like iron, other "well-behaved" elements. These would include Fe, Th, Cr, Na, K. In this group, the standard deviation taken across the six or four (or two for Cr) *mean ratios* is around 1% — indicating that, for these elements, our "Master Table" values are highly internally consistent. Mn would also belong to this group except for G2, where we have obviously taken too large a standard concentration. Doing almost as well is a group where the ratios agree at a level of 2 to 4%. This would include Co, Ba, Sm, Mn. Then there is a group in the 7 to 10% standard deviation range, Eu, Hf, Ta, Sb, Zn, Ca, Yb, Sc, Cs, Ce, La. Finally there is the atrocious Lu, with a standard deviation of 38%: the standard deviation values discussed here correspond in a certain average sense to the values listed, in the case of a *particular*

Garman Harbottle

Table 4. Internal consistency of various choices for concentrations of Sc_2O_3 in six USGS rock standards

	Concentrations of Sc_2O_3					Mean Ratios				
Standard Rock	Master Table[a]	Katz-Grossman[b] Best Lit.	Least Sq.	Flanagan[c]	Based on Gamma Intensity[d]	Master Table	Katz-Grossman Best Lit.	Least Sq.	Flanagan	Based on Gamma Intensity
PCCl	12.55	12.73	12.58	10.58	12.67	1.1020	1.0508	1.0460	1.2461	1.0063
GSPl	12.19	10.94	10.28	10.89	9.22	.8208	.8845	.9260	.8758	1.0009
DTSl	5.89	5.45	5.38	5.52	5.37	.9829	1.0274	1.0239	.9997	.9939
BCRl	49.93	51.39	50.62	50.62	50.28	1.0983	1.0320	1.0308	1.0326	1.0054
AGVl	18.19	18.87	18.71	20.55	18.44	1.1061	1.0312	1.0232	1.1911	1.0059
G2	6.12	5.57	5.64	5.68	5.29	.9368	.9954	.9672	.8288	.9992
				Standard Deviation, as % of mean[e]		11.6	6.1	4.6	16.6	0.5

[a] Abascal et al. 1974.
[b] Katz and Grossman 1976. "Best Literature" is Table 56. "Least Squares" is Table 57.
[c] Flanagan 1976, Table 107.
[d] A set whose values are calculated from ratios of scandium gamma ray intensities, averaged over 45 intercomparisons, with BCRl arbitrarily taken to have $Sc_2O_3 = 50.28$ ppm.
[e] Table 3, above.

bombardment, in the next to last column to the right in Table 2.

Thus far, I have discussed only the mutual consistency of concentration values more or less arbitrarily chosen by us for our "Master Table." But Table 3, based as it is upon the six-way intercomparison of standards repeated fifty or more times with many variables and errors randomized, can equally well, by a slight mathematical manipulation, enable us to test *any* other table of concentration values, and to compare its consistency with that of our "Master Table." In Table 4 the BNL mean ratios for scandium (Table 3) are recomputed to what they would have been had they been based on the "best literature" values of Katz and Grossman (1976, Table 56), the final least-squares fitted values of the same authors (Table 57), the Flanagan 1972 compilation "Estimates" (Flanagan 1976, Table 107) and to a synthesis of self-consistent ratio-determined values, taking an arbitrary value for BCRl.

To test the internal consistency of the various choices of concentrations mentioned above, one need only calculate, as before, the standard deviation of the six ratios. These are given in Table 4 below the mean ratios: the results indicate that the Katz-Grossman least-squares fitted values are a substantially better choice of scandium concentrations than our "Master Table," that the Flanagan 1972 values are the least consistent, and that it is possible, by using

our average observed ratios of line intensities, to calculate a set of values that are very, very self-consistent. This last set is based on Sc_2O_3 in BCRl arbitrarily equal to 50.28 ppm. Any change in this figure would require a proportionate change in the other five standards.

It may be argued that this last set is "good" by circular methods: the same procedures are used to generate and then to test the numbers. This is certainly so, but that is the goal: to find a set that will be consistent with the gamma intensities, as expressed through the mean ratios. However, the data processed in Table 3 can tell us more than a message about mutual consistency of concentrations: it can also provide a measure of precision.

The fifty or so intercomparison runs that form the basis of Table 3 each involved the preparation of samples of each of six different standards by drying and precise weighing (about 40 mg), bombardment together, but not in any very precisely defined geometry — counting in a geometry that was made to be the same, as well as possible, for all six — processing the spectra, correction for various periods of decay, and various degrees of dead time in the counting device, etc. All these error sources, including the ever-present counting statistics, along with the more subtle possibility of inhomogeneity in the standards themselves, are included in the "standard deviation" values in the table: this is the square root of the vari-

Table 3. Mean ratios of elementary calibration constants to geometric means

Element Oxide	Number of Runs	Standard	DTSI	GSPI	PCCI	BCRI	AGV1	G2	Std. deviation of mean ratios as % of mean
Eu₂O₃	45	Mean Ratio		.9143		1.0316	1.0901	.9832	7.4
		Std Deviation		.0609		.0677	.0616	.1059	
		Std Error		.0090		.0101	.0091	.0157	
Lu₂O₃	39	Mean Ratio		1.5797		1.0781	.8054	.7502	38.
		Std Deviation		.1554		.1712	.0902	.0805	
		Std Error		.0248		.0274	.0144	.0129	
HfO₂	49	Mean Ratio		1.1491		1.0088	.8948	.9681	10.7
		Std Deviation		.0753		.0550	.0318	.0556	
		Std Error		.0107		.0078	.0045	.0079	
ThO₂	50	Mean Ratio		.9912		1.0059	.9886	1.0087	1.0
		Std Deviation		.0476		.1006	.0414	.0360	
		Std Error		.0067		.0142	.0058	.0051	
Ta₂O₅	41	Mean Ratio		.9264		1.0434		1.0532	7.1
		Std Deviation		.1204		.1209		.1087	
		Std Error		.0188		.0188		.0169	
Cr₂O₃	45	Mean Ratio	1.0102		.9954				1.0
		Std Deviation	.0303		.0350				
		Std Error	.0045		.0052				
Fe₂O₃	50	Mean Ratio	.9954	.9949	1.0130	1.0061	.9979	.9947	0.76
		Std Deviation	.0251	.0257	.0282	.0330	.0250	.0269	
		Std Error	.0035	.0036	.0039	.0046	.0035	.0038	
CoO	44	Mean Ratio	1.0503	.9691	1.0348	1.0218	.9960	.9401	4.2
		Std Deviation	.0329	.0852	.0438	.0449	.0377	.0426	
		Std Error	.0049	.0128	.0066	.0067	.0056	.0064	
Sb₂O₃	44	Mean Ratio		1.0600			.9495		7.8
		Std Deviation		.0801			.0814		
		Std Error		.0120			.0122		
ZnO	28	Mean Ratio	1.2100	.9198	.9962	1.1026	.9804	.8689	12.4
		Std Deviation	.1066	.0555	.0695	.0986	.0743	.0872	
		Std Error	.0201	.0105	.0131	.0215	.0140	.0164	
CaO	37	Mean Ratio		1.0503		1.1100	.9596	.9109	8.9
		Std Deviation		.1897		.1388	.0696	.1097	
		Std Error		.0311		.0228	.0114	.0180	
Yb₂O₃	52	Mean Ratio				1.0337	1.0852	.8994	9.6
		Std Deviation				.0642	.0642	.0734	
		Std Error				.0088	.0089	.0101	

Oxide		Statistic							
Na₂O	62	Mean Ratio		.9839		1.0179	1.0033	.9970	1.4
		Std Deviation		.0326		.0400	.0373	.0331	
		Std Error		.0041		.0050	.0047	.0042	
K₂O	53	Mean Ratio		.9969	.9829	1.0289	.9996	.9931	1.6
		Std Deviation		.0716	.0265	.1025	.0769	.0618	
		Std Error		.0098	.0039	.0140	.0105	.0084	
Sc₂O₃	46	Mean Ratio	1.1020	.8207		1.0982	1.1060	.9367	11.6
		Std Deviation	.0353	.0225		.0435	.0296	.0273	
		Std Error	.0052	.0033		.0064	.0043	.0040	
Rb₂O	43	Mean Ratio		1.0026		1.0253	1.0208	.9751	2.3
		Std Deviation		.0541		.1346	.0785	.0681	
		Std Error		.0082		.0205	.0119	.0103	
Cs₂O	38	Mean Ratio		1.0042		.8876	1.0261	1.1263	9.8
		Std Deviation		.1254		.1395	.1077	.1149	
		Std Error		.0203		.0226	.0174	.0186	
BaO	45	Mean Ratio		1.0036		.9600	1.0063	1.0358	3.1
		Std Deviation		.0400		.0607	.0386	.0435	
		Std Error		.0059		.0090	.0057	.0064	
CeO₂	54	Mean Ratio		.9692		1.1760	.9002	.9786	11.8
		Std Deviation		.0382		.0648	.0415	.0382	
		Std Error		.0052		.0088	.0056	.0052	
La₂O₃[a]	51	Mean Ratio		.8822		1.0424	1.1194	.9749	10.1
		Std Deviation		.0308		.0513	.0606	.0393	
		Std Error		.0043		.0071	.0084	.0055	
Sm₂O₃	20	Mean Ratio		.9499		1.0057	1.0210	1.0332	3.7
		Std Deviation		.0832		.0557	.0498	.0647	
		Std Error		.0186		.0124	.0111	.0144	
MnO	40	Mean Ratio	1.0175	.9842	1.0110	1.0292	1.0061	.9399	3.2
		Std Deviation	.0840	.0557	.0713	.0533	.0585	.0650	
		Std Error	.0132	.0088	.0112	.0084	.0092	.0102	

[a] The Master Table values differ from those published in Abascal et al. 1974. We now use for La₂O₃ in GSP1 244.4, BCR1 29.6, AGV1 42.5, and G2 108 ppm.

ance in the distribution of ratios sampled by the fifty intercomparison runs, and measures the variance to be expected in a real laboratory (namely, BNL) working day-to-day with routine neutron activation analysis procedures.

As expected, the elements present in large concentration and well-activated (Fe, Cr, Na) show standard deviations that are small, averaging 2.7, 3.3, and 3.6% respectively. A number of other elements, though present at trace concentrations, show small standard deviations: Sc, Ba, Ce, La (Table 3). These relatively small values reassure us that the elements themselves must be reasonably homogeneously distributed in the samples of standard rock supplied to us by the USGS.

Several elements, though present at large concentrations (K, Ca) show substantial standard deviations. In these cases the lack of precision is surely not due to inhomogeneity but, very simply, to the weak activation of the radioisotope of interest, leading to poor counting statistics. The same is, at first sight surprisingly, true of Mn: although this element is strongly activated, our counting procedures result in some standards being counted when the Mn^{56} has already much decayed: it has a short half-life.

In summary, it would appear that the best routine precision attainable at BNL is around ±2.5 to 3%: of this standard deviation I would guess that about 1% is due to the spectrum processing and counting statistics, and the (combinatorially speaking) remainder comes from many small errors such as counting geometry and flux gradient.

The discussion of analytical precision and self-consistent standards has perhaps been overlong: what we are concerned with is what effect this may have on application of the analyses to provenience location. Reverting to questions (a) through (d) asked earlier, of which we answered (c) in advance, it would appear that the available intralaboratory precision is adequate at present [question (b)]. "Natural" groups rarely have a uniformity of under 8 to 10%: more typically they are 15 to 20%. Sampling and measurement error inevitably add something to this (see std. deviations in Table 3) but the *measured* extension of the multivariate group is close enough to the *natural* variance to yield, in most cases, a significant resolution from neighboring groups. A more subtle reason for seeking enhanced analytical precision is that many natural ceramic clays have highly correlated element pairs and multiplets. These correlations, operating through factor and discriminant analysis provide a powerful tool for the resolution of closely similar archaeological groups (Harbottle 1976). The methods work better, the more nearly the analysis reveals the full extent of correlation.

From the practical standpoint, analytical precision is a trade-off with production. If you wish to analyze many samples, you can only count each one for a certain time, and that determines the statistical error.

Question (d), the placing of samples by a second laboratory, using its own standard, into a multivariate group established by the first laboratory, with *its* (different) standards, is the crux of this essay. I believe that we are already quite close to valid interlaboratory data exchange. At BNL we have analyzed, as mentioned above, 161 sherds of "Nile Mud" ware (Kaplan 1978). Perlman and Asaro (1971, Table 13.6) report the analysis of thirty-two sherds of "Nile Mud" — and it must be remembered that these are different sherds from ours, coming from different proveniences. Nonetheless, it will be seen in Table 5 that there is a high degree of correspondence, with no attempt made to adjust for differences in the two standardization techniques. If, at our present state of experience we examined the data in Table 5, with no knowledge of the material analyzed, we would have a strong suspicion that we are both dealing with the same pottery paste type.

Another example, the analysis of three completely different groups of Mycenaean sherds in three laboratories, is given in Table 6. Again, no adjustment for standardization was made, and good similarity is noted.

Still another example concerns analyses of ceramics from Cerro Portezuelo in Mexico, carried out by Branstetter (1979) at Berkeley. She kindly forwarded her data to us, and when it was examined it was found that her main group was readily recognizable as our Valley of Mexico composition (Abascal et al. 1974; Sayre and Harbottle, forthcoming).

In the past the conversion of one laboratory's analyses to another's standardization has often been discussed, and the proposal has usually been either (a) for everyone to use the same standard or (b) to exchange and mutually analyze each other's standards and thus arrive at a matrix of intercomparisons. I now feel that (a) is impractical in that there is already so much data referenced to existing standards, and that (b) is useful, but only as an interim measure. In fact, at BNL we are at present engaged in a project to provide an intercomparison between the Asaro-Perlman and six USGS rocks standards, carried to the highest possible precision. My new proposal is that, given the kind of data seen in Tables 5 and 6, what we should aim for is that anyone wishing to analyze archaeological ceramics should simply use his own standard, but attempt to calibrate that standard as nearly as possible to absolute (i.e., accurate) concentration values. The proposal arises not merely from the fact that we seem to be approaching absolute cali-

Garman Harbottle

Table 5. Concentrations of oxides in "Nile Mud" ware measured in two laboratories

Element Oxide	Berkeley[a] n = 32	BNL[b] n = 161	
MnO	1555 ± 88	1545 ± 540	ppm
La_2O_3	38.4 ± 2.0	33.8 ± 4.5	ppm
Fe_2O_3	9.75 ± .50	9.74 ± .94	%
Sc_2O_3	35.45 ± 1.47	36.2 ± 3.7	ppm
CoO	44.45 ± 2.0	42.9 ± 5.6	ppm
Cs_2O	1.47 ± .22	1.54 ± .48	ppm
HfO_2	10.22 ± .88	7.46 ± 1.21	ppm
ThO_2	7.90 ± .56	7.25 ± .90	ppm
Na_2O	1.80 ± .29	1.70 ± .42	%
Cr_2O_3	264 ± 23	226 ± 46	ppm
BaO	550 ± 83	592 ± 169	ppm
Rb_2O	66.7 ± 7.7	53.4 ± 13.1	ppm

[a] Perlman and Asaro 1971, Table 13.6.
[b] Kaplan 1978.

brations anyhow, but also from the accumulation of error that results from procedure (b).

If laboratory A using standard M wants to compare analyses with laboratory B using standard N then we have comparisons not merely of samples to standards but of M to N also, with errors adding up all along the line. The same argument applies to the idea of a new, universal standard. If existing standards are calibrated to a higher absolute accuracy, on the other hand, I believe that they will be quite adequate in permitting meaningful intercomparison. Of course, the exchange of reference material should continue, but the goal should be not the over-all shifting of all of A's analyses to B's standards but rather the pointing up and elimination of errors or discrepancies in all standardization systems.

The important question is, Will this every-man-for-himself procedure really provide data adequate for the archaeometrist to establish ceramic provenience? I believe that it will, after the discrepancies are ironed out. I base this belief on our experiences in studying a large number of archaeological "systems," i.e., geographic areas in which several ceramic groups involving tempered and/or untempered pastes have been analyzed and resolved from one another, and on our recent use of a "search" computer program, UPDPL (Bernstein 1979, unpub.). In this program, with which we are only beginning to gain experience, the analytical data for a specimen for which the archaeologist wishes to establish origin, or match with other ceramic specimens, is considered element-by-element. The concentration in each element is taken as the center of a plus-minus range which can be specified. For example, if the iron concentration is 5% and the range is set at ±10%, then any other specimen is a "match" if its iron concentration falls between 4.5 and 5.5%. The program then searches the entire data bank, utilizing as many elements as desired, and records those specimens which are "hits," i.e., fall within the specified ranges for all elements, or have one or two "misses," i.e., agree on all but one or two elements. These are recorded, as are "hits" and "misses" in which the error ranges are increased by a specified factor — let us say a factor of two, to ±20%.

What we are finding is that, at least in the few examples studied, if the ranges are set at ±5% and the search is carried out through a few thousand Old-World analyses, there are almost no authentic "hits" and certainly no accidental ones, if about fifteen to twenty elements are being considered. At a level of ±10% there are still very few accidentals. At ±20% one begins to see matches, and if the sherd happens to belong to a well-defined group, for example Attic Black Glaze, many hits, with none, one, and two misses, are recorded from members of that group. It must be emphasized that the search algorithm in UPDPL is Euclidean, that is, the groups are assumed to be spherical in multidimensional space. The actual ellipsoidal shape would further reduce the chance of accidental "hits," if one were to incorporate that feature.

It is not difficult to see why there are so few accidentals even with rather broad "error" ranges: Sneath and Sokal (1973, pp. 124–25) have demonstrated how an increase in the number of dimensions in a multivariate coordinate system decreases the variance in the expected Euclidean distances between points, hence "tightens" the grouping.

This, then, is the bottom line on both the "Provenience Postulate" (Weigand et al. 1977) and the accuracy of analysis needed. If enough elements are analyzed, the Provenience Postulate, which amounts to a statement about the relative sizes of within-groups and between-groups multivariate variance, is more readily fulfilled. Because the "accidentals" occur so infrequently in a population of ceramic analyses searched at the ±10% level, it would seem that, for intercomparison of data, absolute standardizations may not have to agree down to ±1%. It may well be that more modest levels of accuracy, perhaps ±3 to 5%, are perfectly adequate. In any case, we

Table 6. Concentrations of oxides in Mycenaean sherds measured in three laboratories[a]

Element Oxide	Berkeley[b]		BNL[c] 1	Mycenae 2	Subgroup 3	McGill[d]
	n = 16		n = 13	n = 10	n = 6	n = 45
Rb_2O	159.	± 15	164.	126.	142.	139.
Cs_2O	9.8	± .9	8.8	6.3	7.6	9.6
Sc_2O_3	32.4	± .9	34.8	30.3	34.	33.4
La_2O_3	40.0	± 1.4	39.8	36.1	39.1	39.9
Lu_2O_3	.425	± .018	.51	.49	.50	.457
ThO_2	12.2	± .4	13.4	11.6	13.0	13.2
HfO_2	3.78	± .4	3.64	3.72	3.69	4.65
Ta_2O_5	1.00	± .05	1.22	1.20	1.27	1.11
Cr_2O_3	323.	± 20	340.	352.	324.	418.
Fe_2O_3	7.38	± .26	7.51	6.70	7.63	7.89
CoO	35.9	± 1.8	36.7	36.3	35.0	39.4
BaO			427.	502.	444.	1028.
CeO_2			81.9	73.	82.7	78.7
Eu_2O_3			1.62	1.55	1.56	1.46

[a] All concentrations in ppm, except Fe_2O_3 in percentage.
[b] Karageorghis et al. 1972, p. 196 (Asaro-Perlman std.).
[c] Bieber et al. 1976a, 1976b (6 USGS rocks).
[d] Attas et al. 1977, Table 3 (Asaro-Perlman std.).

are already in a position to put these questions to the test, given the size of the Old- and New-World data banks on hand.

In closing, and because there are so many archaeologists present, it is worth mentioning tempered ceramics as a separate class. Temper analysis alone is often not adequate for unequivocal provenience assignment. We make use of it, however, as a preliminary separator of great value — in other words, if the ware is carbonate-tempered, for example, we try not to insert it into taxonomical procedures involving classes of nontempered wares. On the other hand, a knowledge of the type and quantity of the temper is enormously helpful in connecting the clay matrix portion of the ceramic to its proper fine-paste grouping or raw-clay provenience (Bishop 1980).

Although the limits tend to be somewhat broader, many of the procedures ordinarily used in the formation and testing of ceramic groups will work equally well with tempered wares. Our extensive investigations of Thin Orange and Granular wares from Mexico are in this category. The assignment of tempered wares to clay source is, however, a much more difficult problem (Olin and Sayre 1971).

Acknowledgments: I wish to thank my colleague E. V. Sayre for many of the ideas on data treatment involved in Table 3, and R. L. Bishop for continued discussion and helpful suggestions, and writing of the program that generated Table 3.

References

Abascal, R.; Harbottle, G.; and Sayre, E. V. 1974. Correlation between terra-cotta figurines and pottery from the Valley of Mexico and source clays by activation analysis. In Beck, C. W., ed. *Archaeological Chemistry*. Advances in Chemistry, no. 138. Washington, D.C.: American Chemical Society.

Attas, M. 1980. Analyse par activation neutronique de la ceramique de Lerne (Grece) a l'age du bronze ancien: productions locales et echanges commerciaux. Ph.D. dissertation, University of Paris-South, Orsay Center.

Attas, M.; Widemann, F.; Fontes, P.; Gruel, K.; Laubenheimer, F.; Leblanc, J.; and Lleres, J. 1979. Early Bronze Age ceramics from Lerna in Greece: Radiochemical studies. *Archaeophysika* 10:14-28.

Attas, M.; Yaffe, L.; and Fossey, J. M. 1977. Neutron activation analysis of early Bronze Age pottery from Lake Vouliagmeni, Perakhora, Central Greece. *Archaeometry* 19:33-43.

Garman Harbottle

Bernstein, H. L. [1979, unpublished.] UPDPL Version 1.2. A program for creating multielement chemical analytical data bases and for searching such bases for samples having analytical profiles similar to that of a given sample. Chemistry Department, Brookhaven National Laboratory, Upton, New York.

Bieber, A. M., Jr.; Brooks, D. W.; Harbottle, G.; and Sayre, E. V. 1976a. Application of multivariate techniques to analytical data on Aegean ceramics. *Archaeometry* 18: 59–74.

_____. 1976b. Compositional groupings of some ancient Aegean and eastern Mediterranean pottery. In *Applicazione dei Metodi nucleari nel campo delle opere d'arte*, pp. 111–43. Rome: Accademia Nazionale dei Lincei.

Bishop, R. L. 1980. Aspects of ceramic compositional modeling. In Fry, R. E., ed. *Models and methods in regional exchange*. Washington, D.C.: Society for American Archaeology.

Blackman, M. J. 1980. *See* De Atley et al. 1980.

Branstetter, B. 1979. Ceramics of Cerro Portezuelo, Mexico: an industry in transition. Ph.D. dissertation, University of California at Los Angeles [1978].

Brougniart, A. 1854. *Traité des arts céramiques*. 2d ed. Paris: Alphonse Salvetat.

Caley, E. R. 1962. *Analysis of ancient glasses 1790–1957*, p. 13. Corning: Corning Museum of Glass.

Caley, E. R. 1964. *Analysis of Ancient Metals*. Oxford: Pergamon Press.

De Atley, S.; Blackman, M. J.; and Olin, J. S. 1980. Comparison of data obtained by neutron activation and electron microprobe analyses of ceramics. In Olin, Jacqueline S., and Franklin, Alan D., eds., *Archaeological ceramics*, Sec. II, chap. 7. Washington, D.C.: Smithsonian Institution Press, forthcoming [1982].

Fillieres, D. 1980. Unpublished research.

Flanagan, F. J. 1976. Descriptions and analyses of eight new USGS rock standards. Geological Survey Professional Paper, no. 840, pp. 131–83. Washington, D.C.: U.S. Government Printing Office.

Fouque, M. 1869. Une Pompei antehistorique. *Revue des Deux Mondes* 83:923–43.

Hansen, B. A.; Sorensen, M. A.; Heydorn, K.; Mejdahl, V.; and Conradsen, K. 1979. Provenance study of medieval, decorated floor-tiles carried out by means of neutron activation analysis. *Archaeophysika* 10:119–40.

Harbottle, G. 1976. Activation analysis in archaeology. In Newton, G.W.A., ed., *Radiochemistry*, Vol. 3. London: Chemical Society.

Kaplan, Maureen. 1978. The origin and distribution of Tell-el-Yahudiyeh ware. Ph.D. dissertation, Brandeis University.

Karageorghis, V.; Asaro, F.; and Perlman, I. 1972. Concerning two Mycenaean pictorial sherds from Kouklia (Palaepaphos), Cyprus. *Archäologischer Anzeiger* 87: 188–97.

Katz, A., and Grossman, L. 1976. In Flanagan, F. J. 1976. Descriptions and analyses of eight new USGS rock standards, pp. 49–57.

McGovern, P. 1979. Private communication.

Murray, J. 1900. *Murray's Guide to Greece*, p. 928. London, 7th ed.

Newton, G.W.A., and Krywonos, W. 1974–75. Society of Libyan Studies, report no. 6:30.

Olin, J. S., and Sayre, E. V. 1971. Compositional categories of some English and American pottery of the American colonial period. In Brill, R. H., ed., *Science and archaeology*, chap. 14. Cambridge: M.I.T. Press.

Perlman, I., and Asaro, F. 1969. Pottery analysis by neutron activation. *Archaeometry* 11:21–52.

Perlman, I., and Asaro, F., 1971. Pottery analysis by neutron activation. In Brill, R. H., ed., *Science and archaeology*, chap. 13. Cambridge: M.I.T. Press.

Redmond, E. 1981. A fuego y sangre: early Zapotec imperialism in the Cuicatlán Cañada. Ph.D. dissertation, Department of Anthropology, Yale University.

Richards, E. E. 1959. Preliminary spectrographic investigation of some Romano-British mortaria. *Archaeometry* 2:23–31.

Richards, T. W. 1895. The composition of Athenian pottery. *Journal of the American Chemical Society* 17:152–54.

Sayre, E. V., and Harbottle, G. The analysis by neutron activation of archaeological ceramics related to Teotihuacan: Local wares and trade sherds. In Millon, R., ed., *Urbanization at Teotihuacan*. Austin: University of Texas Press, forthcoming.

Sneath, P.H.A., and Sokal, R. R. 1973. *Numerical taxonomy*. San Francisco: W. H. Freeman.

Swift, E. H. 1940. *A system of chemical analysis*. New York: Prentice-Hall.

Weigand, P. C.; Harbottle, G.; and Sayre, E. V. 1977. Turquoise sources and source analysis: Mesoamerica and the Southwestern U.S.A. In Earle, T. K., and Ericson, J. E., eds., *Exchange systems in prehistory*. New York: Academic Press.

Yellin, J.; Perlman, I.; Asaro, F.; Michel, H. V.; and Mosier, D. F. 1978. Comparison of neutron activation analysis from the Lawrence Berkeley Laboratory and the Hebrew University. *Archaeometry* 20:95–100.

7. Comparison of Data Obtained by Neutron Activation and Electron Microprobe Analyses of Ceramics

SUZANNE P. De ATLEY,
M. JAMES BLACKMAN, and
JACQUELINE S. OLIN
Conservation Analytical Laboratory
Smithsonian Institution

Introduction

In general, chemical analyses of ceramic composition have focused on trace elements because, on the whole, they most readily facilitate discrimination among ceramics from different areas. However, there are types of problems which benefit from an understanding of the major and minor element composition of the constituent clays and tempers, since these can affect the various properties of the finished vessel. It is in this respect that the use of the electron microprobe in the analysis of archaeological or art historical samples can provide data which is supplementary to that obtained using other analytical methods. The microprobe is especially useful in conjunction with petrographic studies to obtain compositional data for specific constituents within the ceramic body. In addition, the demonstrated utility of the microprobe for major element whole-rock analysis (Arrhenius et al. 1964; Gulson and Lovering 1968; Rucklidge et al. 1970; Reed 1970; Mori et al. 1971; Nicholls 1974) suggests that such an approach also may be applicable to ceramic materials and may provide a method of analysis that is less time consuming than a method such as atomic absorption spectrometry. This paper describes procedures of sample preparation which may be used to obtain quantitative bulk composition data on ceramic samples and the problems and advantages of each. The data obtained to date are compared to those from samples analyzed by neutron activation analysis for elements which can be determined by both methods. The comparability of results is considered to be important in anticipation of the reporting and use of the results of such analyses in data banks and in combining the results obtained by different methods.

Procedure

Archaeological ceramics from southwestern United States and southwestern Iran and also Mexican and Spanish majolica ceramics were analyzed by instrumental neutron activation analysis and by electron microprobe using several different preparation methods.

Samples for neutron activation analysis were drilled from the edges of sherds using clean tungsten carbide bits. When possible, at least one gram of sample was taken. Each sample was thoroughly mixed and subsampled for analysis. Irradiation and counting of the samples were carried out at Brookhaven National Laboratory and the National Bureau of Standards. Table 1 shows the nuclides sought and the standards used in the analysis.

The analyses of the majolica ceramics for sodium, potassium, and iron were carried out at Brookhaven using the parameters described in Bieber et al. (1976).

79

Table 1. Standards used in the neutron activation analysis

A. List of nuclides

Oxide	Nuclide	Half-life	Energy (keV)	Standards Used
Al_2O_3	Al-27	2.2405M.	1779	NBS SRM 1633
Na_2O	Na-24	14.96 H.	1369	AGV, GSP, BCR, G-2, SRM1633
K_2O	K-42	12.40 H.	1524	AGV, GSP, BCR, G-2, SRM1633
CaO	Sc-47	3.40 D.	159	AGV, GSP, BCR, SRM1633
Fe_2O_3	Fe-59	45.6 D.	1099 & 1292	AGV, GSP, BCR, G-2, SRM1633

B. List of standard concentrations

Standard	Concentrations Used SI	Brookhaven
U.S.G.S. AGV-1	Flanagan 1973	Bieber et al. 1976
U.S.G.S. GSP-1	Flanagan 1973	Bieber et al. 1976
U.S.G.S. BCR-1	Flanagan 1973	Bieber et al. 1976
U.S.G.S. DTS-1	Flanagan 1973	Bieber et al. 1976
U.S.G.S. PCC-1	Flanagan 1973	Bieber et al. 1976
U.S.G.S. G-2	not used at SI	Bieber et al. 1976
NBS SRM 1633	Ondov et al. 1975	not used at BNL

The analyses of the southwestern United States and Iranian ceramics for sodium, potassium, iron, and calcium were carried out at the NBS reactor using the parameters described in Blackman (1979). The aluminum analyses for all three ceramic groups were undertaken at the NBSR. Twenty-five milligram subsamples of the ceramics and of the standard, SRM1633 coal fly ash, were used in the aluminum determination. Samples and standards were dried for 24 hours at 110 °C, weighed into clean polyethylene microcentrifuge tubes, and individually packaged in polyethylene rabbits for irradiation. Each rabbit, containing a single sample or standard, was irradiated at a flux of 1.6×10^{11} ncm^{-2} sec^{-1} for 5 minutes. Irradiations took place midway through the reactor fuel cycle with the reactor operating at a constant power of 9.9 MW. Each sample or standard was counted three times for 100 seconds per count at intervals of two, seven, and ten minutes after the end of the irradiation. Decay time was controlled to the nearest second. The counting was done with an Ortec γ-x intrinsic germanium detector (FWHM at 1332 keV of 1.72 keV) interfaced to a Nuclear Data 6620 using 8192 data channels. Data were stored on disk and processed using the ND data reduction programs.

The microprobe analyses were done on the ARL microprobe at the Mineral Science Department, Smithsonian Institution. This probe has nine spectrometers, which were set for silicon, aluminum, iron, magnesium, calcium, potassium, sodium, titanium, and phosphorus. Operating parameters used for all the analyses were 15 kV accelerating potential, 30 microamp beam current, 10 second counting times, and a defocused beam of 50 microns in diameter.

The first microprobe method used standard polished thin sections of ceramics from the American southwest, such as the thin section illustrated in Figure 1. The samples were carbon coated, placed in the sample chamber, and ten 10-second scans were run across the section. The concentrations reported for each element were the means determined from the ten scans. This was done to average the large-scale inhomogeneities that were likely to be present in a ceramic thin section.

There are several advantages to using a polished thin section. It provides a sample of reasonable size and the structure of the ceramic is preserved. If desired, the chemical data can be used in combination with petrographic analysis, and it is then possible to see which particles contribute to the concentrations of each element. It is also feasible to analyze the clay matrix, avoiding inclusions of a size determined appropriate to the particular problem investigated. In this study the entire section was scanned so the data would be comparable to that obtained by neutron activation, where ceramic powders include both the clay matrix and inclusions.

There are also disadvantages associated with the sections. As can be seen in Figure 1, the ceramics are usually extremely heterogeneous, and it is possible that in random scans an important area or mineral will be missed. This can be controlled to some extent by prior petrographic analysis to determine the sam-

S. P. De Atley, M. J. Blackman, J. S. Olin

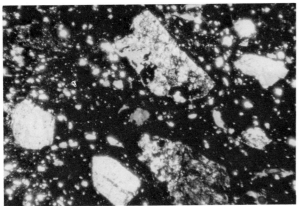

Figure 1. A standard polished thin section of an andesite tempered ceramic from the southwest United States, showing the heterogeneity of the sample.

Figure 2. Apparatus used for fusing ceramic powder samples.

pling strategy for a particular section and by making a sufficient number of scans. Another problem is that the varying porosity of ceramics results in low sums, even if all elements present are accounted for. This will be discussed in some detail later.

The second probe method employed fused samples. Several edges on each sherd were drilled using a clean tungsten carbide bit and the resulting powder was well mixed. Several milligrams were fused according to the procedure outlined for silicate rocks with compositions ranging between 45 and 65 weight percent SiO_2 (Jezek et al. 1979). The procedure involved the following steps. The powder was placed in a tungsten boat which was then mounted between the two bars in the apparatus shown in Figure 2. After a nitrogen atmosphere was introduced into the bell jar, the powder was rapidly heated for not more than 20 seconds, to prevent sodium volatilization. When the powder fused, it was quenched by shutting off the power and directing a stream of nitrogen onto the bottom of the boat. The resulting glass samples were mounted in a leucite disk and a 50 micron defocused beam was used to analyze ten spots on each sample.

The homogeneity of the glasses was much greater than that of the thin sections, and consequently there was less variation in concentration from analysis to analysis. However, several problems were encountered in using the fusion technique. Many of the ceramic powders were less refractory than the silicate rocks, and adjustments were necessary to prevent the volatilization discussed below. Also, the small sample size was as much a drawback as an asset because chances of sampling error increased markedly.

The third probe method, pressed pellets made from powder samples, was adapted from that used for meteorite samples. Powder drilled from sherds

was ground to finer than 100 mesh, and one mg or less was mounted on a cylinder and pressed to form a pellet. The pellet had to have a minimum of surface cracks and be of even thickness. Two pellets were made for each sample and they were mounted on a metal washer (shown in Figure 3) with silver paint for conductivity. The pellets were analyzed using a 50 micron defocused beam to scan the surface of the pellets. Ten scans were performed.

The pellets have two advantages. There is no volatilization problem and the porosity problem of the sherd thin sections is reduced. However, the sur-

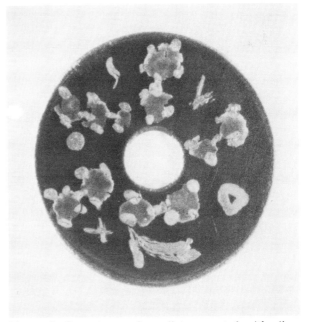

Figure 3. Ceramic powder pellets mounted with silver paint on a metal washer. Washer is 2.5 cm in diameter.

Table 2. Effect of standard selection on electron microprobe concentration values

Standard	SiO_2	Al_2O_3	FeO	MgO	CaO	K_2O	Na_2O	TiO_2	P_2O_5
Kakanui hornblende	46.03	17.18	6.91	5.94	13.72	2.78	0.42	0.84	0.45
BCR–1	45.36	16.03	7.09	6.71	14.69	2.24	0.40	0.79	0.23
G–2	47.14	15.42	6.82	4.98	12.63	2.56	0.40	0.98	0.30
INAA	N.D.	17.43	6.71	N.D.	12.43	2.96	0.45	N.D.	N.D.

Electron microprobe data obtained by analysis of a ceramic pellet using three different standards are compared with data obtained by neutron activation analysis.

face of the pellet is irregular, so the concentration values may be affected because of scattering and absorption properties different from those found with polished thin sections or glass. Once again, the small sample size requires cautious sampling and interpretation of results.

Calculation of Concentrations and Standard Selection for Electron Microprobe Analysis

The data in the form of X-ray intensities were corrected and quantified by an on-line computer. There are several alternative methods of reducing the data, but the shortest method for satisfactory results is calibration by known standards. There is general agreement that the highest accord is obtained by comparing an unknown specimen with a standard whose composition is as close to the unknown as possible, particularly for complex specimens. This is because the required interpolation between the standard and unknown is smaller and introduces less error. When such standards are unavailable, materials which are different in composition must be used, and this may involve additional computations. When similar standards can be used, they generally give results concordant within 5 to 10% of the amount present (Adler 1966; Birks 1971).

The data reduction procedures involve several steps. First, the detector dead time and background corrections are made for the measured counting rates. For extended measurements it may also be necessary to make a drift correction, and therefore during the analysis the standard is remeasured frequently. If the total change in signal intensity for the standard is no more than approximately 5% per hour, then the drift is assumed to be linear, and the data are corrected by recording the time of measurement and correcting for elapsed time (Adler 1966). The resulting intensity values are then converted to concentrations using the Bence and Albee (1968) method to control for matrix effects. The precision and accuracy of these values can be evaluated by running internal standards during analysis of the unknowns. Comparisons between the probe analyses of

these standards and wet chemical analyses permit correction of the unknowns through a method of normalization which brings the internal standard values to values determined by wet chemistry (Melson et al. 1976).

Data

Results for the ceramics analyzed illustrate the ways that preparation methods and standard selection affect the concentration values resulting from electron microprobe analysis. As noted above, the choice of standards is important. Because ceramics can vary widely in concentrations of major and minor elements, they present an initial problem in choosing, a priori, which may be the best set of standards for a particular run. In addition, it can be difficult to find a single standard that matches the ceramics closely in over-all composition. Table 2 shows the concentration values obtained when the same sample, MAP073, was analyzed using three different standards. When compared to neutron activation values, microprobe analyses using Kakanui hornblende as the standard were in good agreement for aluminum, potassium, and sodium, while those using G2 as the standard gave better agreement for iron and calcium. For the subsequent analyses reported here, BCR–1, G2, and Kakanui hornblende were used as standards for silicon, aluminum, iron, magnesium, calcium, sodium, potassium, and titanium. Apatite was used for phosphorous. The weight percent values for these standards are reported in Jarosewich et al. (1979).

Uncertainties in the concentration values of the ceramics may also be introduced by other factors. In the fusion technique of sample preparation for electron microprobe bulk analysis several problems may arise during the heating of the sample. Jezek et al. (1979) were concerned about possible sodium loss during prolonged fusion. They found experimentally that fusion times of 20 seconds or less produced minimal sodium volatilization in several silicate minerals of compositions that approach those of highly fired ceramics. A potentially much more serious problem arises from the breakdown and loss of volatile com-

S. P. De Atley, M. J. Blackman, J. S. Olin

Table 3. Comparison of carbonate bearing samples analyzed by INAA and by fused sample EM

Constituent	(n)	Mean Conc. INAA (wt%)	Mean Conc. EM (wt%)	Average Absolute Difference (wt%)	Average Relative Difference %	Average Ratio probe/INAA
CaO	(6)	20.55	26.82	6.26	26.4	1.31 ± .05
Fe_2O_3	(7)	4.52	5.83	1.32	25.5	1.30 ± .07
Na_2O	(7)	0.57	0.50	0.08	14.8	0.88 ± .14
K_2O	(7)	1.85	1.81	0.33	18.0	0.98 ± .23

Table 4. Interpretation of low concentration sums from electron microprobe analyses

Sample	SiO_2	Al_2O_3	FeO	MgO	CaO	K_2O	Na_2O	TiO_2	P_2O_5	Total
SW005										
Random Scan	54.61	19.67	2.94	1.21	1.60	2.04	0.58	0.58	0.04	83.27
Recalculated	65.57	23.62	3.53	1.45	1.92	2.45	0.70	0.70	0.05	99.99
Pressed Pellet	67.32	23.51	3.75	1.21	1.72	2.51	0.86	0.62	0.08	101.58
MAP001										
Pressed Pellet	33.86	11.93	5.39	5.61	21.12	1.88	0.38	0.53	0.12	80.02
Fused	43.24	12.35	5.44	7.26	26.06	1.40	0.41	0.67	0.18	97.02

SW005 shows the effect of porosity on concentration sums while the low total value in the pressed pellet of MAP001 is due to the presence of unmeasured CO_2.

ponents such as structural water in hydrated mineral phases and CO_2 in carbonate minerals. In ceramics fired at high kiln temperatures this process has already occurred in the initial firing. However, a great deal of the ceramics of interest to archaeologists have been fired to temperatures that do not exceed 600 °C. Some of these low-fired ceramics contain carbonate minerals either as contaminants in the clays or intentionally added as a tempering agent. The fusion of these ceramics at temperatures in excess of 1600 °C results in the loss of CO_2, producing anomalously high yields for other elements in the microprobe analysis. In Table 3, the yields from INAA and fused sample microprobe data are compared for seven low-fired ceramics containing calcite and dolomite. The CaO and Fe_2O_3 concentrations display average relative differences of about 26%, indicating poor agreement between the two analytical techniques. The average ratio of probe data to INAA data for both oxides shows values 1.31 and 1.30 respectively, both with small standard deviations. This indicates a nearly constant analytical discrepancy between the two methods. This discrepancy of about 24% to 26% by weight can be accounted for almost solely by the loss of CO_2 during fusion of the samples. The oxides of sodium and potassium should behave in the same manner as the oxides of calcium and iron; however, the probe to activation analysis ratios for Na_2O and K_2O are both less than one, and both show much greater variance than CaO or Fe_2O_3. Apparently the evolution of CO_2 during the fusion facilitates the volatilization of the oxides of sodium and potassium.

Another problem involves the significance of low sums obtained in analyses of polished thin sections and pressed pellet samples. The first situation is represented by sample SW005 in Table 4. This is a run on a polished thin section of a southwestern United States ceramic, and it shows a low sum owing to the porosity of the ceramic body. The values obtained from the random scans were normalized to 100%, and were compared with values obtained on a pressed pellet from the same sample, where the porosity would not be a problem. The agreement is good enough to support the contention that the low sum was due to porosity. It suggests that if carbonates or other nonoxides are not present in substantial amounts, the values for thin sections can be normalized to 100% for comparison with other bulk analyses.

The second example in Table 4 illustrates the pres-

Table 5. Comparison of fused sample EM and INAA data

Constituents	(n)	Mean[a] Conc. (wt%)	Range of Analyzed Samples (wt%)	Mean Absolute Diff. (wt%)	Range of Absolute Diff. (wt%)	Mean C.V. INAA %	Mean C.V. EM %	Mean Relative Diff. %
Al_2O_3	(10)	18.93	14.28–24.47	1.23	0.41–2.86	1	3.2	6.5
Fe_2O_3	(41)	5.86	2.27–14.71	0.41	0.01–1.52	0.5	7.1	7.0
CaO	(12)	7.97	0.99–13.52	0.56	0.02–1.79	9	5.9	7.0
Na_2O	(50)	0.84	0.13– 2.08	0.11	0.00–0.60	2	12.0	13.1
K_2O	(41)	2.11	0.75– 3.83	0.21	0.00–1.09	8	9.6	10.0

[a]Mean concentration is the mean of the value obtained by both methods.

ence of nonmeasured elements in a ceramic. The pressed pellet and fused sample sums for sample MAP001 do not agree, and the assumption is that the components volatilized during fusion were present, but not measured in the pellet sample. In this case, normalization of the values to 100% would be misleading.

Comparison of INAA and Electron Microprobe Data

Because results obtained by electron microprobe analysis might be used as a complement to that obtained by neutron activation, the results of the two methods were compared for those elements that can be measured by both. Table 5 shows the concordance for fused ceramic samples analyzed by microprobe and powders analyzed by INAA. The low-fired, high carbonate samples have been excluded from the group to eliminate the problems discussed above. The mean relative difference was calculated to show the agreement of the two techniques on an average. This is the mean of the absolute differences divided by the mean concentration and expressed as a percent. The mean relative difference is 6.5% for aluminum, 7.0% for iron and calcium, 13.1% for sodium, and 10.0% for potassium. The mean coefficient of variation for the probe samples shows the heterogeneity of the samples analyzed, and it may contribute to the lack of agreement.

Table 6 compares our fusion data with fusions done on silicate rock powders. The rock powders have been ground to finer than 100 mesh to produce more homogeneous glasses. Under ideal conditions this procedure of sample preparation has been shown to give results which have an average accuracy of better than 5% relative for all major components studied, when compared to results obtained by wet chemical methods (Jezek et al. 1979). The mean rela-

Table 6. Comparison of electron microprobe data with chemical data for silicate rocks and with INAA data for ceramics

	Silicate Rocks[a] Mean Relative Difference %	Ceramics[b] Mean Relative Difference %
Al_2O_3	0.9	6.5
Fe_2O_3	2.2	7.0
CaO	1.9	7.0
Na_2O	4.5	13.1
K_2O	4.5	10.0

[a]Electron microprobe and wet chemical data from Jezek et al. 1979.
[b]From Table 5, this paper.

tive differences for ceramics may be improved in this way and by tailoring the unknowns and the standards more effectively.

To summarize, the electron microprobe can only be employed to get useful bulk chemical composition if the standards are appropriate and if limitations presented by sample preparation techniques are borne in mind. Preliminary sorting of ceramic samples using petrographic analysis, and independent chemical analysis of a member of each group can establish the approximate concentrations of the elements to be included in the analysis group. The most appropriate standard set can then be determined for further microprobe analysis of each group of samples.

While the fusion technique provides the greatest agreement with neutron activation results, the advan-

S. P. De Atley, M. J. Blackman, J. S. Olin

	Na$_2$O	K$_2$O	TiO$_2$	Fe$_2$O$_3$	SiO$_2$	P$_2$O$_5$	Al$_2$O$_3$	MgO	CaO
Spanish majolica									
geometric mean	0.82	1.65	0.65	4.7	51	0.30	13.7	3.8	21.3
alog group std. dev.	1.441	1.259	1.292	1.072	1.023	1.179	1.034	1.304	1.108
Mexican majolica									
geometric mean	1.39	0.92	0.65	4.2	50	0.36	16.3	3.9	19.3
alog group std. dev.	1.326	1.147	1.161	1.145	1.089	1.380	1.097	2.192	1.337

Table 7. Concentrations (ppm) for CeO$_2$, La$_2$O$_3$, ThO$_2$ in majolica

Site	CeO$_2$	La$_2$O$_3$	ThO$_2$
Group I			
Convento de San Francisco, Dominican Republic			
geometric mean	77 ± 18	39 ± 4.0	11.8 ± 0.73
Juandolio, Dominican Republic			
geometric mean	87 ± 5.4	43 ± 4.0	12.7 ± 1.0
La Vega Vieja, Dominican Republic			
geometric mean	90 ± 5.5	42 ± 3.0	13.0 ± 1.0
Isabela, Dominican Republic			
geometric mean	82 ± 4.6	43 ± 2.7	12.6 ± 1.2
Nueva Cadiz, Dominican Republic			
geometric mean	82 ± 4.8	38 ± 2.7	11.8 ± 0.8
Jerez, Spain			
geometric mean	80 ± 3.3	45 ± 1.9	11.7 ± 0.7
Group II			
Mexico City, Mexico			
geometric mean	40 ± 8.6	22 ± 3.9	5.6 ± 0.7

tages of polished thin sections recommends their use in certain cases. They are ideally suited for analysis of inclusions. In addition, they provide the potential for discriminating the extent to which inclusions or clay matrix are responsible for concentrations of particular elements through the use of scanning techniques.

The Combined Use of Neutron Activation and Electron Microprobe Analysis

As noted above, trace element data provide clear differences which enable one to distinguish ceramics from different sources. While major constituents are occasionally useful in this regard, they are also a complement to INAA analysis. They provide an understanding of the kinds of clays (e.g., calcareous and noncalcareous) and inclusions present which make ceramic groups appear similar to or different from one another.

Two hundred and nine majolica sherds from sites of the fifteenth and sixteenth centuries in Spain, the Dominican Republic, Venezuela, Mexico, and from later sites in Central and South America have been analyzed by neutron activation analysis (Olin et al. 1978). Two distinctive groups of pottery could be identified on the basis of neutron activation analysis and petrographic examination. Three oxides in particular distinguish the groups very definitely: CeO$_2$, La$_2$O$_3$ and ThO$_2$. The average composition of these oxides for the samples of the first group for sherds from six different sites and for samples from the second group which are from Mexico are listed in Table 7.

Fourteen sherds from the "Spanish" group and ten sherds from the "Mexican" group were analyzed by electron microprobe analysis. The average compositions (as geometric means) and the anti-logs of the group standard deviations for the oxides analyzed listed in tabular form at the top of this page.

The concentrations of the elements analyzed by microprobe analysis — *see* Figure 4 — do not differ in such an obvious way. Although there are slight differences for the elements sodium and potassium, which were analyzed by both neutron activation and electron microprobe analysis, they do not provide as clear-cut a distinction between the two groups as do cerium, lanthanum, and thorium.

By more careful study of the petrographic data, the differences in the concentrations of Na$_2$O and K$_2$O might be explained. The close similarity of the CaO concentrations and the relatively high levels in both Spanish and Mexican majolica are important in

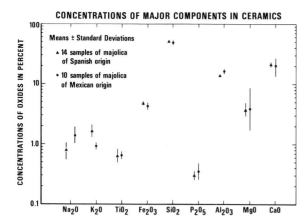

CONCENTRATIONS OF MAJOR COMPONENTS IN CERAMICS

Means ± Standard Deviations
▲ 14 samples of majolica of Spanish origin
● 10 samples of majolica of Mexican origin

Figure 4. Concentrations of major components in Spanish-Colonial majolica obtained by electron microprobe analysis.

that they show that the presence of a high calcium concentration in the Mexican majolica could be a consequence of purposeful selection or preparation of a calcareous clay rather than the deposition of secondary calcite after burial as postulated earlier (Olin et al. 1978). The decomposition of gehlenite could be suggested as the source of secondary calcite in these ceramics (Kupfer and Maggetti 1978).

Conclusions

We have discussed some of the possible sources of error in electron microprobe analysis of ceramics and pointed out the problem of standard selection in such analyses.

As a consequence of the possible use of electron microprobe data for quantitative purposes, even in papers where it is reported but not used in that manner, it is important to report the sample preparation procedures and the standards used. Without this information it is difficult to evaluate the precision or accuracy of the concentration data, and therefore how it should be "weighted" when combined or compared with results from other methods.

Acknowledgments: We would like to thank the Staff of the Reactor Radiation Division, National Bureau of Standards. We are also grateful to the following people from the Mineral Sciences Department at the Smithsonian Institution for their advice and assistance in sample preparation and standard selection for the microprobe analyses: W. G. Melson, K. Fredriksson, E. Jarosewich, P. Brenner, J. Nelen, F. Walkup, R. Johnson, and C. Obermeyer.

References

Adler, Isidore. 1966. *X-ray emission spectrography in geology.* Methods in Geochemistry and Geophysics, no. 4. Amsterdam: Elsevier Publishing Co.

Arrhenius, G.; Fitzgerald, R.; Fredriksson, K.; Holm, B.; Sinkankas, J.; Bonatti, E.; Bostrom, K.; Lynn, D.; Mathias, B.; Ceballe, T.; and Korkisch, J. 1964. Valence band structure and other La Jolla problems in microprobe analysis. (Abstr.). *Electrochem. Soc. Meeting. Wash.* 214:100–103.

Bence, A. E., and Albee, A. L. 1968. Empirical correction factors for the electron microanalysis of silicates and oxides. *Journal of Geology* 76:382–403.

Bieber, A. M., Jr.; Brooks, D. W.; Harbottle, G.; and Sayre, E. V. 1976. Application of multivariate techniques to analytical data on Aegean ceramics. *Archaeometry* 18 (1):59–74.

Birks, L. S. 1971. *Electron probe microanalysis.* 2d ed. New York: Wiley-Interscience.

Blackman, M. J. 1979. The mineralogical and chemical analysis of Banesh Period ceramics from Tal-i Malyan, Iran. A paper read at the 19th International Symposium on Archaeometry and Archaeological Prospection, March 1979, London, U.K.

Brown, Roy W. 1977. A sample fusion technique for whole rock analysis with the electron microprobe. *Geochimica et cosmochimica Acta* 41:435–38.

Flanagan, F. J. 1973. 1972 values for international geochemical samples. *Geochimica et Cosmochimica Acta* 37:1189–200.

Gulson, B. L., and Lovering, J. F. 1968. Rock analysis using the electron probe. *Geochimica et Cosmochimica Acta* 32:119–22.

Jarosewich, E.; Nelen, J. A.; and Norberg, J. A. 1979. Electron microprobe reference samples for mineral analyses. In Fudali, R. F., ed., *Smithsonian Contributions to the Earth Sciences*, no. 22.

Jezek, Peter A.; Sinton, John M.; Jarosewich, Eugene; and Obermeyer, Charles R. 1979. Fusion of rock and mineral powders for electron microprobe analysis. In Fudali, R. F., ed., *Smithsonian Contributions to the Earth Sciences*, no. 22.

Kupfer, T., and Maggetti, M. 1978. Die Terra Sigillata von La Peniche (Vidy) Lausanne. *Schweiz. mineral. petrogr.*, Mitt. 58:189–212.

Melson, W. G.; Vallier, T. L.; Wright, T. L.; Byerly, G.; and Nelen, J. 1976. Chemical diversity of abyssal volcanic glass erupted along Pacific, Atlantic, and Indian Ocean sea-floor spreading centers. In *The geophysics of the Pacific Ocean Basin and its margin.* Geophysical Monograph, no. 19. American Geophysical Union.

Mori, T.; Jakes, P.; and Nagaoka, M. 1971. Major element analysis of silicate rocks using electron probe microanalyzer. *Sci. Rep. Kanazawa Univ.* 16:113–20.

S. P. De Atley, M. J. Blackman, J. S. Olin

Nicholls, I. A. 1974. A direct fusion method of preparing silicate rock glasses for energy-dispersive electron microprobe analysis. *Chem. Geol.* 14:151–57.

Olin, J.; Harbottle, G.; and Sayre, E. 1978. Elemental compositions of Spanish and Spanish-Colonial majolica ceramics in the identification of provenience. In *Archaeological chemistry II*, chap. 13. Advances in Chemistry Series. American Chemical Society.

Ondov, J. M., et al. 1975. Elemental concentrations in the National Bureau of Standards environmental coal and fly ash standard reference materials. *Analytical Chemistry* 47 (7): 1102–109.

Reed, S. J. B. 1970. The analysis of rocks in the electron probe. *Geochimica et Cosmochimica Acta* 34:416–21.

Rucklidge, J. C.; Gibb, G. F.; Fawcett, J. J.; and Gasparrini, E. L. 1970. Rapid rock analysis by electron probe. *Geochimica et Cosmochimica Acta* 34:243–47.

8. Firing Technologies and Their Possible Assessment by Modern Analytical Methods

ROBERT B. HEIMANN
[Institute for Materials Research
McMaster University]

Significance of Firing Temperature Determination

Production of ceramics is essentially a reversal of the natural weathering process. Nature over the course of millions of years breaks down rocks mechanically and chemically forming new minerals. Potters ingeniously invented methods to recombine the chemical compounds once separated by the weathering process. As a result the potter obtains a more or less rocklike material shaped and decorated according to man's need and preference. Nature also consolidates clays during an extremely long-lasting process known as "cycle of rock formation." Man invented a "short-cut" which affects the state of equilibrium of the system to be thermally transformed. The solidified rocklike ceramic material inherits a nonequilibrium and statistical state which is best described as "frozen-in." As we will see, this apparent drawback furnishes us with methods to estimate firing conditions. Essentially, the firing applied to a clay results in a distinct state of sintering, which is also dependent on the time of firing and the composition of the clay. We have to assess the properties of the ceramic in a temperature-time-composition space. Composition encompasses additional variables which complicate the temperature-property-relationship. Therefore no 1:1 correspondence is to be expected between the firing temperature and a particular property like mechanical strength, thermal expansion, or thermal conductivity.

A similar state of sintering can be achieved either by firing at a higher temperature for a short time or at lower temperature held for a considerably longer period. So comparable states of sintering do not necessarily mean identical firing temperatures. Nevertheless, "state of sintering" is a useful reference point to assess and describe ancient ceramics. It is useful to further distinguish clearly between firing temperatures and state of sintering. The possibility of achieving a given state of sintering in a variety of ways through manipulation of composition and/or time allows an assessment of the skill and of the technology of those who made the pottery.

It is the purpose of this paper to analyze and describe the techniques available for the determination of firing temperatures and the evaluation of states of sintering at different levels of analytical sophistication. This offers two approaches to the retrospective estimation of firing conditions (Heimann and Franklin 1979). One is to assess temperature-dependent properties of the particular clay and deduce from them the state of transformation reached; that means maximum firing temperatures. The second approach is to continue the trip "back to the rock." It requires the refiring of the ancient object, and monitoring the change of suitable properties with temperature. Once

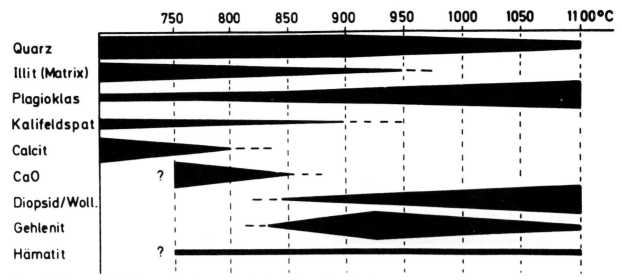

Figure 1. Thermal stability ranges of minerals during firing a clay (Küpfer and Maggetti 1978).

the original firing temperature has been exceeded, there should be a pronounced change of the property in question.

Phase and Textural Changes of Fired Clay Bodies

Thermal treatment causes the clay minerals to change their crystalline lattice arrangement toward a more or less amorphous transient phase. Consequently, no X-ray diffraction analysis which relies on three-dimensional lattice order is applicable in this transition region. The details of the transient phase are highly disputed. Most important is the concept of "metakaolinite" phase which is formed by gradual dehydration of kaolinite. Accordingly, the spatial arrangement of clay mineral platelets of a ceramic object changes because of the onset of sintering processes. In the first instance, consolidation takes place in the solid state, most probably by grain boundary diffusion. With increasing temperature, liquid state sintering starts owing to formation of partial melts. Minor constituents of the clay like lime, feldspar, and ferrous oxide lower the onset of liquid-state sintering. Above 950°C, more and more parts of the clay sample become vitrified, dependent on the composition of the clay, the relative proportion of fluxes, and the kiln atmosphere. A consequence of the increase of the molten phase is the change of the total porosity and the porosity distribution function. On cooling the fired sherd, this molten phase may solidify as a glass.

The material is left in a characteristic but necessarily incomplete state of transformation. So its bulk properties in terms of relative amount of newly formed minerals, glass phase and size, shape and distribution of pores yield information on the firing temperature and the kiln atmosphere.

Methods to Assess States of Sintering
Mineralogical Temperature Scale (MTS)

The decomposition and formation of minerals during firing a clay can be investigated by thin section microscopy, differential thermal analysis, and X-ray diffraction analysis (Fig. 1). Calcite breaks down between 700 and 800°C; potassium feldspar is stable up to 900°C. Clay minerals and micas change their optical properties. Certain minerals sensitively mark firing temperature ranges, as for example does gehlenite. But there are serious restrictions of the applicability of a fixed mineralogical temperature scale, because the thermal stability of a particular mineral is a function of the kiln atmosphere, the amount of molten phase, and the concentration of mineralizers. The existence of minerals far beyond their stability ranges owing to kinetic retardation of the decomposition reactions, and the neoformation of minerals during burial, must be taken into account.

Texture Analysis by Scanning Electron Microscope (SEM)

Quantitative texture determination of ceramic sherds by means of a microscope is difficult mostly because of the inhomogeneous pore distribution. Often the small size of some of the constituents brings us beyond the range of optical microscopy. The latter problem can be overcome with the use of a scanning electron microscope. With some experience it is possible to compare sintering states and, therefore, firing temperatures of ancient sherds by comparing their textures as obtained by a SEM. Figure 2a shows an experimentally fired clay from Rheinzabern, Germany, while Figure 2b shows a Roman terra sigillata

Robert B. Heimann

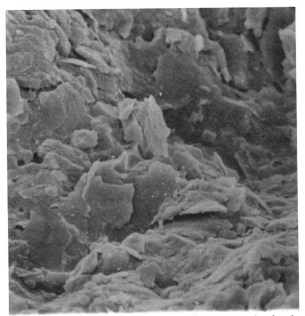 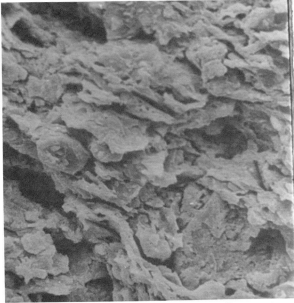

Figure 2. Comparison of texture of two ceramic sherds. (a) Experimentally fired clay (Rheinzabern, Germany). 850°C; 5.2% CaO, 4.6% Fe₂O₃. (b) Terra sigillata plate (Secondinus Aviti, Rheinzabern, 2d century A.D.).

plate from the same location. The firing temperature of the clay was 850°C; the sherd's firing temperature was determined by the thermal expansion method to be 866°C ±25. The texture similarity between the two is striking and is particularly well documented in the pseudomorphically maintained illite platelets.

Ultrasound Velocity Measurements (UVM)

The increasing compaction of a ceramic sherd with increasing firing temperature can be made evident by measurement of the ultrasound velocity which is a function of the density and the elastic constants E and G of the material. Inasmuch as the elastic constants are an indication of the state of sintering, this technique measures the state of sintering nondestructively. Figure 3 shows the calculated E and G values plotted against the firing temperature of test samples and terra sigillata sherds. The ancient sherds are located in the temperature range between 980 and 1060°C which is thought to be typical for high-fired Roman terra sigillata. The steep slope above 900°C is an indication of the increasing glass formation which in turn leads to an increase in elastic constants.

Methods to Assess States of Sintering and Firing Temperatures

In the previous examples the temperature is a derived parameter. Test firings establish a relationship between the state of sintering observable by the methods described above and the actual firing temperature of comparison standards.

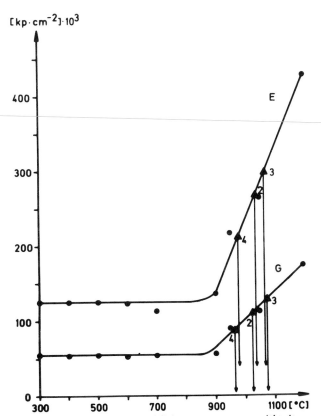

Figure 3. Determination of firing temperatures with ultrasonic attenuation method (from Hennicke 1977). E = modulus of elasticity. G = shear modulus. The force is given in kilopond (kp): 1 kp = 9.81N. O = experimental fired clay (Rheinzabern, Germany). Δ = terra sigillata sherds, Rheinzabern.

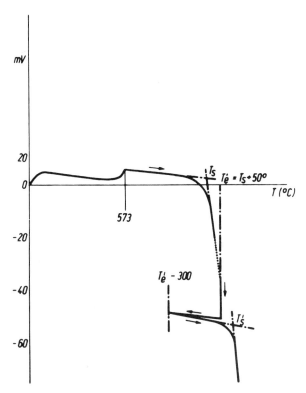

Figure 4. Temperature schedule during a refiring experiment according to Roberts (1963) and Tite (1969).

Thermal Expansion Method (DS-curve)

A direct assessment of the ancient firing temperatures is possible through measurement of thermal expansion. This technique involves a refiring of the sherds. By continuing the ancient firing process beyond the original temperature, it becomes possible to extrapolate back and derive the maximum temperature to which the sherd was subjected in antiquity.

As shown in Figure 4, the procedure is as follows. The sherd is heated slowly in a dilatometer up to a point at which sintering begins. This will erase any alterations that the material might have suffered during burial. The onset of sintering indicates that one has exceeded the original firing temperature. We therefore get a first approximation of the "real" temperature.

According to Roberts (1963) and Tite (1969), the recorded temperature demands a correction which considers the deviation of the refiring rate from the original but unknown firing rate. After refiring the sample at a temperature (T_e') approximately $50°$ above the "original" sintering temperature (T_s) for 1 hour, the sample is quenched by $300°$. In that way the newly established state of sintering is maintained. When the sherd is then heated again, sintering will begin at a higher sintering temperature (T_s') which is now related to the known refiring temperature, T_e'. A

simple reciprocity relation yields an equivalence temperature (T_{eq}) which is claimed to be close to the original firing temperature. The physical processes involved are so complex that one can deal with them only in comparative terms: equivalent states of sintering are produced and firing temperature values are extrapolated from them.

Figure 5 shows calculated equivalence temperatures for test firings versus the known firing temperature (T_w). Agreement for temperatures above $800°C$ is excellent. However, below $800°C$ equivalence temperatures were recorded too high. This is likely because of the relative high vitrification temperature of the particular clay of about $825°C$.

However, by plotting the higher sintering temperature (T_s') versus firing temperature we obtain a linear relationship down to $700°C$ (Fig. 6). This can serve as a calibration curve for the evaluation of firing temperatures of ancient materials. The different signatures refer to clays with different lime content (1–6% CaO). In contrast to all other methods here we get real temperatures. Furthermore, it is possible to get some estimation of the uncertain variable of time which is not easily accessible. A plot of log T_s − T_w versus log T_w (T_w = experimental firing temperature) yields a linear relationship. This is possibly due to the exponential dependence of the sintering rate on the temperature. The term T_s − T_w is essentially the error caused by the deviation of the experimentally applied refiring rate from the unknown original firing rate. This error increases with decreasing firing

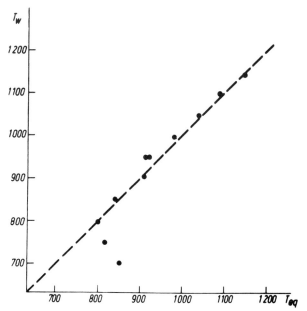

Figure 5. T_{eq} against firing temperature T_w for experimental firings (clay 049, Rheinzabern).

Robert B. Heimann

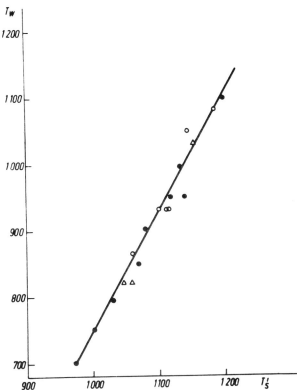

Figure 6. Calibration curve of higher sintering temperature T_s' against T_w for different clays (lime content 1–6% CaO).

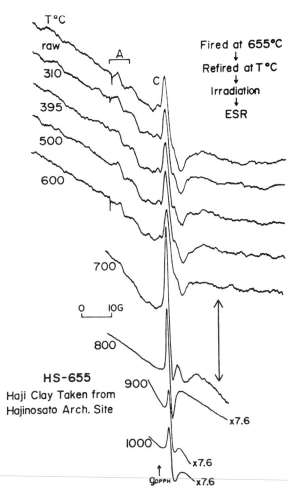

Figure 7. Color center electron spin resonance (ESR) spectrum of an archaeological clay, fired at 655°C (from Warashina et al. 1979).

temperature because the time required for approaching an equilibrium state greatly increases at lower firing temperatures.

The remaining techniques are related to the change in electronic configurations within and between atoms that are indicative of temperature.

Electron Spin Resonance (ESR)

In a fired clay there are a large number of crystal imperfections. Their structure depends on firing temperature. When a clay is irradiated with gamma rays, color centers are formed by trapping secondary electrons or holes at imperfections. The trapped electrons show ESR signals which contain information on the temperature-dependent structure of the imperfection.

Stepwise refiring of a fired clay and likewise an ancient sherd leads to a release of the electrons and a reorganization of the matrix. The clay sample (Fig. 7) was fired at 655°C, irradiated with a Co-60 source, and stepwise refired. Between each refiring cycle the sample was irradiated again. If the refiring temperature exceeds the original firing temperature, the ESR spectrum changes considerably. The same procedure can be applied to sherds (Fig. 8). The change of the spectrum indicates an original firing temperature between 655° and 745°C.

Mössbauer Spectroscopy

Mössbauer spectroscopy allows the determination of valence states and state of bonding of some atoms in a solid. Most important in this context is iron as a Mössbauer-active element. Its state of valence and its crystallographic environment in a ceramic sherd change with firing temperature and kiln atmosphere. Figure 9 (Kostikas et al. 1976) shows an Attic clay heated in air up to 900°C. The spectrum at 400°C indicates the transformation of the initially present lepidocrocite to hematite. At 600°C the central doublet decreases and broadens owing to the loss of hydroxyl ions which were bound to the iron at octahedral sites. Finally, at 900°C the central doublet has completely disappeared. Only the sextet of pure hematite is left.

Quite recently, Bakas, Gangas, and coworkers (1980) investigated pottery found at Glozel, France. They measured Mössbauer spectra before and after refiring between 400° and 1000°C. The quadrupole

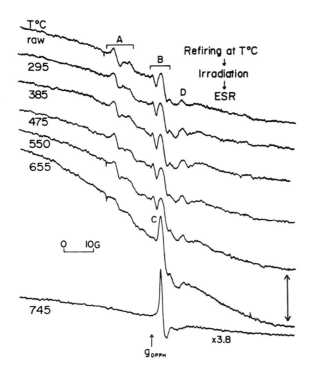

Haji Pottery, HS-5 (Hajinosato Arch. Site)

Figure 8. Color center electron spin resonance (ESR) spectrum of Haji pottery, Hajinosato Archaeological Site, Japan (from Warashina et al. 1979).

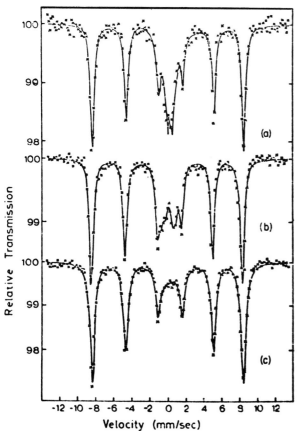

Figure 9. Mössbauer spectra of an Attic clay fired at (a) 400°C, (b) 600°C, (c) 900°C at a measuring temperature of 4.2 K (from Kostikas et al. 1976).

splitting of the first doublet between 400° and 600 °C indicates the continuation or the onset of the dehydroxylation of the clay minerals, thus giving a possible original firing temperature between 500° and 600 °C.

Radial Electron Density Function (RED)

As mentioned before, owing to the amorphous nature of the metakaolinite compound, no appreciable X-ray diffraction pattern is to be expected. There is, however, an at least theoretically possible method to deal with more or less amorphous aluminum silicates in fired clays. In an unfired kaolinite, Al is surrounded by six oxygen atoms (Fig. 10). During firing, OH-ions are expelled in form of water thus leaving behind metakaolinite with only fourfold coordinated Al. At 800 °C, metakaolinite has a theoretical content of Al in tetrahedral coordination of 100%.

Figure 11 shows the radial density distribution of electrons of kaolinite and its thermal decomposition products. The pronounced peaks refer to characteristic bond lengths in the structure which in general are functions of the firing temperatures. During heating, the SiO_4-tetrahedra are deformed thus changing the Si–O distance from 1.61 Å in kaolinite to 1.67 Å in metakaolinite at 800 °C. Accordingly, the bonds related to the sixfold coordinated Al gradually disappear between 100 and 600 °C, indicating a breakdown of the octahedral layer of the kaolinite structure.

Figure 12 shows the experimental profile and the superimposed best-fit values (crosses) as obtained by Leonard in 1977. An automatic least-square procedure splits the cation-oxygen vector band between 1.4 and 2.1 Å into elementary Gaussian contributions. The area under the Gaussian for Al(4)–O is a measure of the relative amount of metakaolinite present in the region up to 800 °C. Above that temperature, the picture becomes obscured by the decomposition of metakaolinite into γ-alumina and amorphous silica, and Al-Si spinel respectively. The maximum of the distribution curve corresponds to the mean Al–0 distance within an (AlO_4)-tetrahedron. The changes of that distance, normalized and plotted against temperature, should give estimates of firing temperatures in the otherwise inaccessible range of low-fired ceramics between 600 and 800° C. However, many constraints affect these measurements, mostly because of the highly defective octahedral layer of the metakaolinite, and the sluggish collapse of the sixfold coordination of aluminum towards the fourfold arrangement in metakaolinite. As a result, the Al(4)–0 bond lengths of metakaolinite are very close to the original Al(6)–0 distances of kaolinite, thus showing a memory of the original structure. Better

Robert B. Heimann

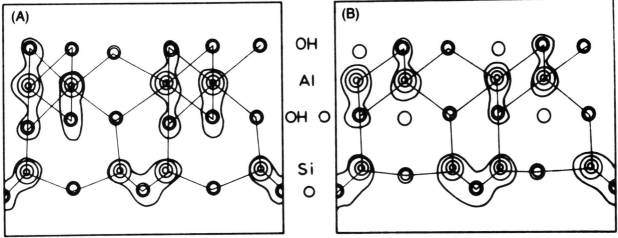

Figure 10. Structural change of kaolinite by dehydroxylation (according to Iwai et al. 1971).

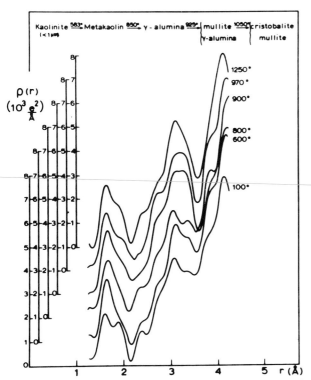

Figure 11. Distribution of radial electron density (RED) of kaolinite and its thermal decomposition products (from Leonard 1977).

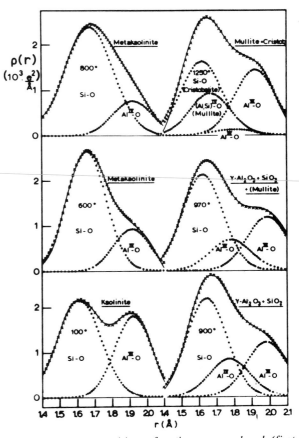

Figure 12. Decomposition of cation-oxygen band (first nearest neighbor bonds) of RED curves of Figure 11 (from Leonard 1977).

quantitative measurements are therefore required to obtain more reliable results (Leonard 1980; Wasada 1980).

Conclusions

Owing to the complexity of the interactions among the components of a ceramic mixture, the same state

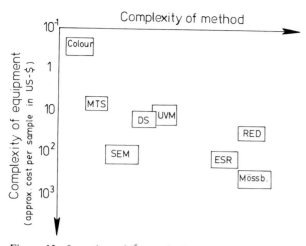

Figure 13. Location of the methods described in a field of different levels of complexity.

of sintering can be achieved in different compositional systems at quite different temperatures. For this reason the relationship between firing temperature and mineralogical composition of ancient ceramics is particularly interesting. Faced with a large collection of excavated sherds, the investigator will deal with the material on different levels of analytical sophistication. Figure 13 may clarify this point. Color determination, low magnification microscopy, and scratch or fracture tests are diagnostic tools to group the material. The next level of sophistication is introduced by phase analysis using X-ray diffraction and/or thin section microscopy. SEM investigation provides evidence on textures and elemental compositions. If well-provenanced reference clays are available, a comparison of textures via SEM, ultrasonic attenuation, or thermal expansion measurements may be adequate. The highest level of complexity for both the equipment and the method is demanded for electron-, nuclear-, or X-ray spectroscopy. It should be noted that a third coordinate, the complexity of evaluation, tends to obscure the picture. For example, the seemingly simple SEM method requires great experience in interpretation of the textural analysis of a particular sherd. On the other hand the RED data, once acquired by complex and difficult measurements, yields a relatively straightforward explanation of the structure of the metakaolinite phase.

But whatever experimental approach is chosen, the results will be useful only if they are interpreted in the total context of materials and techniques.

Acknowledgments: The author gratefully acknowledges Dr. Ursula M. Franklin, Professor, Department of Metallurgy and Materials Science, University of Toronto, for stimulating discussions and for critical reading of the present manuscript.

References

Bakas, T.; Gangas, N. H.; Sigalas, I.; and Aitken, M. J. 1980. Mössbauer study of Glozel tablet 198 bl. *Archaeometry* 22:69–80.

Heimann, R., and Franklin, U. M. 1979. Archaeothermometry: The assessment of firing temperatures of ancient ceramics. IIC–CG 4(2): 23–45.

Hennicke, H. W., 1977. Lect. Symp. Brenntechniken von Keramik und ihre Wiedergewinnung durch experimentelle Archäologie. Berlin.

Iwai, S.; Tagai, H.; and Shimamune, T. 1971. Procedure for dickite structure modification by dehydration, *Acta Cryst. Sect. B.* 27: 248–50.

Kostikas, A.; Simopoulos, A.; and Gangas, N. H. 1976. Analysis of archaeological artifacts. *Appl. Mössbauer Spectrosc.* 1:241–61.

Küpfer, T., and Maggetti, M. 1978. Die Terra Sigillata von La Péniche (Vidy, Lausanne). *Schweiz. Min. Petr. Mitt.* 58:189–212.

Leonard, A. J. 1977. Structural analysis of the transition phases in the kaolinite-mullite thermal sequence. *J. Am. Ceram. Soc.* 60:37–43.

Leonard, A. J. 1980. Private communication.

Roberts, J. P. 1963. Determination of the firing temperature of ancient ceramics by measurement of thermal expansion. *Archaeometry* 6:21–25.

Tite, M. S. 1969. Determination of the firing temperatures of ancient ceramics by measurement of thermal expansion. *Nature* 222:81.

Warashina, T.; Higashimura, T.; and Maeda, Y. 1979. Determination of the firing temperature of ancient pottery by means of ESR spectrometry. *Brit. Mus. Occas. Papers*, in press.

Wasada, Y. 1980. Private communication.

9. The Investigation of Ancient Ceramic Technologies by Mössbauer Spectroscopy

Y. MANIATIS, A. SIMOPOULOS,
and A. KOSTIKAS
Nuclear Research Center Demokritos

Introduction

Ceramics represent one of the earliest and most significant innovations of mankind. Their first appearance marks the beginning of a new period in man's evolution during which important technological developments rapidly succeeded one another. The technology of the ancient ceramics reveals the level of technical background of the people and can be used as an index of ancient civilizations and their interactions. The technology is also dependent on the locality and historical time. The locality factor is mainly determined by the clay deposit from which the ceramic article is manufactured, while the texture, color, and style, attained by more or less well-defined manufacturing procedures, are usually characteristic of a historical period. The foregoing considerations explain why the study of the ancient ceramic technology has always been the subject of amateur and professional scientific investigations. A variety of techniques have been used up to now for these studies, including thermal expansion (Tite 1969), differential thermal analysis, DTA (Cole and Crook 1962; Kingery 1974), X-ray powder diffraction, XRD (Perinet 1960), optical microscopy (Cowgill and Hutchinson 1969), scanning electron microscopy, SEM (Maniatis and Tite 1978), and Mössbauer spectroscopy (Kostikas et al. 1976) which is the subject of the present report.

This last addition to the group of physicochemical techniques used in ancient pottery investigations has the common feature with the other methods that it can provide some unique pieces of information, not obtainable otherwise; yet it has also severe limitations. We shall try to delineate these features in the following exposition, and at the same time substantiate once again the view that the combination of complementary results of various techniques, including Mössbauer spectroscopy, can provide much more reliable results of archaeological significance than the use of a single technique.

Mössbauer spectra of ancient pottery were first reported by Cousins and Dharmawardena (1969). Work up to 1974 has been reviewed by Kostikas et al. (1976). The Mössbauer technique has been used to study the iron-containing phases in the clay and their transformations upon firing (Simopoulos et al. 1975). Since practically every clay contains 5–10% iron, Mössbauer spectra can be readily obtained with a~100 mg sample. The physical and chemical state of iron oxide phases and their interactions with the other constituents of the clay correlate with color and texture of the pottery (Bouchez et al. 1974; Chevalier et al. 1976) and can be associated with major parameters of the manufacturing procedure as, e.g., firing temperature and atmosphere. They also characterize the initial clay so that they may be used for provenance studies as well. To what extent this is possible in a way that permits unambiguous assignment of specific spectral features to particular pottery types is a question that should be systematically investigated before approaching archaeological problems.

We shall be reporting here, first, our recent studies on clays with varying composition, collected mainly near Greek archaeological sites and, therefore, most likely resembling the raw material used for pottery making in ancient times. The scope of this work was to establish patterns of variation of parameters in relation to composition and firing temperature. In the second part of the paper these results are applied to the investigation of two groups of ancient ceramics, i.e., a series of samples of Iraqi pottery and a group of amphorae found in Corinth (Punic amphorae).

Mössbauer Spectra of Iron in Clays

The Mössbauer effect originates in the ability of an excited nucleus to emit a γ-quantum without recoil which in turn can be resonantly absorbed by another nucleus of the same isotope in the ground state. The recoil-free emission and absorption is possible only when the corresponding nucleus is embedded in a solid and thus the effect is limited in the solid state or in systems with very high viscosity. On the other hand, the high resolution that this resonance technique provides allows the study of the interactions of the atomic nucleus with its surrounding electrons (the hyperfine interactions) and through them the electronic and magnetic properties of the solid. (For an introduction to the technique of Mössbauer spectroscopy, *see* Cohen 1976.)

Unlike the analytical spectroscopic techniques applied in the fields of clays and ceramics, Mössbauer spectroscopy yields data that pertain to only one element, the iron. The unique feature of Mössbauer spectroscopy, however, is the detailed picture that it can provide about the iron chemistry in various clays with regard to its dependence on the constitution of the unfired clay and the heat treatment that led to the finished pottery item.

Iron in clays appears *(a)* in the form of paramagnetic ions (ferric Fe^{3+} or ferrous Fe^{2+}) substituting Al or (less frequently) Si sites in the clay minerals, and *(b)* in the form of magnetic iron oxides or hydroxides usually dispersed as small particles with sizes of the order of 100 Å. Figure 1 displays a typical Mössbauer spectrum with spectral features corresponding to the iron phases mentioned above.

The most common experimental arrangement for recording Mössbauer spectra includes a source of ^{57}Co (the mother nucleus to ^{57}Fe), an absorber as,

e.g., the clay sample under investigation and a detector. The energy of the emitted γ-rays is modulated by imparting an oscillatory motion to the source and the transmission is recorded as a function of velocity. The transmission minima in Figure 1 correspond to resonance absorption at specific velocities which are determined by the hyperfine splittings of the ground and excited states of the ^{57}Fe nucleus.

In the absence of a magnetic field the Mössbauer spectrum is typically a doublet arising from the interaction of the nuclear quadrupole moment with the electric field gradient of the chemical environment. Two "quadrupole doublets" assigned to paramagnetic Fe^{2+} and Fe^{3+} ions are indicated by the stick diagrams in the central part of the spectrum of Figure 1 (components I and II). Each doublet is parametrized by the velocity of the center of gravity known as isomer shift (IS) and the separation of the two lines known as quadrupole splitting (QS). The former parameter depends on valence and is typically about 1 mm/sec and 0.2 mm/sec for ionic Fe^{2+} and Fe^{3+} respectively. The quadrupole splitting of Fe^{2+} in clays is always larger than that of Fe^{3+}.

A six-line pattern (component III) is observed in magnetically ordered materials (e.g., magnetic iron oxides and hydroxides in clays) owing to Zeeman splitting of nuclear energy levels by an internal magnetic field. Their spectral features (i.e., line positions) depend on the particular oxide, its particle size and temperature.

The temperature variation of the Mössbauer spectra can also be quite informative in particular with respect to the magnetic iron phases. Spectra of a clay taken at room (300K), liquid nitrogen (77K) and liquid helium (4.2K) temperatures are shown in Figure 2. The major difference observed in these spectra is an increase of the magnetic component at the cost of the paramagnetic ferric doublet as the temperature of measurement is lowered. This change has been attributed (Gangas et al. 1973) to superparamagnetic effects displayed by small iron oxide particles with large surface to volume ratio. At a temperature T, lower than the magnetic ordering temperature, the total magnetic moment of each particle fluctuates with a frequency given by

$$f \sim \exp \left(-\frac{KV}{kT} \right)$$

where K is the magnetic anisotropy constant of the material of the particle and V its volume. If the frequency is high (i.e., small V and/or high T) with respect to the Larmor precession frequency f_L of the Fe^{57} Mössbauer nucleus ($f_L \sim 100$ Mc), the magnetic hyperfine interaction vanishes and a paramagnetic doublet appears in place of the expected magnetic

Y. Maniatis, A. Simopoulos, A. Kostikas

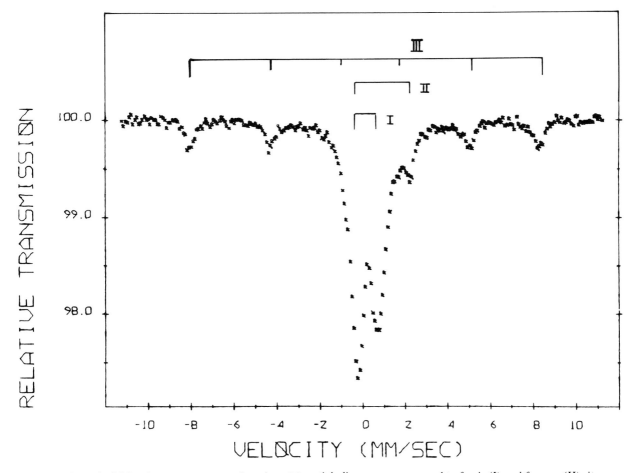

Figure 1. A typical Mössbauer spectrum of a clay. The stick diagrams correspond to ferric (I) and ferrous (II) sites and a magnetic iron oxide or hydroxide phase (III).

sextet. Lowering of the temperature results in a decrease of the fluctuation frequency f and an enhancement of the magnetic sextet at the cost of the (super) paramagnetic doublet. Thus the appearance of a "paramagnetic" doublet cannot be attributed to the presence of only paramagnetic iron ions in the clay unless the measurement is done at very low temperatures. A useful quantity in such measurements is the *magnetic ratio*, which is defined as the ratio of the magnetic component to the total absorption area. Its temperature variation can give valuable information regarding the particle size of the iron oxide phases (Gangas et al. 1973).

The variation of the spectral parameters which are extracted from spectra of pottery samples as described above is the basis of applications of Mössbauer spectroscopy to ancient ceramics. Thus, e.g., the quadrupole splitting of the ferric doublet seems to depend on the firing temperature although the elemental composition of the clay introduces complications to this correlation. As another ex-

ample, the ratio of the intensities of ferrous and ferric doublets is indicative of the prevailing atmosphere during firing. Finally the spectral parameter of the magnetic components (magnetic field, quadrupole interaction, isomer shift) can be used for identification of the iron oxide phases although factors like particle size, degree of crystallization, and impurities can often lead to incorrect conclusions. It must be emphasized, therefore, that both raw and fired clays are very complex multiphase systems and considerable caution must be exercised in using parameter values for classification, especially when the number of samples is small. We shall consider some of these questions in detail in the following sections.

Mössbauer Studies of Raw and Fired Clays

The general idea in several investigations of ancient pottery by Mössbauer spectroscopy reported until now is to compare results obtained from clays fired at various temperatures with measurements on ancient ceramics. Clay samples were usually collected

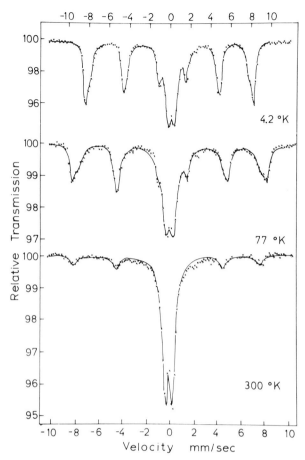

Figure 2. Mössbauer spectra of a clay taken at room, liquid nitrogen, and liquid helium temperatures.

lation of Mössbauer parameters with the details of the elemental constitution of the clays before firing and the physical and chemical origin of the variations observed upon firing. With these outstanding questions in mind we have undertaken a systematic study of a group of thirteen clay samples collected near archaeological sites in Greece. To these were added two British clays and one illitic clay from the United States. The elemental constitution of these samples, as determined by optical emission spectroscopy, is listed in Table I. Mössbauer measurements were made on the raw clays and on clay samples fired at 700 °C, 900 °C and 1080 °C. The variation with firing temperature of the most informative parameters, i.e., the magnetic ratio (MR) and the quadrupole splitting (QS) of the central ferric doublet, are shown in Figure 3 and Figure 4 respectively.

A detailed analysis and discussion of these measurements will appear elsewhere (Maniatis et al. 1980). We shall summarize here the results that are most significant for the applications to ancient pottery studies. We note first in Figure 4 the increase in QS when the clays are fired at 700 °C. A similar increase is observed in the magnetic ratio (Fig. 3) in agreement with results of previous investigations. These changes are attributed to dehydroxylation of the clay minerals and concomitant disorganization of the lattice which results in larger electric field gradients at the nucleus. The increase in the MR is due to the growth of iron

near the corresponding archaeological site in the expectation that they would be similar to the raw material used by the ancient potters. Typically, the comparison involved characteristic spectra parameters which vary during firing, most notably the quadrupole splitting of the central doublet (component I in Fig. 1). Rough estimates of the firing temperature were obtained in this way and conclusions were drawn concerning local or foreign provenance of the pottery. Investigations of this type have been reported by Bouchez et al. (1974) on Iranian pottery and by Aburto et al. (1978) on Mexican pottery. An interesting study of the effect of firing conditions and the provenance of clay on the color of the final product was carried out by Hess and Perlman (1974). Finally the transformations of iron oxides in an Attic clay upon firing have been examined by Simopoulos et al. (1975).

Although the above investigations have produced valuable data, the number of samples is too small to allow the formulation of general rules for use in the evaluation of ancient pottery spectra. It is clear that systematic work is necessary to understand the corre-

Table 1. Chemical composition of the studied clays (% weight as the oxide)

Code No.	Clay	Al_2O_3	Na_2O	MgO	Fe_2O_3	CaO
1	KARFI	20.2	0.45	2.15	8.0	0.1
3	ILLITE	18.1	0.14	1.0	5.1	0.2
6	VOLOS	15.3	1.00	3.1	8.3	1.0
5	PHILAKOPI 3	6.0	2.90	0.6	3.7	1.3
7	LONDON	19.1	0.20	1.8	7.6	0.8
8	PHILAKOPI 1-2	7.8	2.35	1.0	4.4	2.4
9	NAXOS	26.3	1.55	3.0	12.0	3.0
10	CHALKIS	13.4	2.15	1.6	6.7	3.8
11	NICHORIA 2b	19.0	1.25	1.6	8.4	7.0
12	NICHORIA 7	14.5	0.48	2.9	9.2	8.8
13	GAULT	27.8	0.15	1.4	7.2	8.0
14	CORFU	13.2	1.6	4.0	6.6	15.0
15	NICHORIA 4	16.1	0.52	1.7	7.5	15.4
17	CORINTH 2	15.3	0.49	2.9	7.9	21.6
18	PIRGOS	14.3	1.55	4.8	6.4	32.0
19	CORINTH 4	9.2	0.27	3.2	3.1	37.0

Y. Maniatis, A. Simopoulos, A. Kostikas

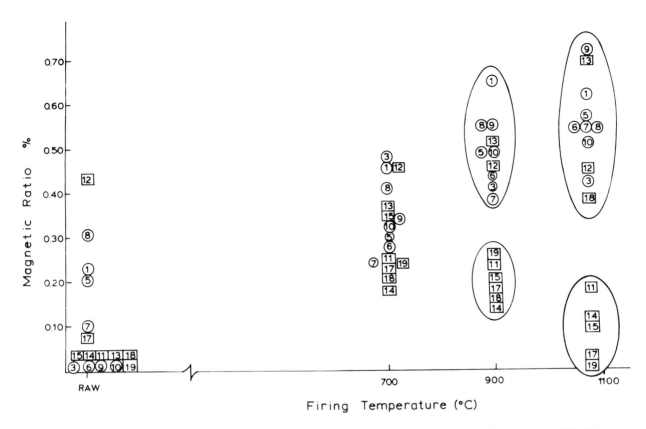

Figure 3. Variation of the magnetic ratio of the R. T. Mössbauer spectra of the various clays with firing temperature. The numbers correspond to the code numbers of the clays referred in Table I.

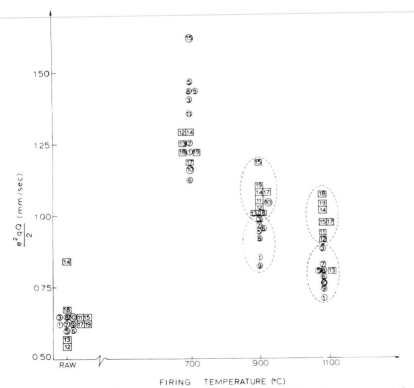

Figure 4. Variation of the quadrupole splitting with the firing temperature of the paramagnetic doublet of the R. T. Mössbauer spectra. The numbers correspond to the code numbers of the clays referred in Table I.

oxide particles (mainly haematite) resulting from three possible sources: *(a)* thermal transformation of the hydroxide phases, *(b)* phase separation and oxidation of the lattice iron, and *(c)* agglomeration of small haematite particles.

Of greater interest are the changes observed upon firing at higher temperatures. The MR (Fig. 3) shows a well-defined separation of the clays into two groups which is most pronounced for the samples fired at 1080 °C. Referring to the elemental constitution of the clays (Table I), we find a clear correlation with the calcium content, i.e., the group with the highest magnetic ratio contains less than 4% Ca (noncalcareous clays) while the other group contains between 7 and 37% Ca (calcareous clays). However, there are a number of exceptions which will be discussed later. When the QS values (Fig. 4) are examined in light of this result, a separation into two groups is also found in correlation with Ca content, with the group of calcareous clays showing higher QS.

These results, in conjunction with XRD and SEM data not discussed in detail here, can now be related to the refractory properties of the clays and the phase transformations that control the color and texture of the finished ceramic product. In calcareous clays, if the calcium-bearing minerals (calcite or dolomite) are in fine particle form they dissociate easily by 850° and the resulting CaO reacts with the clay minerals and forms a stable calcium-aluminosilicate matrix (Tite et al. 1979) which can inhibit the growth of iron oxide particles and/or trap iron in the lattice. On the contrary, noncalcareous clay vitrify continuously with increasing temperature; the lattice being constantly destroyed, the iron can easily move out and react with oxygen, provided the atmosphere is oxidizing, to form iron oxide particles. Thus, in the noncalcareous clays there is a continuous increase in the magnetic ratio while in the calcareous a constancy or decrease is observed. Mossbauer measurements at temperatures down to 1.5 K (Maniatis et al. 1980) give evidence that the size of oxide particles is smaller in calcareous clays. This result is consistent with the behavior of the quadrupole splitting since it is known that the QS of α-Fe_2O_3 small particles increases as the particle size decreases (Van der Kraan 1973). It should be noted, however, that if calcite is present in large particles, e.g., as temper in a clay product, it would remain unreacted during firing (Peters and Jenny 1973; Maniatis 1976) and although the analysis would show a large amount of Ca, the behavior of the clay would in fact be noncalcareous.

The information concerning the iron oxide phases in the fired clays, obtained from Mössbauer parameters, is also relevant to the color of the ceramic product. It is well known that iron oxides are one of the principal causes of pottery color and their influence depends not only on the percentage present in the clay but also on the particle size and distribution of the oxides (Hess and Perlman 1974; Shepard 1968; Matson 1971).

In the case of the clays studied in the present work, the detailed results obtained from the Mössbauer measurements regarding the type and particle size of iron oxides may be used to understand the development of color as the firing temperature changes. In the noncalcareous clays where the iron oxides appear as large well-crystallized haematite particles, their size increasing with firing temperature, the color develops generally from red or brown red for firing at 700 °C to red or dark red at 1080 °C. In contrast, in calcareous clays where the growth of iron oxides is inhibited the color is generally much lighter. As an example the Corfu clay which is gray in its raw form becomes buff-cream when fired at 700 °C, then buff at 900 °C, and almost white at 1080 °C. The Corinth–2 clay — which is also calcareous but in its raw form contains most of the iron in the form of oxides — is brown unfired and becomes pink at 700 °C and red at 900 °C but turns again into pale yellow at 1080 °C in agreement with the observed drop in particle size.

Three of the clays studied deviate from the general pattern of variation of Mössbauer parameters presented above and it is worth discussing the causes for these aberrations in order to be aware of possible complications in cases of ancient ceramics. The first of these is clay No. 14 (Nichoria 7) which is calcareous but exhibits a high magnetic ratio in the range of noncalcareous clays, over the whole range of firing. This is because it already contains a large amount of haematite particles in its raw state, giving it a red color uncharacteristic of calcareous clays.

The second exception is Gault clay (No. 13) from England which contains about 10% Ca but behaves as noncalcareous developing large iron oxide particles upon firing and having a small QS and a large MR which place it in the noncalcareous range. The behavior of this clay was partially understood after XRD measurements and comparison with the other clays fired at 1080 °C (Maniatis et al. 1980). The results showed only the mineral anorthite from the calcium aluminosilicate spectrum as opposed to gehlenite, wollastonite, and diopside that the other calcareous clays contained. It is known that anorthite cannot trap iron in its lattice and therefore Fe can form iron oxide particles during firing. Moreover, this clay develops more vitrification than the other calcareous clays as revealed by scanning electron microscope results (Maniatis 1976). The final exception is the calcareous Pirgos clay (No. 18) which be-

Y. Maniatis, A. Simopoulos, A. Kostikas

haves normally except for a high magnetic ratio in the noncalcareous range after firing at 1080°C arising from a nonidentifiable magnetic phase.

With the above results in mind, we may return now to the questions posed at the beginning of this section, i.e., What can be learned from Mössbauer measurements on ancient ceramics both individually and in comparison with measurements of fired clays of similar constitution? It has been found that two Mössbauer parameters, the magnetic ratio and the quadrupole splitting of the Fe^{3+} doublet are fairly well correlated to firing temperature when the effect of the calcium content is also taken into account. Mössbauer measurements, therefore, can be effective in firing temperature determinations especially if refiring procedures are also used, as will be discussed in the next section. When these measurements are combined with results by other techniques, notably XRD and SEM, they provide a fairly complete characterization of the ceramics under study with regard to the technology of their production. It should be noted here that these results pertain to firings in oxidizing atmospheres. Data for reducing atmospheres are limited (Chevalier et al. 1976) and work on this problem is now in progress at our laboratory.

The above results also show that little information can be obtained concerning provenance since the Mössbauer parameters used for differentiation are mainly determined by elemental constitution and more specifically Ca content as well as other refractory properties of the clay. As the data of Figures 3 and 4 show, the dependence on provenance, if any, is washed out by the dispersion introduced by the other factors.

Refiring Procedures

It is known that once a clay is fired at a certain temperature and then cooled down, it freezes at a stage which can not be altered by subsequent refirings unless the initial temperature is exceeded. This property of ceramics is very helpful because it provides a means for determining the firing temperature reached by a certain ware in antiquity. This determination, of course, is approximate since the original firing schedule and atmosphere are not known to be imitated. The fact that the various parameters of the ceramics do not alter with refirings up to the original temperature has been shown with the SEM (Kingery and Frierman 1974; Maniatis 1976), differential thermal analysis (Cole and Crook 1962), and dilatometry (Tite 1969). It is, therefore, plausible that Mössbauer parameters will show similar behavior and this has been demonstrated in a number of applications. As an example, recently reported refirings were performed on a Glozel tablet (Bakas et al. 1980)

and its very low initial firing temperature was determined.

Another example is shown in Figure 5 with the Mössbauer spectra of a Neolithic sherd from the Greek site Servia as received (ASR) and refired at 700°C and 1000°C. It is obvious that the spectra of the ASR sample and after refiring at 700°C are identical, while a dramatic change occurs after refiring at 1000°C. It is fairly certain, therefore, that this pot was initially fired above 700°C since refiring at this temperature did not change at all the Mössbauer parameters. Similarly the change at 1000°C indicates that this temperature is well above the original firing temperature, so that this item must have been fired at a temperature above 700° and below 1000°C. Refirings at intermediate temperatures could define better the original firing temperatures. Further examples will be discussed in the following sections.

Applications to Ancient Pottery

Iraqi Pottery

Five sherds of pottery have been selected from a large group of ceramics from various sites in Iraq spanning the period from 6000 B.C. to 650 A.D. These sherds have been examined previously with SEM (Tite and Maniatis 1975a) and XRD (Maniatis 1976) and their firing temperatures and degree of vitrification have been determined. Although they span an extended time and site range, they are all calcareous (amount of Ca between 15 and 29%) and their SEM patterns show the characteristic microstructure (Tite and Maniatis 1975b) of calcareous clays fired in the temperature range of 850° to 1050°C. As noted earlier, clays that contain finely divided calcite develop calcium aluminosilicates during firing which inhibit the further development of vitrification. Thus, a stable microstructure is observed between 850°C and 1050°C. Above 1050°C new mineral phases appear with the development of more glass. It is plausible, therefore, that ancient pottery found to exhibit this type of structure would have been initially fired within the 850°–1050°C range. The 200°C uncertainty cannot be narrowed down with the SEM since the microstructure does not change in this range. Figures 3 and 4, however, indicate that the Mössbauer parameters do vary in this temperature range and this could be a way for a finer determination of the firing temperature for pottery of this type.

For this purpose the five sherds, after measurement in the as-received state, were refired at 950°C in an oxidizing atmosphere. The firing temperature was selected as being in the middle of the 850° to 1050°C range. The spectra of the ASR and refired sherds are shown in Figure 6. One can immediately see that the corresponding spectra in pairs are identical. The

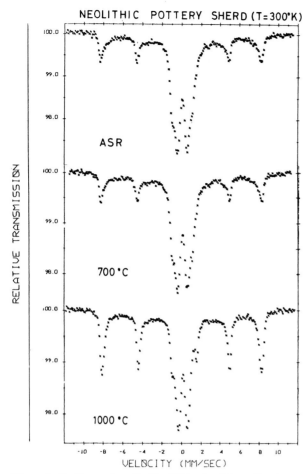

Figure 5. R. T. spectra of a Neolithic sherd from Servia, as received (ASR), refired at 700° and at 1080°C.

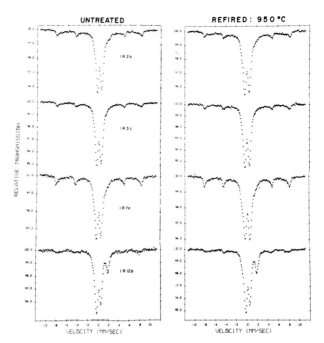

Figure 6. Spectra of pottery from Iraq taken at room temperature as received and refired at 950°C.

Table 2. Mössbauer parameters of Iraqi pottery, as received (ASR) and after firing at 950°C

Sample	$\dfrac{e^2qQ^a}{2}$ (Fe^{3+}) mm/s		Magnetic ratio[b] (%)	
	ASR	950°C	ASR	950°C
IR2a	0.91	0.93	31	36
IR3c	0.92	0.94	20	17
IR7a	0.96	0.97	37	32
IR4e	0.80	0.80	21	21
IR12b	0.79	0.78	14	17

[a]Errors of $\sim \pm 0.01$ mm/s.
[b]Errors of $\sim \pm 4\%$.

Mössbauer parameters are listed in Table 2 and they are also equal within the experimental errors suggesting that the original firing temperature for all sherds has not been exceeded with the refiring at 950°C. With the upper limit defined by the SEM results, the initial firing temperature for these five sherds can be now placed between 950° and 1050°C. Closer determination could be obtained with repeated refirings and Mössbauer measurements but it is archaeologically meaningless since the initial firing cycle is not known and the variation of the kiln temperature during the same firing between the center and the sides could be greater than 100°C (Mayes 1961, 1962). These results demonstrate the very interesting and promising combination of Mössbauer spectroscopy and scanning electron microscopy for studies of the ancient ceramic technology.

Another way of determining the firing temperature of these sherds would be to compare the quadrupole splitting and the magnetic ratio of the ASR Möss-

bauer spectra with the calibration curves of the sixteen fired clays mentioned earlier (Figs. 3 and 4). The classification of the sherds as "calcareous" is useful in this respect but the lack of knowledge of the firing atmosphere is an essential limitation. For example, the quadrupole splitting of sherds IR2a, IR3c, and IR7a fall within the calcareous region of clays and by comparison we can obtain firing temperatures between 900°C and 1080°C (and possibly closer to

Y. Maniatis, A. Simopoulos, A. Kostikas

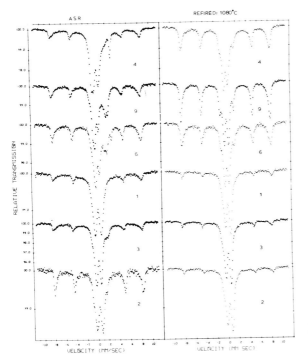

Figure 7. Spectra of Punic amphorae taken at room temperature as received and refired at 1080°C.

1080°C) which is in agreement with the refiring experiments despite the different provenance of the examined ceramics and the control clays. However, sherds IR4c and IR12b where a ferrous doublet is present, indicating a degree of reduction during the initial firing, display quadrupole splitting values for the ferric doublet falling outside the range of calcareous clays. Comparison in this case is therefore not possible.

Another word of caution regarding this second method of the firing temperature determination refers to the accuracy of the Mössbauer parameters. This depends strongly on the procedure followed for fitting the spectra and it is rather difficult to attain better error limits of ± 0.01 mm/sec for the quadrupole splitting. The situation gets more complex when other components overlap with the ferric doublet, as for instance a ferrous doublet. The χ^2 distribution criterion and a number of fits with varying initial parameters can be useful in such cases for obtaining reliable parameters.

X-ray diffraction data obtained for the five Iraqi sherds showed, as expected, the presence of calcium aluminosilicates such as gehlenite, diopside, and wollastonite and a mixture of high-temperature plagioclase feldspars such as anorthite and albite. The minerals gehlenite, diopside, and wollastonite are known to be able to accommodate Fe in the lattice — especially diopside — in the place of Mg.

Punic Amphorae

During the excavation at the ancient site of Corinth under the direction of Charles Williams, a store house was unearthed which was full of broken amphorae, dated from 470 to 430 B.C. The house was assumed to belong to a Corinthian merchant who was importing fish, because on the inside of a number of amphorae scale and fish bones were discovered. The shapes of the amphorae were also foreign to Corinth and to the rest of Greece so they must almost certainly have been manufactured outside Greece and probably in Spain or Africa. The study of these wares is still in progress and has been extended to a large number of samples. Here we report preliminary results of a Mössbauer study of ten representative samples covering all the different types available. Elemental analysis by optical emission spectroscopy showed that the compositions fall in a broad but homogenous range without any distinct grouping. Calcium content varies considerably among the samples from about 10% to 20% but the trace elements (Ni or Cr) are fairly close.

We carried out Mössbauer measurements of the amphorae at room temperature in the as-received state and also after refiring at 1080°C. The refiring at a high temperature and under controlled atmosphere is assumed to level off all the factors depending on initial temperature and atmosphere and reveal the real properties of the clay. That is, assuming the amphorae were made of the same clay, firing at the same temperature and at the same atmosphere should develop the same minerals and microstructure and therefore the same Mössbauer parameters.

Figure 7 shows some typical spectra of the ASR and refired at 1080°C samples. As it can be seen the variation in the ASR spectra is fairly random. However, after the refiring the samples tend to fall into two categories, one developing large iron oxide particles as witnessed by the high magnetic ratio and the other small ones. Note that the samples developing the large oxides contain an amount of ferrous iron indicating a degree of reduction in the initial firing cycle. Figure 8 and Figure 9 show the quadrupole splitting and magnetic ratio results of the refired samples superimposed on the results for the clays of section 3. The ranges shown by broken and solid lines correspond to the calcareous and noncalcareous respectively. It can be seen that the amphorae separate into two groups according to their QS values and much more so according to their magnetic ratio. One group overlaps with the range of the calcareous clays and the other with the noncalcareous range.

The results of the refiring experiments show that the amphorae were manufactured from at least two kinds of clays with different refractory properties,

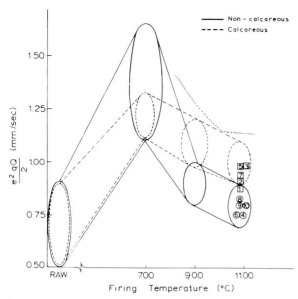

Figure 8. Quadrupole splitting of the paramagnetic doublet of Punic amphorae after refiring at 1080°C superimposed on the results for the fired clays. Broken lines: calcareous region. Solid lines: noncalcareous region.

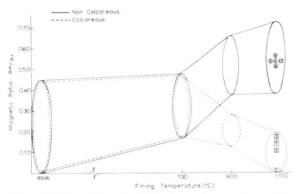

Figure 9. Magnetic ratio of Punic amphorae after refiring at 1080°C superimposed on the results for the fired clays. Broken lines: calcareous region. Solid lines: noncalcareous region.

one behaving as noncalcareous and the other as calcareous. This result is at first sight surprising since the calcium content of the clays is high in both groups.

The amount of Ca, however, can be misleading since it can be contained in large calcite particles as grit which does not react with the clay minerals to produce different refractory properties as mentioned earlier. This is probably the case for the group of amphorae behaving as noncalcareous. If this is verified — selective compositional analysis is in progress now — it will bring out an interesting technological aspect in the manufacture of these articles. It is

known that calcium in the clay produces a more porous and light body while its absence facilitates vitrification and results in denser ceramics, especially if the firing takes place in a reducing atmosphere (Tite et al. 1979). The latter effect may be desirable, e.g., for storing liquids. Thus, if calcium is contained in large calcite particles as grit, it may not react with clay minerals so that the refractory properties are similar to noncalcareous clays. It is interesting to note that the Mössbauer parameters which give information on a microscopic scale are effective in resolving the difference in refractory properties.

Conclusions

Many applications of Mössbauer spectroscopy in the field of ancient ceramics are based on the conclusions reached by research carried out on raw and fired clays. Of primary importance among these conclusions is the result which correlates the Mössbauer spectra with the form of the iron oxide phases and in particular their particle size. This in turn has been correlated successfully with the firing temperature and the Ca content of the clay.

The firing temperature of an ancient ware can in principle be derived by direct comparison of its magnetic ratio and ferric quadrupole splitting with the calibration curves of the fired clays. Only one example, however, has been demonstrated so far and the possibility of other factors, i.e., other than firing temperatures and Ca content, has to be further investigated.

Refiring experiments seem to be more practical and safer for firing determination, in particular if they are combined with other techniques, like SEM, which provide a rough estimate of the firing temperature.

Refiring at high temperatures can also be useful for grouping of ancient wares and possible provenance determination.

Finally one should stress the point that Mössbauer spectroscopy is a sophisticated technique which, above all, is rather time consuming. Thus, problems that require measurements of large numbers of samples, like provenance identification, should be confronted with more routine-based techniques. The Mössbauer spectroscopy, on the other hand, can be particularly useful in pottery studies which are closely related with the state of the iron in the clay — like color and firing temperature.

Future Outlook

So far background work on fired clays has been completed only under oxidizing conditions (Maniatis et al. 1980). A large number of pottery pieces have, however, been fired in reducing (or partially reduc-

Y. Maniatis, A. Simopoulos, A. Kostikas

ing) atmosphere as can be judged by their color. We have recently initiated work on clays fired under reducing atmosphere in order to have a complete picture. It seems that the Mössbauer technique is very useful in this direction since it can easily detect the degree of reduction from the amount of a ferrous component appearing in the spectra.

Other factors should be also investigated in order to increase the degree of confidence in comparisons between clays fired in the laboratory and ancient pottery. Aging effects, for instance, have been reported (Kostikas et al. 1976; Danon et al. 1976) to affect the magnetic ratio through physicochemical processes (Sigalas et al. 1978) but this factor has not yet been investigated systematically.

Acknowledgments: We would like to thank Dr. Richard Jones of the Athens British School of Archaeology who provided most of the clays and their chemical composition. We also like to thank Dr. V. Perdikatsis of the Institute of Geological and Mining Research for consultation on the X-ray diffraction data.

References

Aburto, S.; Cruz, S.; Gomez, R.; and Jimenez, M. 1978. Mössbauer studies of ancient Mexican pottery. *Proceedings of the 18th International Symposium on Archaeometry and Archaeological Prospection*, pp. 1–7. Rheinland-Verlag GmbH Köln.

Bakas, T.; Gangas, N. H.; Sigalas, I.; and Aitken, M. J. 1980. Mössbauer study of Glozel tablet 198 bl. *Archaeometry* 22:69–80.

Bouchez, R.; Coey, J. M. D.; Coussement, R.; Schmidt, K. P.; van Rossum, M.; Aprahamian, J.; and Deshayes, J. 1974. Mössbauer study of firing conditions used in the manufacture of the grey and red ware of Tureng Tepe. *J. de Physique* 35, C6:541–47.

Chevalier, A.; Coey, J. M. D.; and Bouchez, R. 1976. A study of iron in fired clay: Mössbauer effect and magnetic measurements. *J. de Physique* 37, C6:861–65.

Cohen, R. L., ed. 1976. *Applications of Mössbauer spectroscopy*, vol. 1. London: Academic Press.

Cole, W. F., and Crook, D. N. 1962. A study of fired-clay bodies from Roman times. *Trans. Brit. Ceram. Soc.* 61:299–315.

Cousins, D. R., and Dharmawardena, K. G. 1969. Use of Mössbauer spectroscopy in the study of ancient pottery. *Nature* 223:732–33.

Cowgill, M. U., and Hutchinson, G. E. 1969. A chemical and mineralogical examination of the ceramic sequence from Tikel, El Peten, Guatemala. *Amer. J. Science* 267:465–77.

Danon, J.; Enriquez, C. R.; Mattievich, E.; and Beltraro, M. da C. de M. C. 1976. Mössbauer study of aging effects in ancient pottery from the mouth of the Amazon river. *J. de Physique* 37, C6:866.

Gangas, N. H.; Simopoulos, A.; Kostikas, A.; Yassoglou, N. J.; and Filippakis, S. 1973. Mössbauer studies of small particles of iron oxides in soil. *Clays and Clay Minerals* 21:151–60.

Hess, J., and Perlman, I. 1974. Mössbauer spectra of iron in ceramics and their relation to pottery colours. *Archaeometry* 16:137–52.

Kingery, W. D. 1974. A note on the differential thermal analysis of archaeological ceramics. *Archaeometry* 16:109–112.

Kingery, W. D., and Frierman, J. D. 1974. The firing temperature of a Karanova sherd and inferences about South-East European Chalcolithic refractory technology. *Proc. Prehistoric Soc.* 40:204–205.

Kostikas, A.; Simopoulos, A.; and Gangas, N. H. 1976. Analysis of archaeological artifacts. In Cohen, R. L., ed., *Applications of Mössbauer spectroscopy*. London: Academic Press.

Maniatis, Y. 1976. Examination of ancient pottery using the scanning electron microscope. Ph.D. dissertation, University of Essex, England.

Maniatis, Y., and Tite, M. S. 1978. Ceramics technology in the Aegean world during the Bronze Age. In Dumas, C., ed., *Thera and the Aegean World, I: Papers presented at the 2d International Scientific Congress*, pp. 483–92. [London, 1979.]

Maniatis, Y.; Simopoulos, A.; and Kostikas, A. 1980. Mössbauer study of the effect of calcium content on the iron oxide transformations in fired clays. *J. Amer. Ceram. Soc.*, in press.

Matson, F. R. 1971. A study of temperatures used in firing ancient Mesopotamian pottery. In Brill, R. H., ed., *Science in Archaeology*. Cambridge: M.I.T. Press.

Mayes, P. 1961. The firing of a pottery kiln of a Romano-British type at Boston, Lincolnshire. *Archaeometry* 4:4–30.

Mayes, P. 1962. The firing of a second pottery kiln of Romano-British type at Boston Lincolnshire. *Archaeometry* 5:80–92.

Perinet, G. 1960. Contribution de la diffraction des Rayons-X à l'evaluation de la temperature de cuisson d'une ceramique. *7th Int. Ceram. Congress*, pp. 371–76.

Peters, T., and Jenny, J. P. 1973. Mineralogical investigation of transformations upon firing of bricks. Geological contributions of Switzerland. *Gestechnische serie, Liefaring* 50:5–59.

Shepard, A. O. 1968. *Ceramics for the archaeologist*. Washington, D.C.: Carnegie Institute of Washington.

Sigalas, I.; Gangas, N. H.; and Danon, J. 1978. Weathering model in paleomagnetic field intensity measurements on ancient fired clays. *Phys. Earth Plan. Int.* 16:15-19.

Simopoulos, A.; Kostikas, A.; Sigalas, I.; Gangas, N. H.; and Moukarika, A. 1975. Mössbauer study of transformations induced in clay by firing. *Clays and Clay Minerals* 23:393-99.

Tite, M. S. 1969. Determination of the firing temperature of ancient ceramics by measurement of thermal expansion: A reassessment. *Archaeometry* 11:131-43.

Tite, M. S., and Maniatis, Y. 1975a. Examination of ancient pottery using the scanning electron microscope. *Nature* 257, No. 5522:122-23.

Tite, M. S., and Maniatis, Y. 1975b. Scanning electron microscopy of fired calcareous clays. *Trans. Brit. Ceram. Soc.* 74:19-22.

Tite, M. S.; Maniatis, Y.; Meeks, N. D.; Bimson, M.; Hughes, M. J.; and Leppard, S. C. 1979. Technological studies of ancient ceramics. In Wertime, T. A., and Wertime, S. F., eds., *Early Pyrotechnology*. Washington, D.C.: Smithsonian Institution Press, forthcoming [1982].

Van der Kraan, A. M. 1973. Mössbauer effect studies of surface ions of ultrafine α-Fe$_2$O$_3$ particles. *Phys. Stat. Solidi* 18:215-26.

10. The Use of Scanning Electron Microscopy in the Technological Examination of Ancient Ceramics

M. S. TITE, I. C. FREESTONE, N. D. MEEKS, and M. BIMSON
British Museum Research Laboratory

Introduction (section 1)

The primary aim of this paper is to survey the range of technological information that can be obtained from the scanning electron microscope (SEM) examination of ancient ceramics, the technique being supplemented as appropriate by electron microprobe analysis, X-ray diffraction, and thin section optical microscopy.

The data obtained from the SEM examination of fractured and polished sections on the structural and mineralogical changes occurring in ceramics during firing is first summarized (section 2). The use of these data to estimate the effective firing temperatures employed in antiquity is indicated (section 3). This approach to the estimation of firing temperatures is compared with other methods that have been used, and the archaeological significance of a precise estimate of the maximum temperature reached during firing is discussed.

The use of the SEM in the study of the high gloss surface finish applied to ancient ceramics is then considered (section 4) and the results obtained from the examination of the surface finish observed on a selection of pottery from the Aegean area, the Near East, India, and France ranging in date from the Chalcolithic to the Roman period are presented.

SEM Examination (section 2)

Both fresh fracture surfaces and resin-impregnated polished sections from ceramics can be examined with the SEM. The examination of fresh fracture surfaces — which is the approach previously used by the present authors (Tite and Maniatis 1975; Tite et al. 1979; Maniatis and Tite 1981) and the majority of other workers (Kingery 1974; Noll et al. 1975) — has the advantage that the sample preparation required is minimal. However, in some cases the greater time involved in preparing polished sections is justified by the additional information that can be obtained.

The fracture of ceramics tends to occur through the glass phase when this is present and, therefore, in fresh fracture surfaces, the glass phase is clearly visible under the SEM as smooth-surfaced areas (Fig. 1). The continuity or extent of the glass phase increases with increased firing temperature (Fig. 2), and the firing temperatures employed in the manufacture of the ceramics can therefore be estimated by comparing the vitrification structures observed in their as received state and after refiring in the laboratory at known temperatures for a standard period. In polished sections from ceramics, the degree of continuity and interconnection within the clay matrix (Figs. 3 and 4) provides a measure of the extent to which vitrification has progressed and can similarly be used to obtain an estimate of the firing tempera-

Figure 1. Extensive vitrification structure (fracture section) in TIM 2 (copper smelting tuyere from Timna, Israel).

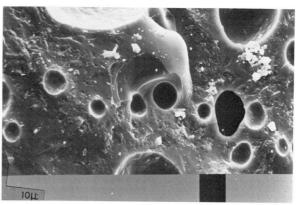

Figure 2. Continuous vitrification structure (fracture section) in TIM 2 (copper smelting tuyere from Timna, Israel).

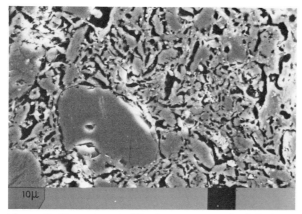

Figure 3. Extensive vitrification structure (polished section) in TIM 2 (copper smelting tuyere from Timna, Israel).

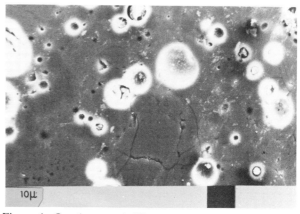

Figure 4. Continuous vitrification structure (polished section) in TIM 2 (copper smelting tuyere from Timna, Israel).

ture employed in antiquity. However, the degree of interconnection also depends on the original texture of the clay and it is therefore sometimes less easy to establish whether or not vitrification has begun from a polished section (Fig. 3) than from a fresh fracture surface in which the smooth-surfaced areas of glass are clearly visible (Fig. 1).

Fresh fracture surfaces, depending as they must on the vagaries of fracture, do not, however, necessarily provide a representative picture of the distribution of inclusions within the clay/glass matrix, nor as a result of the irregularity of the surface are they suitable for quantitative electron microprobe analysis; in these contexts polished sections are preferable. In the SEM, the different phases present can be distinguished on the basis of their atomic number contrast and if polished *thin* sections are prepared, the data obtained with the SEM can be readily supplemented by that from optical microscopy. In addition, polished sections are more suitable for the study of

the surface finish applied to ceramics since it is much easier to control the position of the section through the surface layer, and the surface finish / body interface is more clearly revealed.

Microprobe Analysis

A selection of ceramics fired at a range of temperatures has been studied in polished section using the SEM in conjunction with electron microprobe analysis (Table 1).

In the case of the low fired ceramics in which no glass phase or only a limited amount of glass phase had developed, the clay fraction was analyzed using the electron microprobe in an attempt to identify the clay minerals originally present. Using the technique outlined by Courtois and Velde (1981), a series of analyses with a spot 1–2 μm diameter was made of areas in the clay matrix from which nonplastic inclusions such as quartz and feldspar were, on the basis of light optics, apparently absent. Analyses with the

M. S. Tite, I. C. Freestone, N. D. Meeks, M. Bimson

Table 1. Microprobe analyses of pottery body clays and slips

Oxide (% wt)	TIM2	BRH16	IND4		GR4e		GAlc		BRHl	
			Body	Slip	Body	Slip	Body	Slip	Body	Slip
SiO_2	50.55	53.77	56.43	57.14	57.32	52.79	48.19	43.35	51.00	43.49
TiO_2	nd	0.94	0.65	0.78	0.38	1.62	0.64	0.51	0.41	0.88
Al_2O_3	42.63	36.64	23.77	20.92	17.56	27.10	25.10	30.89	21.01	32.92
FeO	2.18	3.28	7.97	8.94	10.60	9.94	9.81	12.93	5.85	12.38
MgO	0.32	1.45	3.55	3.43	6.14	2.17	6.22	2.28	17.17	0.79
CaO	0.17	0.45	0.86	2.22	2.17	1.67	4.12	0.43	17.17	2.32
Na_2O	0.54	0.38	1.39	0.84	1.57	0.85	1.12	0.64	0.78	0.34
K_2O	3.61	3.09	5.38	5.73	4.26	3.86	4.80	3.97	1.37	6.88
Analysis total[a]	91.46	83.11	77.45	91.21	82.67	83.95	81.71	96.88	82.84	98.93

[a] For ease of comparison, the analyses have been normalized to 100%. The analysis totals are also given. The low totals are due to the irregularity of the polished surface formed by the fine grained and porous clay bodies. In general, the totals increase with increasing degree of vitrification; thus, totals for slip analyses are higher than those for the clays of the corresponding body.

highest alumina to silica ratio were readily repeatable and were therefore taken as representative of the clay composition. Evidence in support of this conclusion was the similarity of the peak size and distribution in X-ray spectra of confirmed clay minerals using the semiquantitative X-ray spectrometer attached to the SEM and the spectra of the analyses obtained using the microprobe. However, in using these data, it must be appreciated that a proportion at least of the calcium and iron contents is present as distinct mineral phases which are intimately mixed in with clay minerals. In Figure 5, the analytical data for the four ceramics examined is plotted on a ternary diagram together with fields defined by corresponding analytical data for standard clay minerals and theoretical clay formulae (Deer et al. 1962). The results indicate that the clay fraction in TIM2 (copper smelting tuyere: Timna, Israel) and BRH16 (Roman mortarium: Hartshill, England) contained a high proportion of the two-layer kaolinite mineral whereas the clay fraction in IND4 (black slip ware: Kausambhi, India) and GR4e (Early Bronze Age: Servia, Greece) consisted predominantly of the three-layer illitic or montmorillonitic clay minerals. This conclusion is consistent with data obtained previously (Tite et al. 1979) which established that the former two ceramics were high refractory in that the development of a glass phase did not begin until the ceramics were fired to about 1000 °C in an oxidizing atmosphere whereas the latter two were low refrac-

tory with a glass phase beginning to be formed after firing at 800 °–850 °C.

In the case of the high fired ceramics in which an essentially continuous glass phase was visible in the polished section, the crystalline and amorphous phases present within the glass were investigated either in the section as prepared or after etching in dilute hydrofluoric acid. For the ceramics made from both low and high refractory noncalcareous clays (i.e., clays containing less than about 5% CaO) and fired or refired to temperatures in the range 1150 °–1200 °C, etching revealed that the apparently continuous glass phase (Fig. 4) consisted of partially dissolved quartz grains embedded in a matrix made up of both a glass phase and a high alumina phase (Figs. 6 and 7). The high alumina phase generally has the form of shapeless, interconnected grains, and in the case of the tuyere, TIM2, the proportion of this high alumina phase decreases with the increasing effective firing temperature towards the surface of the tuyere, which suggests that this phase consists mainly of unreacted relict but almost certainly amorphous clay minerals. However, the X-ray diffraction data, together with the presence of at least a proportion of acicular crystals in the glass phase, suggest that the high temperature phase, mullite, is also present in TIM2 as well as in BRH16 (Roman mortarium: Hartshill, England) and T3b (Middle Bronze Age: Thessaly, Greece). Conversely, no acicular mullite crystals were visible in the glass phase in a low refrac-

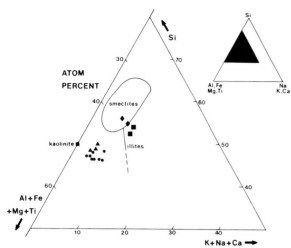

Figure 5. Compositions of clays from ceramics compared with those of major clay mineral types. The field of smectites is based on analyzed montmorillonites from Deer et al. (1962) and the point for kaolinite and the line defining illites are based on theoretical formulae for those minerals. Each point represents a single spot analysis on the clay (TIM 2–circles; BRH 16–triangles; GR4e–diamonds; IND 4–squares).

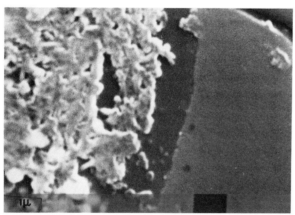

Figure 6. Continuous vitrification structure after etching (polished section) in TIM 2 (copper smelting tuyere from Timna, Israel). The high alumina phase, the partially dissolved quartz grain, and the glass phase are visible as increasingly dark areas.

tory London clay sample fired at 1160 °C and this is again consistent with only a very weak mullite line at 5.39 Å being detected by X-ray diffraction.

For ceramics made from calcareous clays containing more than about 15% calcium oxide and again fired or refired in the range 1150°–1200°C, a calcium-rich phase was normally clearly visible within the glass phase prior to etching (Fig. 8). However, in some cases, this phase could be more easily seen after etching. On the basis of analysis using the energy dispersive X-ray spectrometer attached to the SEM

and the X-ray diffraction data, the calcium-rich phase was identified as wollastonite with some diopside (Fig. 9) in AH5 ('Ubaid ware: 'Ubaid, Iraq) and as a mixture of wollastonite with some diopside and anorthite in IR3b (Halaf ware: Arpachiyah, Iraq). In the case of JR2a (Pottery Neolithic B: Jericho, Jordan), two distinct calcium-rich phases were detected in different areas of the ceramic. The first (which predominated) was probably a mixture of gehlenite and wollastonite and the second was wollastonite by itself.

Firing Temperature Determinations (section 3)

The determination of the extent of vitrification observed with the SEM is only one of many methods that have been used to estimate the firing temperatures employed in the manufacture of ancient ceramics. These other methods are normally based either on the measurement of macroscopic properties such as porosity (Sanders 1973), hardness (Fabre and Perinet 1973), and thermal expansion (Tite 1969; Heimann 1978), which are again dependent on the extent of vitrification or on the use of a mineralogical temperature scale. In the latter case, differential thermal analysis, X-ray diffraction or thin section optical microscopy are used to identify the mineral phases present in the ceramics, and the presence or absence of certain diagnostic minerals (e.g., hydrated clay minerals, calcite, mica, calcium silicates) then provides a basis for establishing the maximum or minimum values for the firing temperature. Alternatively, the state of the iron oxides present in the ceramics as revealed by Mössbauer spectroscopy (Chevalier et al. 1976) or color (Matson 1971) can provide an estimate of both the firing temperature and the atmosphere.

The precision with which the firing temperature can be determined with the above methods, including that of SEM examination, is typically 50°–100°C. The estimation of the firing temperature with the SEM is, however, less precise in those cases where the extent of vitrification is either essentially stable such as in the 850°–1050°C firing temperature range for ceramics made from calcareous clays (Tite et al. 1979) or changing only slowly with increasing temperature such as in the firing temperature range below 800°–850°C prior to the appearance of a definite glass phase. Although other methods such as thermal expansion (Maniatis and Tite 1978; Heimann 1978) and Mössbauer spectroscopy in principle provide a more precise estimate of the firing temperature in these circumstances, uncertainty regarding the firing atmosphere and firing time employed in antiquity tends to limit the precision irrespective of the inherent accuracy of the method.

Also, the question that must be asked is, What, if

M. S. Tite, I. C. Freestone, N. D. Meeks, M. Bimson

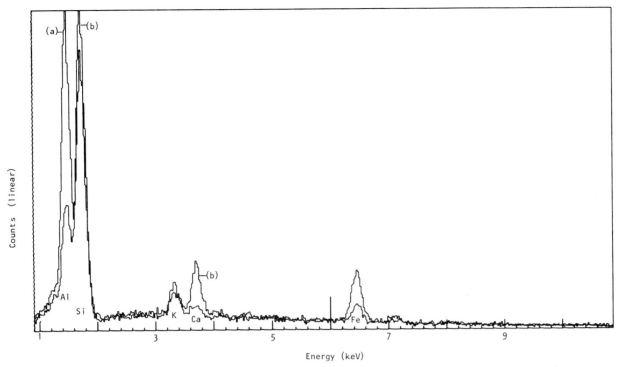

Figure 7. Energy dispersive X-ray spectra for (a) the high alumina phase and (b) the glass phase observed in the continuous vitrification structure of TIM 2 after etching (see Fig. 6).

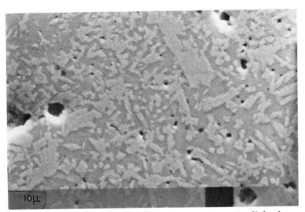

Figure 8. Continuous vitrification structure (polished section) in AH 5 ('Ubaid ware from 'Ubaid, Iraq). The calcium-rich phase (wollastonite with some diopside) is visible as light-colored areas within the darker glass matrix.

any, is the archaeological significance of attempting to determine the firing temperature employed in antiquity with a high precision? In this context, it should be noted that experimental firings of Roman and medieval kilns (Mayes 1961, 1962; Bryant 1970, 1978) have indicated that the temperatures reached in different parts of a kiln can vary by more than 100 °C. We would therefore argue that it is normally adequate to provide a rough estimate of the firing temperature sufficient merely to distinguish between

the different primary pyrotechnologies: that is, firing in a bonfire or clamp to temperatures less than 800 °-850 °C, a normal kiln firing to temperatures in the range 800 °-1000 °C, or a high temperature kiln firing to temperatures in excess of 1000 °C. Experimental firings have clearly demonstrated that temperatures up to about 1000 °C can be achieved in kilns without any great difficulty. Also for firing temperatures up to 1000 °C, careful selection of the clay used is not necessary although the examination of a wide range of ancient ceramics has suggested that for pottery fired in the 800 °-1000 °C range, calcareous clays were preferred (Tite et al. 1979). Controlled firing to above 1000 °C obviously required greater technological expertise and, with the exception of the occasional kiln "waster" and Early Bronze Age pottery of 'Ubaid type from Iraq (Tite and Maniatis 1975), these high firing temperatures do not appear to have been employed in Europe or the Near East during the prehistoric periods.

We would further suggest that, in future, much greater emphasis should be placed on establishing the effect of the different types of clay and firing conditions on those physical properties of the resulting ceramics which are relevant to their suitability for the various uses to which they would have been put in antiquity (Shepard 1956). Such a project would involve the measurement of the strength, toughness, permeability, porosity, and thermal shock resistance of a

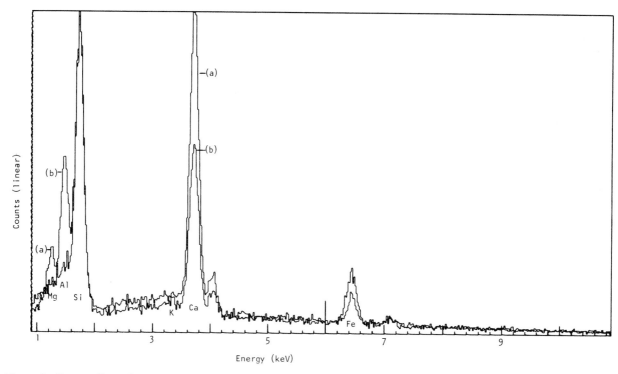

Figure 9. Energy dispersive X-ray spectra for (a) *the calcium-rich phase (wollastonite with some diopside) and* (b) *the glass phase observed in the continuous vitrification structure of AH5 (see Fig. 8).*

range of ceramics, and the investigation of the relationship between these properties and the microstructures of ceramics. The data would then need to be assessed in the context of the properties required for the different uses to which the ceramics would have been put, the extent to which the observed properties match these requirements, and the production methods employed to achieve the different properties. In interpreting these data, one would, of course, have to be very careful to avoid assuming a greater degree of technological sophistication on the part of the ancient potters than is justified in the context of what is essentially a craft tradition.

High Gloss Surface Finish (section 4)

High gloss surface finishes have been a feature of pottery essentially from its earliest production through to the Greek Attic black and red figure ware and Roman Samian ware (terra sigillata). The reasons for applying these surface finishes were both practical, in that they provide a more impermeable surface layer, and decorative.

A selection of pottery from the Aegean area, the Near East, India, and France ranging in date from the Chalcolithic to the Roman period were examined in order to characterize the burnishing techniques and the different types of slip used to achieve a high gloss surface finish. No attempt has, however, been made to establish the chronological development or

Table 2. Provenance and chronological data for pottery with high gloss surface finish

Sherd No.	Provenance	Period/type
H3a	Toszeg, Hungary	Early Bronze Age
GR4e	Servia, Greece	Early Bronze Age
IND1	Kausambhi, India	Black slip ware c500 B.C.
IND4	Kausambhi, India	Black slip ware c500 B.C.
IND2	Rajghat, India	Black slip ware c500 B.C.
IND3	Kausambhi, India	c500 B.C.
ANla	Hacilar, Anatolia	Chalcolithic
G3b	Korakou, Greece	Early Bronze Age
GAlb	Attica, Greece	Greek black or red figure ware
GAlc	Attica, Greece	Greek black or red figure ware
BRHl	Central Gaul	Roman Samian ware
BMl	Central Gaul	Roman Samian ware

Table 3. Results for pottery with high gloss surface finish

Sherd no.	Body Clay type[a]	Body Vitrification stage[b]	Body Firing temperature	Surface finish Color	Surface finish Thickness (μm)	Surface finish Composition (compared to body)
H3a	NC	NV	<750 °C	Black	—	—
GR4e	NC	NV	<750 °C	Black	30–40	High Al
IND1	NC	IV	750–800 °C	Black	∼15	High Al
IND4	NC	IV	750–800 °C	Black	∼10	High Al
IND2	NC	IV/V	∼800 °C	Black	5–10	High Al
IND3	NC	NV	<800 °C	Red	15–20	High Al
ANla	C	NV	<800 °C	Red	10–30	Low Ca, Fe, K
				White	∼100	High Ca
G3b	C	V	850–1050 °C	Red	20–30	High Al — Low Ca, K
GAlb	C	V	850–1050 °C	Black	∼15	High Al — Low Ca
GAlc	C	V	850–1050 °C	Black	20–25	High Al — Low Ca
BRHl	C	V(+)	1000–1100 °C	Red	5–10	High Al, Fe, K — Low Ca
BMl	C	V	850–1050 °C	Red	∼20	High Al, Fe, K — Low Ca

[a] NC, noncalcareous clay; C, calcareous clay.
[b] NV, no vitrification; IV, initial vitrification; V, extensive vitrification; CV, continuous vitrification.

the geographical distribution of the different techniques that have been identified.

Fresh fracture surfaces and resin impregnated polished sections through the pottery were examined with the SEM. The former were used to determine the extent of vitrification in the pottery body and hence estimate the effective firing temperature employed in manufacture. The latter, however, provided a clearer picture of the surface finish / body interface and, in some cases, further information was obtained by reexamining these sections after etching in dilute hydrofluoric acid. The compositions of the surface finish and body were compared in terms of the peak heights of the X-ray spectra obtained by analyzing areas approximately 10μm and 1 mm diameter respectively in the polished sections using the energy dispersive X-ray spectrometer attached to the SEM. The ratio of the peak heights for aluminum and silicon in the surface finish and body respectively were taken as a measure of the relative amounts of clay and quartz, and the aluminum peak heights were used as normalizing factors when comparing the peak heights for the other elements detected (K, Ca, Fe). In addition, spot analyses (1–2 μm diameter) of the clay phase in the surface finish and body were undertaken for some sherds using an electron microprobe (Table 1). The polished sections were also examined in reflected light and, when polished thin sections were available, in transmitted light under a polarizing microscope. Details of the provenance, chronology, and pottery type are given in Table 2 and the information obtained on the surface finish and body is given in Table 3 for a representative selection of the sherds examined.

Sherd H3a is an example of direct burnishing without the prior application of a surface slip. In general, the appearance of this surface, both visually and under the SEM, was very similar to that of a clay sample which had been burnished and fired in the laboratory. No surface layer was visible in polished section in the SEM (Fig. 10), although there tended to be fewer quartz inclusions at the surface, presumably as a result of their having been pushed back by the burnishing action.

Sherds GR4e, IND1, IND4, IND2, and IND3 are examples of burnishing after the application of a noncalcareous surface slip to a body which was also made from a noncalcareous clay. In each case, a clearly defined, fine textured surface layer which contained a lower concentration of quartz inclusions than the body was visible in polished section in the SEM (Fig. 11). In the fresh fracture surfaces through the slips, the flaky structure of the clay particles was still visible and the absence of vitrification was further confirmed by the birefringence observed in thin section under the polarizing microscope. Except for their higher clay contents (i.e., higher aluminum), the compositions of the surface slips were similar, on the

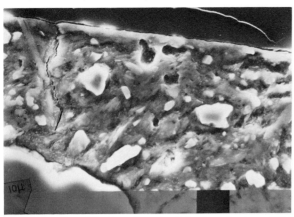

Figure 10. Burnished surface (polished section) on H3A (Early Bronze Age sherd from Toszeg, Hungary).

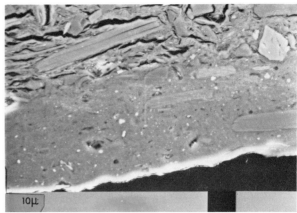

Figure 11. Slip / body interface (polished section) in GR4e (Early Bronze Age sherd from Servia, Greece).

basis of X-ray peak heights measured in the SEM, to those of the bodies. Electron microprobe analyses (Table 1) showed that the compositions of the clay phase in the slip and body of IND4 were essentially the same, which suggests that the fine-particle fraction from the body clay was used for this slip. In contrast, the compositions of the slip and body clays were different for GR4e but this fact does not necessarily exclude the possibility that the fine-particle fraction from the body clay was again used for the slip. Although the slip of IND4 contains a slightly higher concentration of iron oxide than the body, these results do not really confirm the suggestion made by Hegde (1979) that the slip for the black slip ware from India (IND1, IND4, and IND2) was prepared from a mixture of clay and red ochre. However, the slip on the black slip ware was clearly different from that used for the northern black polished ware from India which, on the basis of analyses and electron microscopy, was shown by Hegde (1979) to have been prepared using a mixture of clay, red ochre, and *sajjimatti* (a natural efflorescence rich in sodium carbonate) and fired to a sufficiently high temperature to produce vitrification.

The remaining sherds are examples of a slip prepared from a noncalcareous clay which was applied to a body made from a calcareous clay. In the case of sherd AN1a, the surface finish was produced by applying a double layer of slip which was then burnished. These two slip layers were clearly visible in terms of color differences in polished section under the optical microscope and were detected in the SEM by their compositional differences (Fig. 12), although no clear textural difference between the slips and the body was visible. It appears that a thick layer of white slip ($\sim$100μm) which contained a much higher concentration of calcium than the body was first

applied. This was then covered with a thinner layer of a second slip (10–30 μm) which contained a negligible amount of calcium and which fired to a definite red color. Burnishing of the slipped surface produced the high gloss mottled red and white finish. In the case of sherd G3b, the slip layer, which was clearly visible in polished section in the SEM, consisted of fine textured noncalcareous clay containing some quartz inclusions and its structure contrasted with the more open structure of the calcareous clay body.

The high gloss black slip on the Greek Attic black and red figure ware (GA1b, GA1c) consists of a very fine textured noncalcareous clay (Fig. 13) in which the flaky structure of the clay particles is not visible even in the fresh fracture section. However, the examination of thin sections under the polarizing microscope revealed birefringent clay minerals set in an isotropic glassy matrix. Furthermore, some texture associated with clay particles was visible in the SEM after etching polished sections with dilute hydrofluoric acid (Fig. 14) and in addition, etching resulted in a large increase in the relative concentrations, as measured with the electron microprobe, of aluminum and silicon (0.6 to 1.4 for GA1c) as well as a decrease in the potassium concentration. These observations therefore suggest that the slip layer is partially vitrified and that the etching has preferentially dissolved the glass phase. In contrast to the slips, the bodies exhibit the characteristic open structure associated with calcareous clays which have been fired to a sufficiently high temperature (850°–1050°C) to produce extensive vitrification. Apart from their significantly lower calcium contents and their higher clay contents (i.e., higher aluminum), the compositions of the slips were, on the basis of the X-ray peak heights measured in the SEM, similar to those of the bodies. Electron microprobe analyses (Table 1)

M. S. Tite, I. C. Freestone, N. D. Meeks, M. Bimson

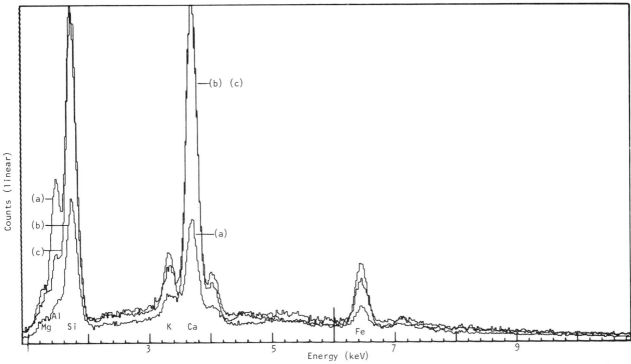

Figure 12. Energy dispersive X-ray spectra for (a) red slip, (b) white slip and (c) body of ANla (Chalcolithic sherd from Hacilar, Anatolia).

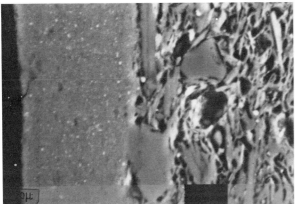

Figure 13. Slip / body interface (polished section) in GA1c (Greek Attic black or red figure ware).

Figure 14. Slip / body interface after etching (polished section) in GA1c (Greek Attic black or red figure ware).

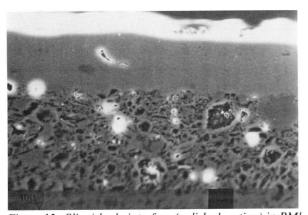

Figure 15. Slip / body interface (polished section) in BMl (Roman Samian ware).

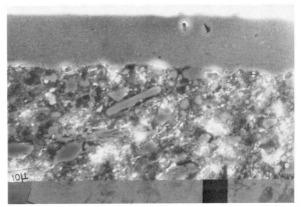

Figure 16. Slip / body interface after etching (polished section) in BMl (Roman Samian ware).

showed that the slip clay of GA1c contained lower magnesium and calcium contents but a higher iron content than the body clay. However, since the aluminum to silicon ratio was only slightly higher in the slip (0.64 as compared to 0.52 in the body) and there was no significant difference in the potassium content, the clay used for the slip did not contain a significantly higher proportion of illitic clay minerals than that used for the body. Further, and in spite of these differences in composition, it is possible that the fine-particle fraction from the body clay was used for the slip (Harbottle 1980).

The high gloss red slip on the Roman Samian ware (BRH1 and BM1) again consists of a very fine textured noncalcareous clay (Fig. 15) with no clay structure visible even in the fresh fracture section. In the case of BRH1, the slip appeared isotropic in thin section under the polarizing microscope and only slight birefringence was observed for other Samian slips examined. Furthermore, no texture associated with clay particles was visible in the SEM after etching in dilute hydrofluoric acid (Fig. 16) and the increase in the relative concentrations, as measured with the electron microprobe, of aluminum to silicon (0.8 to 1.0 for BRH1) and the decrease in the potassium concentrations were less pronounced after etching than in the case of the Greek Attic slip. Therefore, on the basis of the examples examined, the Roman Samian slip appears to be more fully vitrified and homogeneous than the Greek Attic slip. The bodies of the Roman Samian ware again exhibit the characteristic open structure associated with calcareous clays. Etching of the bodies in dilute hydrofluoric acid resulted in some increase in the relative concentration of aluminum to silicon and a significant increase in the calcium content. Hence the etching appears to have preferentially removed the glass phase to leave the relict clay minerals as well as the calcium aluminosilicates (e.g., anorthite) which were formed during firing and which were detected by X-ray diffraction. Electron microprobe analyses (Table 1) showed that the compositions of the clay phase in the slip and the body of BRH1 were very different. In addition to the significantly lower calcium content and higher iron content in the slip, the aluminum to silicon ratio (0.76 as compared to 0.41) and the potassium content were also much higher in the slip. Hence the clay used for the slip contained a significantly higher proportion of illitic clay minerals than that used for the body. However, it is again possible that the fine-particle fraction from the body clay was used for the slip (Heimann 1980).

The techniques used in the production of the Greek Attic and Roman Samian wares have been the subject of extensive investigations (Binns and Frazer 1929; Schumann 1942; Bimson 1956; Hofmann 1962, 1966). On the basis of this work it is now generally accepted that an illitic clay was selected for the slips and that a reducing-oxidizing firing cycle was used to produce the Greek Attic black and red figure ware, while an oxidizing atmosphere was maintained throughout the firing in the case of the Roman Samian ware. The current analytical data confirm the use of illitic clays for the slip although in the case of Greek Attic sherds examined, the proportion of illitic clay minerals was not significantly greater in the slip than in the body. Similarly, the open structure of the calcareous clay body of the Greek Attic ware is consistent with its being more readily oxidized than the impermeable slip during the oxidizing phase of the firing cycle. However, Bimson (1956) has pointed out that this purely physical explanation is inadequate since, after slight exposure to a reducing atmosphere, the Roman Samian red gloss is reduced to a black color while reoxidation even to a reddish-brown color was correspondingly difficult. The differential oxidation of the slip and body in the case of the Greek Attic ware must therefore be due, at least in part, to the different stabilities of the associated ferrous iron phases and not merely to the lower porosity of the partially vitrified slip layer. Mössbauer spectroscopy (Longworth and Warren 1975; Longworth and Tite 1979) has confirmed that, in the black slip, the iron is present as a spinel (i.e., a member of the $Fe_3O_4 - FeAl_2O_4$ series), and this phase may be less readily oxidized than the calcium iron silicates in which the iron exists in the calcareous clay body.

General Discussion

The results presented above establish that the slips used to produce high gloss surface finishes were prepared almost exclusively from noncalcareous clays. This observation is consistent with the fact that a noncalcareous clay is necessary in order to produce an impermeable slip without firing to very high temperatures since calcareous clays exhibit an open, porous structure when fired in the $850°-1050°C$ temperature range. This open structure is most probably due to the disruption of the clay particles when carbon dioxide is released in association with the decomposition of the calcite. In addition, when fired in an oxidizing atmosphere, a noncalcareous clay is likely to produce a more attractive red color than a calcareous clay since the iron will remain as haematite rather than forming calcium iron silicates. Also, when a noncalcareous clay slip is used with a calcareous clay body, a more definite color contrast between the slip and the lighter colored body will be achieved.

A further question that needs to be considered is why, other than for reasons of color contrast, were

M. S. Tite, I. C. Freestone, N. D. Meeks, M. Bimson

calcareous clay bodies used in conjunction with noncalcareous clay slips? As discussed above, this combination of clays is probably necessary for the Greek Attic ware in order to achieve the differential oxidation of slip and body during the oxidizing phase of the firing cycle. However, the benefits of a calcareous clay body are less obvious in the case of Samian ware. Picon et al. (1971) have shown that calcareous clays were used almost exclusively for Samian ware from both Gaul and Arezzo even when other pottery types from the same manufacturing center were being made from noncalcareous clays. There is, therefore, no doubt that calcareous clays were being deliberately selected for the production of Samian ware. Picon and Vichy (1974) have further suggested that it is possible that calcareous clays were selected for historical reasons and that the Roman potters were continuing a long-established tradition for the production of pottery with a slipped surface even though the original reasons (e.g., color contrast, permeable body) were no longer relevant.

There are, however, a number of technological advantages to be gained from the use of calcareous clays for the body. First, a calcareous clay body will tend to have a higher thermal expansion coefficient ($4.5-7.0 \times 10^{-6}/°C$) than that of comparable noncalcareous clay bodies ($2-3.5 \times 10^{-6}/°C$). Its thermal expansion coefficient will therefore more closely match that of the partially vitrified slip which is likely to be in the range $5-10 \times 10^{-6}/°C$ and consequently there will be less risk of the slip crazing during cooling. Second, as a result of the formation of crystalline phases, calcareous clays produce bodies which have a higher rigidity and compressive strength than those produced from comparable noncalcareous clays (Peters and Iberg 1978). The resulting pottery is therefore more practical when used as domestic tableware as was the case with Samian ware. A further advantage of calcareous clays is that their vitrification structure remains essentially unchanged over the 850°–1050°C firing temperature range and therefore the control of the firing temperature needed to produce pottery of a consistent quality is less critical than would be the case for a comparable noncalcareous clay.

Conclusions (section 5)

The above examples indicate that the SEM examination of fresh fracture and polished sections through ceramics when used in conjunction with hydrofluoric acid etching, electron microprobe analysis, optical microscopy, and X-ray diffraction provides a powerful technique for elucidating the structural and mineralogical changes occurring when ceramics are fired and hence for obtaining information on the raw materials and procedures used in the production of ancient ceramics. For example, the clay type used for the body and slip can be identified and the effective firing temperature employed can be estimated. In addition, the detailed information obtained on microstructure would be relevant to an understanding of the physical properties of ceramics (e.g., strength, toughness, permeability, porosity, thermal shock resistance) determined by direct measurement.

Acknowledgments: We are indebted to Dr. A. C. Bishop, Keeper of the Department of Mineralogy, British Museum (Natural History), for allowing us to use the electron microprobe in his department, and to Mr. R. F. Symes and Mrs. J. Bevan for advice and guidance in the operation of his instrument. Assistance from Mrs. S. La Niece in the preparation of the polished sections is gratefully acknowledged.

References

Bimson, M. 1956. The technique of Greek black and terra sigillata red. *Antiquaries Journal* 36: 200–204.

Binns, C. F., and Frazer, A. D. 1929. The genesis of the Greek black glaze. *American Journal of Archaeology* 33:1–10.

Bryant, G. F. 1970. Two experimental Romano-British kiln firings at Barton-on-Humber, Lincolnshire. *Journal of the Scunthorpe Museum Society* 3:1–16.

———. 1978. Romano-British experimental kiln firings at Barton-on-Humber, England, 1968–75. *Acta Praehistorica et Archaeologica* 9/10:13–22.

Chevalier, R.; Coey, J.M.D.; and Bouchez, R. 1976. A study of iron in fired clay: Mössbauer effect and magnetic measurements. *Journal de Physique* 37, C6:861–65.

Courtois, L., and Velde, B. 1981. Petrographic and electron microprobe studies of Cypriot white slip ware. *Revue d'Archéométrie Supplément:* 37–43.

Deer, W. A.; Howie, R. A.; and Zussman, J. 1962. *Rock-forming minerals.* Vol. 3, *Sheet Silicates.* London: Longmans.

Fabre, M., and Perinet, G. 1973. Mesure de la dureté de pâtes céramiques calcaires. *Bulletin de la Société Francaise de Céramique* 99:39–49.

Harbottle, G. 1980. Private communication.

Hegde, K.T.M. 1979. Analysis of ancient Indian deluxe wares. *Archaeo-physika* 10:141–55.

Heimann, R. B. 1978. Mineralogische Vorgänge beim Brennen von Keramik und Archaeothermometrie. *Acta Praehistorica et Archaeologica* 9/10: 79–102.

———. 1980. Private communication.

Hofmann, U. 1962. The chemical basis of ancient Greek vase painting. *Angewandte Chemie* 1: 341–50.

_____. 1966. Die Chemie der Antiken Keramik. *Naturwissenchaften* 53: 218-23.

Kingery, W. D. 1974. A technical characterization of two Cypriot ceramics. In Bishey, A., ed., *Recent Advances in Science and Technology of Materials*, Vol. 3, pp. 169-86. New York: Plenum Publishing Corporation.

Longworth, G., and Warren, S. E. 1975. Mössbauer spectroscopy of Greek "Etruscan" pottery. *Nature* 255: 625-27.

Longworth, G., and Tite, M. S. 1979. Mössbauer studies on the nature of red or black glazes on Greek and Indian painted ware. *Journal de Physique* 40, C2:460-61.

Maniatis, Y., and Tite, M. S. 1978. Examination of Roman and Medieval pottery using the scanning electron microscope. *Acta Praehistorica et Archaeologica* 9/10: 125-30.

Maniatis, Y., and Tite, M. S. 1981. Technological examination of Neolithic-Bronze Age pottery from Central and Southeast Europe and from the Near East. *J. Archaeological Science* 8: 59-76.

Matson, F. R. 1971. A study of temperatures used in firing ancient Mesopotamian pottery. In Brill, R. H., ed., *Science and Archaeology*, pp. 65-79. Cambridge: M.I.T. Press.

Mayes, P. 1961. The firing of a pottery kiln of a Romano-British type at Boston, Lincolnshire. *Archaeometry* 4: 4-30.

_____. 1962. The firing of a second pottery kiln of a Romano-British type at Boston, Lincolnshire. *Archaeometry* 5: 80-92.

Noll, W.; Holm, R.; and Born, L. 1975. Painting of ancient ceramics. *Angewandte Chemie* 14: 602-613.

Peters, T., and Iberg, R. 1978. Mineralogical changes during firing of calcium-rich brick clays. *American Ceramic Society Bulletin* 57: 503-509.

Picon, M.; Vichy, M.; and Meille, E. 1971. Composition of Lezoux, Lyon and Arezzo Samian ware. *Archaeometry* 13: 191-208.

Picon, M., and Vichy, M. 1974. Recherches sur la composition des céramiques de Lyon. *Revue Archeologique de l'Est et du Centre-Est* 25: 37-59.

Sanders, H. P. 1973. Pore size determinations in Neolithic, Iron Age, Roman, and other pottery. *Archaeometry* 15: 159-61.

Schumann, T. 1942. Oberflächenverzierung in der antiben Töpferkunst, Terra Sigillata und Griechische Schwarzrotmalerie. *Berichte Deutscher Keramischen Gesellschaft* 23: 408-426.

Shepard, O. A. 1956. *Ceramics for the archaeologist,* pp. 113-36. Washington, D.C.: Carnegie Institution of Washington.

Tite, M. S. 1969. Determination of the firing temperature of ancient ceramics by measurement of thermal expansion: a reassessment. *Archaeometry* 11: 132-43.

Tite, M. S., and Maniatis, Y. 1975. Examination of ancient pottery using the scanning electron microscope. *Nature* 257: 122-23.

Tite, M. S.; Maniatis, Y.; Meeks, N. D.; Bimson, M.; Hughes, M. J.; and Leppard, S. C. 1979. Technological studies of ancient ceramics. In Wertime, T. A., and Wertime, S. F., eds., *Early Pyrotechnology*. Washington, D.C.: Smithsonian Institution Press, forthcoming [1982].

11. Phase Analysis and Its Significance for Technology and Origin

MARINO MAGGETTI
Institute for Mineralogy and Petrography
University of Fribourg (Switzerland)

Abstract

This paper presents the results of investigations on temper, paste, and porosity of ancient ceramics by application of optical microscopy, X-ray diffractometry, and measurement of porosity. Porosity data must be interpreted carefully; the results of controlled firing and refiring of illitic calcareous and kaolinitic noncalcareous clays show how difficult their interpretation in terms of ancient firing temperatures and initial granulometry can be. The effect of reducing atmosphere is also discussed. Much more research work is needed, however, before porosity data can be interpreted correctly. The mineralogical changes during firing of the paste are very useful for an estimation of the ancient firing temperature, the nature of the raw material, the technology of the processing and firing atmosphere. Firing experiments on kaolinitic noncalcareous and illitic calcareous clays are discussed. There is a great need for more detailed research, especially with respect to reducing firing conditions. A review of the mineralogical changes during burial leading to secondary products as calcite, montmorillonite, mixed-layers, and zeolites is presented. Finally, the application of temper analysis for identification of local or foreign production of coarse ware is discussed and arguments for identifying artificially added temper are presented.

Introduction

If an archaeologist gives a sherd to an archaeoceramist for analysis, then the sherd has reached the fifth step of its long life (Fig. 1). These steps are: *(1)* extraction of the clay from a clay pit ("origin"); *(2)* manufacture of the ceramic object (processing, firing); *(3)* use with subsequent breakdown; *(4)* burial stage; and *(5)* analysis. From the first four steps the sherd has stored information and it possesses a memory which can be activated by the analysis (step 5) gaining the "sleeping" information about the steps 1 to 4. This can be done by a lot of physicochemical methods based on the analysis of the chemistry, mineralogy, and other physical parameters as magnetism, thermoluminescence, etc., of the sherd. Considering the *chemical composition*, it is obvious that the chemistry is a function of the composition of the original clay, of its processing (the extraction of coarse particles or addition of temper fragments can change the chemistry), of the use (the chemistry of a cooking pot can be affected by reaction processes between the pot itself and the food), of the burial stage (infiltration of foreign matter in the sherd body, extraction of sherd matter due to solvents from invading solutions) and of the archaeological treatment (cleaning with acids can lead to dissolution of carbonates). Therefore, the chemical analysis *alone* can-

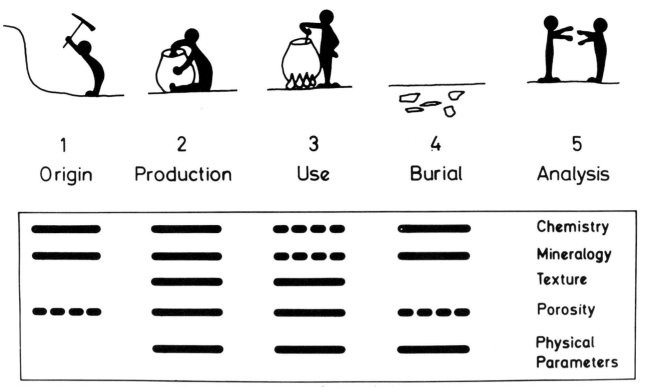

Figure 1. The five steps in the life of a ceramic object and the types of information that can be found using a defined scientific method.

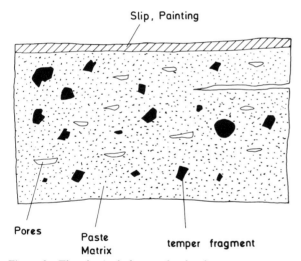

Figure 2. The physical phases of a sherd.

tions such as: *(a)* origin of temper and matrix (origin of the ceramic body); *(b)* technology of the ceramic process (artificial additions, treatment of the clay, molding, firing, etc.); *(c)* function (use) of the ceramic object; *(d)* age; and *(e)* burial conditions.

This paper will not give a complete review of all methods and applications of phase analysis on ancient ceramics. The aim is to present and discuss some archaeologically important aspects of phase analysis based on the results of recent research of the working group on ''Archaeoceramics'' from the University of Fribourg (Switzerland). Therefore literature is cited only when needed and the reader interested in other aspects and more information is referred to the papers of Courtois (1976), Farnsworth (1964), Frechen (1972), Peacock (1970), and Shepard (1968).

The following sections deal with the porosity of the ancient sherds and with the mineralogy of paste and temper. To avoid misinterpretation, some general remarks are outlined at the start.

Porosity includes all pores or voids of a sherd and is mainly due to the firing process, the initial porosity, the chemistry/mineralogy of the starting material; by addition of outburning organic substances (e.g., straw), an artificial porosity can be produced (Rye 1976). During use and/or burial the porosity can be affected by cementation (e.g., crystallization of gypsum; Courtois 1976) or leaching processes (calcite

not show which parameter (original clay, processing, use, burial, treatment) affects which chemical element. This can be done by other methods only, involving the physical phases of the sherd: *voids* (pores) and solid *matter* (temper and matrix/paste); *see* Figure 2.

The combination of both *chemical* and *physical analysis* leads to a better understanding of all the factors involved in the long history of an archaeological sherd and is the key to solving archaeological ques-

Marino Maggetti

dissolution; Kuepfer and Maggetti 1978; Marro 1978; Rottlaender 1973).

The distinction between *temper* and *paste* (matrix) is based on two criteria: granulometry and the plastic/nonplastic behavior of the initial nonfired material. By definition, temper includes all phases with a diameter greater than 0.015 mm (Maggetti 1979). The matrix predominantly contains the initially plastic phases with minor amounts of nonplastic ones, the temper predominantly nonplastics. Mineralogically, matrix and temper consist of solid phases which can be amorphous or crystalline. The initial plastic phases are sheet silicates (e.g., kaolinite, illite, montmorillonite); the nonplastic phases are either natural rock and/or mineral fragments, natural organic or artificial inorganic materials (e.g., fired brick). The temper can be added artificially (artificial temper) or was present in the initial clay (natural temper).

From the genetic point of view the solid phases can be classified into three groups: *(1)* primary or prefiring minerals (relictic minerals inherited from the initial clay); *(2)* firing minerals (formed during the firing process); and *(3)* secondary minerals (postfiring minerals, formed during the use or the burial stage).

The Interpretation of Porosity Data

Quantitative analyses of porosity include the measurement of specific and apparent weight, the pore size distribution, and the subsequent calculation of total open and closed porosity as well as the specific surface. Only few people have used these parameters for studies on archaeological ceramic objects (Cabotse 1964; Heimann 1976, 1977; Sanders 1973; Strunk-Lichtenberg et al. 1973). The porosity depends on many factors. According to Maggetti and Kahr (1980) the following parameters are important: mineralogical composition of the clay, chemical composition of the clay, granulometry of the clay, firing temperature, firing atmosphere, processing of the clay, and burial changes (interaction of the sherd and invading solutions resulting in cementation or dissolution).

An example of the application of simple measurements of specific and apparent weight for technological purposes is given by the paper of Beckmann et al. (1971). In this paper the increase of the apparent weight of medieval ceramics from Siegburg from 1,62 g/cm³ (1150 A.D., earthenware) to 2,35 g/cm³ (1450 A.D., stoneware) is clearly related to an evolution in ceramic technology. The paper also discusses other porosity parameters such as open porosity, total porosity, and so on. The changes of porosity with increasing firing temperatures could in principle be used for the estimation of ancient firing temperatures. This will now be reviewed critically.

Porosity of Kaolinitic Noncalcareous Clays

The work of Maggetti and Rossmanith (1981) on fourteen kaolinitic clays (noncalcareous) showed the importance of *granulometry* and *firing temperature* on porosity data, the former being the decisive one (Figs. 3–7). It can be inferred from this study that for

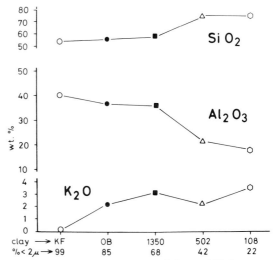

Figure 3. Granulometry: SiO₂, Al₂O₃, and K₂O content of five kaolinitic noncalcareous clays (nos. KF, OB, 1350, 502, and 108).

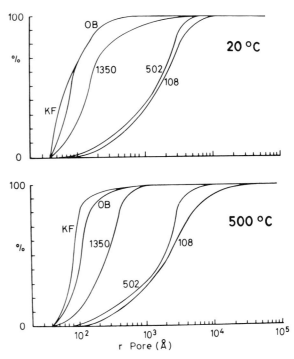

Figure 4. Pore size distribution curves (PSDC) of the clays from Figure 3 at room temperature and 500°C. The fine grained clays have markedly finer pores than the coarse grained ones and their PSDC are much steeper.

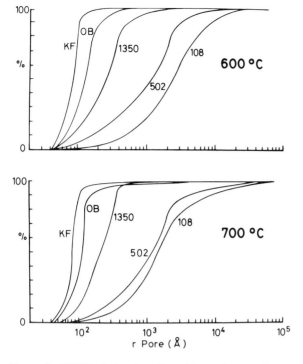

Figure 5. PSDC of the clays from Figure 3 at 600°C and 700°C.

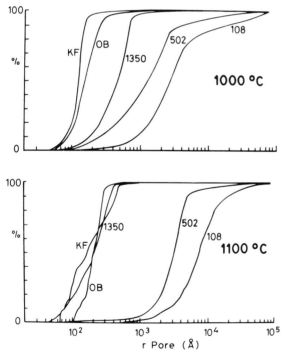

Figure 7. PSDC of the clays from Figure 3 at 1000°C and 1100°C.

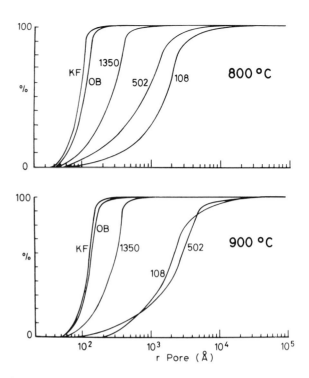

Figure 6. PSDC of the clays from Figure 3 at 800°C and 900°C.

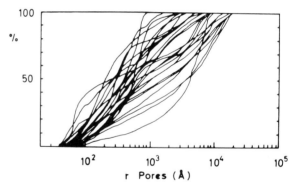

Figure 8. PSDC of Iron Age sherds from the Heuneburg, Germany (Maggetti and Galetti 1980). The curves are steep or lesser inclined, indicating the existence of two sherd populations. Since the chemical compositions of the two populations are identical, the differences in the PSDC can be explained by different granulometry of the raw materials (n = 25).

a given firing temperature and a known chemical or mineralogical composition of two ceramic objects, the differences in porosity data — especially the pore size distribution curves — can be explained by different granulometric composition of the starting materials; fine grained clays have steeper pore size distribution curves (PSDC) than the coarser grained

Marino Maggetti

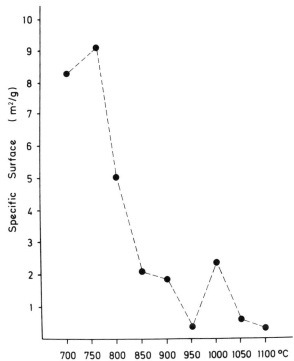

Figure 9. Variation of the specific surface of an illitic calcareous clay with firing temperature. The specific surface generally decreases with increasing firing temperature.

Table 1. Chemical analysis of an illitic calcareous clay (no. LP 142, Maggetti 1981)

SiO_2 (wt %)	55.83	Ba (ppm)	409
TiO_2	0.67	Cr	68
Al_2O_3	16.78	Cu	37
Fe_{tot} as Fe_2O_3	5.63	Ni	74
MnO	0.09	Rb	127
MgO	2.77	Sr	235
CaO	13.53	Zn	98
Na_2O	1.07	Zr	116
K_2O	3.36		
P_2O_5	0.21		
	99.94		

loss by ignition (1100 °C) 13.14 wt. %

ones. This result was used by Maggetti and Schwab (1982) to explain differences in PSDC of Iron Age sherds from the same locality and the same chemical/mineralogical composition as a function of differing granulometry. These differences could be due to differing original clay or to differing treatment of the material before firing (Fig. 8).

A second result of the cited work on kaolinitic clays is the hypothesis that it would be likely that by refiring of pieces of a kaolinitic archaeological object at different temperatures (say 600°, 700°, 800°C, etc.) the porosity changes could be used to find out the original firing temperature. However, this hypothesis has not been tested by experimental refiring of modern samples with known previous firing temperature.

Porosity of Illitic Calcareous Clays

As in the case of the kaolinitic clays (with exceptions; *see* Maggetti and Rossmanith 1981), illitic calcareous clays show considerable porosity changes with increasing firing temperature. These changes are mainly due to sintering phenomena as well as crystallization of new firing minerals. As an example the behavior of the illitic calcareous clay from La Péniche (Switzerland) is shown in Figure 9. The chemical composition is given in Table 1. With increasing fir-

ing temperature the specific surface diminishes and the mean diameter of the pores increases in general, both phenomena being explained by sintering processes leading to a closure of the micropores. The reason why the sample 1000°C does not follow the general trend is not well understood. The open microporosity and the shape of the pore size distribution curves (PSDC) are not much affected by the firing temperature.

The more or less regular decrease of the specific surface and increase of the mean pore radii (Fig. 10) lead to the hypothesis that a refiring of an object with known firing temperature would not change its mean pore size and its specific surface at refiring temperatures below the original firing temperature, but would change it at refiring temperatures higher then the original firing temperature. If this assumption is correct, then the unknown original firing temperature of an ancient object could be inferred by refiring some portions of it and determining at which temperature the mean pore radii increase and the specific surface decreases (with respect to the parameters of the starting material). This temperature should be higher than the original firing temperature. In order to test this hypothesis, experimental refiring of previously heated (800°, 900°, 1000°C) clay samples LP 142 were performed. The refiring temperatures were lower and higher than the original firing temperature, the atmosphere was oxidizing, and the samples were held 1 hour at maximum temperature in an electric furnace. The results are summarized in Table 2 and can be interpreted as follows:

(1) Refiring temperatures below the original firing temperature: The mean pore radius as well as the specific surface are not identical to the one of the start-

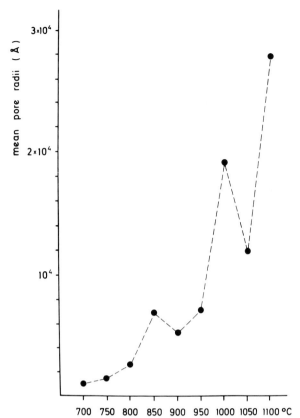

Figure 10. Variation of the radii of the pores of an illitic calcareous clay with firing temperature. A general increase of the pores with increasing firing temperature is to be seen.

Table 2. Refiring of three fired (800°, 900°, 1000°C) illitic calcareous clay samples (LP 142). Specific surface (m²/g) and mean pore radii (Å).

Firing temperature: 800°C

	800	750	800	850	900	950°C
m²/g	5.09	4.47	2.59	1.75	2.10	1.64
Å	2600	2000	2300	4200	3800	3000

Firing temperature: 900°C

	900	800	850	900	950	1000	1050°C
m²/g	1.93	2.78	2.79	2.06	1.99	1.03	0.93
Å	5500	2600	2600	3000	3200	3900	26 '000

Firing temperature: 1000°C

	1000	800	900	950	1000	1050°C
m²/g	2.40	1.78	1.56	1.64	2.45	1.44
Å	19 '000	3600	2900	3100	3000	3600

ing material; they can be higher or lower.

(2) Refiring temperatures above the original firing temperature: Both parameters follow the trend of the LP 142, with exception of the refired 800°C sample.

(3) If the values of the starting material are compared with the ones from the refired specimens, no reliable extrapolation to the original firing temperature can be made based on both parameters.

In conclusion the promising hypothesis is to be abandoned, at least for the studied calcareous illitic clay. It seems that no reliable original firing temperature estimation can be made by refiring experiments and subsequent porosity analyses.

The Influence of Firing Atmosphere

Experimental work on the influence of a reducing atmosphere on porosity data of fired clays is very scarce. Heimann et al. (1980) studied one single calcareous illitic clay: the samples show a strong correlation between apparent weight and open porosity. The apparent weight as well as the mean pore radius increases, and the open porosity decreases with increasing firing temperature. These phenomena are explained by sintering processes which are stronger at higher oxygen fugacities ($fO_2 > 10^{-4}$atm).

Conclusion

The application of porosity data in archaeoceramic research is surely very useful, but must be done with caution, because many factors are involved. At present, more experimental work is urgently needed on kaolinitic, illitic, montmorillonitic (calcareous and noncalcareous clays) in oxidizing and reducing atmosphere. This is the only way to understand and interpret porosity data correctly.

Paste Analysis

In our research, the paste is studied by optical microscopy (polarizing petrographic microscope), differential thermal analysis (DTA), and X-ray diffraction techniques. These methods yield data on texture and mineralogy of the paste which can be interpreted with regard to the origin of the clay, ceramic technique, firing temperatures, firing atmosphere, and burial conditions. Among others, the following authors successfully used paste analysis: Isphording (1974); Isphording and Wilson (1974).

Nature of the Initial Clay

The fact that the ancient potters used differing clays at the same site has been recognized by Maggetti (1979), Nungaesser and Maggetti (1978), and Maggetti and Schwab (1982) by identification of the mineralogical composition of low fired sherds. These sherds can be classified — with respect to the presence or absence of carbonatic minerals — into

Marino Maggetti

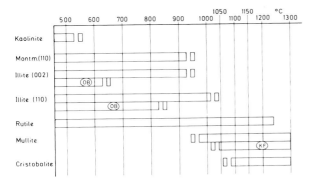

Figure 11. Stability of minerals in five kaolinitic noncalcareous clays during controlled firing; (110) and (002) are selected reflections.

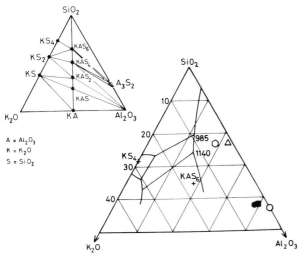

Figure 12. Position of five kaolinitic noncalcareous clays (see Fig. 3) in the SiO₂, K₂O, Al₂O₃ diagram. LEFT: possible subsolidus relations. RIGHT: liquidus relations.

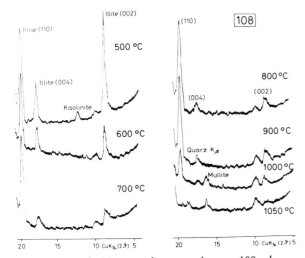

Figure 13. Kaolinitic noncalcareous clay no. 108: changes of intensity of illite basal reflections (002, 004) with increasing firing temperature.

three main groups: *(a)* sherds with carbonatic matrix; *(b)* sherds with silicatic matrix; and *(c)* sherds with carbonatic-silicatic matrix. In these sherds the firing temperatures were estimated not to have exceeded 600°–700°C; so the carbonates and silicates are mostly primary minerals and the differing mineralogical compositions of the pastes are therefore due to the use of marly clays (calcareous clays), moderately calcareous clays, or noncalcareous clays. Additionally, the textural features of these three clays give indications if a starting clay was well or poorly processed (Maggetti 1979).

Firing Temperatures

The firing temperature of an ancient sherd can be estimated by various approaches using the mineralogical changes occurring during a controlled refiring of the sherd itself and comparison of the transformations with the starting materials, or by refiring of an identical clay and comparison of the results obtained on the ancient sherd with those obtained on the clay. The changes in mineralogical composition of various clays dependent on the firing temperature were studied by many workers. An excellent review is given by Grim (1968).

The refiring experiments (Fig. 11) on five *noncalcareous kaolinitic clays* from the Westerwald region (Maggetti and Rossmanith 1981) shows the breakdown of kaolinite between 500°–600°C; the basal reflections of illite are stable up to 900°–1000°C, the (110) reflections to 1000°–1050°C. Rutile is stable up to 1200°C and probably dissolves in the glassy phase at higher temperatures. (Fig. 12). These observations are in good agreement with those of other authors. Kaolinitic clays therefore seem to be not so useful for archaeothermometric purposes since no pronounced mineralogical changes occur between 600°–1000°C. However, if a 2M illite is present, additional information can be gained. As shown by Figure 13, the intensity of the basal reflection of illite decreases with increasing firing temperature; in contrast the (110) reflection is not essentially affected below 900°–950°C. Therefore the ratio (height of the 002-peak/height of the 110-peak) of illite can be used for temperature calibration in the range of 500°–950°C. For the considered clay 108, this ratio is greater than 0.3 for temperatures below 600°C and lies between 0.2–0.1 for temperatures between 600°–950°C. Another ratio can close up the temperature estimation; Figure 14 gives an example for two clays showing the decrease of the ratio (height of the peak 110/half height width of the peak 110) with increasing firing temperatures. It seems plausible that by refiring kaolinitic objects containing 2M illites, a rough estimation of the ancient firing temperature (under

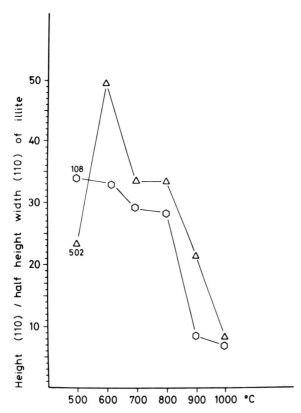

Figure 14. *Kaolinitic noncalcareous clays no. 108 and 502. Variation of the ratio: height of (110)-peak/half height width (110)-peak of illite with firing temperature.*

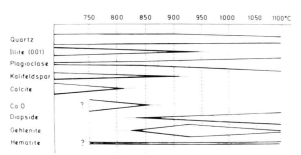

Figure 15. *Mineralogical changes during firing of illitic calcareous clays.*

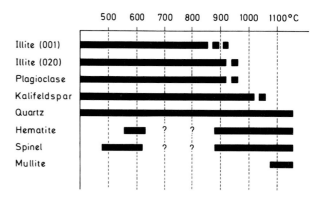

Figure 16. *Mineralogical changes during firing of illitic noncalcareous clays.*

850°–900°C. The so-called gehlenite problem (absence or presence of gehlenite) was studied by Heimann and Maggetti (1981) and Maggetti and Heimann (1979); these studies showed that the absence of the gehlenite phase is due to three possible reasons: *(a)* fine-grained initial clay; *(b)* decomposition of gehlenite to various secondary minerals during the burial stage (especially zeolites and calcite); or *(c)* very high firing temperatures or very long holding at maximum temperatures. It seems that the first point is the controlling factor, but the exact relations to granulometry are still unknown.

The noncalcareous illitic clays do not show so spectacular changes in mineralogy as the calcareous one (Fig. 16) and therefore mineralogical analysis of the paste is not very useful for archaeothermometry.

Firing Atmosphere

Up to now all cited experiments were carried out under oxidizing conditions. But what about mineralogical changes of the matrix in a reducing firing atmosphere? In this context very little information can be found in literature. Heimann and coworkers (1980) have shown that a calcareous illitic clay yields differing paragenesis for differing reducing conditions:

(a) $fO_2 < 10^{-4}$ atm, 1000°C
sanidine + magnetite + ferro-cordierite + biotite + fayalite + quartz + plagioclase
(b) fO_2 10^{-4} to 2.10^{-1} atm , 1000°C
sanidine + magnetite + tridymite + quartz + plagioclase.

Up to now no author has noticed the presence of ferro-cordierite in a black or grayish calcareous illitic sherd. So the assumption suggests itself that the oxy-

oxidizing conditions) is possible.

The firing experiments carried out on *illitic calcareous and noncalcareous clays* yielded very useful information. The calcareous illitic clays are ideal for archaeothermometric purposes because of the important mineralogical transformations during firing. Figure 15 summarizes the experiments of Peters and Jenny (1973); Peters and Iberg (1978); Kuepfer and Maggetti (1978); and Maggetti (1981). It shows that calcite decomposes at 750°–800°C in a natural clay and that calcium-silicates (gehlenite, diopside/wollastonite, plagioclase) appear in the range

Marino Maggetti

gen fugacity of the ancient kilns was greater than 10^{-4} atm. However, much more basic work is needed, because Maggetti et al. (1981) inferred from the coexistence of two Fe-spinels (magnetite$_{ss}$ + hercynite$_{ss}$) in black coatings of campanian sherds that the fO_2 was between 10^{-12} and 10^{-21}! The starting material of these coatings was most probably a very fine grained, noncalcareous, and highly ferrous illitic clay suspension.

Mineralogical Changes during Burial

Fired ceramic bodies are very sensitive to environmental conditions, especially low fired sherds (500°–700°C) which react with invading solutions. The following reaction processes can be listed: extraction of sherd material (dissolution phenomena); deposition of minerals in pores and voids (cementation phenomena); and decomposition of existing primary or firing minerals to secondary minerals. The secondary products are mostly carbonates (calcite), hydrates (hydration of hematite to goethite: Enriquez et al. 1979), hydrosilicates (zeolites, clay minerals), and sulfates (gypsum: Courtois 1976).

Secondary calcite is clearly identifiable if present in high fired products (e.g., terra sigillata which was fired between 900°–1000°C) or in pores (Courtois 1976; Kuepfer and Maggetti 1978). The origin of this calcite can be either completely allochthonous (crystallization directly from invading, carbonatic solutions without contribution of matter from the sherd itself) or partly allochthonous (crystallization of secondary minerals by reaction between existing minerals in the sherd and invading solutions). An example for the latter case is the reaction of gehlenite + solutions to secondary calcite, which was postulated by Kuepfer and Maggetti (1978) for the explanation of the presence of calcite and the absence of gehlenite in high fired terra sigillata sherds. This reaction was successfully performed in experiments by Heimann and Maggetti (1980).

Rehydration of incompletely destroyed clay minerals in low fired sherds is another possible process and was noticed by several authors (Courtois 1973; Noll 1977; Maggetti and Schwab 1982; Nungaesser and Maggetti 1978, 1981). Regarding montmorillonite the secondary nature of this mineral is obvious, since montmorillonite and/or mixed layer minerals containing a smectite phase lose the water layer between the silicate units below 300°C, the sherds having been fired at temperatures of 500°–600°C; however X-ray diffractograms of low fired sherds frequently show a large peak between 5°–10°2θ (for CuK$_\alpha$ radiation) — see Figure 17. In some cases this peak represents mixed-layer phases containing montmorillonite, as detected by the glycolation technique. In other cases,

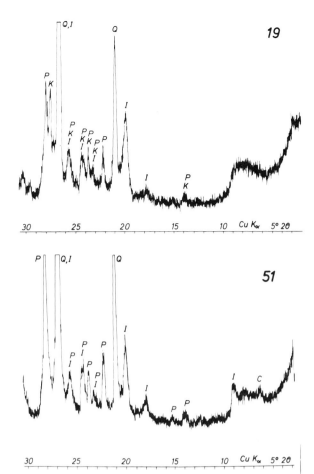

Figure 17. X-ray diffractogram of two neolithic sherds (nos. 19 and 51) from the Burgäschisee, Switzerland (Nungaesser and Maggetti 1978). C = chlorite, I = illite, K = kalifeldspar, P = plagioclase, Q = quartz. The large peak between 5 and 10°2θ is due to rehydration during burial of clay minerals which were partially destroyed by firing.

however, the large peak shows no variation by glycolation but is reduced by firing at 200°–300°C to a single illite peak or split into an illite + chlorite basal peak. It must therefore be assumed that the large peak is caused by the presence of very fine grained clay particles of a mixed layer type (probably chlorite-illite), all particles having different chemical compositions and being poorly crystalline. The disappearance of these large peaks by firing above 300°C is an indication that these mixed layers were formed during burial.

Conclusion

The previous sections have shown how useful paste analysis can be for archaeological questions; however, as in the case for porosity, more basic research on various types of clays with varying firing atmosphere is needed. Only by this approach can the technology of reduced fired gray or black ware be fully understood.

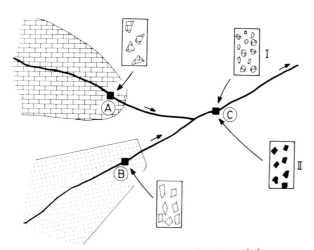

Figure 18. Principle of source localization of the temper fragments by petrographic analysis. [See text for explanation.]

Temper Analysis

The use of temper analysis (by optical microscopy) to identify local or foreign production of a ceramic object is a powerful method especially for coarse grained sherds. Additionally, morphological criteria can be used for technological aspects, e.g., to find out whether or not a certain temper has been added artificially to a clay during processing. In the following section a discussion of these two applications is presented.

Importation or Local Production

The analysis and identification of temper for product localization has been the object of many studies (e.g., Arnold 1972; Aumassip et al. 1969; Frechen 1958; Hays and Hassan 1974; Koehler and Morton 1954; Lais 1957; Maggetti et al. 1979; Maggetti and Galetti 1980; Marro et al. 1979; Nungaesser and Maggetti 1978; Okrusch et al. 1973; Peacock 1967, 1970; Schmid 1966; Slatkine 1972; Stauffer et al. 1979; Williams 1979). The method is based on the assumption that a potter uses local material for tempering his clay. This assumption has been corroborated by ethnological studies. The temper of a local pottery must therefore reflect the geology of the site; an imported vessel can be recognized if it contains a temper not found in the neighborhood. The approach is made in two steps: *(1)* identification of the temper; and *(2)* comparison of the nature of the temper fragments with local geology and subsequent establishment if the temper in the sherd can be from a local source or not.

A schematic explanation is given with the aid of the sketch in Figure 18 which shows two rivers and three archaeological sites (A, B, C). Rectangular diagrams represent schematic thin sections of ceramic objects with schematic temper fragments found at each site. The local geology of site A is dominated by one single rock type, for instance granite. A local potter will use local material for his pottery; the temper will therefore consist of fragments of granite or fragments of mineral derived from weathered granite. If the microscopical analysis of a sherd from station A reveals the presence of granite or granitic minerals, a local production of this object would be highly probable.

The thin section of the ceramic ware from site B contains temper fragments of material (say limestone) found at or in the vicinity of the station. Here, too, a local production is probable based on the possible derivation of the temper fragments from local rocks. At the station C, two sherds were analyzed. The sherd number I contains temper fragments of granite and limestone, whose outcrops are found upstream; fluvial transport has rounded these fragments and reduced their grain size. The temper of this sherd can easily be explained by the local geology. The ceramic body could therefore be of local production. In contrast, the sherd number II has rock fragments (e.g., basalt) as characteristic temper which are not to be found in the local or upstream geology. This sherd cannot have been produced locally and must therefore be imported. A local production of the ceramic with use of imported temper is theoretically possible, but has not been recorded by ethnological research work until now.

Artificial Temper

Adding artificial temper is a common practice among ancient potters. An artificial temper can readily be identified in the following cases:

(1) Calcite fragments. The presence of fresh rhomboedric calcite crush fragments with angular, sharp outlines is possible only if the ancient potters used crushed calcite; naturally present calcite would be very fine grained owing to the splitting behavior of calcite and would also have rounded edges because of transport by water during the deposition of the clay.

(2) Fired brick. Fired brick, too, is an indication of artificially added temper and can be recognized — with respect to the embedding sherd — by differing color, mineralogical composition, or texture (Maggetti 1979).

(3) Organic material. Addition of straw, etc., was also frequently used by ancient potters and can be identified by the presence of an abnormally high and coarse porosity and/or relicts of the organic matter, often as black carbonaceous substance.

Marino Maggetti

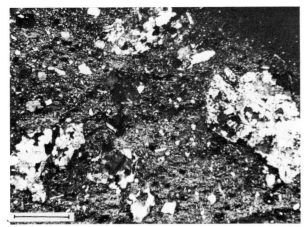

Figure 19. Angular gneissic temper fragments in a thin section of a Bronze Age sherd from Montlingerberg, Switzerland (Marro 1978; Marro et al. 1979). Sample Me 24, crossed polars, bar = 1 mm.

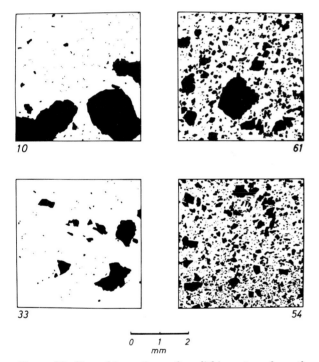

Figure 20. Four thin sections of neolithic pottery from the Burgäschisee, Switzerland. The nos. 10, 33, and 61 show — with respect to the grain size of the temper fragments — two populations, a fine grained one and a coarse grained, the latter having sharp edges and representing therefore crushed rock fragments. These fragments were added artificially to a natural fine grained temper.

(4) Shape of the fragments. Angular fragments with sharp edges are often an indication that crushed material has been used (Marro 1978); see Figure 19. However, regarding finer grained particles the naturally present quartz grains in some alpine clays have angular shapes, too! This is due to the fact that a short distance of transport does not allow a rounding of the grains.

(5) Granulometry. The presence of two populations of grain sizes (the so-called hiatal structure) is also an indication that the coarser particles were added artificially (Figure 20; Nungaesser and Maggetti 1978).

Conclusion

Chemical analysis is a very powerful method for identifying the origin of an ancient object, but it must not be forgotten that the actually analyzed chemical data are a function of many processes affecting the chemistry of the original clay (e.g., processing, tempering, firing, use, burial, cleaning of the object). These aspects can be elucidated by the phase analysis based on the identification of the mineralogical nature of temper and paste, their texture, the porosity, and other physical parameters. The phase analysis can be used, too, for localization in suitable cases, as for coarse ceramics. But the most important application is the elucidation of ancient technology. Actually, the method suffers some severe limitations, since fundamental basic research is still lacking. Much more work on typical, widely used clays (calcareous and noncalcareous illitic, montmorillonitic, kaolinitic clays with varying granulometry) at different firing temperatures and atmospheres is needed urgently. Only then can the technology of, for instance, the "reduced" grayish and black ware be understood.

Acknowledgments: The author thanks A. D. Franklin and B. Stoeckhert for revising the English text, and J. Charrière and A. Jornet for the drawings, as well as the whole staff of the Mineralogical and Petrographical Institute of the University of Fribourg for their help. The participation at this symposium was partly financed by a grant of the Swiss National Foundation (1.844-0.78). Thanks are due also to G. Piller for her helpful typing of the manuscript.

References

Arnold, D. E. 1972. Mineralogical analyses of ceramic materials from Quinua, Department of Ayacucho, Peru. *Archaeometry* 14, 1:93–102.

Aumassip, G.; Marmier, F.; and Trecolle, G. 1969. Dégraissants et forme des poteries. *Libyca A.P.E.* 17: 267–69.

Beckmann, B.; Strunk-Lichtenberg, G.; and Heide, H. 1971. Die frühe Siegburger Keramik und ihre Entwicklung zum Steinzeug. Naturwissenschaftliche Analysen zur Geschichte der mittelalterlichen Keramik. *Keramische Zeitschrift* 23: 656–59.

Cabotse, Jean. 1964. Essai d'application d'un test physique à l'étude de la céramique antique. *Revue archéologique de l'Est et du Centre-Est*, 358–67.

Courtois, L. C. 1973. Phénomènes de "régénération" après cuisson de certaines céramiques anciennes. *Comptes Rendus de l'Académie des Sciences*, Paris. Série D, 276: 2931–33.

_____. 1976. Examen au microscope pétrographique des céramiques archéologiques. *Notes et Monographies Techniques*, no. 8. Centre de recherches archéologiques.

Enriquez, C. R.; Danon, J.; and Beltrao, M. 1979. Differential thermal analysis of some amazonian archaeological pottery. *Archaeometry* 21, 2: 183–86.

Farnsworth, M. 1964. Greek pottery: a mineralogical study. *American Journal of Archaeology* 68: 221–28.

Frechen, J. 1958. Die petrographische Untersuchung der Keramik. In K. Böhner, *Die fränkischen Altertümer des Trierer Landes*, 63–68.

_____. 1972. Petrographische Untersuchungen an römischer Keramik aus Neuss. In Filtzinger, P., ed., *Die röm. Keramik aus dem Militärbereich von Novaesium*. Novaesium V = Limesforschungen Bd. 11: 41–45.

Grim, Ralph E. 1968. *Clay mineralogy.* 2d ed. New York: McGraw Hill.

Hays, T. R., and Hassan, F. A. 1974. Mineralogical analysis of Sudanese neolithic ceramics. *Archaeometry* 16, 1: 71–79.

Heimann, R. 1976. Moderne Poren- und Gefügeuntersuchungen an Keramik. *Informationsblätter zu Nachbarwissenschaften*, Petrographie 7.2: 1–2; 16.

_____. 1977. Korrelation von Porenkenngrössen und chemischer Zusammensetzung von Provinzialrömischer Keramik. In Hennicke, H. W., ed., *Mineralische Rohstoffe als kulturhistorische Informationsquelle*: 234–48. Hagen: Verlag des Vereins Deutscher Emailfachleute.

_____. 1978/79. Mineralogische Vorgänge beim Brennen von Keramik und Archaeothermometrie. *Acta Praehistorica et Archaeologica* 9/10: 79–102.

_____; Maggetti, M.; and Einfalt, H. C. 1980. Zum Verhalten des Eisens beim Brennen eines kalkhaltigen illitischen Tones unter reduzierenden Bedingungen. *Berichte der Deutschen Keramischen Gesellschaft* 57, 6–8: 145–52.

_____, and Maggetti, M. 1981. Experiments on simulated burial of calcareous terra sigillata (mineralogical changes). *British Museum Occasional Paper*, 19: 163–77.

Isphording, W. C. 1974. Combined thermal and X-ray diffraction technique for identification of ceramicware temper and paste minerals. *American Antiquity* 39: 477–83.

_____, and Wilson, E. M. 1974. The relationship of "volcanic ash," SAK LU'UM, and palygorskite in northern Yucatan Maya ceramics. *American Antiquity* 39, 3: 483–88.

Koehler, A., and Morton, F. 1954. Mineralogische Untersuchung prähistorischer Keramik aus Hallstatt im Zusammenhang mit der Frage nach ihrer Herkunft. *Germania* 32: 66–72.

Kuepfer, T., and Maggetti, M. 1978. Die Terra Sigillata von La Péniche (Vidy/Lausanne). *Schweizerische Mineralogische und Petrographische Mitteilungen* 58: 189–212.

Lais, R. 1957. Ein keramischer Brauch im Breisgau des frühen Mittelalters. *Schau-ins-Land* 75: 157–66. Freiburg im Breisgau: Jahresheft des Breisgau-Geschichtsvereins.

Maggetti, Marino. 1979. Mineralogisch-petrographische Untersuchung des Scherbenmaterials der urnenfelderzeitlichen Siedlung Elchinger Kreuz, Landkreis Neu-Ulm/Donau. München: *Kataloge der Prähistorischen Staatssammlung* 19: 141–67.

_____, and Heimann, R. 1979. Bildung und Stabilität von Gehlenit in römischer Feinkeramik. *Schweizerische Mineralogische und Petrographische Mitteilungen*, 59, 3: 413–17.

_____; Marro, C.; and Perini, R. 1979. Risultati delle analisi mineralogiche-petrografiche della ceramica "Luco." *Studi trentini di scienze storiche LVIII* 1: 3–19.

_____. 1981. Composition of Roman pottery from Lausanne (Switzerland). *British Museum Occasional Paper*, 19: 33–49.

_____, and Galetti, G. 1980. Composition of Iron Age fine ceramics from Châtillon-s-Glâne (Kanton Fribourg, Switzerland) and the Heuneburg (Kr. Sigmaringen, West Germany). *Journal of Archaeological Science* 7: 87–91.

_____, and Kahr, G. 1980. Homogenität archäologischer keramischer Objekte: Teil I. Porosität und Porenradienverteilung. *Archäologie und Naturwissenschaften* 2: 1–20.

_____, and Rossmanith, M. 1981. Archaeothermometry of kaolinitic clays. *Revue d'Archéometrie*, III: 185–94.

_____, and Schwab, H. 1982. Iron Age fine pottery from Châtillon-s-Glâne and the Heuneburg. *Archaeometry*, 24, 1: 21–36.

_____; Galetti, G.; Schwander, H.; Picon, M.; and Wessicken, R. 1981. Campanian pottery: the nature of black coatings. *Archaeometry*, 23, 2: 199–208.

Marino Maggetti

Marro, Christian. 1978. Recherches en archéocéramiques. Diplomarbeit, Universität Fribourg.

_____; Maggetti, M.; Stauffer, L.; and Primas, M. 1979. Mineralogisch-petrographische Untersuchungen an Laugener Keramik — ein Beitrag zum Keramikimport im alpinen Raum. *Archäologisches Korrespondenzblatt* 9, 4: 393-400.

Noll, W. 1977. Hallstattzeitliche Keramik der Heuneburg an der oberen Donau. *Archäologie und Naturwissenschaften* 1: 1-19.

Nungaesser, Wolfgang, and Maggetti, Marino. 1978. Mineralogisch-petrographische Untersuchung der neolithischen Töpferware vom Burgäschisee. *Bulletin Société Fribourgeoise des Sciences Naturelles* 67, 2: 152-73.

_____, and Maggetti, Marino. 1981. Etude minéralogique et petrographique de la poterie néolithique du Burgäschisee (suisse). *Revue d'Archéométrie*, III: 225-26.

Okrusch, M.; Strunk-Lichtenberg, G.; and Gabriel, B. 1973. Vorgeschichtliche Keramik aus dem Tibesti (Sahara). I. Das Rohmaterial. *Berichte der Deutschen Keramischen Gesellschaft* 50, 8: 261-67.

Peacock, D. P. S. 1967. The heavy mineral analysis of pottery: a preliminary report. *Archaeometry* 10: 97-100.

_____. 1970. The scientific analysis of ancient ceramics: a review. *World Archaeology* 1: 375-89.

Peters, T., and Jenny, J. P. 1973. Mineralogische Untersuchungen über das Brennverhalten von Ziegeltonen. *Beiträge zur Geologie der Schweiz*, Geotechnische Serie, 50: 1-59.

_____, and Iberg, R. 1978. Mineralogical changes during firing of calcium-rich brick clays. *American Ceramic Society Bulletin* 57, 5: 503-506.

Rottlaender, R., and Schröter, R. 1973. Magerungseffekte an Schussenrieder Gefässen von Riedschachen. *Archaeologisches Korrespondenzblatt* 3, 5: 177-79.

Rye, O. S. 1976. Keeping your temper under control: Materials and the manufacture of Papuan pottery. *Archaeological and Physical Anthropology in Oceania* XI, 2: 106-137.

Sanders, H. P. 1973. Pore-size distribution determinations in Neolithic, Iron Age, Roman and other pottery. *Archaeometry* 15, 1: 159-61.

Schmid, Elisabeth. 1966. Ton und Magerung urgeschichtlicher Keramik vom Schönberg, Gemeinde Ebringen, Landkreis Freiburg. *Mitteilungen des badischen Landesvereins für Naturkunde und Naturschutz*, new series 9, 2: 325-28.

Shepard, A. O. 1968. *Ceramics for the archaeologist*. 5th ed. Washington, D.C.: Carnegie Institution.

Slatkine, A. 1972. Comparative petrographic study of ancient pottery sherds from Israel. *Museum Haaretz Yearbook* 15/16: 101-111.

Stauffer, L.; Maggetti, M.; and Marro, C. 1979. Formenwandel und Produktion der alpinen Laugener Keramik. *Archäologie der Schweiz* 2: 130-37.

Strunk-Lichtenberg, G.; Gabriel, B.; and Okrusch, M. 1973. Vorgeschichtliche Keramik aus dem Tibesti (Sahara). II. Technologischer Entwicklungsstand. *Berichte der Deutschen Keramischen Gesellschaft* 50, 8: 294-99.

Williams, D. F. 1979. Petrological analysis of some mica-dusted and "London ware" pottery. In Shelton, H., ed., *Excavations in Southwark, 1972-1974*, forthcoming.

12. The Proton Probe as a Tool in the Elemental Analyses of Archaeological Artifacts

C. P. Swann
Bartol Research Foundation of the Franklin Institute
University of Delaware

Abstract

A proton probe system for elemental analysis has been used in preliminary studies of archaeological copper-based alloys, glasses, and potsherds. Protons generated in a 2 MeV Van de Graaff accelerator and passed into the atmosphere through a pinhole were used to induce the characteristic X-rays for elements from Na to Pb. For the lighter elements a helium atmosphere with no X-ray filter was used, whereas for the heavier elements air or nitrogen with a combination of selective filters was used. This technique is essentially nondestructive, is primarily a surface analyzer, and allows for mapping of the elements. Selected samples from Egypt, Jordan, and Crete were studied to demonstrate the feasibility of the method.

Introduction

The use of proton induced X-rays (PIXE) for the study of archaeological artifacts began with the work of Folkman (1975) and Ahlbert et al. (1976). Since then a number of other reports have appeared, the most recent being those of Fleming and Crowfoot-Payne (1979) on Egyptian bronzes, Duerden et al. (1979) on obsidians from the Pacific region, and Betancourt et al. (1979) on Vasilike ware. All of these studies were performed with the sample in vacuum with the spatial resolution being defined by the beam size. The system being discussed in this report makes use of an external beam generated by passing the protons through a pinhole. The advantages of such a technique have been discussed by Grodzins et al. (1975) and later by Cookson (1979). It is not, however, the intent to claim that this method is better than or even a substitute for other methods of analysis. All systems have their own advantages and disadvantages but all should be considered complementary.

The importance of knowing the elemental composition of archaeological artifacts is basic. The amount of Zn, As, Sn, Pb, and other elements in copper-based alloys says much about the period of time: the culture, the technology, and the foreign relations. Obviously, all of these require a dating technique which is only indirectly arrived at through the chemistry. Similar comments can be made concerning glasses and pottery in which the development of pigments or colorants for surface patterns relates to the period of time.

The remainder of this report is divided into two parts. The first deals with the technique itself and gives a description of the Bartol-Delaware proton probe. In the second section some results for archaeological artifacts are given. Needless to say, this technique has been and is being used in many other

135

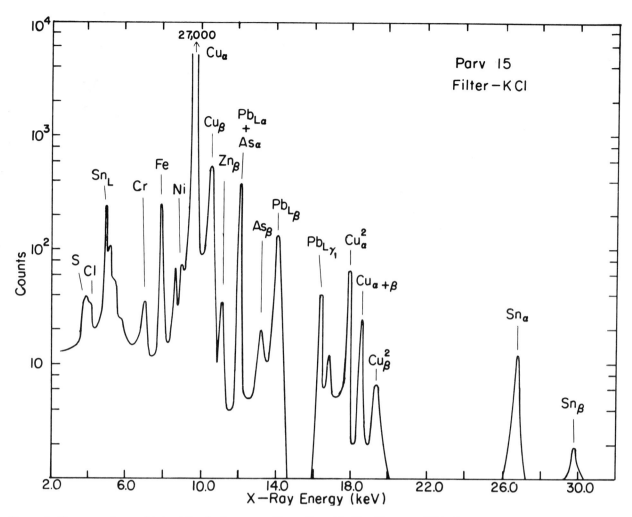

Figure 1. X-ray spectrum obtained for the bronze artifact, Parv 15. The filter was KCl; the environment, air; and the proton energy, 2.0 MeV. Note the pile-up peaks labeled Cu_α^2, $Cu_{\alpha+\beta}$, and Cu_β^2. All lines are K lines unless indicated as L lines.

disciplines. Here at the Bartol-Delaware additional investigations are being pursued in the fields of geology, marine biology, surface physics, and environmental sciences.

Proton Probe

There are many reports in the literature describing the various types of ion probe systems. That of Cookson (1979) is probably the most comprehensive and includes a very thorough list of references. The Bartol-Delaware microprobe itself has been described elsewhere (Fou et al. 1979; Van Patter et al. 1980). For the purposes of this paper only a brief description will be given with the emphasis on aspects important to the present studies.

The source of exciting protons is the Delaware TN200 Van de Graaff accelerator which can provide protons with energies up to 2.5 MeV. For the present work the two energies of 1.3 and 2.0 MeV have been

used; the reasons for two separate energies are given below.

The beam transport consists of initial steering into the magnetic analyzer system followed by a pair of magnetic quadrupoles for focusing the beam into the final stage of the probe. This stage consists of a 0.5 mm aperture, a 1.25 mm antiscattering aperture, and a graphite tip through which a small hole has been drilled; a 7.5 mm Kapton film serves as the vacuum-atmosphere interface. The effect of this film on proton beam scattering is negligible for the hole size used in these experiments of approximately 0.45 mm. Of course, much smaller hole sizes are possible but for the studies described herein such fine spatial resolution is not required. However, the effect of the atmosphere cannot be neglected. The range of 2 MeV protons in air is about 5 cm and the scatter over this range is significant. To minimize the energy loss and the scattering, the distance between the Kapton film

C. P. Swann

and the sample under study is kept to within a few mm. Within the sample itself the proton range is very limited, the effective depth for an average medium being only 10 to 15 μm for 2 MeV protons. Consequently only the surface of the sample is analyzed.

The characteristic X-rays induced by the proton bombardment are observed in a Si (Li) detector with an area of 30 mm^2 and an active depth of 3 mm. In order to get the optimum efficiency the diode must be cooled to liquid nitrogen temperature which, of course, requires that the system be in vacuum. A 7 μm Be window acts as the vacuum/atmosphere interface. This window in itself, because of absorption, limits the observable X-rays to those from sodium.

The electronics of the detector system is quite standard and has a measured energy resolution of 160 eV (FWHM) at 5.89 keV with a 10 μsec pulse-shaping time. The sample itself is attached to a pair of precision translational stages with 50 mm, 100-turn micrometer heads. The horizontal stage is driven by a stepping motor in 2.5 μm steps whereas the vertical stage is hand operated. This arrangement allows one to average over a limited region or, by appropriate storage, to scan a region for mapping.

As pointed out above, two separate conditions were established in obtaining the data. First, measurements were made in a helium atmosphere with a proton energy of 1.3 MeV. This lower energy favors the low energy X-rays, i.e., the low Z elements, and the helium atmosphere allows for the observation of Na and Mg. Second, measurements were made in air or a nitrogen atmosphere with different combinations of filters between the sample and the detector; the proton energy was 2.0 MeV. The purpose of the filters is to reduce, selectively, the effect of the most prominent low energy X-rays. Consequently, a significantly higher beam current can be used without introducing serious problems resulting from high counting rates. The major effect, of course, is pile-up of the intense X-rays. Pile-up results when two X-rays impinge upon the detector within the resolving time of the electronics; this looks like a pulse with an energy equal to the sum of the two incident X-rays. Figure 1 shows a spectra obtained using a KCl filter in which pile-up effects are very clear. Figure 2 demonstrates the benefit of using two selective filters, Co (15 mg/cm^2) followed by V (7.5 mg/cm^2). The Co acts on the strong Cu lines and the V acts in the resultant fluorescent Co lines. A Cr filter would be preferable but was not available. The large enhancement of the Ag, Sn, and Sb lines is obvious. Typical times for obtaining this data were 10 to 20 minutes.

Of course, it must be realized that the end results desired are actual percentages of the elements observed in the material under study. One method for accomplishing this is to measure the cross sections for excitation. However, this requires a precise knowledge of the proton beam current striking the sample, the effective depth of penetration, and the absorption of the emitted X-rays. Resolving the first of these is very difficult. Only a fraction of the beam hitting the graphite tip passes through the hole, and a measurement of the beam intensity passing through this pinhole is complicated because of the ionization of the surrounding medium. Consequently, we have gone the route of using "standards." These "standards" are prepared as close in composition to the material under study as reasonably possible in order to allow for the absorption of the incident protons and the outgoing X-rays. Some of these "standards" are obtained commercially; others are prepared in the laboratory.

It is quite clear from the above discussion that the proton probe has the distinct advantage of allowing one to deal with almost any size sample and to study any particular surface region of interest. Furthermore, no sample preparation is required beyond simple cleaning and any possible damage is negligible. Some radioactivity can be induced at 2 MeV but for the beam currents used of the order of nano-amperes the radioactivity would be minimal. It is true, of course, that the chemical form is not determined by this method. In some cases the chemical form is obvious but for other cases other techniques must be applied.

Some Experimental Results

Copper-based Alloys

These studies are a preview of a more extensive investigation which will hopefully be undertaken in collaboration with Drs. S. Fleming and V. Pigott of Museum Applied Science Center for Archaeology (MASCA), University Museum, University of Pennsylvania. Of the number of examples of Cu-based alloys we have selected two for this report. The first (Tut) is a sliver of near-pure Cu from the tomb of Tutankhamun, Luxor, Valley of the Kings in Egypt (ca. 14th century B.C.). The second sample (Parv) is a fragment of a Parvati Shiva from southern India; the date of this sample is unknown.

The importance of these studies lies in the early development of bronzes and brasses. By observing the trend in the use of Pb, Sn, and Zn one can chronologically determine the transition from bronzes to brasses and can also establish the flow of technology from one geographic region to another. An additional important aspect behind such elemental analyses is the determination of the authenticity of early bronze and brass castings.

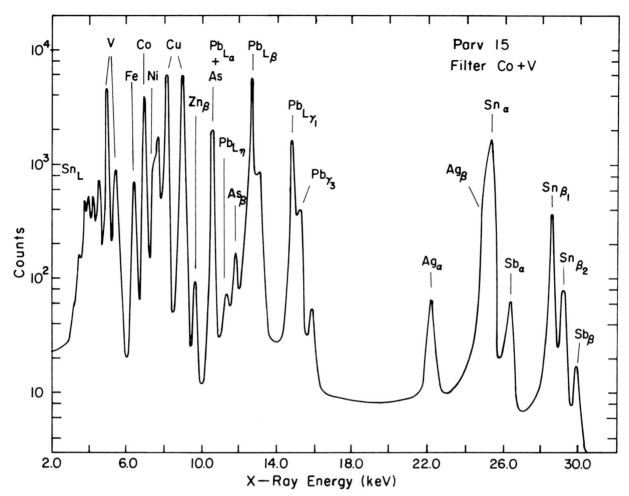

Figure 2. X-ray spectrum obtained for Parv 15 using a double filter of Co followed by V. Note the absence of the pile-up peaks and the much intensified Ag, Sn, and Sb K lines. [See text for other details.]

The data for the two castings examined in the present measurements were obtained using a Co filter followed by a V filter with a proton energy of 2 MeV. The significance of this double filter was given earlier in this report and Figure 2 shows the spectrum obtained for Parv. Certain elements of these copper-based alloys are difficult to observe by the proton probe method because of the intense Cu K$_\alpha$ line and the possibility of strong L lines from Ag and Sn. The former tends to block out the Co and Zn lines and the latter conceals the K and Ca lines. A measurement using a helium atmosphere and a lower proton energy would help but this has not been tried as yet. The absolute values were obtained by comparison with metal standards.

The results for these measurements are given in Table 1. Also given are previous published results for one of the samples, Tut (Coghlin 1975). The Tut sample is indeed quite pure Cu although our results show more elements present especially in the lighter element region. Otherwise the two sets of data compare favorably. The interesting feature of the Parv data is the low Zn content; whereas the amount of Pb and Sn is rather normal. Consequently, the dating of this specimen will have to await further studies.

It should be pointed out that to determine the origin of a particular sample of copper-based alloys is complicated by the possible variations in composition of the raw materials. As will be seen for the case of sherds of pottery, statistical variations are possible, and it is likely that such effects would appear in Cu-based alloys as well. Of course, this depends on the artisans and the care with which they carried out their processing.

Glass Beads

These studies were undertaken in collaboration with Drs. S. Fleming and P. McGovern of MASCA as part of a more concerted future investigation. The beads analyzed are from the Umin ad-Dananir of the northwestern Bagcah Valley, ca. 20 km northwest of Amman, Jordan, and were discovered in burial caves

C. P. Swann

Table 1. Elemental composition in percent by weight of copper-based alloys

Element[a]	Tut[b]	Tut[c]	Parv[d]
Al	nd	nd	1.82
Si	0.08	nd	1.46
S	0.11	nd	0.51
Cl	0.04	nd	0.79
Ti	nd	nd	0.38
Cr	0.03	nd	0.55
Mn	0.01	nd	0.01
Fe	0.11	~0.05	0.39
Co	nd	0.003	nd
Ni	0.15	0.02	0.07
Cu	97.6	99	77.8
Zn	nd	nd	0.70
As	0.13	0.1	0.35
Pb	nd	0.01	7.42
Bi	nd	0.0004	0.20
Ag	nd	0.001	0.20
Sn	1.80	>0.5	7.42
Sb	nd	0.003	0.19

[a]Over-all errors for present results range from 10 to 50% depending on element and level of effect.
[b]Present data — a sliver of near-pure copper from Tut's tomb.
[c](Coghlin 1975) — same material as in [b].
[d]Present data — a fragment from a Parvati Shiva provided by Spinks of London.

of the Late Bronze Age (LBA). Since the LBA is very poorly represented in Transjordan at this time, these artifacts are potentially important towards understanding the cultural level and foreign relations, particularly with Egypt, of the period. These beads compare well with New Kingdom Egyptian beads and were either produced locally under the stimulus of Egyptian traditions or imported. Since the Egyptians were most involved in pigment experimentation during this era, one important question is the extent to which Egyptian political control may have influenced similar developments in Syria-Palestine. All beads can be dated to LB1 (ca. 1550–1400 B.C.). Another interesting point is that these beads represent some of the earliest glass developed in Transjordan; in this regard it should be noted that glass was first produced in northern Mesopotamia (ca. 1600 B.C.).

Examples of seven beads were analyzed. Two sets of measurements were made, one in a helium atmosphere with no filter and at a proton energy of 1.3 MeV, the other in air with a double filter of Al (5

Table 2. Description of beads from Bagcah Valley (Jordan) and Beth Shan (West Bank)

Registration No.[a]	Description
B77, A2, 3	Bead. Beck type XXIII.A.2.a (fluted spheroid), I.B.1.b (circular short barrel) — small, VIa. Gray glass. P. 77–18–1.
B77, A2, 33	Bead. Beck type I.A.1.a (circular oblate disc), VIa. Gray and white variegated glazed faience. P. 77–18–20.
B77, A2, 50	Bead. Beck type I.B.1.a (circular oblate) — small, VIa. Mottled green, white, and pink glass. P. 77–18–31.
B77, A2, 56	Bead. Beck type I.A.1.a (circular oblate disc), VIa. Red glass. P. 77–18–36.
B77, A2, 61	Bead. Beck type XLVI.A.7.a (stratified flush eye well-separated), I.B.1.a (circular oblate) — small, VIa. Mottled white and yellow eyes in greenish white glass matrix. P. 77–81–41.
B77, A2, 102	Bead. Beck type XXIII.A.2.a (fluted spheroid), I.B.1.a (circular oblate) — small, VIa. "Egyptian Blue." P. 77–18–68.
B77, A2, 137	Bead. Beck type XLVI.A.d (flush crumbs), I.C.1.a (circular circular) — large, VIa. Black and gray variegated glass with yellow, gray, and white spots. P. 77–18–95.
27–10–296 (Beth Shan) Level VII, Locus 1251	Fragment of "Egyptian Blue" chunk, probably from workshop.

[a]B77 refers to cave excavation (1977); Cave A2. P. number refers to Pennsylvania University Museum numbers.

mg/cm2) and V. For this latter case the Al acts to reduce the intense Si K-x-ray and the V acts likewise on the moderately strong Fe K-x-rays. For the cases of beads no. 61 and no. 137 on the surfaces of which yellow design eyes were apparent, measurements were made at the location of the yellow eyes and on the white fabric. For the remaining beads the color was uniform and, consequently, only one location

Table 3. Elemental analysis of glass beads (percent by weight) described in Table 2

Element[a]	Egyptian Blue	#61 White	#61 Yellow	#137 White	#137 Yellow	#3	#50	#56	#33	#102
Mg	0.99	2.22	1.63	2.16	2.00	1.08	2.29	0.81	0.82	0.73
Al	2.62	13.8	6.81	7.79	7.52	6.40	4.91	4.19	4.05	5.66
Si	57.7	62.2	45.8	76.18	70.50	76.98	81.04	51.90	79.17	52.15
S	0.29	0.84	0.91	0.31	0.40	0.51	0.42	0.14	0.27	0.09
Cl	0.13	0.13	0.21	0.51	0.88	1.44	0.29	0.33	0.24	0.06
K	1.22	0.51	0.40	—	0.57	3.14	0.41	0.58	0.95	0.58
Ca	19.3	11.3	6.81	8.11	7.55	4.67	5.46	8.30	2.72	15.45
Ti	—	0.50	—	0.40	0.49	—	0.30	0.18	0.34	0.38
Cr	1.42	—	—	0.31	0.48	—	—	—	—	0.53
Mu	—	2.61	0.62	1.41	0.75	2.12	—	—	2.82	0.46
Fe	0.79	3.17	1.92	1.89	2.58	0.71	3.11	30.59	1.90	2.50
Ni	—	—	—	0.01	0.03	0.10	0.04	0.03	0.45	—
Cu	11.0	1.43	0.22	0.12	1.36	2.59	0.37	1.14	4.79	20.66
Zn	—	0.02	0.02	0.03	0.04	0.19	0.08	0.07	0.37	0.11
Ga	—	0.02	0.09	—	—	—	—	—	—	—
Pb	0.05	1.57	7.13	0.04	1.13	0.03	0.46	0.47	0.08	—
Br	—	—	—	—	—	0.01	—	—	0.01	—
Rb	—	—	—	0.01	—	0.01	0.01	—	0.03	—
Sr	0.13	0.15	0.08	0.03	0.04	0.02	0.06	0.55	0.08	0.46
Zr	—	—	—	0.03	0.04	—	0.04	—	—	0.12
Sn	4.46	—	—	—	—	—	—	—	0.90	—
Sb	—	—	27.3	0.67	3.63	—	0.74	0.74	—	—

[a]Over-all errors range from 10 to 40% depending on the element and the level detected.

was examined. In all cases an area of about 1.25 mm² was scanned. For calibration purposes a "standard" prepared in our laboratory was used.

Descriptions of the seven beads studied are given in Table 2 and the elemental analyses are given in Table 3. Also shown is an analysis of a piece of Egyptian Blue. The Beck type refers to the standard publication on bead typology (Beck 1927). From a quick review of the data one can suggest which colorants were used in preparing the glasses: the yellow of the eyes of no. 61 and no. 137 are from an Sb compound, the red of no. 56 is an Fe compound, and the blue of no. 102 is from a Cu compound. Beyond this not much can be concluded at this time. More samples will have to be studied in order to obtain statistically meaningful results.

Sherds of Pottery from Gournia

This report on the elemental analysis of white-painted pottery of Early Minoan III (ca. 2200–1950 B.C.) is part of an interdisciplinary project under the direction of Prof. Philip Betancourt of Temple University. This phase of the investigation is being performed in collaboration with Prof. T. K. Gaisser also of the Bartol Research Foundation and is the outgrowth of feasibility studies made previously (Betancourt et al. 1979). Professor Betancourt has already reported on many aspects of the over-all project, but for the purposes of orientation a few brief comments are in order.

The thirty-one sherds examined are from Gournia, a settlement in eastern Crete. This region is regarded as the type-site for this pottery because of the large quantity found there in good stratigraphically datable context. A study of this white-painted ware is a very good indicator of the formative stages of Minoan art and culture. This in turn is important since the Minoan culture of this period greatly influenced the early Greek civilization of North Aegean.

The two sets of measurements at three different locations on each of the thirty-one sherds were per-

C. P. Swann

Table 4. Average composition of 31 pottery sherds from Gournia

Element[+]	Edge		White		Glaze	
	Mean	SD*	Mean	SD*	Mean	SD*
Na[a]	1.9	0.8	1.5	0.6	1.8	0.6
Mg[b]	11	2	8.5	4	7.3	1.3
Al[c]	22	2	26	4	32	4
Si[d]	39	4	36	5	33	4
S	0.5	1.4	1.6	3.4	1.3	1.8
Cl	0.17	0.18	0.23	0.32	0.18	0.18
K[e]	2.3	0.5	2.0	0.8	3.4	1
Ca[f]	11.9	4	13.2	6	8.3	3.5
Ti	0.50	0.13	0.54	0.10	0.58	0.11
Cr	0.48	0.22	0.48	0.21	0.26	0.15
Mn	0.22	0.08	0.18	0.10	0.19	0.16
Fe[g]	9.8	3	9.6	2	12	2
Ni	0.054	0.023	0.028	0.01	0.035	0.009
Cu	0.013	0.009	0.013	0.008	0.011	0.006
Zn	0.016	0.008	0.04	0.019	0.046	0.014
As	0.002	0.007	0.003	0.006	0.003	0.007
Pb	0.007	0.019	0.022	0.023	0.023	0.027
Rb	0.020	0.013	0.018	0.010	0.028	0.012
Sr	0.045	0.025	0.048	0.015	0.039	0.014
Y	0.008	0.016	0.010	0.006	0.012	0.01
Zr	0.045	0.026	0.069	0.05	0.057	0.02

[a]percent by weight as Na_2O.
[b]% by weight as MgO.
[c]% by wt. as Al_2O_3.
[d]% by wt. as SiO_2.
[e]% by wt. as K_2O.
[f]% by wt. as CaO.
[g]% by wt. as Fe_2O_3.
*SD = standard (r.m.s.) deviation.
+ elemental % by weight unless noted.

formed. The locations were on the fabric at a fresh break, on the white-painted decoration, and on the glaze. The first set of measurements was made in a helium atmosphere with no filter and at a proton energy of 1.3 MeV, while the second set was made in air with a double filter of V and Al as for the case of the glasses. In all, twenty-one elements were observed. In accumulating the data an area of about 1.25 mm[2] was scanned.

Table 4 is a summary of the average concentrations and corresponding dispersions for twenty-one elements detected. The results are quoted as percentages by weight. In the case of some of the light elements the percentages refer to an assumed chemical form, as noted; for example, it is assumed that Al appears as Al_2O_3. These assumptions were made for consistency with the form in which concentrations of elements in standard geological samples are presented (Flanagan 1969). The dispersion is measured by the standard deviation (S.D.). [Recall that the standard deviation is defined as the square root of the mean of the squared deviations from the average value.] The error in determining the concentration of an element in a particular sample is negligible compared to the S.D. of the results for all samples.

Inspection of Table 4 shows some systematic effects: (1) Mg and Ni are depleted in both surface areas, the white and the glaze, compared to the fabric (edge), whereas Zn, As, and Pb are enhanced on the surface. The concentration of aluminum increases from edge to white to glaze. (2) There is also a group of elements with similar concentration in fabric and in the white paint but with differing concentrations in the glaze. The elements K, Fe, and possibly Rb are enhanced in the glaze, whereas Ca and Cr are depleted.

The trends for a few of the elements are illustrated pictorially in the set of histograms, Figures 3–5. It should be noted also, for example, that the results for concentration of Zn on the surfaces show much greater scatter than for the fabric.

A search has been made through the data to find samples that appear to be anomalous in some way. Four sherds stand out from the rest. (The number refers to the Pennsylvania Museum cataloging.)

MS 4615–39 This sample has a very high concentration of Pb on edge, white and glaze: about 15 times above average in the fabric and 6 times higher than average in the glaze and white paint.

MS 4615–21 This sample has a similarly high concentration of As: about 20 times normal in the fabric, 10 times normal in the white and 5 times normal in the glaze.

MS 4615–7 The concentration of sulphur is anomalously high in the fabric (about 15 times normal) and also somewhat enhanced on the surface.

MS 4615–32 Both Ca and Cr are significantly enhanced relative to the average in the edge of this sample.

These examples illustrate the way in which the data collected so far may be used to search for distinguishing features and anomalies among other samples to be studied in the future. All the data obtained is stored on computer discs and so is available for further statistical analysis.

Conclusion

It has not been the intent of this paper to give conclusive results for artifacts of copper-based alloys, glass beads, and pottery sherds, but rather to demonstrate

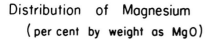

Distribution of Magnesium
(per cent by weight as MgO)

Distribution of Aluminum
(per cent by weight as Al₂O₃)

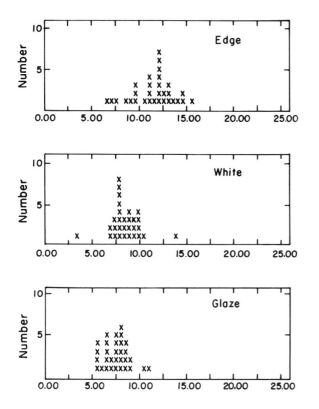

Figure 3. Histograms of the distributions of magnesium for the 31 sherds as one goes from the fresh fractured edge, to the white on the surface, to the glaze.

Figure 4. Same as Figure 3 except for aluminum. Note *the opposite trend.*

the feasibility of using the proton probe as a tool in such studies. The method does not have the sensitivity of other techniques, i.e., neutron activation, atomic absorption spectroscopy, spark source mass spectroscopy. The electron probe is certainly capable of a finer spatial resolution but the sensitivity is down by two to three orders of magnitude because of the intense bremsstrahlung background and the sample must be prepared for use in a vacuum. Therefore, it is quite apparent that the nondestructive nature, the spatial resolution capability, and the rapidity of multielemental analyses of the proton probe are of great importance. The variability inherent in the composition of artifacts requires a statistical approach to the analyses as demonstrated by the results for the potsherd studies. This, of course, requires the study of many samples.

Acknowledgments: Sincere appreciations are due Drs. S. Fleming, V. Pigott, and P. McGovern of MASCA for assistance in preparing the sections of this report relating to copper-based alloys and glass beads, to the collaborative efforts of Dr. T. K. Gaisser in the pottery sherds study, and to Dr. P. Betancourt without whom this latter effort would not have been possible.

References

Ahlbert, M.; Akselsson, R.; Forkman, B.; and Rausing, G. 1976. Gold traces on wedge-shaped artifacts from the late neolithic of southern Scandinavia analyzed by proton-induced X-ray emission spectroscopy. *Archaeometry* 18: 39–49.

Beck, H. C. 1927. Classification and nomenclature of beads and pendants. *Archaeologia* 77: 1–76.

Betancourt, P.; Gaisser, T. K.; Matson, F. R.; Myer, G. H.; and Swann, C. P. 1979. Vasilike ware. *Studies in Mediterranean Archaeology* 56: 3–11.

C. P. Swann

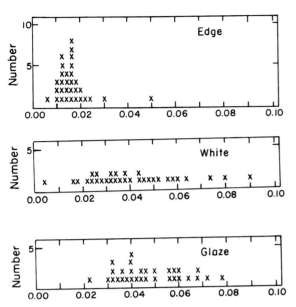

Figure 5. Same as Figure 3 except for zinc. Note *the trend and the increased scatter as one moves to the surface.*

Van Patter, D. M.; Swann, C. P.; and Glass, B. P. 1980. Proton probe analysis of an irghizite and a high-magnesium Java tektite. *Geochimica et Cosmochimica Acta*, in press.

Coghlin, H. H. 1975. Copper artifacts from Tutankhamun's tomb. *Journal Historical Metalogy Soc.* 9: 64–67.

Cookson, J. A. 1979. The production and use of a nuclear microprobe of ions at MeV energies. *Nucl. Instr. and Methods* 165: 477–508.

Duerden, P.; Cohen, D. D.; Clayton, E.; Bird, J. R.; Ambrose, W. R.; and Leach, B. F. 1979. Elemental analysis of thick obsidian samples by proton induced X-ray emission spectroscopy. *Analytic Chemistry* 51: 2350–54.

Flanagan, F. J. 1969. U.S. Geological Survey standards–II. First compilation of data for new USGS rocks. *Geochimica et Cosmochimica Acta* 33: 81–120.

Fleming, S. J., and Crowfoot-Payne, J. 1979. PIXE Analyses of some Egyptian bronzes of the Late Period. *MASCA Journal* 1: 46–47.

Folkman, F. 1975. Analytical use of ion-induced X-rays. *Journal Phys. E, Scientific Instr.* 8: 429–44.

Fou, C. M.; Rasmussen, V. K.; Swann, C. P.; and Van Patter, D. M. 1979. The Bartol-University of Delaware proton microprobe. *IEEE Trans. Nucl. Sci.* NS-26: 1378–80.

Grodzins, L.; Horowitz, P.; and Ryan, J. 1975. The scanning proton microprobe in an atmosphere environment. *Science* 189: 795–97.

13. Xeroradiography of Ancient Objects: A New Imaging Modality

RALPH E. ALEXANDER, M.D., and ROBERT H.
JOHNSTON, Ph.D.
Rochester Institute of Technology

Introduction

This study deals with the application of xeroradiography to the examination and study of ancient materials. Technological and analytical studies of excavated material and material housed in museums have played an increasingly important role in the study of cultures past. With the early work of Sir Flinders Petrie at Tel Hesi in 1891, excavators began to develop chronologies of civilizations by ceramic typology. With the broad vision of excavators such as Dr. G. Ernest Wright, Dr. James L. Kelso, and Dr. William F. Albright, the study of ancient material was widened to encompass early technological analysis of processes and products. Early writers began to call for material studies. Among these scholars were Professor R. U. Sayce, whose book *Primitive Arts and Crafts* contained data from his lectures delivered at the University of Cambridge (England) in the 1930s, and G. Ernest Wright whose thesis entitled *The Pottery of Palestine from the Earliest Times to the End of the Bronze Age* was completed and published in 1937 by the American Schools of Oriental Research. Both men were prophetic about the need to broaden the study of excavated material and the need for multidisciplinary study of archaeological sites.

In 1965 Dr. Frederick R. Matson published his landmark book *Ceramics and Man* and stated his ecological approach to the study of ancient ceramics. In 1970 he instituted the phrase "archaeological present" to describe his ethnographic and ecological studies, all of which added new dimensions to the study of ancient material. Museums have vast deposits of material to be studied and conservators require more nondestructive analytical processes that would enable them to conserve and restore this great wealth of material. Xeroradiography offers such a new analytical process. This paper will be the first of a series that will explore the applicability of the xeroradiographic process to the solution of many of the technical problems encountered when one deals with a complex contemporary excavation. It is one more tool — a most important one — available to assist the excavator, the conservator, the art historian, the museum curator, the student, the anthropologist and the ethnographer in the search to unravel the mysteries of the past. It is a tool that can help in the hermeneutic interpretation vital to presenting a clear picture of man past. In the words of Professor Sayce (1933, p. 2):

> One of the principal characteristics of modern thought is a realization of the essential unity of all knowledge. Few nowadays would waste time in trying to define the exact scope and limits of the various branches of study. Scarcely any subject is

self-contained and self-sufficing. Each borrows from, and may in return throw light upon, many others.

Xeroradiography is an example of an interdisciplinary, interpretative, analytical, and technical process that can be of great value to all who labor in the vineyards of ancient cultures.

Xeroradiography has been in use for several years as a supplement to conventional film radiography. Its ability to delineate edges even in the presence of minimal density differences has significantly enhanced the medical radiologist's imaging abilities. The authors have therefore decided to investigate the potentials of this process in the study of ancient artifacts, and of ceramics in particular.

Technical Aspects of the Radiographic Process

Almost by definition any ideal method of analysis should be nondestructive in nature. Thus, it is no accident that many of the great advances in radiography have occurred in the field of medicine. Preservation is no less important when dealing with irreplaceable archaeological material. One would expect, therefore, that radiographic analysis would have assumed major importance in the archaeologist's armamentarium. That it has not done so is a result of significant deficiencies in film radiographic images. Fortunately, many of these deficiencies may now be overcome by the use of electrostatic imaging, i.e., xeroradiography. To understand just what this relatively new mode of X-ray imaging can bring to our perception of the structure of ancient artifacts, we must first consider the basic virtues and vices of the radiographic process.

Ever since the discovery of X-radiation by Roentgen in 1895, the classical method of producing X-ray images has involved the use of a silver halide photographic type of emulsion as the recording medium. X-radiation comprises a broad spectrum of electromagnetic radiation of extremely short wave length starting with the far ultraviolet and extending into the realm of gamma radiation. This radiation is incapable of producing any form of response, color or black and white, in the photoreceptors of the eye, but may be made apparent by use of the inherent sensitivity of silver halides to X-rays in proportion to the amount absorbed, or, alternatively, by the conversion of the X-radiation to the ultraviolet and visible spectrum through absorption and conversion by an appropriate fluorescent screen.

Visible light is imaged by refraction. Lenses are capable of bending the rays to produce a crisp (i.e., high contrast) image which is then recorded on photographic film. In contrast, there is no lens or other device capable of refracting X-rays. In practice, images may be produced by two means only — diffraction or absorption. Diffraction will only be produced in the examination of submicroscopic structures such as crystal planes (in keeping with the extremely short wave lengths of X-radiation) and thus is not a technique of value in producing images of macroscopic objects. It is therefore necessary to resort to the crudest of image formation methods — the shadowgraph — to utilize the absorption characteristics of materials of differing densities to produce a radiographic image. Thus, our radiographic images are in every sense of the word just shadows and it is a tribute to the ingenuity of the equipment designers that such finely detailed shadows can be secured, although in no manner can these images be compared to the refinement of a high quality refracted (i.e, photographic) image.

More than three quarters of a century have been devoted to the improvement of radiographic images. Insofar as generating sources are concerned, the early primitive gas tube (as temperamental a beast as any in recent history) gave way to the reliable tungsten filament (Coolidge) tube in the twenties only to be dramatically upgraded into the rotating anode tube of the thirties. This rotating anode tube successfully distributed the enormous heat developed by the sudden stoppage of the high speed electrons over an arc rather than to a localized spot. A smaller target could thus be used with an inversely proportional improvement in detail at energy levels which would otherwise melt the tungsten target and destroy the tube.

Thus, image generation has undergone continuous and significant refinement. Yet this is only half the story. The other half is of equal or greater importance: the medium upon which this image is recorded. Here the obstacles are as great or greater, for the X-ray shadowgraph is a most imperfect image in a new sense. The problem is simple and basic: X-rays, with all their legendary ability to penetrate matter, do so most imperfectly. To consider the photographic parallel once more, the atmosphere for all practical purposes is completely transparent to visible light. In contrast there is nothing short of a vacuum completely transparent to X-rays, so much so that soft (low voltage) X-rays escape the X-ray tube with difficulty if at all, and are significantly absorbed and scattered by air.

The world as depicted by X-ray imagery is, therefore, translucent rather than transparent in character. This problem would be manageable if the absorbed or deflected X-rays merely disappeared from the image-forming process. Unfortunately they do not. The key word is *scatter* — for these rays are dispersed in every direction adding up to an over-all

R. E. Alexander, R. H. Johnston

haze through which, at times, the basic image may be barely discernible. The scatter is everywhere: within the X-ray tube, in the air, from any equipment upon which the X-ray beam impinges, in the object under study, in the film holder, in the fluorescent screen, if used, and in the film itself. The measures used to control scatter include limitation of field size as far as practical since a small volume of matter will scatter less than a large volume, use of filters to eliminate the softer and more easily scattered radiation, development of the Bucky diaphragm (a grid composed of lead strips tangential to the primary beam whose function is to absorb any radiation deviated more than a few degrees from the primary beam as a result of scatter), and the use of intensifying fluorescent screens to enhance contrast.

The magnitude of the problem becomes obvious when the photographic analogy is again employed. The contrast of a photographic system customarily expressed as the "gamma" (slope of the density versus exposure curve) is usually considered to be at an optimum in the 0.7 to 0.8 range. An uncommonly flat or obscure subject might call for a gamma of 1.0. Compare this to an X-ray imaging system where a gamma of 3.0 is mandatory to overcome the deleterious effect of scatter and produce an optimal image. Photographically, a gamma of 3.0 would represent a black and white line copy devoid of intermediate tones; yet this gamma is necessary to bring the scatter-degraded X-ray image to a near optimum visual range. In photographic parlance, radiographs would be considered to have a notably poor "modulation transfer function" (MTF). The MTF of a system is currently considered to be one of the more sophisticated measures of image quality, measuring, as it does, the degree of contrast attainable for a given level of resolution.

The essential feature of this analysis is that film radiography is an additive process. Film might be likened to an elephant that neither forgives nor forgets, and the resultant image represents a summation of all factors, good and bad, that have occurred in the image-forming process.

To sum up, many years of refinement have vastly improved the quality of radiographic film images; nevertheless significant gaps persist in our imaging capabilities.

Xeroradiography (Electrostatic Imaging)

It is against this analysis of the successes and failures of classical radiology that one must measure the newer modality "Xeroradiography." Xerography is electrophotography; xeroradiography is the radiographic application of electrophotography. Fortunately the image-forming characteristics of xero-radiography are in many respects diametrically opposed to those of film radiography. As will be shown, xeroradiography in no way replaces film radiography but does possess unique characteristics which supplement film radiography in just those areas where the latter is most deficient.

In electrophotography, advantage is taken of the ability of a selenium-coated plate to hold a charge of positive ions. This charge may then be depleted by exposure of the plate to visible light or to X-radiation. Partial depletion of the charge results in a demonstrable, though as yet invisible, electrostatic image. This plate is capable of attracting charged pigment particles, thus creating a visible image which may then be transferred to a permanent support. Thus far the method of image formation and preservation demonstrates no obvious fundamental differences as compared to film radiography. Nevertheless, there are two crucial differences in the mode of image formation:

1. Whereas the film absorbs incident radiation and thereby builds up a latent image, the xeroradiographic image is produced by a partial destruction of the electrostatic charge of the selenium plate. The film image is additive; all of the factors, favorable and unfavorable, are integrated into the formation of the final image. It is the authors' opinion that the crucial difference lies in the fact that xeroradiography is subtractive: the charge is dissipated and many of the factors influencing film image formation simply disappear and play no further part in image formation. Thus the diffusing effect of scatter is minimized. It is true that excessive scatter might, for instance, drop the residual charge from 150 to 125 volts at a given point. Nevertheless, the image is formed by voltage differential between one point and the next, and if the reader will permit an anthropomorphic approach, the plate could not care less whether scatter has reduced the charge to 150 or 125 volts; all it cares about is the residual difference between charges. Thus xeroradiographic images, through a wide range of densities, are almost impervious to the effect of scatter and thereby often avoid the image degrading effects so detrimental to film images.

2. The gamma of a xeroradiographic system is incredibly low — as measured by Wagner (Wagner et al. 1974), only 0.2. This low level of contrast would, in film images, be flat to the point where detail would be barely discernible. However, since the xeroradiographic image is electrostatic, build-up of lines of force on one side of an interface deplete those on the other side, producing the phenomenon known as "edge enhancement." This enhancement is controllable by adjusting the factors affecting the plate,

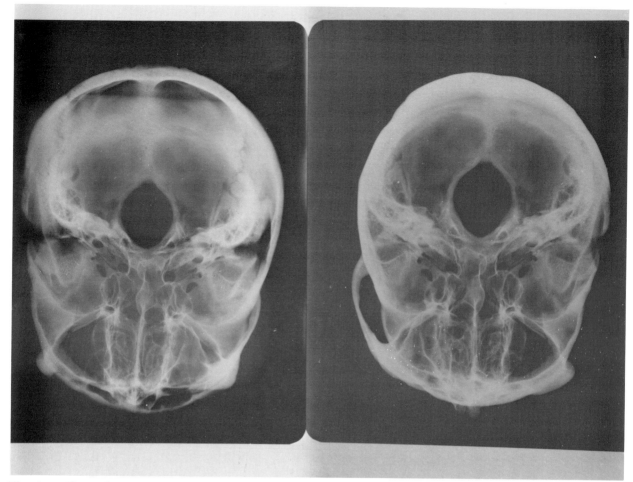

Plate 1. *a*. Film radiograph of dried skull. *b*. Film radiography with water bottle with added scatter.

thereby allowing the visualization of fine interfaces, although broad area response suffers in consequence. The result is an image of amazing tonal range (consonant with a gamma of 0.2) in which edge enhancement is utilized to render fine detail. This it does remarkably well, but with the caveat that one should not rely on the process to render comparative densities with precision. For this function, one may still rely upon the basic film radiograph.

It might be mentioned in passing that the dramatic success of the newest of X-ray modalities, the CAT scanner, is also based in part on its ability to bypass the effect of scatter in image formation. Briefly, the CAT scanner measures the density at any given point within the image plane by triangulation with computer analysis for reconstruction. Sensitive determinations of object density are possible far beyond the range of conventional radiography. However, spatial resolution capability is poor and for this reason the

process offers little in the study of ancient artifacts and therefore will not be considered further in this context.

Summary

Xeroradiography represents a new imaging modality that differs from conventional film radiography in several crucial aspects. These unique characteristics, as applied to the study of ceramics, provide the investigator with the ability to demonstrate the following features to a degree not previously attainable by nondestructive methods:

1. The demonstration of crisp, accurate, scatter-free profiles of ceramic vessels of sufficient precision to replace current caliper-controlled hand sketching techniques.

2. The ability to show textures produced by a-plastics or other inclusions within ceramics even when these inclusions closely resemble the basic clay

R. E. Alexander, R. H. Johnston

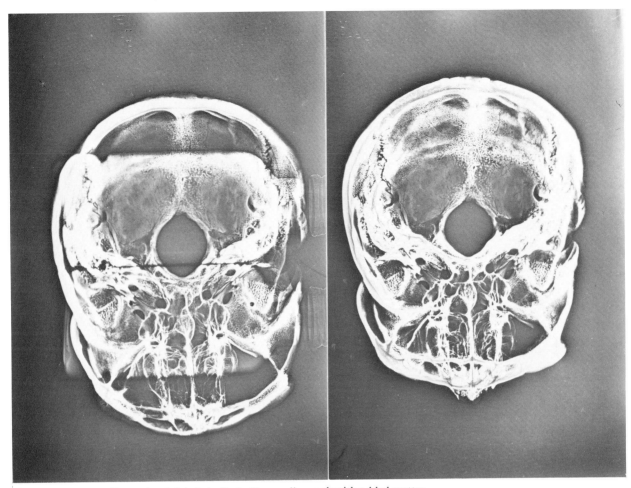

Plate 2. *a*. Xeroradiograph of dried skull. *b*. Xeroradiograph with added scatter.

in their radiographic densities. The ability of xeroradiography to demonstrate edges to a greater degree than relative density makes this possible.

3. As a derivative of *(2)*, modes of manufacture including (but not limited to) hand- versus wheel-formed, direction of rotation of the wheel, technique of joins, repairs, later additions to ancient pottery, and so on, may now be studied with great precision.

It should be noted too that xeroradiography also finds applications in related fields through its ability to demonstrate the grain of woods, structural details in weavings even when imbedded in materials which would preclude ordinary radiographic study, the differentiation of some metals from their corrosion products, and many other applications where edge delineation may be helpful. The history and principles of the xeroradiographic process are admirably reviewed by John M. Wolfe (1972). Note should also be made of the early work of S. Heinemann (1976) in

which the application of xeroradiography to the study of archaeological material is first suggested.

Analysis

Plate 1 demonstrates the degrading effect of scatter produced by the soft tissues of a living skull as contrasted to the critically sharp image of a dried skull. With xeroradiography (Plate 2), no such degrading effect is evident. Plate 3 is an example of a so-called magic pot that is quite common throughout the ancient world. The piece that we are using is a modern-made village pot that one can find in bazaars in many parts of the world, of a type usually sold to tourists. But behind the modern pot is a long history of double-chambered pots or connected pieces of pottery which were probably used in the Bronze and Iron Ages by shamans to impress people with ritual and magic phenomena that to the person in antiquity would be inexplicable. The piece of pottery at hand

a.

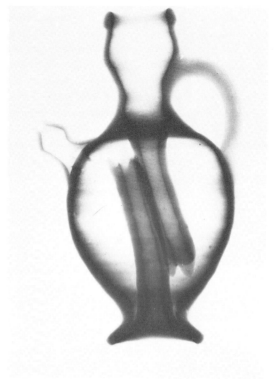

b.

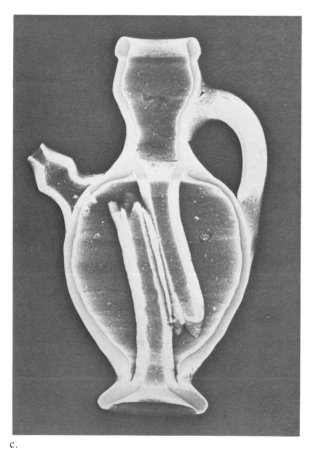

c.

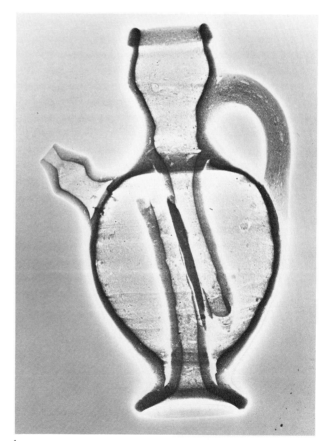

d.

R. E. Alexander, R. H. Johnston

a.

b.

c.

d.

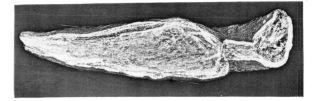

e.

Plate 3. *a*. Magic pot. *b*. Film X-ray of magic pot. *c*. Xeroradiograph of magic pot (negative). *d*. Xeroradiograph of magic pot (positive).

Plate 4. *a*. Mummified fish (Egypt). *b*. Mummified bird (Egypt). *c*. Film X-ray of mummified bird and fish. *d*. Xeroradiograph of fish (negative). *e*. Xeroradiograph of bird (negative). *f*. Xeroradiograph of bird and fish (positive).

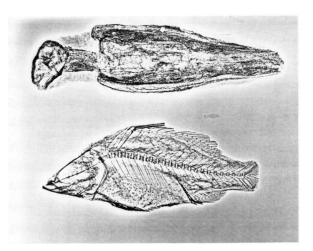

f.

has a hole in the top into which water can be poured in the usual manner, but in addition a hole in the bottom so that the piece can be turned upside down and water poured into the bottom as well. One uses this pot by pouring water into the top, turning the piece upside down (at which point the water mysteriously does not run out), so that one can now pour some water into the hole at the bottom, turn the piece of pottery right side up — and lo and behold the water stays inside the vessel. At this point the shaman could have taken the piece of pottery by the handle and poured the water from the spout, very much to the awe of all who would be witnessing the experiment.

A modern "magic pot" was used to show how the process of xeroradiography can clearly demonstrate the workings of such a container, and show the various construction techniques used in making the vessel. One can readily see by the indication of throwing marks that the body of the vessel was thrown on a centrifugal potter's wheel. It is easy to see how two tubes were placed inside, one from the top and one from the bottom. The bottom tube also constitutes the base since the join of the base and the bottom tube is clearly visible. The neck was added as a separate piece thereby welding together the entire upper section of the vessel including the upper tube, and afterwards the rolled handle was added. In fact, one can see some air pockets at the join of the handle. Thus, without having to damage this piece by cutting or drilling, it is easy to see how the "magic pot" functions and how it was constructed.

The size, distribution, and comparative aplastic tempering material is quite visible in the xeroradiograph. If one compares the xeroradiograph to the X-ray of the same piece, the capacity of the xeroradiograph to define edges of materials of comparable densities offers a wealth of information not visible in film radiography. The edge effects characteristic of the process also produce incomparable profiles of objects and vessels, clear delineation of wall thickness, and the dynamic effect of the manufacturing processes on the material. A secondary benefit is the ability of the process to replace endless hours of drudgery by the staff artist responsible for delineating the profile.

Plate 4 is an example of using xeroradiography to study some mummified material dating to approximately 2000 B.C. from the area of Luxor in Egypt. As indicated in the illustration captions, we have an X-ray and a xeroradiograph of a mummified fish and a mummified bird. Through application of the technique of xeroradiography it is quite evident that the bird really does not contain any actual material of an ancient bird at all; as a matter of fact, there is a wooden plug in the neck and head of the bird and the

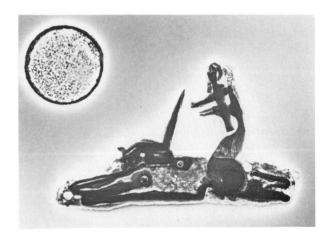

Plate 5. *a.* Colonial gunlock (corroded). *b.* Film X-ray of corroded gunlock. *c.* Xeroradiograph of corroded gunlock.

152   R. E. Alexander, R. H. Johnston

rest of the mummified bird is simply wrapped emptiness. No one knows whether a fake such as this was made in ancient times or whether this was something made more recently and sold on the antiquities market or to the tourist trade. It is quite possible that with the press of time the ancient mortician would at times produce mummified material that in fact did not contain the remains of any species which would be buried with the deceased pharaoh or member of the royal family. The fish is very intriguing because not only can you see the skeletal remains of the fish — which, by the way, show equally well in the traditional film radiograph — but in the xeroradiograph one can actually notice the fish scales and actually see parts of the fins and other details of the mummified fish not shown in the film radiograph.

Plate 5 is an example of a badly corroded colonial gunlock. The purpose was to use xeroradiography to help the conservator clean and conserve this ancient flintlock. When working with badly oxidized metal, using a variety of cleaning techniques including an air abrasive gun, one must be very careful that undue cleaning does not occur in areas where the metal has been so badly oxidized that its integrity is impaired. The film did not indicate some of the more eroded, sensitive areas. The xeroradiograph clearly indicates the details and mechanics of the flintlock and shows those areas where the metal has been so badly eroded by oxidation that an attempt to clean that particular area would simply destroy the piece.

Plate 6 is an example of the use of xeroradiography as a nondestructive method of reading ancient cuneiform clay tablets without harming the sealed fired clay envelopes. In conducting this experiment the authors were well aware of the fact that much of the information placed on tablets inside of such fired cases is cuneiform material that can in part be read on the exterior of the case. Nevertheless, it was a challenge to see if xeroradiography could be used to read tablets through the cases without having to cut into or damage the fired clay envelopes. It must be explained to those not so familiar with clay envelopes that these envelopes are covered with valuable cylinder seal impressions as well as cuneiform inscriptions which provide invaluable documentation of the individuals and time period involved. It took considerable experimentation before techniques were found that allowed us to bring out the image of the tablet inside the fired case, and as the xeroradiograph example shows, one can readily translate the tablets — a feat heretofore not possible without removing the inner tablet. We hope to carry this experiment further by using computer enhancement to make the inscription even more legible.

In conclusion, it is hoped that by using the tech-

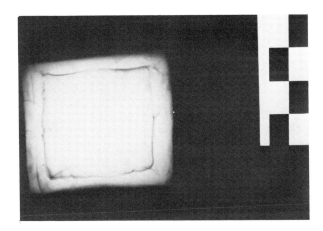

Plate 6. *a*. Cuneiform tablets in fired cases. *b*. Film X-ray of cuneiform tablet. *c*. Xeroradiograph of cuneiform tablet.

nique of xeroradiography, images and techniques can be developed that will be of great use to all those who have to work with and study the vast finds from excavated sites without having to damage the objects themselves. Our experiments will continue and we look forward to receiving problems and material from those in the field who would like to have us attempt to apply our technique as an additional tool for the excavator.

NOTE: Anyone having material that might benefit by xeroradiographic examination should feel free to contact the authors.

Acknowledgments: The authors would like to acknowledge with great appreciation the assistance of the Xerox Corporation for its willingness both to assist us in our research and to share all sorts of technical information with us that helped make this research project possible. The authors would also like to acknowledge Professor Robert Kushner and Ms. June Alexander for their photographic assistance and expertise. Special thanks are due also to Ms. Barbara Albrecht who prepared and assisted in editing this manuscript.

References

Heinemann, S. 1976. Xeroradiography: a new radiological tool. *American Antiquity* 41, no. 1.

Matson, Frederick R. 1965. *Ceramics and man.* New York: Wenner-Gren Foundation for Anthropological Research.

Sayce, R. U. 1933. *Primitive arts and crafts.* Cambridge University Press (reprinted 1965), p. 2.

Wagner, R. F.; Weaver, E. E.; Denny, E. W.; and Bostrom, R. G. 1974. *Med. Phys.* 1:11.

Wolfe, John H. 1972. *Xeroradiography of the breast.* Springfield, Ill.: Charles C. Thomas.

Wright, G. Ernest. 1937. *The pottery of Palestine from the earliest times to the end of the Bronze Age.* Dissertation, American Schools of Oriental Research.

14. Photoacoustic Examination of Ceramic Surface Layers

ALBERT D. FROST
Department of Electrical and Computer Engineering
University of New Hampshire

Abstract

The periodic illumination of a solid sample results in cyclic heating and cooling which in turn produces an acoustic signal at the same frequency as the illumination rate. The strength of this signal is dependent on the light source, the absorption spectrum of the material, and the optical and thermal properties of the surface layers. The variation in the strength of the photoacoustic signal as the illumination rate is changed can provide information on the number and color of any surface layers present. The variation in acoustic signal observed as various points on the sample surface are illuminated can provide a sensitive detector of changes in surface condition or composition. This method has been applied to selected East Cretan white on dark ware sherds and the results of the examination of outer decorated surfaces as well as inner surfaces are reported.

Introduction

The photoacoustic (or optoacoustic) effect was first reported in 1881 (Bell 1881). It was noted that an audible sound was produced when a transparent cell containing carbon black was exposed to a periodic illumination. Other investigators (Tyndall 1881; Rayleigh 1881) speculated on the possible thermal mechanisms involved. Despite this early interest, the matter was not pursued and indeed disappeared from the literature for nearly a century. It reappeared in 1963 in connection with studies of the atmospheric absorption of laser beams. Since 1975 numerous investigations (Rosencwaig 1975; Rosencwaig and Gersho 1976; Monahan and Nolle 1977; Adams and Kirkbright 1977) have demonstrated that the effect, under appropriate conditions, can make a significant contribution to the analysis of solids.

Under steady illumination the temperature of an object will rise as nonradiative de-excitation processes convert part or all of the light absorbed by the solid into heat. In time the target will arrive at a temperature distribution in equilibrium with the surroundings. With a periodic interruption or "chopping" of the illumination, the average incident flux level will produce a corresponding equilibrium temperature with a superimposed fluctuating component. It is this time-varying term in the surface temperature that is responsible for the photoacoustic effect. The gas layer in contact with the target surface is heated at the periodic rate and the subsequent expansion and contraction cycles provide the boundary conditions necessary to launch an acoustic wave having the same fundamental frequency (f) as the illumination or chopping rate.

The acoustic energy level is very low and must be conserved by enclosing the test sample and a micro-

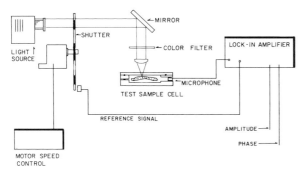

Figure 1. Block diagram of photoacoustic system for solid samples.

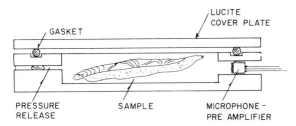

Figure 2. Test cell for photoacoustic samples.

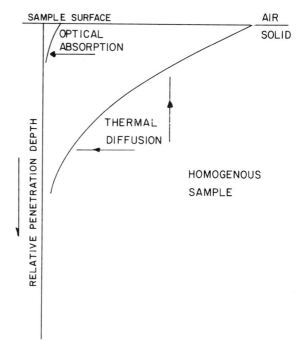

Figure 3. Relative distribution with depth of (a) optical absorption; the relative radiant energy absorption and (b) thermal diffusion; the relative amplitude of the time varying component of the sample temperature, for an opaque, thermally thick, homogenous sample.

phone in a sealed test cell which also serves to exclude a portion of the external ambient noise. The system used to collect the data presented in this paper is shown in schematic form in Figure 1. The light source (GE ELH 300 W.) is interrupted by a rotating Plexiglas shutter having six opaque and six clear sectors. A front surface mirror directs the light beam through a color filter and a condensing lens. The combined optical system produces a circular illumination spot approximately 3 mm in diameter. The sample test cell (Fig. 2) uses a rectangular cavity milled in a mild steel block. A clear Lucite cover plate and gasket are attached as shown. Sealed access holes are provided for an electret condenser microphone and a pressure release passage. The photoacoustic signal component of the microphone/preamplifier output is measured with the aid of a coherent lock-in amplifier (PAR Model 5204). A reference signal, locked-in frequency and phase to the shutter rotation rate is obtained using a secondary light source and photocell.

Acoustic Signal Analysis

The strength of the photoacoustic (PA) signal is a complex function of the intensity and color of the illuminating source, the chopping rate (f), the volume of the test cell in addition to k_s thermal conductivity, C_s specific heat, ϱ density, and β the optical absorption coefficient of the sample. While it is possible to adjust the cell geometry so as to resonate the air vol-

ume at the designated chopping frequency, this was not done since (as will be discussed in subsequent sections) it was found advantageous to observe the PA signal for various values of chopping rate. The cell used was arranged to have a minimum residual air volume to enhance the signal while at the same time avoiding resonance effects.

In a homogenous material the PA signal is a result of the absorption, in a thin surface region, of the incident illumination. The consequent heating effects extend into the sample with an exponential decrease in amplitude as a function of depth below the surface. Figure 3 shows in schematic format, for the case of a homogenous material, *(a)* the relative distribution with depth of the radiant energy absorbed and subsequently released as heat during each illumination interval, and *(b)* the relative amplitude of the fluctuating component of sample temperature. Through thermal diffusion the periodic energy input is translated into a temperature profile decreasing from a maximum at the surface and composed of an average value (constant in time) on which is superimposed an alternating component having the frequency of the illumination rate. The value at the air-sample interface of the latter component is directly related to the pressure fluctuations in the test cell and hence determines the intensity of the observed photo-

Albert D. Frost

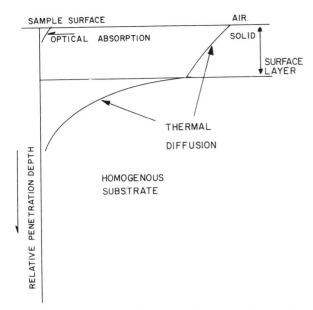

Figure 4. *Relative distribution with depth of (a) optical absorption; the relative radiant energy absorption and (b) thermal diffusion; the relative amplitude of the time varying component of the sample temperature, for a sample having a single surface layer, optically thick at the illuminating wavelength over a homogenous substrate with a lower thermal diffusivity.*

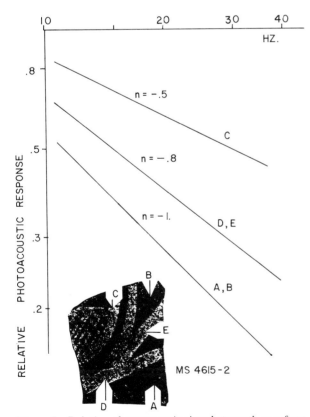

Figure 5. *Relative photoacoustic signal strength as a function of f, the illumination rate, using a yellow filter, measured at the surface points indicated. Design surface: East Cretan sample MS 4615-2.*

acoustic signals. For a given illumination rate and absorbed flux, higher amplitudes of surface temperature fluctuations are observed in materials in which low conductivity and low specific heat tend to concentrate the available energy into a surface layer and reduce the thermal penetration into the body of the sample. A measure of this penetration is provided by the thermal diffusion length L_s of a sample (Rosencwaig 1975), where L_s is given by the equation

$$(1) \qquad L_s^2 = \frac{\varrho\, C_s}{\pi\, f\, k_s}$$

Since the surface heating results from an integration of the energy input, the PA signal produced in any particular case will vary as

$$(2) \qquad PA_s = A\, f^n$$

with n = −1 for a sample homogenous in both color and physical properties.

Extensive application of the photoacoustic effect has been made in the area of absorption spectroscopy. The PA signal will vary with the wavelength of the illumination since absorbed wavelengths will produce a strong PA response, while reflected ones will produce a weak or zero response. In these cases chopping rates from 10 to 20 Hz are used.

Examination of Laminar Samples

If a test sample has a distinct surface layer over a thick body or substrate then several additional considerations are involved in the production of a photoacoustic signal. If the entire illumination is absorbed in the upper layer which is substantially thicker than the length L_s then the exponent in *(2)* will be −1 and there will be no observable difference when compared with a nonlayered sample. If however the surface layer is thermally thinner while remaining optically thick there will be a redistribution in heating effects (Fig. 4) if the thermal properties of the substrate differ from those of the surface layer or there is a discontinuity in the heat transfer across the interface. In this case the rate of change of surface temperature as a function of f is reduced and n will be in the range from 0 to −1.

An example of these conditions is shown in Figure 5. Photoacoustic signal measurements were made at several points on an East Cretan sherd MS 4615-2. PA signal levels were recorded as a function of f, the illumination chopping rate. The dark areas gave values for n of −1 while various portions of the design had n values of −.5 and −.8. The difference noted at various positions might relate to either the thickness of the colored layer, its density, or its bonding to the substrate. If there is a color difference between the surface layer and the sample body and the surface layer is translucent, then a combined effect

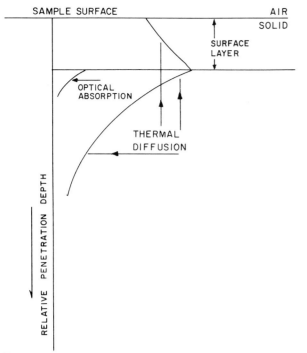

Figure 6. Relative distribution with depth of (a) optical absorption; the relative radiant energy absorption and (b) thermal diffusion; the relative amplitude of the time varying component of the sample temperature, for a sample having a single surface layer which is translucent at the illuminating wavelength.

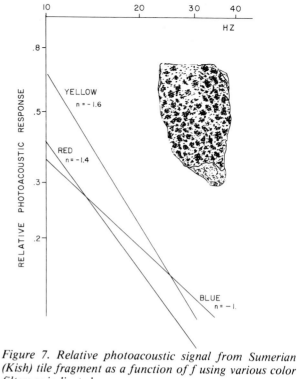

Figure 7. Relative photoacoustic signal from Sumerian (Kish) tile fragment as a function of f using various color filters as indicated.

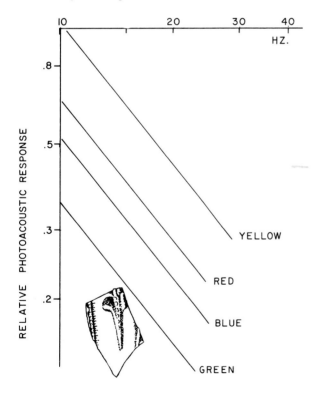

Figure 8. Relative photoacoustic signal from pottery fragment (Central Gaul) as a function of f using various color filters as indicated.

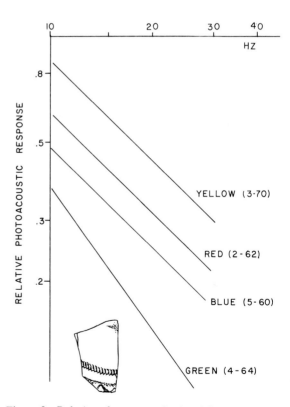

Figure 9. Relative photoacoustic signal from pottery fragment (East Gaul) as a function of f using various color filters as indicated.

158

Albert D. Frost

can be observed in which illumination at a wavelength absorbed in the surface layer results in a PA signal which varies as n = −1 or less while illumination with a color transmitted by the surface but absorbed by the substrate results in a condition where the PA signal varies as n in a range from −1 to −2. The rate of decrease with frequency is greater since the heat production in the latter case is below the first surface. This is illustrated by Figure 6.

A glazed Sumerian pottery fragment was examined photoacoustically using several color filters as shown in Figure 7. With a blue filter the value of n over the range from 10 to 40 Hz is −1. In red light this changes to −1.4 and in yellow to −1.6. This suggests that the upper levels of the glaze absorb blue light but are translucent to red and yellow which are absorbed at deeper glaze levels or in the case of the yellow possibly in the pottery body.

While stylistic difference in design and decoration can in many cases be used to distinguish between East and Central Gaul sources of Rhenish ware of the second century, a study was undertaken to determine if other tests could be found for the identification of sherds from these sources (Symonds 1978). Samples from each area were examined and the results are shown in Figure 8 and Figure 9. For samples from Central Gaul sources, plots of the photoacoustic signal vs. f had the appearance shown in Figure 8, i.e., all colors red, yellow, green, and blue are absorbed at the same layer, at or below the surface. In the case of East Gaul samples as shown in Figure 9, the absorption level for green is greater than for the other colors. In all, nineteen samples were examined. Central Gaul samples gave n values which differed by no more than .05 for red, yellow, green, and blue illumination when compared at 10 and 30 Hz. Actual slope determinations were made on the basis of a "best fit" line through eight to ten measurements made in the range from 10 to 40 Hz. East Gaul samples exhibited a similar clustering of n values for red, yellow, and blue but the magnitude of n for green was .3 to .4 greater. For example, a sample in which the red, yellow, and blue slope vs. frequency corresponded to n = −1.05, the green slope was −1.4.

Measurements on fifteen of the samples were in agreement with the stylistic assignment to East or Central Gaul sources. Three were incorrectly assigned and one did not fit the PA model and was not assigned. There was time to measure only one spot per sample. This was selected visually as being of uniform and representative appearance, away from the sherd edges and any surface decorations. Specialists in this type of pottery have declared that a visual check on the two pottery sources can in some cases be made on the basis of a "greenish cast" to the surface

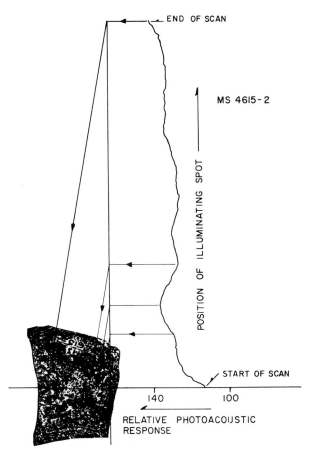

Figure 10. Surface distribution of relative photoacoustic response, yellow filter, f = 19 Hz. Rear surface East Cretan MS 4615-2.

color. Our observations would seem to support this comment and provide greater potential sensitivity in an objective measurement.

Surface Mapping Observations

If the light level and chopping rate are held at fixed values as the illumination spot position is moved over the sample surface, changes in the PA signal strength (if any) will be due to changes in surface color or in the composition of the surface or substrate. Several sherds which form a portion of those studied by the white-on-dark ware group (Betancourt 1980) were examined in this manner. The results are presented as photoacoustic signal amplitude plots projected along the spot path across the sample as shown in Figure 10. In this example the PA signal (arbitrary units) is plotted on the x axis and spot position on the y axis. With appropriate orientation of the sample image it is possible to relate spot location and PA levels. Note that the scale zero for the PA signal is off the page to the right.

The effect of decoration or patterns is shown in Figure 11 where, as might be expected, distinct

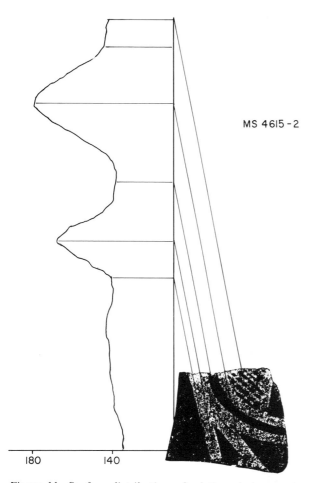

Figure 11. Surface distribution of relative photoacoustic response, yellow filter, f = 19 Hz. Design surface East Cretan MS 4615-2.

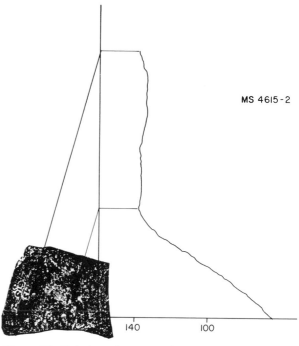

Figure 12. Relative photoacoustic response, MS 4615-2, rear surface, yellow filter, 19 Hz.

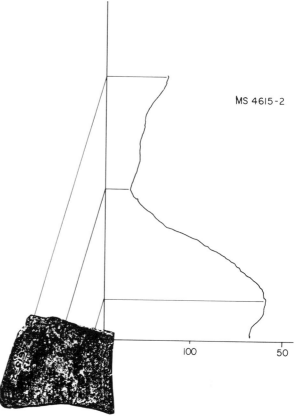

Figure 13. Relative photoacoustic response, MS 4616-2, rear surface, yellow filter, 19 Hz.

changes in surface color result in corresponding changes in the photoacoustic signal. As a consequence of the spot size, the edges of the design are somewhat smeared but the two bands traversed are clearly evident. In general if a surface design coloration is thin and well bonded to the body of the sample, it would be expected that dark regions, being more absorptive, would produce a stronger PA signal level than lighter ones would. This is not the case in sample MS 4615-2 seen in Figure 11. In this case, the reverse is true, with stronger signals being obtained when the spot is on the light design bands and lower levels on the dark background areas. This is the same sherd shown in Figure 5. One of the bands scanned is in region marked "E" in Figure 5 having an n value of $-.8$ which suggests that since the design is a distinct layer, the energy is concentrated in the layer and not dissipated into the body of the sample.

A subsequent examination of the rear (inside) sur-

Albert D. Frost

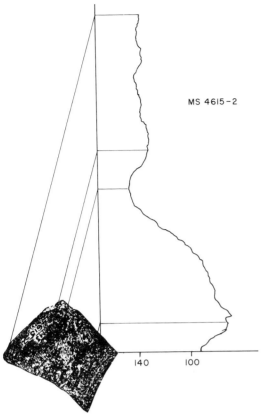

Figure 14. Relative photoacoustic response, MS 4615-2, rear surface, yellow filter, 19 Hz.

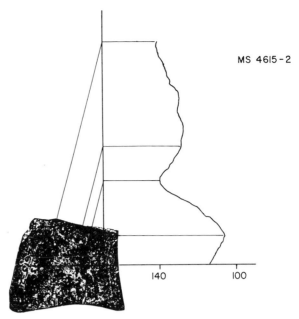

Figure 15. Relative photoacoustic response, MS 4615-2, rear surface, yellow filter, 19 Hz.

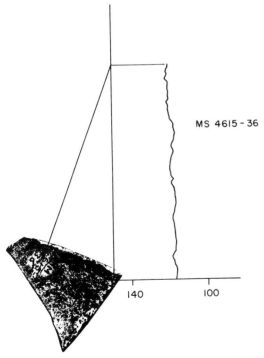

Figure 16. Relative photoacoustic response, MS 4615-36, rear surface, yellow filter, 19 Hz.

face of this same sherd is shown in Figure 12. The surface is smooth with a slightly mottled appearance. The PA signal shows two regions of interest, a plateau to the left and a sharp transition to the decreasing PA values to the right as one moves to the rim edge. This same pattern could be seen in other scanning paths across the back of MS 4615-2 (Figs. 13, 14, and 15) and suggested a rim-related change in the rear surface. Discussion with Dr. Betancourt (Temple University) and close visual inspection of this and others of the East Cretan sherds studied in this project disclosed that the transition in PA levels corresponded to an interior region of burnishing parallel to the rim.

Examination of the rear surface of MS 4615-36 (Fig. 16) showed no evidence of the change in level in the vicinity of the rim, seen in other samples. The design side was examined (Fig. 17) along a path of uniform color and surface appearance. Despite this there was a region of substantially lower PA signal owing possibly to an inclusion in the base material hidden by the surface color. Rear surface PA characteristics similar to those seen on MS 4615-2 are to be seen in Figure 18, MS 4615-45, and Figure 19, MS 4615-28. In most cases the rear surfaces of these samples had *not* been cleaned. As a further test of these observations, the rear surfaces of MS 4615-20 and MS 4615-21 were mapped. The former sherd was not cleaned while the latter had been cleaned and some evidence of burnishing was detected on close visual

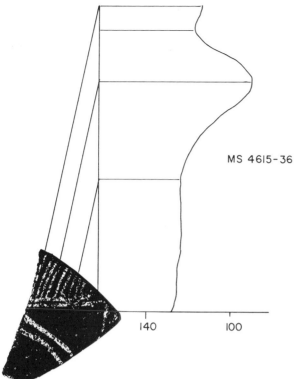

MS 4615-36

Figure 17. Relative photoacoustic response, MS 4615-36, design surface, yellow filter, 19 Hz.

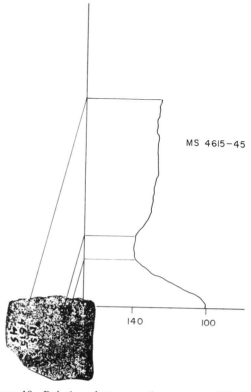

MS 4615-45

Figure 18. Relative photoacoustic response, MS 4615-45, rear surface, yellow filter, 19 Hz.

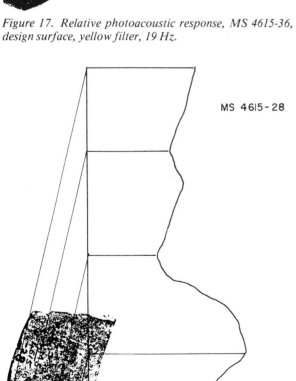

MS 4615-28

Figure 19. Relative photoacoustic response, MS 4615-28, rear surface, yellow filter, 19 Hz.

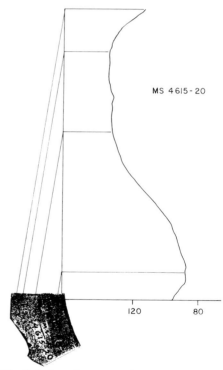

MS 4615-20

Figure 20. Relative photoacoustic response, MS 4615-20, rear surface, yellow filter, 19 Hz.

Albert D. Frost

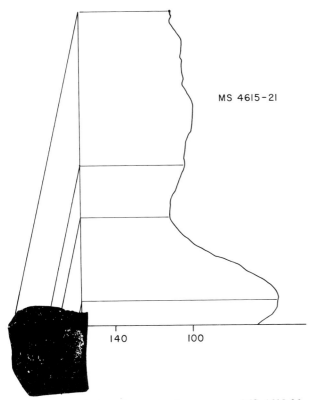

Figure 21. Relative photoacoustic response, MS 4615-21, rear surface, yellow filter, 19 Hz.

examination. The results (Figs. 20 and 21) show that while the rim effect is more clearly defined for the cleaned sample, the photoacoustic effect does penetrate the surface layer accumulation and can disclose changes in the ceramic material below.

Conclusion

Photoacoustic examination techniques can, under suitable condition, reveal in a nondestructive manner possibly significant surface layer characteristics of ceramic materials. Depending on the need, photoacoustic examination can be applied to explore the number and color of layers in surface glazes, to determine subtle variations in surface coloration, or to detect changes in the physical properties of the base material which may be hidden under pigment layers or accumulated surface coatings. As with any physical or chemical analytic technique applied to an archaeological investigation, these observations must be made in the context of other parallel studies to which the surface layer characteristics or anomalies can contribute another parameter, a physical fingerprint that may assist in determining the source of samples or the technology that created them.

Acknowledgments: Much of the initial theoretical and experimental work relating to the application of photoacoustic techniques to the examination of ceramic materials was carried out in 1978–1979 at the Research Laboratory of Archaeometry and the History of Art, Oxford University, with the kind permission of Prof. E. T. Hall and Dr. Martin J. Aitken. Thanks are due to Dr. Robert Hedges for the Sumerian samples, to Ms. Helen Hatcher and Mr. Robin Symonds (Institute of Archaeology) for the Rhenish ware, to the entire RLAHA staff for their courtesy and interest, and to Stacey Frost for archaeological drafting. Continuing work on the East Cretan white-on-dark ware is the result of an invitation from Dr. P. Betancourt (Temple University) with samples from the University Museum, Philadelphia.

References

Adams, M. J., and Kirkbright, G. F. 1977. Thermal diffusivity and thickness measurement for solid samples using the opto-acoustic effect. *The Analyst* (London) 102:(1218) 678–82.

Bell, A. G. 1881. *Philosophical Magazine* 11: 510.

Betancourt, Philip P. 1980. Preliminary results from the East Cretan white-on-dark ware project. In Olin, Jacqueline S., and Franklin, Alan D., eds., *Archaeological ceramics*, Sec. IIIB, chap. 16. Washington, D.C.: Smithsonian Institution Press, forthcoming [1982].

Monahan, J., and Nolle, A. W. 1977. Quantitative study of a photoacoustic system for powdered samples. *Journal of Applied Physics* 48: (8) 3519–23.

Rayleigh. 1881. *Nature* 23: 274.

Rosencwaig, A. 1975. Photoacoustic spectroscopy of solids. *Physics Today* 28: 23–30.

Rosencwaig, A., and Gersho, A. 1976. Theory of the photoacoustic effect with solids. *Journal of Applied Physics* 47: 64–69.

Symonds, Robin. 1978. Private communication.

Tyndall, J. 1881. *Proc. Royal Society* 31: 307.

Archaeological Examples
A. Faience

15. Technological Change in Egyptian Faience

PAMELA VANDIVER
Department of Materials Science and Engineering
Massachusetts Institute of Technology

Abstract

The technology of Egyptian faience was studied in order to characterize the diversity of manufacturing techniques and to understand the sequence of technological development. A survey of six hundred Egyptian faience objects from Predynastic to early Roman times was undertaken using collections at the Ashmolean Museum and the Museum of Fine Arts, Boston. Three different methods of producing glazes and many techniques of body manufacture are described and differentiated by period. Study by optical microscopy revealed temporal differences in glaze morphology and in body characteristics, such as hardness, particle size distribution, porosity, coloration, and the occasional presence of layered body structures. A number of minute samples were destructively analyzed with the scanning electron microscope with energy dispersive X-ray attachment. Laboratory tests aimed at duplicating manufacture were conducted, analyzed, and compared with analyses of the artifacts.

Problem Statement: Characterization of Egyptian Faience Technology

Egyptian faience is a glazed ceramic material which consists of a crushed quartz or sand body with minor amounts of lime and either natron or occasionally plant ash. Natron is a naturally occurring mixture of sodium carbonate, sodium bicarbonate, sodium chloride, and sodium sulphate. The body is coated with a glassy layer which consists of a soda-lime-silica glaze, most often colored by CuO, MnO_2, or an Fe_2O_3 and MnO_2 mixture. A composite range of chemical analyses of the body shows 92–99% SiO_2, 1–5% CaO, and 1/2–3% Na_2O with minor amounts of CuO, Al_2O_3, TiO_2, MgO, and K_2O (Lucas 1962; Kiefer 1971; Noble 1969; Kühne 1969; Kaczmarczyk 1981). Although the composition of Egyptian faience remained relatively constant through the time period surveyed, the ways in which the body and the glaze were formed changed. Characterizing the diversity of manufacturing techniques and understanding the sequence of technological development are the aims of this study.

A survey of about six hundred Egyptian faience objects from Predynastic, ca. 4000 B.C., to Roman times, ca. A.D. 30, was undertaken using the collections of the Ashmolean Museum, which are representative of faience produced in the Predynastic, Old Kingdom, and New Kingdom periods, and the collections of the Museum of Fine Arts, Boston, in which Middle Kingdom faience is well represented. Study by low-power optical microscopy revealed temporal differences in glaze morphology and in body characteristics such as hardness, particle size distribution,

Application of Glaze Slurry

• Thickness Depends On Body Porosity and Water Content Of Slurry.

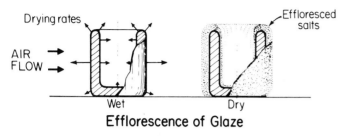

Efflorescence of Glaze

• Thickness Depends On Drying Rate.

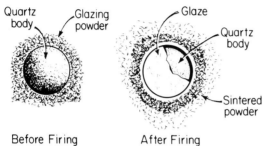

Cementation of Glaze

• Thickness Depends On Firing Time and Temperature.

Figure 1. Methods of glazing Egyptian faience.

porosity, coloration, and the occasional existence of layered body structures. A small number of samples were destructively analyzed with the scanning electron microscope with an energy dispersive X-ray attachment. Laboratory tests aimed at duplicating manufacture were conducted, analyzed, and compared with analyses of the artifacts.

Three methods of glazing Egyptian faience have been proposed in the archaeological literature (Wulff 1968; Kiefer 1971; Noble 1969; Binns 1932). Characteristics of these glazing processes were identified in the literature and then replicated in the laboratory. Studies of faience objects from museum collections were then made in order to determine the relationship of the three glazing processes to different time periods and sites. These three glazing methods are depicted in Figure 1 as *(a)* the application of a glaze as a liquid slurry or powder which is followed by firing to melt and form the glaze (Petrie 1909; Beck 1934; Lucas 1962); *(b)* the firing of a layer of soluble salts which are effloresced or deposited on the surface from the body during drying (Binns 1932; Noble 1969); *(c)* the cementation method of glazing which involves the slow roasting of a body of crushed quartz in a glazing powder (Kiefer 1968, pp. 395–402;

Wulff 1968). Evidence for the ancient use of each of these methods has been found in this study. Before this evidence is cited, a description of the criteria for recognizing each of these types is given.

The first method of application of a glaze is that in which raw materials of fine particle size are mixed with water to form a slurry that is applied onto the surface of the faience body by pouring, dipping, or brushing. (No direct observation of brush marks of the glaze slurry was made, although brush marks of polychrome decoration on New Kingdom ware were observed.) One criterion for recognition of applied glazes is the uneven thickness of the glazes. If an over-all glaze occurs, one finds setter or kiln marks. The flow of the glaze during application in the form of drips or runs often is evident. If only the top surface is glazed, a thick rim at the base of the glaze often occurs and no setter marks occur as there is no glaze on the bottom. The glaze can be applied directly to the unfired body. A primary or bisque firing of faience is unnecessary.

The second method involves the incorporation of water soluble salts as raw materials in the body. These salts are precipitated or effloresced on the surface of the body as water evaporates at the surface.

Pamela Vandiver

Figure 2a. *Laboratory replication of cementation process. TOP: fired beads are still embedded in glazing powder. BELOW: bead and broken cross section. All scales are in millimeters unless otherwise indicated.*

Figure 2b. *Contemporary modeled bead with drilled hole from Qom, Iran, glazed by cementation process.*

Figure 2c. *Molded discs and modeled inlaid bead, all glazed by efflorescent method as replication of process.*

Figure 2d. *Reverse side of effloresced glaze discs showing drying and firing marks. Glaze has not formed where faience rested during drying. Firing marks are indicated by arrows.*

This process is analogous to the precipitation of salts from saline water, for instance, at the edge of a low lying pan or depression in the desert which had filled with flood water. The firing of such a layer of efflorescent salts to form a glaze is a process which was termed self-glazing by Binns in 1932. The thickness of the fired glaze varies with the amount of soluble salts which effloresce during drying. Thus, the drying rate is of critical importance, a thicker coating being deposited in those areas which are exposed to a greater flow of air and have a faster drying rate.

The third method of glazing is also termed self-glazing, as no glaze slurry is applied prior to firing. This process can be termed cementation because the body is surrounded with a powder and heated so that the body becomes glazed by a chemical combination at the surface with a fraction of the powder. The crushed quartz or sand is placed in a high flux content powder which partially melts and reacts with the body to form a glaze. The time of firing for the reaction to occur is much longer than with the other two glazing processes. After cooling the faience object is easily removed from the friable and porous glazing powder, as shown in Figure 2a. The glaze thickness is fairly constant over the entire body but tends to be thickest in those areas where glaze materials have interacted with areas of least dense quartz grain packing (a phenomenon similar to the pitting corrosion of refractories by glass attack). No firing or setter marks are found. The example in Figure 2 was fired to 900 °C for 8 hours. In concave areas and holes, a glazed surface results only where there has been contact with the glazing powder during firing. The replication compares well with beads from Qom, Iran, reported in the ethnographic description of Wulff (1968). An example of a Qom bead is shown in Figure 2b in which the over-all glaze has no drying or firing marks.

The laboratory reproduction of the second process whereby efflorescent salts are heated to form a glaze is portrayed in Figure 2c. These salts consist of Na_2CO_3, $NaHCO_3$, $NaCl$, and Na_2SO_4 in various mixtures similar in composition to naturally occurring natron (Lucas [1962] gives a range of composition for natron as follows: $NaCO_3$, 10-75 wt.%; $NaHCO_3$, 1.5-34%; $NaCl$, 2-57%; Na_2SO_4, Tr-70%; pp. 267, 493-94). The reverse side — Figure 2d — shows drying marks where no salts could be precipitated owing to contact with a support. Also evident are firing or setter marks where the glaze adhered to the kiln support during cooling. Kiefer and Allibert (Kiefer 1968, p. 115) demonstrate that objects with an effloresced layer can be fired in a glazing powder or on a nonwetting substrate. External characteristics which would differentiate such a process from cementation could not be isolated. Therefore, there was no possibility in this study of separating such a combined process into another category.

Results: Summary by Period

In this study clear examples of each glazing process were located by using the criteria of the existence or lack of drying marks, firing marks, and glaze thickness and evenness. The evidence of these glazing processes and a description of how these techniques and methods of body manufacture vary by period is

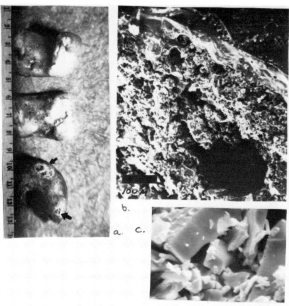

Figure 3a. Predynastic faience beads, Ashmolean no. 1895.880a, Naqada I or II, Naqada, grave 1783. Arrows indicate firing marks.

Figure 3b. SEM micrograph showing glaze layer at top and body below. Sintered quartz grains appear light; porosity appears as dark voids.

Figure 3c. Enlargement of Figure 3b.

given. The data are limited to observations of two major collections, and the conclusions should be verified and expanded by study of other collections. I had hoped to investigate the question of how conservative the tradition of Egyptian faience manufacture was during a 4000-year period. This question is more complex than originally believed, and the survey technique used is inadequate to fully articulate fine differences. More study of the technology of Egyptian faience will be required as well as study of Near Eastern accomplishments and craft. The results presented here are sufficient to discern coarse differences with time. The tentative conclusion set forth here is that within a conservative framework, experimentation and development did occur which allowed the uses of faience to be expanded to include a variety of functions previously relegated to other materials and that using faience allowed the elaboration of decoration in a material which was a substitute for more costly and difficult to obtain semiprecious stones.

Predynastic Period Faience

The wares of the Predynastic period are characterized by a great deal of variability, as one might expect in the early developmental phases of a technology (Smith 1978; Edwards 1971). Whether these early beads and amulets were produced in Egypt or, as G. Brunton and others have suggested (Brunton 1928; Stone 1956), were imports from the Near East, really does not affect recognition of the experimental nature of the objects, although it certainly hinders interpretation. Of the Naqada I and II faience beads, all exhibit an over-all glaze. However, half have firing marks, and half do not have such marks — Figure 3a — and the glazes are sometimes uneven. Thus, cementation, application, or efflorescence are equally probable. The glaze, porosity, and sintered quartz body can be characterized in the scanning electron micrograph in Figure 3b, 3c. Glaze thickness varies from 20–200 μm; quartz grains measure from about 5–300 μm maximum diameter; and porosity measures about 5–200 μm and is bimodal in distribution depending on whether the source of the porosity is intergranular or included air pockets.

The suggestion of Hornblower (1932) and others (Lucas 1962, p. 41; Maloney 1976) that these early blue-green beads and amulets are substitutes for turquoise, lapis, and malachite, commodities rare in Egypt and for the most part believed to have been imported (Lucas 1962, pp. 170–1), is supported by the observation of techniques of manufacture which use stone bead manufacturing methods. Modeling of a body (which is barely plastic when compared with clays) is followed by surface grinding and drilling of a hole, most often from opposite sides. Impressions of ridges and scratches in holes and on the exteriors are frequently observed. Modeling is always followed by subsequent surface grinding. Examples of beads individually formed and ground are less frequent than beads rounded first as a rod, then segmented, separated, and finally drilled from one or both ends. The technique of using a rod to form several beads is common to stone bead manufacture. Further support is added to the contention of the techniques of stone bead manufacture being used to make faience beads when one realizes the relative numbers of beads being manufactured. In this collection glazed soft stone (steatite, for example) beads outnumber faience (about 100 to 1) with turquoise and lapis being more common than faience. For this study twenty-seven faience objects were examined from the Predynastic period, whereas over five hundred glazed soft stone objects were examined. If the museum collections are representative of excavated and indeed original materials, then stone technology is far more prevalent than faience technology, and faience technology is the more likely to be derivative. However, only some aspects of forming faience can be understood as derivative of stone technology.

The level of experimentation with imitation stone-like materials and the glazing of stones is revealed by

Pamela Vandiver

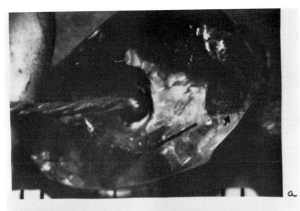

Figure 4. Other Predynastic beads having technological affinities with faience.

Figure 4a. Partially glazed rock crystal (quartz), University College no. 4507, Naqada II, Naqada, grave 1248. Arrow points to glaze.

Figure 4b. Glazed steatite beads ground to shape and drilled from both sides. Ashmolean no. 1911.368, Naqada II, Gerza, grave 133.

Figure 4c. Gold foil wrapped faience body, Ashmolean no. E.E.36, Naqada I or II, El Amrah, grave B62; see MacIver and Mace, El Amrah and Abydos (1902).

the diversity of beads and amulets. The illustrations that constitute Figure 4 show other Predynastic beads having technological affinities with faience. Examples of experimentation with other materials include glazed rock crystal, as in Figure 4a, and the well-known, although little investigated, glazed soft stones, one of which according to Beck (1934) is steatite (a hydrated magnesium silicate, $Mg_3(OH)_2Si_4O_{10}$, often called soapstone [Figure 4b]). Other possibilities requiring future investigation are serpentine and chlorite (Boardman 1970; Kohl 1979). A lesser known example shows the use of a faience body as a substrate for the forming of gold foil, as in Figure 4c. This example of a spherical bead is one of seven from El Amrah; other examples of tubular beads wrapped with gold foil were found at Matmar and Harageh.

An early example of the possible imitation of carved turquoise in faience is the falcon (1895.142,

Naqada I, grave 1774) in the Ashmolean Museum collection. Grains of quartz as seen through a hole in the bottom are angular, vary in size, and have no directional alignment. Although crushed quartz is the most probable source of body material, the possibility exists that the body might have been formed from a surface ground lump of sandstone or from crushed sandstone. If the quartz grains in a sandstone were not transported far from their source, one might find angular grains of varying particle size; however, one would also expect high impurity concentrations which are not present in the bodies of early faience. (In general, orthoquartzites are characterized by rounded grains exhibiting considerable sorting and few impurities.) A search for unusual Egyptian sandstones from geological sources is presently underway and may help to resolve this problem. The impossibility of destructive sampling of early one-of-a-kind objects prevents a petrographic examination which would distinguish crushed quartz from sandstone, either crushed or in bulk. No workshops have been found from this time period, and thus there is no direct information about manufacture external to the objects themselves.

Protodynastic and Old Kingdom Faience

From the Protodynastic and Old Kingdom, one hundred and twenty-five samples were examined primarily from three sites: Hierakonpolis, Saqqara, and Abydos. The size of objects increases from that of beads and amulets to the scale appropriate to the many new functional categories of objects which appear in faience, such as tiles, figures, reliefs, and vessels. The increased scale may be related to a need for larger stonelike blue-green objects as symbols of prestige of the newly formed central authority. However, attempts to substantiate such speculation are beyond the scope of this study. The number of methods of body manufacture increases from modeling and surface grinding to include application of a layer of fine particled white quartz on a body surface, the forming of the body of a vessel on a rod or core, mixing of two different colored bodies to give a marbleized effect, or while in the wet state the decoration of the surface by painting or daubing small areas with a slurry and colorant mixture (see Table 1). The prime focus of technological concern is experimentation not with glaze composition or processing, but, instead, with techniques for manipulation of the body. Efflorescence is the prime means of glazing as evidenced by drying and firing marks. The durability of most Old Kingdom glazes is very poor. Salt deposits, flaking, and powdering are common. Kiefer and Allibert have stated that low hardness and poor durability tend to support efflorescence as the method of glazing (Kiefer 1968, p. 114).

Table 1. Methods of Egyptian faience manufacture

Period	Body Manufacture	Glaze Process	Factory Evidence	Number of Samples Examined	Sites Surveyed
Predynastic (4000–3100 B.C.)	Modeling a core for grinding Surface grinding Free-form modeling (rare)	Experimental period Application (?) (Beck, Petrie) Cementation (?) Efflorescence (?) (Binns)	None	55 faience 125 glazed stone	Naqada, Badari, El Amrah, Matmar, Harageh, Abadiya, Gerza
Protodynastic (3100–2686), Old Kingdom (2686–2181) and First Intermediate (2181–2040)	Modeling Surface grinding Painting with slurry Layering (rare) Forming on a core (rare) Marbleizing (rare) Molding (?)	Efflorescence	None	128	Hierakonpolis, Saqqara, Abydos, Hammamiya, Mahasna, Qau, Matmar, El Kab, Armant
Middle Kingdom (2133–1786) and Second Intermediate (1786–1567)	Modeling Molding on a form Forming on a core Marbleizing Layering Painting with a colored quartz slurry Incising Inlaying Resisting Painting with a pigment wash	Efflorescence (Noble) Cementation (Kiefer and Allibert) Application as a liquid (Reisner)	Kerma Lisht	229	Abydos, Kerma, El Kab, Haraga, Beni Hasan, Mustagidda
New Kingdom (1568–1085)	Molding on a form Pressing into open-face molds Forming over a core Joining of molded parts with quartz slurry Layering Incising Inlaying with quartz slurry Painting with pigment wash Throwing (?)	Efflorescence Application as a liquid Finely powdered glass added to body or inlay to extend color range (Kühne)	Amarna	232	Amarna, Abydos, Serabit el Khadim, Yahudiya, Lahun, Nebesha, Medinet Ghurob, Akhmin
Later Periods (1085 B.C.–A.D. 30)	All of New Kingdom techniques and Throwing (?)	Application as a liquid Efflorescence	Memphis Naucratis	105	Memphis, Abydos, Thebes, Giza, Matmar, Saqqara

172

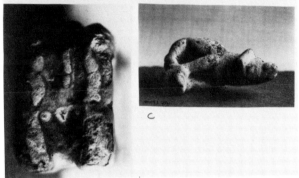

Illustrations of Old Kingdom faience from the main deposit at Hierakonpolis constitute Figure 5. From Hierakonpolis are the small glazed figures, like the baboon formed by modeling and surface grinding in Figure 5a. Drying and firing marks appear on the bottom of the baboon shown in Figure 5b; thus, efflorescence was the glazing method. The thickness of the glaze decreases in the concavities. The contours and details of the bound ram in Figure 5c have been carefully formed by scraping and surface grinding as the body began to dry, and very little salt effloresced in the concavities or in those areas which were heavily ground. There is a range of objects from Hierakonpolis with variable surface grinding and this range corresponds well to glaze thickness: the more grinding that was carried out, the less efflorescent salt collected. The bodies are soft (MOHS hardness of 1–4) and show great variation in particle and porosity size (for instance, quartz grains measure 2 mm and less; porosity measures 4 mm and less maximum diameter). There is a greater proportion of porosity compared with later wares; the porosity consists both of intergranular and semispherical pores. The spherical pores are not burned out organic matter, but are air

Figure 5. Protodynastic faience from the main deposit at Hierakonpolis.

Figure 5a. Glazed baboon, Ashmolean E.5, Dyn. I–II. Glaze is missing behind head.

Figure 5b. Bottom of baboon showing firing and drying marks.

Figure 5c. Calf bound at feet, with residual glaze, Ashmolean no. E.4, Dyn. I–II.

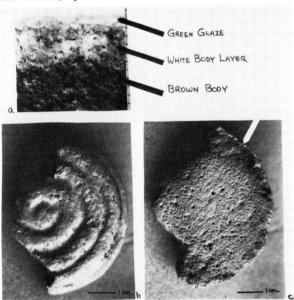

Figure 6. Protodynastic faience object from Hierakonpolis having two-layered body.

Figure 6a. Cross section showing fine white quartz layer separating glaze from brown body interior.

Figure 6b. Object with spiral, perhaps a lid, Ashmolean no. E.4006, Dyn. I–II, Hierakonpolis main deposit.

Figure 6c. Reverse side of object in Figure 6b, with arrow pointing to white body layer. The porous body collects dirt which makes cleaning essential to recognition of this layer.

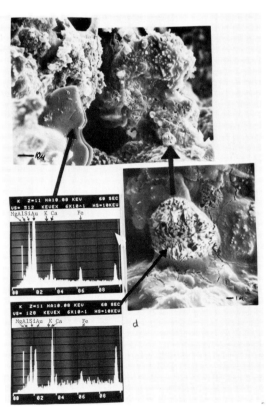

Figure 6d. SEM micrograph of faience body showing areas high in Si above and Ca below, which can be identified tentatively as quartz and calcite, respectively.

Figure 7a. Saqqara tile, Ashmolean no. 1937.115, Dyn. III, Djoser Pyramid.

Figure 7b. Reverse of the tile in Figure 7a, showing ground surfaces and doubly drilled hole.

Figure 8a. Strings of Middle Kingdom beads from Abydos.

Figure 8b. Melon bead with blue-green effloresced glaze, Ashmolean no. E.E.481, E.3.

Figure 8c. Green bead with no firing marks on entire string, cementation process, Ashmolean no. E.E.478, 1900. E.3.

Figure 8d. Edge and back of hand-made Kerma tile fragment showing drips of applied glaze (arrows), Museum of Fine Arts, Boston, Cabinet 13B, Drawer I, KIIa, Middle Kingdom; see G. A. Reisner, Excavations at Kerma (1923), vol. VI, p. 149.

bubbles caused by incomplete mixing, analogous to entrapped air pockets in clay. These air pockets elongate in the direction of body extension. In those rare cases where seeds are added to the body, an impression of the shape of the seeds is clearly present. Petrographic thin sections reveal the bodies consist of fields of alpha-quartz with occasional hematite, biotite, or plagioclase grains. The volume fraction of these occasional impurities is less than 1%. The location of calcite in the body has presented difficulties. No calcite was found in thin sections, but in the interstitial glass of a Hierakonpolis inlay, grains rich in Ca have been located by scanning electron microscopy; *see* Figure 6d.

An exceptional group of objects from Hierakonpolis is represented by the inlay modeled in a brown sand and clay mixture and coated with a layer of fine white quartz beneath the effloresced glaze; *see* Figures 6a, 6b, and 6c. Suggestions of why this layer was added include: *(1)* to increase a limited resource of ground quartz, *(2)* to reduce labor time required to crush quartz, and *(3)* to increase reflectivity of the translucent glaze. From laboratory replications, the blue-green color becomes greenish-brown if an effloresced salt coating is fired onto a ferruginous,

brown clay body or an iron-containing quartz body. In order to maintain the blue-green color, a white quartz layer covering the brown interior is necessary.

The only possible exception to the conclusion of a Protodynastic and Old Kingdom faience technology based on modeling and grinding are tiles from Saqqara — *see* Figures 7a and 7b — which have been described as molded (Lauer 1938, 1976) but when measured are seen to vary in dimension considerably, about 1 cm in 4 cm. The long dimension is 6 cm with less than ½ cm variation. These tiles have extensive grinding on the backs where there is little or no glaze. Because a great many similar tiles (perhaps thirty-six thousand) were made for the reliefs of the Step Pyramid, molding seems most likely. The variation in only one dimension may indicate that a crude mold was used. The only suggestion I can present is the possibility that the body was pressed out between two stationary sticks, thus insuring the one constant dimension measured and a similar thickness. Even though these tiles may have been molded, there is ex-

Pamela Vandiver

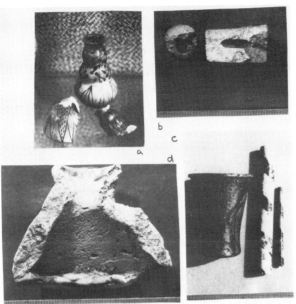

Figure 9a. LOWER LEFT, molded bowl fragment. RIGHT, rod formed vessel and fragment, Ashmolean, Abydos 416, Middle Kingdom.

Figure 9b. Rod formed vessel fragments, Middle Kingdom. LEFT, Kerma, Museum of Fine Arts, Boston, no. 14.2.314; RIGHT, Abydos, Ashmolean Museum, 416.

Figure 9c. Vessel, Ashmolean no. E.2176, Abydos E3, Middle Kingdom, and marbleized tubular beads, Ashmolean no. E.1750 Abydos E30 and no. E.E486 Abydos E2. The vessel and small bead are formed from two different colors of paste, whereas the large bead is made of one color paste with a painted spiral surface decoration.

Figure 9d. Vessel fragment made of molded parts and joined with slurry, M.F.A.B. no. 14.3.1443.B49, Kerma, Middle Kingdom.

tensive hand work involved in grinding the protrusion on back and in drilling a hole through each protrusion from two directions — see Figure 7b. During the Protodynastic and Old Kingdom period, the manufacture of blue-green stonelike materials is greatly expanded as shown in both the size and variety of objects, but the prime technology remains one of modeling and surface grinding. The prime glazing method is the firing of efflorescent salts.

Middle Kingdom Faience

The Middle Kingdom can be characterized by faience manufacture that includes a variety of body-forming techniques (Table 1) and the first clear evidence for all three glazing processes. One can study these three glazing processes by looking at representatives of fairly large groups of beads from Abydos — Figure 8a — and of tiles from Kerma — Figure 8d. In Figure 8b, a melon bead is shown to illustrate the efflorescent method of glazing in which less salt effloresced on concave surfaces. The melon beads were formed by modeling and piercing the bead to form the hole when still wet from the left or more bulbous end. The lack of plasticity of faience is demonstrated by such deformation from spherical shape as is shown by various types of these beads. Cementation is exemplified in the overall-glazed green beads in which no firing marks occur on any of the beads of this type; see Figure 8c. The hole was pierced in a manner similar to the melon bead. As the hole was begun, the faience compressed enlarging the diameter of the right end; as the left side was pierced by the exiting tool, the faience surface developed a tensile crack consisting of a two-, three-, or four-point rip. The forces are only locally present in the faience, whereas in clay the much more plastic body would deform to allow passage of a tool. It is difficult, though not impossible, to rapidly form clay beads of this characteristic faience shape; whereas it is equally difficult to form spherical faience beads without drilling the hole when the bead is dry. Application of a glaze slurry is exemplified on the tile from Kerma shown in Figure 8d, which has two drips down one edge. The glaze composition shows that between 800° and 1000°C this glaze was viscous and should not have flowed in such drips during firing.

Examples of Middle Kingdom forming methods show an increase in number and complexity beyond the forming methods used during the Old Kingdom. The execution is finer and the product more durable during the Middle Kingdom. Forming a vessel on a core is rare in the Old Kingdom, but is common during the Middle Kingdom; see Figures 9a and 9b. Onto a rod the faience body was pressed. Then, the rod was removed once drying had started or was perhaps completed. (Shrinkage in lab replications can vary from about 4 to 12% depending on particle size distribution of the body.) Some spherical shapes were formed over spherical cores. One possibility for such a core is a wound ball of grass which may have been placed over the end of a rod. Another technique common during the Middle Kingdom was molding parts onto a form and joining these parts with ground quartz slurry. The bowl shown in Figure 9a *left* was formed over a male mold which probably resembled a hemisphere. The fragmentary vessel in Figure 9d was formed by joining two hemispheres with slurry and by attaching a preformed lip with slurry. In Figure 9c are examples of the mixing and forming of two different colors of quartz body so that a marbleized effect is attained. There is only one example of this marbleizing process from the Old Kingdom, but many examples from the Middle Kingdom. Another process involves the inlaying of a quartz paste of a different color into channels hollowed out of the fa-

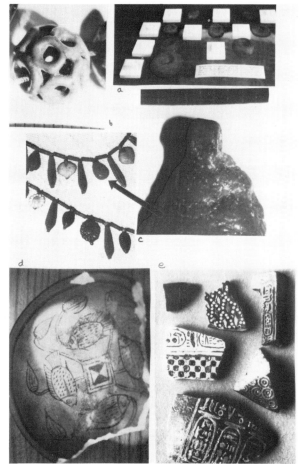

Figure 10a. Group of clay molds with contemporary plaster impressions, Ashmolean Museum, Amarna, New Kingdom.

Figure 10b. Composite faience bead, Ashmolean no. 1933.7201 Amarna, New Kingdom.

Figure 10c. Molded beads having loops joined with slurry; all Amarna, New Kingdom. The magnified bead shows a red loop and molded body joined with blue slurry, Ashmolean no. 1924.124a Amarna.

Figure 10d. Molded bowl, M.F.A.B. no. 1977.619 Amarna, New Kingdom.

Figure 10e. Group of two incised tiles (RIGHT) and four incised and inlaid tiles or vessel fragments (LEFT), Ashmolean Museum, Amarna, New Kingdom.

ience. This process is carried out when the faience is quite wet. If a fairly dry body were used, the inlay would tend to shrink away from the rest of the body. This separation of inlay from body occasionally occurs in the Middle Kingdom, but is used regularly as a controlled decorative effect in the New Kingdom, as can be seen in Figure 10e.

Layering is also commonly observed in Middle

Kingdom bodies. Reproductions show that it is possible to effloresce sufficient salts from only the surface layer, in which case one should be able to locate interstitial glass in the fine quartz surface layer. Attempts to apply microprobe analysis to determine the composition of interstitial glass were unsuccessful, because the glass tended to be removed by grinding of the harder and more durable quartz body. If one could gain a knowledge of the interstitial glass compositions of the body layers, then one could better understand the technology of such layered faience structures. This study of 229 objects of Middle Kingdom faience revealed a proliferation of techniques and forms, an increase in size and numbers of objects, and an increase in technological sophistication. These characteristics are indications of a well-established technological tradition. Two factories have been located at Lisht and Kerma; both of them support the contention that variety, high quality, and large quantity characterize Middle Kingdom objects of faience.

New Kingdom Faience

Study of 232 New Kingdom faience objects revealed that molding replaced modeling as the primary means of body manufacture, and that glazing technology was modified. The *(1)* greater MOHS hardness, *(2)* more vitreous structures viewed by SEM, and *(3)* isotropic colored glass fraction observed in thin sections, are evidence that with the introduction of glass into Egypt, glass was added to some of the faience bodies and to inlays in faience in order to extend the color range — a suggestion first proposed by Kühne (1969).

Processing can be investigated by observing the open-face molds from the factory at Amarna into which beads and amulets were pressed — Figure 10a. In Figure 10c are examples of large groups of similar beads formed by such rapid means as pressing faience into a mold and then joining a small segment from a tubular bead with a slurry onto the back of the molded faience in order to have a hole in the bead for stringing. Usually two such loops are added. No disruption of the pressed form occurred by the action of piercing a hole through the molded body. The bead which serves as a hole was joined onto the pressed faience often with slurry of a different color. This process is easiest to visualize as a set of production steps which are specialized and yet must occur in fairly rapid succession to prevent drying and shrinkage of the parts and to produce an even layer of effloresced salts. Recognition of the complexity of this process does not require that this possible scenario of fairly large-scale production is more than a tentative suggestion, but some reinforcement is added by the

Pamela Vandiver

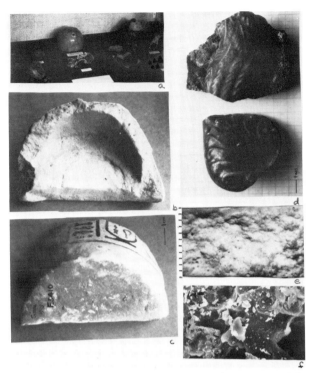

Figure 11a. LEFT TO RIGHT: Fritted glaze spheres, kiln wasters including warped bowl with triple support marks, and setters. Ashmolean Museum, Qom Qalana kiln site near Memphis, Roman.

Figure 11b. Vessel fragment with inlaid decoration, possibly thrown, Ashmolean no. E.3410, Serabit el Khadim, temple, New Kingdom.

Figure 11c. Base of vessel fragment shown in Figure 11b.

Figure 11d. Molded and glazed kiln wasters, Ashmolean nos. 1910.560 (TOP) and 1910.5552 (BOTTOM), Qom Qalana kiln site, Roman.

Figure 11e. Amarna inlay, thin section, low-power optical microscopy.

Figure 11f. Amarna inlay, SEM micrograph.

large numbers of molds and objects found by Petrie (1909) at Amarna.

In addition to production by what may be termed factory methods, one finds tour de force limited production objects, which are exemplified — Figure 10b — by a hollow cagelike bead made of preformed beads built up by joining with slurry. Another technique used as a common means of decoration is incising and inlaying with quartz slurry of a contrasting color, as in Figure 10e. The inlay is applied into the incised groove after the body has begun to dry. The inlay shrinks as it dries and forms an outline around the inlay. All of the means of forming and decorating faience, with the exception of this technique of outlining an inlay, are seen in earlier periods. A bowl

molded over a hemispherical male form — Figure 10d — and coated with a white fine particled slurry was rotated during examination so that the faceted outer contour was revealed. The cross section of the body showed the white surface layer beneath the glaze and decorative lines which were painted in slurry on the body and which are raised from the surface. The bottom surface displays marks of having been fired on a tripod. These combined characteristics are indications of a well-established technological tradition, one which has synthesized diverse elements to produce an excellence in craftsmanship. Methods of forming body and glaze added nothing new to the tradition at this time; where experiments did occur was in the development of new glaze colors.

The lead antimoniate, $2PbO \cdot Sb_2O_5$ (Rooksby 1962), and cobalt aluminate spinel, Al_2CoO_4 (Riederer 1974; Kaczmarczyk 1981), as well as other colorants introduced during the New Kingdom appear to be added as either very fine glassy powders or raw materials to the inlay or surface layer rather than to the entire body, probably in order to minimize the amount of colorant used. A large fraction of the fine particled colorants in replication studies migrate to the surface to deposit the effloresced salts. The New Kingdom faience is highly innovative in increased color range of the faience, but all within the traditional framework of faience manufacturing methods. The large glassy phase can be seen in the SEM micrograph of the Amarna inlay — Figure 11f — in which a considerable amount of glassy fracture is apparent in regions in which the composition is lower in Si compared to fluxes (such as Na, K, Ca and Mg) than would be expected for quartz. In thin section there is considerable isotropic glassy fraction present; and by low-power optical microscopy observation shows a more vitreous cross section than encountered in previous periods (Figure 11e). The need for or possibility of large quantities of brightly colored faience increased production, streamlined many processes, and changed glaze technology to incorporate advances in glass technology.

The late periods incorporate all of the methods of body manufacture seen earlier and several probable examples of thrown ware are encountered. The earliest example of what may be thrown ware is shown in Figures 11b and 11c. The difficulty in assessing whether ware has been thrown arises because the exterior is smoothed and often ground, and concentric throwing ridges on the bottom or parallel ridges on the walls may be less distinct than in thrown clay wares. All potentially thrown wares are thicker and heavier than if made in clay, primarily because of the lack of plasticity of faience. One hundred and five samples from the late periods between 1085 B.C. and A.D. 30 were examined. This sample size was insufficient to characterize the diversity of manufacture over such a long time span. In general, the efflorescence method of glazing is encountered less frequently than in other periods. Techniques common to glazed pottery are seen in wares from the Qom Qalana kiln site near Memphis; see Figures 11a and 11d. For instance, three pointed clay cones are used as setters for the stacking of bowls. Glaze for application was prepared by sintering the raw materials which had been prepared as balls about 1 cm in diameter. A means of developing two-color polychrome faience is shown in molded ware from this kiln site in which varying glaze thickness produced two different colors. The glaze was applied and then wiped to produce such variation: the thinner, lighter color glaze occurred on the raised portions of the molded body, in Figure 11e.

Discussion: Technological Factors Affecting Development

In this study low-power optical microscopy of a large number of faience objects was combined with replication and analysis of a small number of samples to reveal information of technological importance for the understanding of faience manufacture. At the least abstract level of generalization from the data, one can recognize the diversity of manufacturing methods. The major portion of this paper has been concerned with describing such processing techniques by interpreting those groups of external characteristics found by examining the objects, especially those broken and fragmentary objects which allowed study of cross sections of the bodies.

At a more abstract level of interpretation, some of the technological concerns of craftsmen working within a framework of a traditional craft speciality can be detected. For example, the array of different processes carried out on a variety of materials during Predynastic times indicates that beadmakers' concerns involved the physicochemical experimentation necessary to repeatedly produce artificial blue-green beads. During the Old Kingdom, larger objects fulfilling new functions are produced similar in color and texture to semiprecious stones. The external appearances of these objects are related to concern with and developments in processing technology, that is, the physical manipulation of the faience. Developments in glaze technology during the Middle Kingdom are the cause of brighter colored, more durable glazes. The Middle Kingdom objects reflect a concern with chemical composition and heat treatment. During the New Kingdom, the development of large-scale craft production and the close technological ties

with glass technology are isolated as concerns when one examines a large enough sample and tries to make comparisons with previous and later periods. Which of these technological changes were introduced from without and which are indigenous cannot be concluded primarily owing to the lack of knowledge of Near Eastern faience; one can only state that changes in technology are manifest in the objects and that without additional information from manufacturing sites, models, wall paintings, or texts, interpretation is limited. These changes in technology may serve to reveal the concerns of craftsmen in a general sense, but there is no information which would allow one to say whether change in technology was a conscious goal, which craftsmen or how many craftsmen were involved in such change, or even how these changes differed from site to site. The site bias in this study has been toward temples, tombs, and palaces in major administrative centers. Trying to summarize concerns of craftsmen falls short of developing a scenario for the process of technological change and questioning the interaction of technological and aesthetic factors.

Taking the study of Egyptian faience to yet another level of abstraction (implying less certainty in drawing conclusions), one can try to assess the parameters of initial development and those factors which persevered through the development of the technological tradition of Egyptian faience. Beads and amulets flaked and ground from stone were made to look blue like turquoise and lapis lazuli by glazing. The semiprecious stones were also imitated in such easily modeled materials as wetted crushed stone. The iron-bearing clays present in Egypt were probably tried but failed to produce a suitable color when glazed. Satisfactory white clays were not available for making replicas of semiprecious stones. White steatite, uncommon in objects of later times, may have also been difficult to find in Predynastic times. By the Old Kingdom, the method of Egyptian faience was found to predominate over glazed soft stones. Once the best method of producing artificial stone had been found, the early development persisted through years of technological modification and elaboration, but the principal process remained modeled and molded powdered quartz mixed with Na_2O, CaO, and CuO containing materials. One must emphasize the conservative nature of glazing methods in that the efflorescent method of glazing persisted throughout this time span as a means of producing a brilliant, durable glaze with good color quality. The technological factors affecting the development of Egyptian faience which can be perceived by examining the objects include the methods of manufacture, the concerns of craftsmen in a general

Pamela Vandiver

sense, and the possibilities and constraints presented by the raw materials available to craftsmen.

Acknowledgments: The author gratefully acknowledges the criticism of Professors W. D. Kingery and C. S. Smith of M.I.T., and Dr. Robert Brill of the Corning Museum of Glass. This study has benefited greatly from the assistance of Dr. P. R. S. Moorey, Ashmolean Museum, and Dr. Edward Brovarski, Museum of Fine Arts, Boston. The research necessary for the study was made possible by a grant from the Council for the Arts at M.I.T. Permission to photograph and publish objects was kindly granted by the Museum of Fine Arts, Boston, and by "Courtesy of the Visitors of the Ashmolean Museum, Oxford." A full report of this work will be published next year with Dr. Alex Kaczmarczyk as a British Archaeological Report entitled *Egyptian Faience*.

References

NOTE: Works by more than one author are cited in the text by first author's name only and year date.

Beck, H. 1934. Notes on glazed stones. *Ancient Egypt and the East*. June: 19–37.

Binns, C. F. *et al.* 1932. An experiment in Egyptian blue glaze. *Journal of the American Ceramic Society* 15: 71–72.

Boardman, J. 1970. *Greek gems and finger rings*. pp. 373–83. London: Thames and Hudson.

Brunton, G., and Caton-Thompson, G. 1928. *Badarian civilization and Predynastic remains*, pp. 27, 28, 41. London.

Edwards, I. E. S. 1971. The early Dynastic period in Egypt. *Cambridge Ancient History*, vol. 1, part 2: 67, 70. Cambridge University Press.

Hornblower, G. D. 1932. Blue and green in ancient Egypt. *Ancient Egypt*, part 1: 47–53.

Kaczmarczyk, A. 1981. Personal communication.

Kiefer, C., and Allibert, A. 1971. Pharoanic blue ceramics: the process of self-glazing. *Archaeology* 24: 107–117.

––––––. 1968. Les ceramiques bleues pharaoniques et leur procede revolutionnaire d'emaillage. *Industrie Ceramique*, May: 395–402.

Kohl, P. L., *et al.* 1979. Physical and chemical analyses of soft stone vessels from southwest Asia. *Archaeometry* 21: 131–60.

Kühne, K. 1969. Agyptische Fayencen. Part I. In St. Wenig, *Grabungen der deutschen Orient-Gesellschaft*, pp. 6–27.

Lauer, J. P. 1976. *Saqqara: the royal cemetery of Memphis*, pp. 86–136. London: Thames and Hudson.

––––––. 1938. Fouilles du service des antiquites à Saqqarah. *Annales du Service des Antiquities de l'Egypt* 38: 551–65.

Lucas, A., and Harris, J. R. 1962. *Ancient Egyptian materials and industries*. London: Arnold.

Maloney, C., ed. 1976. *The evil eye*, pp. 1–4, 80, 310. New York: Columbia University Press.

Noble, J. V. 1969. The technique of Egyptian faience. *American Journal of Archaeology* 73: 435–39.

Petrie, W. M. F. 1909. *The arts and crafts of ancient Egypt*, pp. 107–119. London: Foulis.

Riederer, J. 1974. Recently identified Egyptian pigments. *Archaeometry* 16: 102–109.

Rooksby, H. P. 1962. Opacifiers in opal glasses. *G.E.C. Journal* 29 (1): 20–26.

Smith, C. S. 1978. Structural hierarchy in science, art, and history. In Wechsler, J., ed., *On aesthetics in science*, pp. 9–53. Cambridge: M.I.T. Press.

Stone, J. F. S., and Thomas, L. C. 1956. Use and distribution of faience in the ancient East and prehistoric Europe. *Proc. of the Prehistoric Society* 22 (5): 40.

Wulff, H. E., *et al.* 1968. Egyptian faience: a possible survival in Iran. *Archaeology* 21: 98–107.

Archaeological Examples
B. Pottery

16. Preliminary Results from the East Cretan White-on-Dark Ware Project

PHILIP P. BETANCOURT
Department of Art History
Temple University

Contributing Authors

P. P. Betancourt, Temple University, stylistic and archaeological analysis

A. D. Frost, University of New Hampshire, photoacoustic spectroscopy

T. K. Gaisser, Bartol Research Foundation of the Franklin Institute, University of Delaware, proton microprobe

N.-H. Gangas, University of Ioannina, Mössbauer spectroscopy

J. Gifford, University of Minnesota, Duluth, geology

G. Gosser, Tyler School of Art of Temple University, reconstruction of the ceramic technology

R. Johnston, Rochester Institute of Technology, xeroradiography

Y. Maniatis, Nuclear Research Center Demokritos, Aghia Paraskevi, Attiki, Greece, analysis of firing temperatures

F. R. Matson, Pennsylvania State University, scanning electron microscopy; physical characterization of fabrics and slips

G. H. Myer, Temple University, ceramic petrography

G. Rapp, Jr., University of Minnesota, Duluth, neutron activation analysis

S. Sapareto, Tyler School of Art of Temple University, reconstruction of the ceramic technology

C. P. Swann, Bartol Research Foundation of the Franklin Institute, University of Delaware, proton microprobe

H. Blitzer Watrous, Buffalo, N.Y., ethnography

M. Voyatzoglou, Athens, Greece, ethnography

Introduction

East Cretan white-on-dark ware is a hand-made pottery used on the island of Crete at the end of the Early Bronze Age and the beginning of the Middle Bronze Age. Its period of use—about a century before and after 2000 B.C.—corresponds to about the First Intermediate period and the early Middle Kingdom in Egypt. In Crete this is known as Early Minoan III and Middle Minoan IA (EM III–MM IA). It is just before the brilliant palace civilization which begins in Middle Minoan IB–II, and the artistic style of white-on-dark ware is thus the immediate predecessor of an elaborate floral and geometric decoration used for the palatial Minoan pottery.

The clay of this ware is always fired to a light buff color, varying toward redder or paler hues in some examples. In the usual system, a dark firing slip (red to black) is painted on the inside of the rim and on the exterior, with white linear designs added on the dark background. Open shapes like shallow bowls may have the interiors painted, and some vases have the dark slip in bands or panels. The ware is most common in the eastern part of the island where it is found both in settlements and in graves.

Most vessels were intended for liquids. Drinking cups are of several types, with simple conical and rounded forms predominating (Plate 1B and 1C). Jugs (Plate 1A) and jars with spouts and two horizontal handles (Plate 1F) are common. Other shapes include open bowls, spouted bowls (Plate 1E), teapots (Plate 1D), and many miscellaneous shapes—including even female figures with hollow interiors, an opening at the head, and pierced breasts.

Simple linear designs are used for ornament. The individual motifs are normally organized in one of two ways, either in circumcurrent patterns which repeat or alternate around the vase, or in facial designs which emphasize particular sides of the vase. Some of the motifs are rectilinear (bands, diagonal lines, chevrons, crossed lines), while others are curved (spirals, arcs, quirks). Endless variations and combinations create a rich ornamental system.

The ware may be traced from simple beginnings at the end of Early Minoan II through the period of its main developments to a final merging with later styles in Middle Minoan IA–B. At Myrtos, a hilltop settlement in southeastern Crete, simple white ornament already appears in EM IIB (Warren 1972, Period II). The decoration in this early phase is always rectilinear, and chevrons and hatched triangles are among the most popular motifs. In the next period, EM III, the ware is known from many more sites. An especially large deposit comes from Gournia, a town on the northeast coast (Hall 1904/5). Because of the

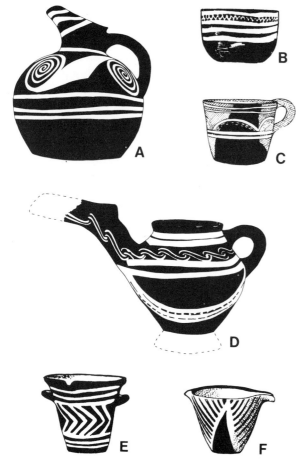

Plate 1. A selection of typical vessels in East Cretan white-on-dark ware, from the mature phase of the style. *A.* Jug from Mochlos. *B.* Rounded cup from Vasilike. *C.* Conical cup from Gournia. *D.* Teapot from Vasilike. *E.* Spouted, conical bowl from Vasilike. *F.* Spouted jar from Vasilike. [These illustrations are derived as follows: After Hall 1904/5, pl. 26, no. 3 *(C)*; Seager 1906/7, figs. 3c *(E)*, 4c *(B)*, and 6 *(F)*; other drawings by the author.]

uniform style of this large deposit, Gournia is the type site for the mature phase of the ware. Other useful groups from this period come from Vasilike (Seager 1906/7, pp. 118–23), Palaikastro (Dawkins 1903/4, pp. 198–99; 1904/5, pp. 269–72; Sackett, Popham, and Warren 1965, pp. 250, 269–72, 277–78), and elsewhere. In this phase curvilinear motifs are added to the repertoire, and the style develops its mature character. The decoration is more complex, and it is careful and well organized. A later phase with more varied designs and a few new vessel shapes (like the cylindrical cup) may be dated to MM I. Closed deposits from the late phase have been excavated from Pyrgos, Myrtou (Cadogan 1978, Period IIa–b), Mochlos (Seager 1909, pp. 290–93), and Vasilike (Seager 1906/7, pp. 126ff.; Betancourt 1977, pp. 345–46 and illus. 1). By the end of this period the

ware has developed into the polychrome pottery of MM IB–II called kamares ware.

Cooperation with Other Laboratories

A team representing several different disciplines is currently studying the white-on-dark ware of eastern Crete. The project is being directed by the writer, and George H. Myer is coinvestigator. It has a number of aims: a better knowledge of the ware's characteristics, based on better founded and more scientifically measurable definitions than have formerly been available; a more complete reconstruction of the technology; a greater understanding of the stylistic development; an increased knowledge of the relation between the pottery from the type site and the stylistically similar ware from other sites in eastern Crete; and a better knowledge of the ware as a whole. In addition, it is expected that the cooperative efforts of specialists in many fields will yield practical knowledge on how better to coordinate and integrate future interdisciplinary studies of this type.

The first year of work terminated in December of 1980. The year's program concentrated on the stylistic investigation, on the ethnographic and geological studies, and on several of the analysis techniques, especially on pottery from the type site. Future work will analyze samples from other sites as well, so that they can be compared and contrasted with the type material. The project has already resulted in new conclusions, and information is now available on several aspects, from the choice of raw materials and their preparation through the manufacturing, decorating, and firing, to the ware's distribution and use.

The potters of eastern Crete were fortunate because this region is rich in clays. Gournia, the type site for the ware under investigation, is located near the northern coast at the Isthmus of Hierapetra. The mountains that extend across Crete from east to west are broken here, and the Miocene marine deposits that make up most of the isthmus are considerably lower than the high peaks to the east and west. Erosion has deposited many clays, easily available to any potter looking for raw material. Several outcrops of granite occur in the town's vicinity, along with the Gavrovo-Tripolitza series of limestones and dolomites (Creutzburg et al. 1977).

Thirty-one sherds from the type site, all considered typical of the ware, have been examined by ceramic petrography. Mineralogically, they all belong to a single group (Table 1). Nonplastic particles include quartz, plagioclase, hornblende, and sometimes biotite. Olivine has been recognized in two samples. Rock fragments containing two or more of these minerals may also be present. Argillaceous globules

Philip P. Betancourt

Mineral Inclusions in Thin Sections
Pottery from Gournia

Museum	Number	Quartz	Plagioclase	Biotite	Yellow-Red Hornblende	Yellow-Green Hornblende	Rock Fragments	Olivine
Penn	MS 4615-6	X	X	X	X	–	X	
	-7	X	X	–	X	–	X	
	-8	X	X	X	–	–	X	
	-9	X	X	–	X	–	–	
	-10	X	X	–	X	–	X	
	-11	X	X A	X	X	–	X	X
	-12	X	X A	–	X	–	X	
	-13	X	X	X	–	X	X	
	-15	X	X	–	–	–	–	
	-16	X	X A, OZ	X	X	X A	X	
	-17	X	X OZ	–	X	–	X	
	-18	X	X	X	X	–	X	
	-20	X	X A	X	X	–	X	
	-21	X	X A	X	–	–	X	
	-22	X	X	X	X	–	X	
	-23	X	X OZ	X	X	–	X	
	-24	X	X A	X	X P	X	X	X
	-25	X	X	X	X	–	X	X
	-26	X	X	X	X P	X	X	
	-27	X	X A	X	X	–	X	
	-29	X	X	X	X S	–	X	
	-31	X	X	X	X S	X	X	
	-32	X	X OZ	–	–	–	X	
	-33	X	X A	X	X S	–	X	
	-34	X	X	X	X	–	X	
	-35	X	X	X	X	–	X	
	-37	X	X A	X	X S	X	X	
	-39	X	X	X	X	–	X	
	-43	X	X A, OZ	X	X	–	X	
	-44	X	X	X	X	X	X	
	-47	X	X	X	X S	X	X	
% of samples that contain inclusion:		100%	100%	77%	84%	26%	97%	

Key:
A — Altered
OZ — Oscillatory Zoning
S — Strongly Pleochroic
P — Plentiful
X — Present
– — Absent

(which were plastic when the vessel was manufactured) and vesicular globules have also been observed. The mineral inclusions are compatible with a residual clay soil profile developed on a metamorphic calc-silicate rock formation. Similar inclusions have been noted in pottery from nearby Vasilike, from the immediately preceding period (by Myer, in Betancourt et al. 1979, p. 5, Table I).

Both the quantity and the coarseness of the inclusions vary considerably, depending on the shape of the vessel. Since cups are fine textured while jars are coarse textured, the variations are obviously deliberate. There is more than one possible explanation. A common way of preparing clay is to mix it with water in large settling pits, a process still in use in Greece today. This refining technique, often enhanced by the addition of a deflocculant, collects coarser particles at the bottom and finer material at a higher level. A potter can then choose his material as desired. Since differential deposition may also occur in nature, it is also possible that the potters chose naturally sorted clays. A third possibility is a mixing of clays, with varying amounts of a coarse clay or soil being added to a fine clay. While it is likely that some of the inclusions were added as temper for the largest vessels, they occur as tiny particles even in the finest textured cups.

The dark-firing slip has been examined by several analytical techniques. The only coloring agent is iron, which means that the color was produced by reduction during the firing rather than by the addition of a pigment. Analysis by proton microprobe has been able to compare the elemental composition of the slip and fabric. The iron content is slightly higher in the slip (it has a mean of 12% by weight, with a standard deviation of 2, as opposed to 9.8% in the fabric, with a standard deviation of 3). Mg, Ni, Ca, and Cr are lower in the slip, while Zn, As, and Pb are lower in the fabric. While the possibility that this difference arises from the preparation of the slip cannot be entirely excluded (since the fineness of the slip would result in a concentration of fine grained minerals and the exclusion of the coarser fragments), it is more likely that the potters chose two different clays or mixtures, one for the fabric and another for the slip. To achieve the desired fineness, the potter would need to make a colloidal suspension of clay in water and allow the mixture to settle. The finest layer from the top would be saved for use as the slip.

The other raw material, the white substance used for the decoration, has also been investigated. Previous researches into the white slips used for EM III and MM I–III pottery have identified both huntite (Stos-Fertner et al. 1979, p. 192, table 1) and talc (Noll 1977, p. 27). At Gournia, however, the elemental analyses have not found the high magnesium content which would indicate one of these minerals. High aluminum, silicon, calcium, and iron contents indicate the white is a calcium rich argillaceous material. Examination by thin section shows it to be transparent and anisotropic, with three phases present. Its original appearance was probably very much like *asprochoma*, a term used in Crete for any white clay of the type used until modern times for roofs.

Since the potter's wheel was not introduced to Crete until MM IB, East Cretan white-on-dark ware is made by hand. The vessels are well finished, and seams are not visible with the naked eye. Xeroradiography, an X-ray technique with a very high resolution, shows that the walls were built up from slabs of clay up to 10 cm or more wide. Cross sections illustrate the remarkable uniformity of the walls, indicating much wet working, a fact that is confirmed by the alignment of inclusions and air bubbles (visible with low-power microscopic examination of cross sections sawed through the walls). The vases were thus made by a slow, careful method, with much turning during the work. Experiments suggest that a skillful potter can make a cup in 20 to 30 minutes.

After drying, the vessels would be ready for firing. The final result was an oxidized pale buff body with a red to black reduced slip and clean white decoration.

Experiments to duplicate these effects were conducted in a small built kiln using gas for the primary heat in combination with wood as an accessory fuel to create the necessary reducing atmosphere. Good results were achieved with a reducing followed by an oxidizing atmosphere, a simple procedure in a kiln stoked with wood. Whenever wood is added to the fire, the smoky, oxygen depleted (reducing) atmosphere causes the iron in the clay to form black ferrous oxide. The fineness of the slip causes sintering and partial vitrification, a process that can be verified in ancient sherds by examining them under the scanning electron microscope. The vitrification traps the black color within the slip, and as soon as the reducing condition clears, the porous clay body reoxidizes to a buff hue while the slip remains dark. The technique has been previously documented in Minoan pottery from both earlier times (Farnsworth and Simmons 1963, pp. 392–93; Betancourt et al. 1979, chapter II) and later times (Noll 1977, pp. 25–26).

As used at Gournia, the pyrotechnology has a high margin of error. Good results were achieved with many different clays, with the best results using a firing temperature of ca. 1000 °C. While the slip must be finer than the body, no real precision is necessary in the settling operation. Good effects were achieved both with slips that have higher iron contents than the body and with the same clay used for both body and slip. Once the basic process is understood, an experienced potter could duplicate the results under primitive conditions with a wide range of raw materials.

Preliminary indications suggest the ware had both secular and funerary uses. It is found in many different contexts, in both settlements and tombs. Modern folk potters in the area suggest a number of possible models for pottery distribution, including traveling craftsmen and sedentary potters who market their wares over a considerable distance. More direct information on the EM III situation is furnished by the vase shapes, which suggest local preferences for particular types, perhaps reflecting particular sources of supply. More evidence should be forthcoming with future analyses of sherds from different sites.

The white-on-dark ware project is still continuing, and the preliminary results are still being evaluated. Scheduled work includes analysis of clay samples from eastern Crete, to contribute more information on the local clay resources. Experiments with Cretan clays will provide information on the elemental depletion or enrichment one may expect with different settling and refining methods, such as the effect of using wood ash as a deflocculant. In particular, the examination and analysis of samples from sites other than the type site should provide more complete knowledge on the range of the ware and on the question of trade as opposed to local manufacture at different centers. Our knowledge of white-on-dark ware is just beginning, and much work remains to be done.

Acknowledgments: Portions of the project are being funded by a grant from the National Endowment for the Humanities, no. RD-000158-79-1363, and by grants from Temple University. Thanks are extended to the following museums for permitting material to be sampled for analysis: University Museum, University of Pennsylvania; Ashmolean Museum, Oxford University; Art Museum, Mount Holyoke College, South Hadley, Mass.; Museum of Fine Arts, Boston, Mass.

References

Betancourt, Philip P. 1977. Some chronological problems in the Middle Minoan dark-on-light pottery of eastern Crete. *American Journal of Archaeology* 81: 341–53.

Betancourt, Philip P.; Gaisser, Thomas K.; Koss, Eugene; Lyon, Robert F.; Matson, Frederick R.; Montgomery, Steven; Myer, George H.; and Swann, Charles P. 1979. *Vasilike ware. An Early Bronze Age pottery style in Crete*. Göteborg: Paul Åströms Förlag.

Cadogan, Gerald. 1978. Pyrgos, Crete, 1970–77. *Archaeological Reports for 1977–78*: 70–84.

Creutzburg, N., et al. 1977. General geological map of Greece. Crete Island. Athens: Institute of Geological and Mining Research.

Dawkins, R. M. 1903/4. Excavations at Palaikastro, III. *Annual of the British School at Athens* 10: 192–226.

———. 1904/5. Excavations at Palaikastro, IV. *Annual of the British School at Athens* 11: 258–92.

Farnsworth, Marie, and Simmons, Ivor. 1963. Coloring agents for Greek glazes. *American Journal of Archaeology* 67: 389–96.

Hall, Edith H. 1904/5. Early painted pottery from Gournia, Crete. *Transactions of the Department of Archaeology, Free Museum of Science and Art* 1: 191–205.

Noll, Walter. 1977. Techniken antiker Töpfer und Vasenmaler. *Antike Welt* 8, 2: 21–36.

Sackett, L. H.; Popham, Mervyn R.; and Warren, Peter M. 1965. Excavations at Palaikastro, VI. *Annual of the British School at Athens* 60: 248–314.

Seager, Richard B. 1906/7. Report of excavations at Vasiliki, Crete, in 1906. *Transactions of the Department of Archaeology, Free Museum of Science and Art* 2: 111–32.

Philip P. Betancourt

_____. 1909. Excavations on the island of Mochlos, Crete, in 1908. *American Journal of Archaeology* 13: 273–303.

Stos-Fertner, Z.; Hedges, R. E. M.; and Evely, R. D. G. 1979. The application of the XRF–XRD method to the analysis of the pigments of Minoan painted pottery. *Archaeometry* 21: 187–94.

Warren, Peter. 1972. *Myrtos. An Early Bronze Age settlement in Crete.* Oxford: British School of Archaeology at Athens, Suppl. Paper 7.

17. Kilns and Ceramic Technology of Ancient Mesoamerica

WILLIAM O. PAYNE

Abstract

Microscopic and chemical analyses were made of specimens recovered from excavations in the Valley of Oaxaca, Mexico, to determine the geologic origins. Field studies were conducted to find the pottery materials for comparison. Contemporary potters were subjected to close scrutiny of their preparation, forming, and firing practices to learn what to look for in ancient wares and to compare the technologies. Kiln structures were examined very closely, resulting in the identification of kilns and kiln sites of approximately 600 A.D.

Introduction

These studies were begun in 1958 in the Valley of Oaxaca and adjacent terrain, in southern Mexico, and are continuing to the present day. The primary object was to reveal as much as possible regarding the technology of pre-Columbian pottery making. First was a thorough study of the geology of the valley. Second, samples were taken of soils suitable for the production of ceramic bodies. (NOTE: The author uses the ceramist's term "body," rather than the limited, and inaccurate, word "paste.") Suitable materials were found in situ where they were formed by the disintegration of rock formations and in places such as alluvial fans, river banks, and flood plains. Third, modern village potters were studied to determine present methods of preparation of bodies and formation of wares. This work revealed clues as to the techniques of ancient potters. Fourth, modern village kilns were examined for clues in the search for ancient firing technologies. As a result, two kilns were recognized from the period of ca. 600 A.D. Fifth, various firing methods of the present day were studied and experimented with in an attempt to duplicate atmospheres and temperatures used for ancient ware.

Raw Materials

Collection of soils and minerals from many formations was made. Alluvial fans were found to produce suitable bodies originating by decomposition of tertiary rocks, such as rhyolite, andesite, and acid granites. The plastic component was supplied largely by decomposed feldspars. The angular shapes of the granular components indicated nearby sources of the above rocks. Cretaceous formations produced compositions of clayslates, limestones, and metamorphic sandstones. Extensive flood plains are made up of mixtures of the above residues in varying amounts depending upon the distances transported and the hydrological history. Most of these soils exhibit deoxygenation resulting in light to dark gray colors. Many of them carry small amounts of angular pyroclastic ash, similar to the fallout produced by Mount St. Helens, Washington. Another source of coarse body is from the decomposition of Precambrian gneisses and schists. These are among the most ancient rocks on the North American continent and are found on the surface only in southern Mexico.

A deposit of high quality kaolinite was found near Mitla, Oaxaca. It is probably a source of the off-white body used in the valley in ancient times. It was formed by the percolation of hot volcanic waters through a very large feldspar dike. Levigation produced a very fine slip clay. A commercial deposit of fine white kaolin is presently producing clay for local factories. It occurs near Nochistlan and may be the source of the white slip clay used on Mixtec polychrome decoration.

Mineral oxides are found in many places in and near the valley. Red iron oxides are common, and the dioxide of manganese occurs as veins at San Pedro el Alto. These along with the white kaolin were the principal colorants for washes and slip painting.

The ratio of plastic components (i.e., clays) to nonplastics (quartz, feldspars, micas) measured by dry weight, after levigation and decanting, was clustered around 50:50, or half and half. That ratio is common today for the industrial production of commercial ceramic bodies.

Samples of soils and lightly crushed fragments of pottery were glued side by side for microscopic determination of mineral content regardless of the color of the specimens. A rubber-tipped pestle was used in a porcelain mortar to avoid crushing of nonplastics. Most of the complicated classifications of Oaxacan pottery have, in the past, been based upon color changes due to firing conditions, rather than upon mineral composition. Of the some eighteen to twenty thousand sherds and fired bodies examined microscopically, not one was found to contain crushed fired pottery as the nonplastic component.

The excavation of Tomb 2 at Lambityeco produced a large quantity of unfired ceramics. Some pieces were made of the coarse red Precambrian material, but most were formed of the gray valley floor soil. The former was found in nearby ravines and the latter was found within a half kilometer of the tomb site. Much of the material had been removed in ancient times, leaving mounds topped by very old trees held up by clusters of roots. Sherds formerly used as scrapers were common in the clay pits.

The author has observed (over many months of field studies of many sites) that almost 100% of the pottery at a given site was made within a 2-kilometer radius of that location. A search within that range will usually reveal the body source, as well as a source of water and of fuel. If the area has not been plowed or covered by vegetation, it may be possible to find old kiln structures.

Body Preparation

Preparation of the material for use is a homogenizing process called "wedging," a method of kneading the wet body. The material is crushed to speed wetting, and rocks, if present, are picked out by hand. Several cones of prepared body were found in Tomb 2 at Lambityeco. These had been shaped in the same way that Oriental potters today prepare body for use in the village potteries.

Forming of Ware

Many clues as to forming methods may be found in ancient ware. "Ropes" of body were laid up in concentric rings for the walls. This technique has been miscalled "coiling" for many years. One may observe the evidence often, on the inside or outside of the ware. The rings are pinched up to thin out the walls which are subsequently scraped and/or burnished on the outside of jars and the inside of bowls and dishes. Some pieces from the Early and Middle Formative periods showed evidence of the lower half of large jars being formed over an existing pot, then finished by adding concentric rings for the upper half. That wood ash was used to prevent sticking is proven by observing pockmarks left by burned-out charcoal fragments. Ash is used today by many potters for the same purpose. Imprints of matting are occasionally seen, showing that slabs were patted out before laying up on the mold. Many large figures were molded entirely by hand, while smaller, mass-produced pieces were partially hand-formed, with mold-made additions. Many of these molds have been found.

Kilns

Extensive studies were made of contemporary village pottery kiln structures. Some potters simply pile the ware loosely, in the open, place fuels under and over the pots, set the mound afire, then wait until combustion is complete. Others make a ring of large pots on open ground, place fuel on the ground, stack the pots on that, cover the pile with more fuel and fire it off. Some build much more elaborate structures for more controlled temperature and atmosphere control. Two pits are dug in the ground about a half meter apart with a hearth tunnel joining them at the bottom. A perforated floor of adobe bricks is made in one pit at the level of the top of the tunnel. The other pit is used for fuel storage and stoking of the fire. In other villages a large cylinder is laid up of rocks and mud mortar on the surface with a covered hearth on one side. The floor of the firing chamber is made in the same way as the subterranean models.

William O. Payne

Figure 1. Consolidated remains of a pottery kiln found in a habitation site on the slopes of Monte Alban, Oaxaca, Mexico. Diameter of the ware chamber is 1.40 M (4'7"). Rocks which formed the cylindrical wall were dispersed downhill to form farming terraces. The kiln was in use ca. 600 A.D.

Measurements made of the firing aperture were found in square area to equal the total area of the perforations in the firing floor. This formula is that used by contemporary Western potters for their up-draft and down-draft kilns. This research led to the identification of two kilns in a residential site on the slopes of Monte Alban (Fig. 1). They were thought to be storage pits until recognized as pottery kilns built about 600 A.D. The larger kiln was semisubsurface with the firing chamber excavated in the bed rock and the ware chamber built on the surface of laid-up local rocks. A very small kiln was cut in a bank of bed rock, but was in such poor condition that its total structure was conjectural in details.

Firing Methods: Fuels, Atmospheres, and Temperatures

Owing to the absence of known kilns suitable for the production of the reduced black ware of the Oaxaca region, reference was made to the methods employed by the Pueblo potters of New Mexico. Experiments were conducted and resulted in duplicate gray-black color of the wares fired and smothered. Since the discovery of the Monte Alban kilns, it is now known that the pre-Columbian potters were using the iron oxide reduction technique. For pots to be fired in the open area, pot-wall techniques were given a "bon voyage" blessing with a burning twig before being packed inside the kiln wall on dried maguey leaves. More leaves were piled on top of the load and it was set alight on the downwind side. More fuel was placed on top to even the burning as it progressed. A thermocouple stuck inside one of the pots recorded a temperature of 700 °C, about 1300 °F, in 50 minutes. The ware was allowed to cool to 300 °C before drawing of the ware began.

The subterranean kilns are loaded to the top of the chamber and laid over with sherds of broken ware. A very low fire is lighted and allowed to burn for about 3 hours to drive off the hygroscopic water; then the principal fuel of oak is added for about 8 hours until the ware seen through the sherds glows a dull red. More fuel is added, often including resinous pine. When the fire is at peak heat, the kiln is sealed quickly with mud on the top over the sherds, an adobe brick is placed in the fire door, and the seal is made air-tight with mud mortar. This technique causes the ware to burn black because of oxygen starvation. The kiln is allowed to cool for about 8 hours, when the chamber is opened for removal of the ware. Recorded temperature was 750 °C, or about 1400 °F.

A large pot was recovered in pieces and reconstructed. The pieces had apparently been used as covering sherds, in different firings. There are varying degrees of reduction of the iron content; some of the fragments are a light brown and others are shaded in values of gray to almost black.

Summary

The application of disciplines in geology, mineralogy, physical chemistry, and a knowledge of the art and craft of the potter have led to some significant revelations in an area hitherto ignored. The truism "it takes one to know one" has never been more applicable than in this research. The author is a potter, not a scientist, and as such relates directly to the craft upon which so much archaeological "evidentia" depends.

It is hoped that this brief review stimulates field archaeologists to depend upon an exhaustive study of the simple, physical evidence of the potters' art, before resorting to expensive and sophisticated analytical processes. Comparative studies, of course, are only useful where there is a probable continuum of cultural pattern. The situation in the Oaxaca Valley is such that it may be used as a pattern for research— the living potters are using the technology developed by their ancestors. Modern ceramic technology has made definite inroads on their craft, but the fundamentals are still there.

The result of these intensive studies of the crafts of the modern potters has led to the presently expanding discoveries of kilns and kiln sites for the making of pottery of earlier times. Without the indispensable device of the kiln, there is no way in which pottery could have been made of the quality found throughout Mesoamerica. The kilns excavated at Monte Alban are presumably identified as the first permanent structures for firing pottery in Mesoamerica. In the past month [9-1-80] another large pottery kiln has been uncovered in the Monte Alban zone; see M. Winter, field notes, INAH Regional Center, Oaxaca, Mexico, personal communication.

Acknowledgments: The author is indebted to Dr. John Paddock of the Institute of Oaxacan Studies, Mitla, Oaxaca, and to Dr. Kent V. Flannery, Director of the University of Michigan Oaxaca Valley Project.

References

Caso, A., and Bernal, I. 1952. *Urnas de Oaxaca*. Oaxaca, Mexico: INAH.

Caso, A.; Bernal, I.; and Acosta, J. R. 1967. *La ceramica de Monte Alban*. Oaxaca, Mexico: INAH.

Cornwall, I. W. 1958. *Soils for the archaeologist*. London: Phoenix House.

Guthe, Carl E. 1925. *Pueblo pottery making*. New Haven: Phillips Academy, Department of Archaeology.

Payne, W. O. 1970. "A potter's analysis of the pottery from Lambityeco Tomb 2." *Boletin de Estudios Oaxaquenos* (Mitla), no. 29.

Winter, M. C., and Payne, W. O. 1976. Hornos para ceramica hallados en Monte Alban. *Boletin INAH*, no. 16.

18. Ceramic Technology and Problems and Prospects of Provenience in Specific Ceramics from Mexico and Afghanistan

CHARLES C. KOLB
Department of Anthropology
The Behrend College of The Pennsylvania
State University

Abstract

The theme of this research follows Frederick R. Matson's statement in *Ceramics and Man* that "unless ceramics studies lead to a better understanding of the cultural context in which the objects were made and used, they form a sterile record of limited worth" (1965a, p. 202). The ultimate goal of ongoing technological investigations of Mesoamerican "Thin Orange" ceramics from central Mexico, and Central Asian "Red Streak-Burnished" ware from northern Afghanistan is to identify the loci of manufacture and determine the sociocultural mechanisms whereby these ceramics were distributed in their respective culture areas. The results of my technological, mineralogical, and petrographic investigations are summarized, and the suggested cultural mechanisms of distribution elaborated. The Mesoamerican ceramic (150 B.C.–A.D. 850) has numerous variants based on aplastic analysis, and was manufactured primarily outside of the Basin of Mexico but also at the metropolis of Teotihuacan, in the main during the Classic Teotihuacan period. The Afghan ware (A.D. 140–550) was apparently made in Baluchistan and transported northward, ultimately destined for the market centers of Central Asia. The results of these studies are discussed, and analytical problems and interpretational difficulties are noted at this interface between archaeological and physical scientific investigations.

Introduction

Recent publications in archaeology have stressed the processual analytical approach as contrasted with a strictly historical analytical approach (Wetherington 1978). Although both viewpoints are valid, the intellectual stimulation derived from their interaction demonstrates the need for archaeologists to become more proficient in relating their own research to ethnographic, ethnohistoric, and archaeological problems. The archaeologist's goal should be to explicate archaeological data within a framework of the social and behavioral sciences as well as the arts and humanities. At the same time the archaeological investigator is reliant upon analytical techniques that derive from the physical sciences, especially chemistry and physics. Therefore the sites, artifacts, and contexts are analyzed and initially interpreted within the physical sciences, yet the ultimate interpretations are social and humanistic. As a result, the archaeologist is present at the interface between these realms, and with a "foot in each camp" attempts to resolve the interface problems whereby both physical scientists and archaeologists benefit from one another's specializations and research interests.

Distribution and exchange systems and mechanisms have been of concern to ethnohistorians and ethnographers for many years (e.g., Polanyi, Arensberg, and Pearson 1957), and during the last decade have become a focus of extensive and intensive archaeological investigations (Wilmsen 1972; Hodder 1974; Wright 1974; Sabloff and Lamberg-Karlovsky 1975; Earle and Ericson 1977; among others). Such interest in prehistoric and early historic exchange systems stems from the recognition of exchange and distribution systems as a factor in the maintenance and dynamics of cultural systems within cultural ecological and both synchronic and diachronic perspectives (Peacock 1977). In addition, innovations in quantification techniques and physical and chemical analyses of artifacts have allowed more detailed and intensive studies, ultimately generating more finite descriptive, ethnohistorical, and systemic models, as for example Kamilli and Lamberg-Karlovsky's (1979) work.

A most beneficial methodology is that of ceramic ecology, previously elaborated by Matson (1965a) in Near Eastern studies, whereby archaeology, ceramic technology (especially the physical and chemical studies), and ethnology are related. In a seminal statement in *Ceramics and Man* Matson proposed that: "Unless ceramics studies lead to a better understanding of the cultural context in which the objects were made and used, they form a sterile record of limited worth" (1965a, p. 202). He elaborated such variables as the environment, water, food, fuel, clay, the potter, the product, and the interactions, noting that the transitory equilibrium existing between the physical, biological, and cultural elements is easily altered (1965a, p. 213). In "Ceramic Queries" Matson enumerated seventeen major variables, each with a series of questions, that the ethnographer should be asking (1965b). I have elaborated these queries and applied them to contemporary Latin American potters (Kolb 1976). The five primary variables in transitory equilibrium were elaborated (1976, pp. 40–47, fig. 2), and are diagrammatically presented here as Figure 1.

Muscarella (1975), among others, has warned that ceramic evidence may be easily misinterpreted, and called for careful handling of the material, and a conservative approach to the interpretation of the pottery and the data derived from technical analyses. He observed that "archaeology is not a science," because the interpretation of the material is subject to human fallibility (1975, p. 65). While his statement is debatable, one cannot deny that the cultural interpretation of ceramic technological data is intriguing and fraught with potential interpretive pitfalls.

In this paper I shall employ two sets of data to illustrate the problems and prospects of provenience studies. One data set is from the Basin of Mexico and environs in Mesoamerica and concerns an important diagnostic ceramic termed "Thin Orange" ware, previously detailed as having two primary types, *Alpha* and *Beta* (Kolb 1973, 1977a, 1978). The second data set is derived from sites in the foothills of the Hindu Kush of Afghanistan in Central Asia, where an unusual ceramic called "Red Streak-Burnished" ware was discerned (Kolb 1977b, 1980). As a participant in the Teotihuacan Valley Project of The Pennsylvania State University from 1961 to 1965, I analyzed Classic Teotihuacan ceramics from 135 sites in the valley. Among these was Thin Orange. From 1965 to 1966 I was a member of the Archaeological Mission of the American Museum of Natural History in northern Afghanistan and directed the excavation of sites which yielded the Red Streak-Burnished ware. In addition, I conducted the initial ceramic studies (Dupree and Kolb 1972). Therefore I had the opportunity of being both the surveyor-excavator as well as the ceramic technologist.

Archaeological investigations and preliminary petrographic analyses by myself and others suggested that *Alpha* type Thin Orange could not have been manufactured at sites in the Basin of Mexico (Kolb 1973; Harbottle et al. 1976). However, the *Beta* type could have been an indigenous product made in the Teotihuacan subvalley of the Basin of Mexico (Kolb 1977a, 1978). The Red Streak-Burnished ware was not manufactured at the sites where it was excavated, nor was it apparently made in other locales in northern Afghanistan or Soviet Central Asia (Kolb 1977b).

Therefore, once basic problems of chronology had been resolved for these ceramics, the primary question of provenience remained. Ultimately cultural mechanisms for the importation of *Alpha* type and Red Streak-Burnished ceramics could be suggested on the basis of ethnohistoric and ethnographic data and analogies. It is hypothesized that *Alpha* Thin Orange was made from clays whose sources are in southern Puebla and adjacent geomorphic regions southeast of the Teotihuacan Valley and Basin of

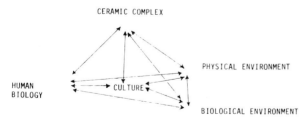

Figure 1. Ceramic complex: Three-dimensional five variable model.

Table 1. Basin of Mexico: Partial chronology[a]

Stage	Chronology	Phase Name
Post Classic	750–850 A.D.	Xometla/Oxtotipac
Classic	650–750	Metepec
	550–650	Late Xolalpan (Maquixco)
	450–550	Early Xolalpan
	350–450	Late Tlamimilolpa
	250–350	Early Tlamimilolpa
	200–250	Miccaotli
	150–200	Apetlac (Early Miccaotli)
	50–150	Teopan (Late Tzacualli)
Preclassic	100 B.C.–50 A.D.	Oxtotla (Early Tzacualli)
	300–100 B.C.	Tezoyuca/Patlachique

[a]After Kolb 1977a, p. 534.

Map 1. Central Mexico and the Teotihuacan Valley

[by CCK]

Mexico. The *Beta* type was made and locally consumed at the urban center of Teotihuacan in the valley of the same name. In addition, it is hypothesized — primarily on the basis of archaeological evidence — that the Red Streak-Burnished ware originated near the site of Sutkagen-dor in present-day Pakistan. I believe that the *Alpha* Thin Orange was imported via a long-distance trading network similar to that of the Aztec *pochteca* from its source in Puebla or adjacent areas into the Basin of Mexico. Red Streak-Burnished ceramics from southern Pakistan were transported into Central Asia by historic Kushan and/or Surashthan peoples. One must, of course, be aware of potential "traps" that exist in suggesting how artifacts are moved from one place to another (Hole and Heizer 1977, p. 227).

The subsequent sections of this paper briefly elaborate the technological, mineralogical, and petrographic investigations of each ware. Sociocultural mechanisms are suggested on the basis of current results for each. Provenience determination is at the crux of the research, and the analytical problems and interpretational difficulties are discerned at this interface between the physical sciences and the archaeological goal of the cultural and humanistic evaluations of ceramic data.

Thin Orange Ware

Introduction

During the course of the Teotihuacan Valley Project in the northeastern section of the Basin of Mexico,

twenty-two excavations were conducted in various rural sites (Sanders 1965). [*See* Table 1 for the various Teotihuacan chronologies, and Map 1 for the location of the Teotihuacan Valley.] Twelve of these sites had Classic Teotihuacan components containing Thin Orange ceramics. In addition, 135 Classic sites were systematically surface-surveyed and ceramic samples collected (Kolb 1969, 1973). The excavations provided 2,890 Thin Orange sherds, while survey samples yielded an additional 1,480 for a total of 4,370 sherds, versus the 854 surface collected sherds studied by Tolstoy (1958, p. 19). The total Thin Orange sample was examined in order to discern typological, chronological, and technological data which were published elsewhere (Kolb 1973); however, only 1,300 of the 2,890 excavated sherds were utilized in original analysis regarding aplastic content. The remaining 1,590 excavated and 1,480 surface sample sherds now have also been intensively examined regarding aplastic material content. Collections of Thin Orange ware in the American Museum of Natural History and Museo Nacional de Antropologia were also studied.

The ceramics collected by Teotihuacan Valley Project personnel were examined in the Department of Anthropology Ceramic Technology Laboratory, The Pennsylvania State University (1968–1969), and/or in the Department of Anthropology's Archaeology Laboratory, Bryn Mawr College (1970–1972). The analysis was conducted by the use of a binocular microscope (60x magnification) and a tangential nonfluorescent lighting source. A "fresh break" in the paste was made with pliers to facilitate the examination of worn sherd edges. The same equipment was employed in both laboratories, and I made all of the evaluations. It was also determined that basic distinctions could be made between the types by using a 20x hand lens in normal daylight. This technique has been used in the field and the same sherds were rechecked in the laboratory to determine accuracy (98.5%). The total Thin Orange ware collection (n = 4,370) was examined in order to discern the kinds, sizes, and relative quantities of aplastics, using the late Anna Shepard's *Ceramics for the Archaeologist* (1968, pp. 25-31, 156-57) and training gained at Penn State in the seminar "Ceramics and Man," taught by Professor Frederick R. Matson, as bases for analysis. The manuscript on the typological, chronological and technological analyses of Thin Orange (Kolb 1973) benefited from written comments made by both of these ceramic technologists.

Thirty Thin Orange sherds (twenty excavated and ten from surface survey collections) were selected for thin section analyses. The sections were commercially prepared, and "control" sherds kept as suggested by Shepard (1968, p. 159). The petrographic microscope examinations followed the procedures suggested by petrographers (Deer, Howie, and Zussman 1962; Heinrich 1965; Mielenz, King and Schieltz 1950; Saggerson 1975; Winchell 1957). The analyses confirmed the binocular microscope (60x) examination, and resulted in the delineations elaborated below.

The analysis of the 4,370 sherds indicated that the Classic Teotihuacan Thin Orange pottery, which was easily discerned from Post Classic Aztec Plain Orange ceramics, had notable characteristics. The light colored clay was thickly strewn with opaque, translucent, lustrous and crystalline aplastics; few clear grains were found. The major constituents included: quartzite, calcined calcite, talc, quartz, muscovite mica, and hematite. Minor inclusions were: feldspars, hornblende, chlorites, and scoria. No vegetable fibers or seeds of any kind were observed. The sherds examined could be divided into two distinctive groups, Type *Alpha* and Type *Beta*.

Specific petrographic and other data on *Alpha* and *Beta* Thin Orange ceramics may be found in Appendix I, end of this chapter.

General Conclusions

Type *Alpha* conformed to Sotomayor y Castillo Tejero's (1963) Group "A" (Subgroups A-1 and A-2). Their initial results were later confirmed by de la Cadena, Franco, and Escobar (1967). It was also identical to "Core Thin Orange," identified by the

neutron-activation analyses of ceramic clays by Harbottle, Sayre, and Abascal (1976, p. 15). The latter concluded that Teotihuacan itself, Acatlan, Izcaquixtla, and the area near the mouth of the Rio Coatzalcoalcos were not the sources of clay and hence the center of manufacture. They consider southern Puebla and adjacent geomorphic regions potential clay sources, confirming earlier suppositions (Sotomayor and Castillo Tejero 1963; Kolb 1973, 1976). Harbottle et al. also discern a small number of "Classic Teotihuacan Thin Orange" sherds as "atypical," but made from local Teotihuacan (San Sebastian) clays. It may be that these specimens conform to Subgroup A-3 (lacking calcite), but further investigations are required. "Classic Teotihuacan Thin Orange" could be restricted to the urban center and does not appear in my sample from primarily rural and urban fringe sites.

Type *Beta* sherds (n = 112) generally had the same aplastics as *Alpha*, but in different percentages. The major temper was muscovite mica rather than biotite mica (as in Sotomayor and Castillo Tejero's Groups B and C). These micas are closely related in structure and properties, occurring in many kinds of granitic rocks and in siliceous metamorphic rocks, but cannot always be distinguished on the basis of color (Saggerson 1975, pp. 354-55). *Beta* Thin Orange has culturally been referred to as "Coarse Thin Orange" to differentiate it from the more common *Alpha* ware (Kolb 1965, 1973). The *Beta* ceramic dated to the terminal Metepec Phase of the Classic and the initial Post-Classic Oxtotipac Phase in the Teotihuacan Valley. It was rare in rural sites but more notably represented in the eastern urban area near modern Hacienda Metepec.

Beta Thin Orange in both phases was associated with only two vessel forms: (1) flared-rim high-necked jars, frequently with strap handles, during the Metepec Phase, and (2) large cylindrical vases (up to 68 cm in diameter) with mold-made tripod supports (solid or hollow types) and occasional stamped or appliqued mold-made decorations. The restricted number of types and chronology as well as sherd frequencies suggest a probable local manufacture, perhaps utilizing local clays and imported aplastics. This is in direct opposition to my earlier hypothesis that the vicinity of Huajuapan de Leon, Oaxaca, was a possible production center of *Beta* Thin Orange (Kolb 1973). Supporting evidence for local manufacture comes from a paper by Rattray (1976), in which a Metepec Phase Thin Orange workshop at Teotihuacan is reported to have specialized in the production of "coarse amphoras" (the high-necked jars). The substantial quantities of mica make neutron activation studies of the archaeological ceramic

Charles C. Kolb

Table 2. Aq Kupruk: Afghanistan chronology[a]

Stage	Chronology	Phase Name
Historic	1800–present	Modern Nomadic
	1200–1800 A.D.	Late Islamic
	700–1200	Early Islamic
	500–700	Late Iron Age
	B.C./A.D.–400 A.D.	Early Iron Age
Neolithic	2000–1700 B.C.	"Goat Burial"
	5200–4200	Ceramic
	6800–5200	Nonceramic B
	9500–9000	Nonceramic A
Upper Paleolithic	14,900–14,400	Kuprukian B
	20,000–15,000	Kuprukian A

[a]After Kolb 1977b, p. 536.

Map 2. Central Asia and Aq Kupruk

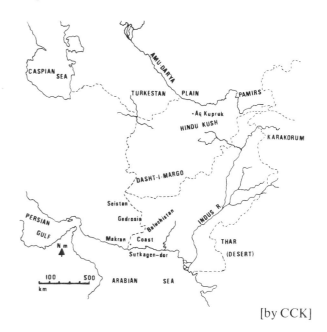

[by CCK]

difficult, but it may be that clays from San Sebastian, a modern and Classic Period pottery-making center, were employed in the manufacture of *Beta* ware. Hacienda Metepec and San Sebastian are less than 3 km apart. A further elaboration is found in Kolb (1978), where seven sociocultural postulates regarding the manufacture and distribution of Thin Orange are evaluated.

Alpha Thin Orange was recognized as an imported ware over forty years ago (Linne 1934; Kolb 1973) and has proven to be a particularly intriguing problem in discerning provenience. Harbottle and his colleagues have been able to discern only where the ceramic was *not* made, and have only been able to suggest the region of southern Puebla and adjacent geomorphic locations as probable sources (Harbottle, Sayre, and Abascal 1976). *Beta* Thin Orange, recognized as a distinct ceramic over fifteen years ago (Kolb 1965, 1973) on the basis of archaeological data and petrographic examination, presents a particular problem of provenience determination because of the cultural addition of muscovite mica as an aplastic. Contemporary potters at the San Sebastian are probably using the same clay sources but the sources have changed in composition over the last 1200 years. We have no archaeological samples of original raw clays to clarify the problem of *Beta* provenience.

Red Streak-Burnished Ware

Introduction

The Archaeological Mission of the American Mu-seum of Natural History in Afghanistan and the Kabul Museum (National Museum of Afghanistan) conducted excavations near the bazaar town of Aq Kupruk, Balkh Province, northern Afghanistan (Dupree et al. 1972). [*See* Table 2 for a regional chronology, and Map 2 for the location of the sites.] Four excavations were carried out in three caves and one open-air site in the gorge of the Balkh River in the northern foothills of the Hindu Kush Mountain Range, a westward extension of the Himalayas, on the fringe of the Turkestan PLAIN OF Central Asia.

The Aq Kupruk sites yielded a total of 21,433 sherds which I have classified into sixty-one types. A total of 1,079 sherds (Types 40–44) were defined on cultural and technological bases as "Aq Kupruk Red Streak-Burnished Ware" (Kolb 1977b). The data may be summarized as follows (Table 3).

A plot of radiocarbon dates for the Aq Kupruk sites during the Iron Age indicated that the earliest occurrence of the Red Streak-Burnished ware would be 140 A.D. and the most recent occurrence would be 550 A.D., a maximal time span of 410 years. The ceramic occurred primarily in deposits of the "Late Iron Age" in northern Afghanistan (Dupree et al. 1972, p. 75), but was also found in "Early Iron Age" strata at Aq Kupruk I. A time span of 150–400 A.D. may be suggested (Kolb 1977b, p. 536).

The ceramics were examined in the Department of Anthropology Ceramic Technology Laboratory, Pennsylvania State University (1969), and/or in the Department of Anthropology's Archaeology

Table 3. Red Streak-Burnished ware types

Site and Type	Subtotal	Total Sherds
Aq Kupruk I		
40, Plate-bowl, plain (burnished motif)	807	
41, Plate-bowl, striations (incised)	13	
42, Jar, plain (undecorated)	212	1,059
43, Jar, punctations	4	
44, Jar, stamped (eight subtypes)	23	
Aq Kupruk II		
40, Plate-bowl, plain (burnished motif)	1	1
Aq Kupruk IV		
40, Plate-bowl, plain (burnished motif)[a]	18	19
42, Jar, plain (undecorated)[b]	1	
Total		1,079

[a]All sherds fit two nearly complete vessels.
[b]Nearly complete miniature vessel (unguent jar).

Laboratory, Bryn Mawr College (1970–72). The analytical techniques employed were identical to those used in the study of the Thin Orange ware from the Teotihuacan Valley, Mexico. The same equipment was employed in both laboratories, and I made all of the evaluations. Five sherds were selected for thin section analyses, and a petrographic microscope examination followed the procedures previously delineated for the Mexican ceramics.

Specific analytical data on Red Streak-Burnished ware may be found in Appendix II, end of this chapter.

General Conclusions

The ceramics indicated a high degree of craft specialization because of consistencies in production methods, size, shape, decoration, slipping, and firing. Potters' signature stamps, roulette decoration, vessel manufacture by molding (terra sigillata), and micaceous paste were *not* characteristic of the ware. Vessel shapes were different than those delineated by Dragendorff, Loeschcke, Ritterling, Hermet, Knorr, and others. It is suggested that this ware was one of the locally manufactured "imitation" Arretine wares. However, the Aq Kupruk materials did not resemble the true or imitation Arretine ceramics found at Arikamedu (Wheeler, Gosh, and Deva 1946), nor

were there strong similarities to the eastern Mediterranean, Syrian, and other Near Eastern Arretine or sigillate pottery, namely Eastern Sigillate A and B Wares (Kolb 1980). It was definitely *not* Late Roman C Ware of the fourth century A.D. (Hayes 1972, pp. 323–70). The northern Afghanistan ceramics differed in form, although not in technology, from Seleucid and Parthian copies or other northwest Indian local renditions.

Therefore, it was probable that the Aq Kupruk Red Streak-Burnished ware represented a local Central or South Central Asian development. It was certain that the ceramic was not made from local Aq Kupruk clays used today, based on a preliminary study of mineral content. Sun-dried mud brick is manufactured in the modern community, but ceramics are not produced (Dupree 1968, p. 21). The archaeological sites near the community of Aq Kupruk (particularly Aq Kupruk I) were convenient stopovers on one of the north–south caravan routes from the Central Asian Turkestan Plain through the Hindu Kush to southern Afghanistan, Baluchistan, and the Indian subcontinent.

While Aq Kupruk I provided the overwhelming bulk of the Red Streak-Burnished ware sample, the more complete specimens came from Aq Kupruk IV. This latter site, "Skull" Cave, was a burial area which contained the remains of ten individuals and associated grave goods in a pit surrounded on three sides by a series of rough limestone blocks and on the fourth by the cave wall. The burial deposit was undisturbed, and was composed of partially disarticulated skeletal remains of male and female adults and child, indicative of secondary multiple interment. The skeletal population was studied by J. Lawrence Angel, John Bear, and Joy Bilharz Kolb at the Department of Physical Anthropology, Smithsonian Institution, Washington, D.C. (Bilharz Kolb et al. 1972). Their study of the adult males' muscle attachment scars indicated that a riding posture (horseback?) was common to their lifeways. Such secondary interments of human skulls with horse skulls and the bones of other animals, including dogs, gazelles, and pigs, have been reported from mud brick vaulted funeral chambers at Shahr-i Qumis, Khursan, Iran (Hansman and Stronach 1970a, 1970b; Matheson 1973, pp. 191–92). These dated to the Parthian period (ca. 70 B.C.) at the site, which is located near Tepe Hissar in north central Iran.

The grave furniture at Aq Kupruk IV included the two nearly complete plate-bowls and small unguent jar. In addition there was a circular bronze mirror of Chinese origin which was studied by Earl Caley at Ohio State University (Dupree et al. 1972, pp. 44–50). It appeared that the mirror dated to the Han

Charles C. Kolb

Dynasty, ca. 200 B.C.–A.D. 200. A silver finger ring with a lapis lazuli setting, a rectanguloid lapis bead, bronze finger rings, and iron and bronze horse (?) trappings were also recovered. A smashed double straphandle amphoralike globular bodied ceramic vessel (base missing), with a black to very dark gray (Munsell 1954) exterior slip on its upper half was also recovered and was designated Type 4. This vessel may be related to the Red Streak-Burnished ware, as it had similar paste color, texture, and hardness, and the same tempering and other nonplastics. The handles differed from those of Type 42 jars, but the rim was a bolstered square type reminiscent of the Red Streak-Burnished jars. This vessel was definitely *not* a Roman amphora (Dupree and Kolb 1972, p. 42, Fig. 134).

The geographical location of Aq Kupruk, south of the modern community of Mazar-i-Sharif on the Balkh River, made it an important commercial and political center on the north–south route from Bactria to the regions south of the Hindu Kush. The village of Aq Kupruk lay in a strategic position and had evidence of occupations dating to at least early Kushan of the first century A.D. Kushan column bases have been incorporated in the construction of a local mosque and in one teahouse (*chaykhanah*), and other column bases are used as tables in another teahouse. The Aq Kupruk sites I, II and IV are located within two kilometers down river, and have substantial ceramic materials dating to the Kushan and more recent culture periods. Buddhist paintings in a cave chamber adjacent to Aq Kupruk I dated to the period 500–700 A.D. Therefore, the locality was of some importance during the first through sixth centuries A.D.

Roman Arretine was produced at Arretium in northern Italy and was a highly prized and widely exported ceramic. It was related to "Pergameme" pottery and "Samian ware," made in the eastern Mediterranean during earlier times. Following the cessation of its manufacture in Italy, local imitations were made in Europe (Gaul, Spain, Germany, and England) and the Near East (especially Syria). Imitation and true Arretine wares reached the Indo-Roman trading station of Arikamedu (Pondicherry) on the Southeast Indian coast by sea routes between 25 and 45 A.D. (Wheeler, Gosh, and Deva 1946; Wheeler 1954). Present evidence suggests that a local imitation — Red Streak-Burnished Ware — was manufactured in the Baluchistan region ca. A.D. 150–400 (Kolb 1980). Strikingly similar ceramics relatively dated to the "Bronze Age" were reported from Gedrosia and in collections from Sutkagen-dor, a former Harappan seaport, by Stein (1931), but the Red Streak-Burnished ware at Aq Kupruk definitely

dates to A.D. 140–550 on the basis of radiocarbon dates and is incontrovertibly associated with the Han Dynasty mirror. It is postulated that one or more sites in Baluchistan or Gedrosia (present-day southeastern Iran and western Pakistan) received Roman material culture and/or influence. Sutkagen-dor or other sites in the region could have been the manufacturing center(s) for a local "pseudo-Arretine" pottery, copying or imitating true or Eastern Mediterranean forms, during late and post-Roman times. These dates would indicate that the assignment of a "Bronze Age" chronology was in error and that the ceramics were in reality "Iron Age." The context at Aq Kupruk is Early Iron Age while a Late Iron Age chronology existed at Sutkagen-dor. It appears that this ceramic, among others (Red/Buff), was traded northward by Kushan and/or Surashthan peoples or others into Central Asia during the first and later centuries A.D. Selucid and Parthian ceramics did not typologically or technologically conform to the Sutkagen-dor specimens.

Aq Kupruk was a stopover on the north–south trade route from Baluchistan to Balkh and the Turkestan Plain and received quantities of the new ceramic. Some specimens of the ware have been found in the collections from Balkh in the Kabul Museum. The ceramic was possibly destined for Antiochia Margiana (Merv), Bokhara, etc., but is not represented in sites from northern Iran. A search of the Soviet Central Asian archaeological literature has failed to uncover a similar ceramic ware. Further typological and technological studies are anticipated.

Extensive sampling of clay sources in southern Afghanistan and especially the Baluch areas of eastern Iran and Pakistan could resolve the Red Streak-Burnished provenience problem, although the compositions of the deposits have undoubtedly altered over the nearly two thousand intervening years. I am unaware of any raw clay samples from excavated sites which could help clarify this provenience problem. The political situation in Pakistan, and also in Afghanistan, for the time being precludes sampling from potential source areas, including Sutkagen-dor.

Problems and Prospects

Introduction

From the viewpoint of the physical sciences, the determination of provenience is a matter of comparing the research samples with materials of known association, a form of cross-locational analysis. In principle the study of potsherds by neutron activation analysis, for example, should yield data which can be related to the actual clay deposits, thereby establishing provenience in an absolute manner. However, this direct approach is one that cannot be generally employed, especially because it is difficult to obtain appropriate clay samples, and also because there may be questions or uncertainties as to how the artisans treated the clays prior to fabrication.

Under uncomplicated circumstances, the relationships between clay sources and ceramic products can be simple. The importation of pottery from distant regions of manufacture to place of use (and excavation) presents serious problems of exact provenience determination. Adequate sampling and systematic examination of all materials — sherds *and* clays — are at the basis for determining provenience. These, in turn, relate to the validity of the cultural mechanisms that are proposed on the basis of ethnographic analogs.

The goals of this paper were threefold: *(1)* to demonstrate that ceramics as archaeological material present unique interface problems of analysis and interpretation, as noted in the seminar prospectus; *(2)* to present data and interpretations on two unique wares: Mesoamerican Thin Orange and Central Asian Red Streak-Burnished; and *(3)* to relate these physical scientific data and interpretations to the archaeological social, behavioral, and humanistic interface. The latter was designed to reflect interface problems and prospects in ceramic investigations.

Two major types of Thin Orange found at urban and rural Classic Teotihuacan sites were discerned. Other investigators, on the basis of neutron activation analysis, have identified subtypes of the more common *Alpha* type (Abascal, Harbottle, and Sayre 1972, 1973; Harbottle 1973; Harbottle, Sayre, and Abascal 1976). *Alpha* Thin Orange / "Core Thin Orange" was manufactured and imported into the Classic Teotihuacan sites from loci external to the Basin of Mexico. I have elsewhere postulated an importation network model and mechanism for the type utilizing a *pochteca* (Aztec long-distance merchant-trader) mercantile model (Kolb 1978). *Beta* Thin Orange / "Coarse Thin Orange" first appeared in the Metepec phase of the Classic Teotihuacan chronology, and could have been produced in the vicinity of San Sebastian, part of the ancient Teotihuacan metropolis. The analytical and interpretive literature on Thin Orange ware is extensive (Kolb 1978).

Red Streak-Burnished ware from three Aq Kupruk sites in northern Afghanistan has been thus far reported only from those sites (Dupree and Kolb 1972; Kolb 1977b). The technological variables have been identified in the present paper. I have postulated that this ceramic was a local imitation of a "pseudo-Arretine" pottery and was a copy of East Mediterrane-

an forms most likely manufactured in Baluchistan or Gedrosia. The ware demonstrates a form of stimulus diffusion, as similar pottery was found and probably made at Sutkagen-dor (Stein 1931). It appears that some of the pottery was traded northward into south Central Asia and destined for market distribution (Kolb 1977b).

As Ehrich (1965) and Matson (1965a) have emphasized, the goal of "ceramics and man" investigations must meld the technological and cultural realms and diffuse the interface between the physical sciences and anthropology, literally defined as the comparative study of humankind. Therefore, the application of physical scientific techniques of analysis to archaeological data requires the critical examination of the assumptions the investigator has made at all levels of analysis and interpretation. In general, the assumptions can be placed into one of two, or both, categories of: *(1)* methodological and/or statistical assumptions which concern the applicability of particular techniques to a particular problem or set of problems; and *(2)* social, behavioral, and humanistic assumptions ("anthropological"), which speak to the validity of variables as accurate measures of human behaviors. These categories require a brief elaboration.

Included within methodological and/or statistical assumptions are the methods of data collection, which, in turn, involve the research design (unit of analysis in time and/or space, problem, hypotheses, dependent and independent variables, operationalization, etc.). Likewise the potential biases of the researcher ("lumping" vs. "splitting" philosophies, for example) and other extraneous variables must be defined and controlled. The rigorous application of the scientific method is an underlying assumption. The applicability of various statistical techniques and/or mathematical models is dependent on the control of variables and the reliability of the data. We all recognize that it is possible to "lie with statistics" because of slanting the data or selecting a particular formula or model which "works."

Human beings as "culture bearing" animals are at the same time homogeneous in certain cultural traits and complexes (the Universal Culture Pattern, for example), yet diverse in others. Biology influences human behavior and vice versa, and there is the influence of culture and social learning plus the processes of socialization or enculturation to be considered. Certainly we cannot deny the influence of situations on human behavior. Also of concern is how to conceptualize and operationally define human behavior in quantitative terms that can be related to the problem and hypothesis. Although human beings are

Charles C. Kolb

greatly varied within and among cultures, we ask our colleagues in the social and behavioral sciences to quantify human societies and behavior ranges within societies, and to discern model behaviors. The quantification of such variables is again underlaid with assumptions as to method and interpretation (Dunnell 1970; Read 1974; Rice 1978). In summary, the researcher concerned with explicating human behaviors associated with archaeological data may be unable to cope with the two categories of assumptions delineated (Cowgill 1970). In dealing with archaeological materials the investigator must consider the limitations of method and theory in the physical scientific and behavioral realms, yet add the longitudinal variations of human society and behaviors as well as possible natural ecological (physical and biological environmental) changes. Therefore alternative hypotheses may be advanced, current interpretations modified, and old "solutions" discarded.

Provenience

Following the excavation of the ceramic vessels and/or sherds, the initial housekeeping (locational data, sherd washing if appropriate, labeling, etc.) precedes classification. Archaeologists and ceramic technologists employ sets of dependent and independent variables in the classification and creation of pottery types. The variables utilized cluster into those defined as physical (paste color, slip color, hardness, paste texture, temper and aplastic inclusions, firing variations, etc.) and those delineated as cultural (method of manufacture, vessel form and function, surface treatment, decoration, dimensions [ranges, means, medians, "ideal"], etc.). Most archaeologists emphasize the cultural set of variables since these are allied to human behavior, the mental template, percepta, mentifacts, and so on — or at least this is assumed.

Some researchers may stop at this point and elaborate the assumed behavior patterns of the artisan who created and the individual who used the pottery. Others, such as myself, seek to discern cultural mechanisms, the how and why, especially when the pottery is not indigenous or is "foreign" to the locale or site(s) where it was recovered. Data from physical geography, geology, sedimentology, petrography, and mineralogy are sought in an attempt to locate the possible or probable areas of origin of manufacture. Here, again, difficulties may arise to diffuse our search for the "truth." Diachronic environmental changes, lack of comparable data, and errors of measurement or calculation are but three prime difficulties.

Alpha Thin Orange ware and Red Streak-Burnished ware are postulated to have been transported to their locations of discovery from external areas, judging from physical scientific data which indicates that the raw materials (clays and/or aplastics) were "foreign" to the locales of discovery. These conclusions in turn may suggest probable areas of origin of manufacture. From the physical scientific viewpoint we must be aware that provenience studies of pottery involve the detection and measurement of minor and especially trace elemental constituents (Rice 1978, p. 513; Goffer 1980, p. 128). Because ceramics consist of fired clay, their classification and identification are similar to those of mineral samples (Deer, Howie, and Zussman 1962; Grim 1967; Heinrich 1975; Larsen and Berman 1964; Ries 1927; Saggerson 1975).

Provenience studies assume that in a given ceramic sample, the materials will have some elements in common but present in different concentrations. Groups or types are initially defined to serve as a basis for later classification. Usually, if complete information is available regarding the origin of the specimens, identification may be required only to assign each sherd to one of a set of subgroups/subtypes. Significantly there are in many instances limited data available concerning the possible origin of a set of samples. Mössbauer spectroscopy and neutron activation analyses are important tools if quantifiable, quality data exist or can be determined to aid in the interpretations. The analysis of contemporary ceramic products and production materials is a useful exercise (Arnold et al. 1978) and gives us valuable insights into human behavior, although the validity of applying such sociocultural models to archaeological phenomena may be questioned because of potential culture changes since the pottery was originally made.

Investigators of contemporary artisans and their materials, whether the researchers are ethnographers, archaeologists, or ceramic technologists, must be cognizant of seven categories of variables in order to extract valid behavioral data (Kolb 1976, pp. 53–60). These categories include geological and mineralogical considerations; selection of the clay(s); processing of raw materials; the behavioral nature of the potter and his/her work; manufacture/production; decorating, drying, and firing; and consumption and distribution of the product.

Unfortunately in many instances there are limited data concerning the potential origin(s) of an archaeological specimen. Ceramics as archaeological materials present unique problems in determining provenience, in contrast to contemporary ethnographic ceramic research. Standard physical scientific methods such as petrographic and mineralogical studies, neutron activation analysis, and optical emission spectroscopy are useful since they indicate where *not* to seek the origins of manufacture. Only rarely can such techniques indicate the exact loci of the clay or aplastic used by the ceramic artisan. Often the investigator lacks the clays for comparison with the archaeological specimens (Arnold et al. 1978, pp. 546–47). The method of analysis should be sensitive to elements or minerals that may be present in very small amounts. Statistically, the number of elements to be determined should be as large as possible in order to identify the source with greater certainty. In addition, a large number of samples should be analyzed (Goffer 1980, p. 130). Therefore, neutron activation analysis, X-ray fluorescence, and optical emission spectroscopy would appear to be the best tools for provenience determination.

A number of raw material variables need to be considered since they may alter the conclusions. Among these is the uniformity of the clay sample. The composition of a clay bed may differ from that of the ceramics made from it because of the sieving or refining of the clay, the addition of aplastics and/or salts to the raw material, the mixing of clays from other deposits, etc. As a result of these practices, the original elements or minerals may be altered (enhanced or decreased in concentrations) into separate subgroups when chemically analyzed (Rice 1978, pp. 514–15, 536–37). An additional problem is that the clays found in a given deposit may change through time because of the exhaustion of resources, erosion, recent sedimentation, or because other or better resources become available. Clays available in antiquity may not be available now because of recent land alterations, construction activities, or environmental changes (such as a shift in the water table). These phenomena have been observed firsthand in the Teotihuacan Valley (Kolb 1978). Precise location cannot be discerned because of diachronic problems.

It is assumed that the techniques of clay preparation used by the artisan do in some instances alter the element or mineral patterns (Kolb 1976, pp. 53–54). The levigation of clays may change concentrations of specific elements owing to the deletion of mineral inclusions (Abascal, Harbottle, and Sayre 1973), a practice which alters the conclusions as to the origin of Thin Orange wares (Kolb 1978). Such washing of the raw clay causes changes in the ratios of elements (Rb, Hf, and Sm) in ceramic samples from Guatemala (Rice 1978, p. 535). Subramanian and Gibbs's (1975) experiments on exchangeable trace metals on clay minerals indicated that Fe and Mn absorption was a function of the initial concentrations of Fe and Mn in *river* water. The initial concentrations influence the ratios of Fe/Ca and Mn/Ca in the exchange sites. They also suggested that Mn, Co, and Cr were variable in selectivity sequence and could replace

each other in exchange sites so that the amounts of these elements in the exchange sites are highly variable for any clay mineral. These factors may result in typological variants in the Red Streak-Burnished ware from Central Asia (Kolb 1980).

The techniques employed by the artisans in producing a vessel also vary with time (Kolb 1976, pp. 56–58). A neglected methodological problem in the chemical analysis of ancient ceramics concerns inclusions which occur naturally in the raw clay and/or aplastics or tempering materials purposefully added by the artisan. Bromund et al. (1976) reported that since these inclusions may vary greatly in size and/or frequency, it is imperative that a practical method be developed to determine the *amount* to be sampled from a specimen. Their method involved the counting of frequency and measuring the sizes of diagnostic inclusions. The investigation required a minimal sample size, proved economical, and tested at the 0.95 confidence level by t-test.

Brooks and Bieber (1973) noted that the mixing of clays resulted in element and mineral alteration. The addition of aplastic materials (organic and/or inorganic), salts, ash, water, or other matter to change the plastic properties of a clay may enhance or decrease elemental concentrations (Matson 1965a, pp. 210–11). Rice (1978, pp. 527–34, 538) found that Guatemalan clay composition was altered by adding 15% ash as an aplastic. Likewise, the clays for *Beta* Thin Orange at Teotihuacan were altered by the addition of micaceous material (Kolb 1973, pp. 522–25). This alters the results of analyses by neutron activation.

The firing temperatures attained and the deviation of such temperatures may also complicate the analysis (Shepard 1968, pp. 74–93; Bromund et al. 1976; Rice 1978, pp. 534–35). Variations of time and temperature, according to Brooks and Beiber (1973), have no effect on the elemental composition of the clays, but may alter highly volatile lead glazes. In this latter instance X-ray fluorescence results are affected (Poole and Finch 1972). Postfiring treatment and deposition may alter the elemental composition, even though the sherds to be analyzed are soaked in distilled water for 24 to 36 hours prior to analysis to remove mineral salts (Shepard 1968, p. 93; Rice 1978, p. 517).

In summary, the provenience studies of ceramic materials must include an analysis of what have been termed physical and cultural variables, and must take into account the limitations of specific methods and their underlying assumptions. Petrographic and mineralogical analyses are as useful as the assumptions on which they are based. The same is true of neutron activation analysis, optical emission spectroscopy,

Charles C. Kolb

and electron microprobe studies. Statistical deviations are a potential source of error. Usually a few dozen or up to a hundred sherds may be selected for analysis. Ultimately the chosen specimens may be selected randomly, or by a stratified random sampling technique, or simply discerned by judgment. Sample size will always be a mitigating factor. Goffer (1980, p. 133) suggested that in order to provide a reliable analysis of an unknown sample, about 10,000 sherds would have to be analyzed!

What is the outcome after the investment of large amounts of time and funds? We hope to achieve a better understanding of the potter and his work; otherwise we have the "sterile record of limited worth" cited by Matson (1965a, p. 202). Muscarella's (1975) warning that ceramic evidence may be easily misinterpreted, and that we should take a conservative approach to data interpretation, should be heeded. Kamilli and Lamberg-Karlovsky (1979), in combining petrographic and electron microprobe analysis, have taken an important step towards the interpretation of ceramic data and human behaviors. Indigenous wares can be discerned more easily than "foreign imports," yet the latter should be explicated ultimately in terms of cultural processes and mechanisms. Indeed, in following the scientific method, the conclusions continue to generate other and new questions as to the how and why of human behavior. Ceramics are an extremely complex product of human behavior.

Acknowledgments: The analyses and conclusions reached in this paper owe much to a number of colleagues; I, however, bear responsibility for the final product. I am indebted to Frederick R. Matson (The Pennsylvania State University) for initial training in ceramic studies, and for his encouragement and helpful criticisms of my past investigations. In addition I wish to acknowledge the assistance of Garman Harbottle (Brookhaven National Laboratory), Dean Arnold (Wheaton College), the late Anna Shepard, Florencia Muller (INAH), Evelyn Rattray (UNAM), William Sanders (Penn State), Anton Kovar (Penn State), Gordon Ekholm (AMNH), William Crawford (Bryn Mawr College), and Eva Tucker (Behrend College). Financial support in the field came from Louis Dupree and William Sanders.

The laboratory analyses were partially funded by The Pennsylvania State University Central Fund for Research (1968-1969), the Madge Miller Fund of Bryn Mawr College (1969-1973), a National Science Foundation Institutional Grant to Bryn Mawr (1979), and The Behrend College Research and Scholarly Activities Fund (1976, 1978, 1980).

The Thin Orange specimens are stored in the Archaeological Laboratory, Department of Anthropology, The Pennsylvania State University, University Park, Pa. The bulk of the Afghan ceramics, including complete vessels, is located in the Kabul Museum, Kabul, Afghanistan. A select sample is to be found in the American Museum of Natural History, Anthropology Department, New York City.

Appendix I: *Alpha* and *Beta* **Types of Thin Orange Ware**

Types *Alpha* and *Beta* were originally discerned microscopically in 1965 and reconfirmed by petrographic analyses (Kolb 1965, 1973). Table 4 summarizes and updates the findings detailed elsewhere (Kolb 1973). One notable inclusion found in both *Alpha* and *Beta* types was scoria or basalt. Scoria is essentially "pyroclastic ejecta, usually of basic composition, characterized by marked vesicularity, dark

Table 4. *Alpha* and *Beta* types: Thin Orange ware

Type *Alpha* (n = 4,258)

Minerals/Other Inclusions	Approximate Percentages
Quartzite (angular and subangular)	35–25
Calcite (angular)	25–20
Talc	15– 5
Quartz (angular and rounded)	10– 5
Muscovite mica	10– 5
Hematite (lumps and crystals)	5– 0
Feldspar (angular)	1– 0
Hornblende (angular)	1– 0
Various chlorites/schists	1– 0
Scoria or basalt	1– 0
Unidentified minerals	Traces

Type *Beta* (n = 112)

Minerals/Other Inclusions	Approximate Percentages
Muscovite mica	65–30
Quartzite (angular and subangular)	30–20
Quartz (angular and rounded)	10– 5
Calcite (angular and subangular)	10– 0
Talc	10– 0
Hematite (lumps and crystals)	5– 0
Feldspar (angular)	1– 0
Hornblende (angular)	1– 0
Various chlorites/schists	1– 0
Scoria or basalt	1– 0
Unidentified minerals	Traces

color, heaviness, and partly crystallized" (American Geological Institute 1960, p. 439). "Basalt" is here defined as a fine grained dark-colored igneous rock composed mostly of microscopic calcium-sodium (plagioclase) feldspar, pyroxene, and olivine (Pough 1955, pp. 15-16; American Geological Institute 1960, p. 41). Scoria and basalt particles may have been natural, fluvially weathered residuals in the raw clays, or accidentally added during the crushing of the clay or grinding of temper when the abrading surfaces of the implements (*manos* and *metates* of basalt, and mortars and pestles of *tezontli*, a scoria) wore away.

Alpha and *Beta* sherds always contained large quantities of opaque particles, cryptocrystalline quartzose fragments, and translucent quartzite which was grayish in color (Sinkankas 1966; Saggerson 1975). The quartzite graded into translucent cryptocrystalline quartz particles (chalcedony or possibly chert) sometimes white, gray, or yellowish in color. "Quartzites are among the hardest and the most resistant of all rocks" (Pough 1955, p. 24), and the particles attained values of 5, 6, or 7 on Mohs' Scale of hardness. Quartzite is abundant and widespread in igneous and metamorphic rocks, especially if the metamorphic class rocks were derived from sedimentary rocks (Sinkankas 1966, p. 443). Quartz crystals were occasionally observed as translucent, rarely opaque, and hexagonal in pattern. Hardness on Mohs' Scale was judged as 7. Most examples were colorless or white, but some were tinted by impurities or had inclusions (especially mica and hematite), rendering the particles cryptocrystalline. The general chemistry was essentially silicon dioxide, SiO_2, and crystals were insoluble in hydrochloric acid (Larsen and Berman 1964, p. 69; Sinkankas 1966, pp. 436-46). The quartzite and quartz fragments ranged in size from "very fine" (1/8-1/16 mm) through "fine" (1/4-1/8 mm), "medium" (1/2-1/4 mm), "coarse" (1-1/2 mm), "very coarse" (2-1 mm), and occasional "granules" (4-2 mm). The grades "medium" and "coarse" were predominant, based on Wentworth's Size Classification (1933).

Calcite, nearly always in its calcined form, with a general chemistry of calcium carbonate, $CaCO_3$, was moderately abundant. This mineral was calcined owing to the firing of the ceramic vessels, indicative of firing temperatures from 650 °C, when carbon dioxide is first released, to 898 °C, when calcination is complete (Shepard 1968, p. 22; Pike 1976). The mineral exhibited typical physical properties of rhombohedral cleavage, was transparent to translucent, and was nearly colorless (sometimes yellowish or grayish, probably because of impurities). Dilute hydrochloric acid dissolved crystals with resultant effervescence. Some examples had traces of hematite interstices.

Calcite is "very common and abundant in all classes of rocks except granitic types and pegmatites; less abundant in diabases, basalts, and related flow rocks except in cavities and fissures" (Sinkankas 1966, p. 361). Preserved crystals exhibited a typical hardness of 3 on Mohs' Scale (Larsen and Berman 1964, p. 229; Sinkankas 1966, pp. 359-64). Calcite fragments ranged in size from "very fine" through "very coarse" (2-1 mm range) on the Wentworth Scale. Most dominant were the grades "medium" and "coarse."

Various amounts of talc, the softest known mineral, were recognizable. This mineral, a phyllosilicate, $Mg_3(OH)_2(Si_4O_{10})$ in pure form was white or whitish green in color, and was fine grained. Particles were insoluble in hydrochloric acid (Larsen and Berman 1964, p. 164). Talc is a secondary mineral formed by the alteration of various magnesium silicates and is often embedded in micaceous flakes and may be associated with quartzites. Talc particles ranged in size from "very fine" (1/8-1/16 mm range) to "fine" (1/4-1/8 mm range) on the Wentworth Scale, with the former predominant.

Small quantities of muscovite mica were always present in *Alpha* sherds, but dominant in *Beta* sherds (*cf.* Saggerson 1975, pp. 354-55). It is a common rock-forming mineral with its general chemistry considered potassium-sodium hydroxyl alumino-silicate, $(K,Na)Al_2(OH)_2(AlSiO_{10})$ (Sinkankas 1966, p. 481). The mineral was most often light yellow or colorless, translucent, and easily cleaved into elastic sheets. Hardness on Mohs' Scale was 2-2 1/2, and the mineral was insoluble in hydrochloric acid (Larsen and Berman 1964, p. 163). Muscovite is "abundant in many kinds of granitic rocks and in siliceous metamorphic rocks but good specimens are obtained only from granitic pegmatites, from microlytic cavities in granites, or from cavities in some quartz veins" (Sinkankas 1966, pp. 481-82). Particles of muscovite graded on the Wentworth Scale were always in the "silt" (1/16-1/25 mm), "very fine," or "fine" grades, with the former two grades most dominant.

Very small quantities of hematite, present as free tabular crystals or in association with quartzite or calcite, were found in all *Alpha* and *Beta* sherds. Hematite, with a general composition of Fe_2O_3 (ferric oxide), is a common substance of general occurrence and was most often dark red or opaque black in color with a variable hardness on Mohs' Scale of 1-6 1/2 (Sinkankas 1966, p. 326). I found that particles were soluble in concentrated hydrochloric acid, also noted by Larsen and Berman (1964, p. 95). The mineral normally occurs in large beds of sedimentary origin, in some metamorphosed sedimentary rocks, and in veins in igneous class rocks (Sinkankas 1966,

Charles C. Kolb

pp. 326-27), and in its many varieties hematite is one of the commonest minerals. Particles in terms of size were classified on the Wentworth Scale as "very fine." Lumps of reddish-brown hematite were conspicuous, but long thin fragments were also distinctive. This was also noted by Shepard (1946, p. 200).

Feldspars, especially orthoclase and the plagioclase group of oligoclase and andesine, were investigated. Orthoclase, $K(AlSi_3O_8)$, and oligoclase and andesine, $Ca(Al,Si)(AlSi_2O_8)$, were not well represented. Feldspars are the principal constituents of igneous and plutonic rocks (Sinkankas 1966, pp. 449-59). Hornblende, $NaCa_2(Mg,Fe,Al)_5(OH_2)(Si,Al)_8O_{22}$, is another mineral abundant in igneous rocks, but is also found in metamorphics as well (Sinkankas 1966, pp. 489-90). Hornblende, like the feldspars, was present (if at all) in minute quantities.

Minerals in the chlorite series were present in variable minute quantities. Chlorite, $(Mg,Fe,Al)_6(OH)_8$ $(Al,Si)_4O_{10}$, is normally dark green in color, but reddish-brown varieties (presumably containing manganese) were sometimes found. Chlorites are common in many kinds of rock and mineral deposits, usually are of secondary origin, and are especially common in metamorphosed siliceous rocks as in schists or partly altered igneous rocks as basalts (Sinkankas 1966, pp. 485-86).

Appendix II: Red Streak-Burnished Ware

Aq Kupruk Red Streak-Burnished Vegetable Fiber Tempered ware was characterized on the basis of an intensive examination of 1,079 sherds and thin sections. Physical properties of color (paste and slip), hardness, paste texture, temper and other aplastic inclusions, firing variations, and the cultural properties of method(s) of manufacture, vessel form and function, surface treatment and decoration, and dimensions were detailed (Kolb 1980), and are briefly summarized.

The fabric or paste color was in the Munsell (1954) range of white through very pale brown, with 91.5% of the sample in the white or pink category. The distinctive slip ranged in color from light red to dusky red, with 85.6% light red or light reddish brown. The ware had Mohs' Scale hardness values of 4 and 5 with the latter predominating, and a microhardness estimated between 143.0 and 577.0 (Shepard 1968, p. 114). Such data would indicate firing temperatures in excess of 850°C.

Paste texture, in terms of Wentworth's Size Classification (1933) recommended by sedimentary petrologists, was consistently in the "silt" category (1/16-1/25 mm diameter grade limit), as measured by means of a 60x binocular microscope. Verification of size was made through the examination of thin

sections by petrographic microscopy. The concentration of aplastic inclusions by percentage of surface area in cross section was in the sparse range (0-15%). The ceramic ware was tempered by an extremely fine vegetable fiber of a size generally *less* than 0.7 mm in length and 0.1-0.05 mm in diameter. It is suggested that the raw clay may have been "naturally tempered," i.e., had a natural fibrous vegetable material in it, or that the potters added small amounts (up to 15%) of fiber to the raw clay. One possibility was the addition of fine fiber, such as cattail "fuzz," from riverine or swamp reeds. Straw or chaff from animal dung, broken down by amino acids during the digestive processes, was too large and apparently not utilized as tempering material.

Other aplastic inclusions found during microscopic examination were present in insignificant amounts in 22.5% of the sherds. These probably were not specifically added by the potters as temper but either were present in the raw clay itself or were accidentally added during preparation of the clay, i.e., the crushing and/or kneading processes, prior to manufacture. The other nonplastics included unidentified small seeds (1.0-0.05 mm in length and 0.4-0.2 mm in diameter) which were neither wheat nor barley, and were represented by exocasts. The genus and/or species could not be identified by a botanist (Kovar 1969). Additional rare aplastics included: crushed limestone (0.5 mm or less in diameter), crushed unidentified granitic and basaltic stone (0.3 mm or less in diameter), and occasional ferric oxide particles (Fe_2O_3).

The firing atmosphere was consistently completely oxidized. Only three of the 1,079 sherds exhibited incomplete oxidation where carbonaceous matter in the paste had not been totally burned out. As was noted, the paste color was normally white to pink, indicative of complete oxidation. Firing temperatures were in excess of 850°C and probably 880°-950°C based on kiln refirings of sherds (Shepard 1968, pp. 74-94; Pike 1976). Kilns may have been employed, but this cannot be confirmed.

The Red Streak-Burnished ware was wheel-turned, but whether on the fast or slow potters' wheel or *tournette* was unclear. Plate-bowl and jar forms were of uniform sizes, indicative of pottery craft specialization. Handles for jars were hand modeled and appliqued to jars without piercing the wall of the vessel. The paste was finger smoothed, and was not scraped or object burnished while "leather hard" prior to the application of red slip and subsequent firing.

References

Abascal, R. 1974. Analysis por activacion de neutrones: Una aportacion para la arqueologia moderna. Dissertation, Escuela Nacional de Antropologia e Historia y UNAM, Mexico.

_____; Harbottle, Garman; and Sayre, E. V. 1972. Neutron activation of Thin Orange. Paper read at the Society for American Archaeology Annual Meeting. Bal Harbour, Florida.

_____. 1973. Correlation between terra cotta figurines and pottery from the Valley of Mexico and source clays by activation analysis. Paper read at the American Chemical Society Annual Meeting, Dallas. Mimeographed. (*See* Beck 1974.)

American Geological Institute. 1960. *Dictionary of geological terms*. 2d ed. Garden City, N.Y.: Doubleday.

Arnold, Dean E., et al. 1978. Neutron activation analysis of contemporary pottery and pottery materials from the Valley of Guatemala. In Wetherington, Ronald, ed., *The ceramics of Kaminaljuyu*. Monograph Series on Kaminaljuyu. University Park: Pennsylvania State University, pp. 343–86.

Beck, Curt W., ed. 1974. *Archaeological chemistry*. (Papers read at the American Chemical Society annual meeting, Dallas, 1973.) Advances in Chemistry Series.

Bilharz Kolb, Joy; Bear, John; and Angel, J. Lawrence. 1972. Prehistoric research in Afghanistan (1959–1966): Human osteology from the Aq Kupruk sites. Paper prepared at the Smithsonian Institution, Department of Physical Anthropology, Washington, D.C.

Bromund, R. H.; Bower, N. W.; and Smith, R. H. 1976. Inclusions in ancient ceramics: An approach to the problem of sampling for chemical analysis. *Archaeometry* 18: 218–21.

Brooks, D. W., and Bieber, A. M., Jr. 1973. Biblical studies through activation analysis of ancient pottery. Paper read at the American Chemical Society annual meeting, Dallas. Mimeographed. (*See* Beck 1974.)

Cook de Leonard, Carmen. 1957. El origin de la ceramica anaranjada delgada. Dissertation, Escuela Nacional de Antropologia, Mexico.

Cowgill, George. 1970. Some sampling and reliability in archaeology. In *Archaeologie et calculaterus: problemes semiologiques et mathematiques*, pp. 161–75. Colloque Internationaux du Centre National de la Recherche Scientifique. Paris: Editions du Centre National de la Recherche Scientifique.

Deer, W. A.; Howie, R. A.; and Zussman, J. 1962. *Rock-forming minerals*. London: Longmans.

de la Cadena, A.; Franco, F.; and Escobar, S. 1967. *Analisis quemico de ceramicas arqueologicas*. Serie Technologica No. 1. Mexico: Departamento de Prehistoria, Instituto Nacional de Antropologia e Historia.

Dunnell, R. C. 1970. Seriation method and its evaluation. *American Antiquity* 35: 305–19.

Dunoyer de Segonzac, G. 1970. The transformation of clay minerals during diagenesis and low grade metamorphism—a review. *Sedimentology* 15: 281–346.

Dupree, Louis B. 1968. Aq Kupruk: A town in Afghanistan. In Associates of the American Universities Field Staff, *City and nation in the developing world*. New York: American Universities Field Staff, pp. 9–61.

_____, and Kolb, Charles C. 1972. Ceramics from Aq Kupruk, Darra-i-Kur, and Hazar Gusfand. In Dupree, Louis et al., *Prehistoric research in Afghanistan (1959–1966)*. Transactions of the American Philosophical Society 62(4): 33–42. Philadelphia.

_____, et al. 1972. *Prehistoric research in Afghanistan (1959–1966)*. Transactions of the American Philosophical Society 62(4). Philadelphia.

Earle, Timothy K., and Ericson, Jonathan E., eds. 1977. *Exchange systems in prehistory*. New York: Academic Press.

Ehrich, Robert W. 1965. Ceramics and man: a cultural perspective. In Matson, F. R., ed., *Ceramics and man*, pp. 1–19. Viking Fund Publications in Anthropology, no. 41. Chicago: Aldine.

Goffer, Zvi. 1980. *Archaeological chemistry: A sourcebook on the applications of chemistry to archaeology*. New York: John Wiley and Sons.

Grim, R. E. 1967. *Clay mineralogy*. New York: McGraw-Hill.

Hansman, John, and Stronach, David. 1970. Excavations at Shahr-i Qumis, 1967. *Journal of the Royal Asiatic Society* 1970: 142–55.

Harbottle, Garman. 1973. Upton, L. I., N.Y.: Brookhaven National Laboratory. Personal communication (letter).

_____; Sayre, E. V.; and Abascal, R. 1976. *Neutron activation analysis of Thin Orange pottery*. Upton, L. I., N.Y.: Brookhaven National Laboratory/U.S. Energy Research and Development Administration.

Hayes, J. W. 1972. *Late Roman pottery*. London: British School at Rome.

Heinrich, E. W. 1975. *Microscopic identification of minerals*. New York: McGraw-Hill.

Hodder, Ian. 1974. Regression analysis of some trade and marketing patterns. *World Archaeology* 6: 172–89.

Hole, Frank, and Heizer, Robert F. 1977. *Prehistoric archeology: a brief introduction*. New York: Holt, Rinehart and Winston.

Kamilli, D. C., and Lamberg-Karlovsky, C. C. 1979. Petrographic and electron microprobe analysis of ceramics from Tepe Yahya, Iran. *Archaeometry* 21: 47–59.

Charles C. Kolb

Kolb, Charles C. 1965. *A tentative ceramics classification for the Teotihuacan Valley (Patlachique through Aztec V phases)*. University Park: Department of Sociology and Anthropology, Pennsylvania State University, pp. 1–48.

———. 1973. Thin Orange ware at Teotihuacan. In Sanders, W. T., ed., *Miscellaneous papers in anthropology*. Occasional Papers in Anthropology, no. 8, pp. 309–377. University Park: Department of Anthropology, Pennsylvania State University.

———. 1976. The methodology of Latin American ceramic ecology. *Eldorado: Bulletin of South American Archaeology* 1: 44–82.

———. 1977a. Technological investigations of Mesoamerican "Thin Orange" ware. *Current Anthropology* 18: 534–36.

———. 1977b. Imitation Arretine pottery in northern Afghanistan. *Current Anthropology* 18: 536–38.

———. 1978. Technological and cultural aspects of Teotihuacan period "Thin Orange" ware. In Rice, Prudence M., ed., *Pots and potters: Current approaches in ceramic archaeology* [Festschrift for Frederick R. Matson]. Manuscript.

———. 1980. A red slipped "Pseudo-Arretine" ceramic from south Central Asia. *East and West*, in press.

Kovar, Anton J. 1969. University Park: Department of Botany, Pennsylvania State University. Personal communication.

Larsen, Esper S., and Berman, Harry. 1964. *The microscopic determination of the nonopaque mineral*. 2d ed. Geological Survey Bulletin, no. 848. Washington, D.C.: U.S. Department of the Interior.

Linne, Sigvald. 1934. *Archaeological researches at Teotihuacan, Mexico*. New Series Publication, no. 1. Stockholm: Ethnographical Museum of Sweden.

———. 1942. The yellowish-red pottery: a problem of Mexican trade relations. *Ethnos* 7: 156–65.

Matheson, Sylvia A. 1973. *Persia: an archaeological guide*. Park Ridge, N.J.: Noyes Press.

Matson, Frederick R. 1965a. Ceramic ecology: an approach to the study of early cultures of the Near East. In Matson, F. R., ed., *Ceramics and man*, pp. 202–17. Chicago: Aldine.

———. 1965b. Ceramic queries. In Matson, F. R., ed., *Ceramics and man*, pp. 277–88. Chicago: Aldine.

Mielenz, R. C.; King, M. E.; and Schieltz, N. C. 1950. Staining tests. In *Reference clay minerals*. *American Petroleum Institute Project*, no. 49 (Preliminary Report, no. 7, section 6). New York.

Munsell, A. 1954. *Munsell soil color charts*. Baltimore: Munsell Color Co.

Muscarella, Oscar White. 1975. Archaeological uses of pottery. *American Ceramic Circle Bulletin: 1970–71* 1: 51–64.

Peacock, D. P. S. 1977. *Pottery and early commerce: characterization and trade in Roman and later ceramics*. London: Academic Press.

Pike, H. H. M. 1976. Pottery firing temperatures. *Archaeometry* 18: 111–14.

Polanyi, Karl; Arensberg, Conrad M.; and Pearson, Harry W., eds. 1857. *Trade and market in early empires: economies in history and theory*. New York: Free Press.

Poole, A. B., and Finch, L. R. 1972. The utilization of trace chemical composition to correlate British post-medieval pottery with European kiln site materials. *Archaeometry* 14: 79–91.

Pough, Frederick H. 1955. *A field guide to rocks and minerals*. 2d ed. Boston: Houghton-Mifflin.

Rattray, Evelyn. 1976. Thin Orange: a Teotihuacan trade ware. Paper read at the Society for American Archaeology annual meeting, St. Louis.

Read, D. W. 1974. Some comments on mathematical models in anthropology. *American Antiquity* 39: 3–15.

Rice, Prudence M. 1978. Clear answers to vague questions: some assumptions of provenience studies of pottery. In Wetherington, Ronald, ed., *The ceramics of Kaminaljuyu*. Monograph Series on Kaminaljuyu. University Park: Pennsylvania State University Press, pp. 511–42.

Ries, Heinrich. 1927. *Clays: their occurrence, properties, and uses*. 3d ed. New York: John Wiley and Sons.

Sabloff, Jeremy, and Lamberg-Karlovsky, C. C. 1975. *Ancient civilization and trade*. Albuquerque: University of New Mexico Press.

Saggerson, E. P. 1975. *Identification tables for minerals in thin section*. London and New York: Longmans.

Sanders, William T. 1965. *The cultural ecology of the Teotihuacan Valley*. University Park: Department of Sociology and Anthropology, Pennsylvania State University.

Shepard, Anna O. 1946. Technological features of Thin Orange ware. In Kidder, A. V. et al., eds., *Excavations at Kaminaljuyu*, pp. 198–201. Publication 561. Washington, D.C.: Carnegie Institution of Washington.

———. 1968. *Ceramics for the archaeologist*. Rev. 6th printing. Publication 609. Washington, D.C.: Carnegie Institution of Washington.

Sinkankas, John. 1966. *Mineralogy: a first course*. Princeton: Van Nostrand.

Sotomayor, Alfredo, and Castillo Tejero, Noemi. 1963. *Estudio petrographico de la ceramica "anaranjado delgado."* Serie Prehistoria, no. 12. Mexico: Instituto Nacional de Antropologia e Historia.

Stein, Mark Aurel. 1931. *An archaeological tour in Gedrosia*. Memoir 43. Delhi: Archaeological Survey of India.

Subramanian, Vaidyanatha, and Gibbs, Ronald J. 1975. Selectivity sequence of exchangeable trace metals on clay minerals. In Verma, V. K., ed., *Recent researches in geology*, vol. 2, pp. 202–211. Delhi: Hindustan Publishing Corp.

Tolstoy, Paul. 1958. *Surface survey of the northern Valley of Mexico: the Classic and Post-Classic periods.* Transactions of the American Philosophical Society 48(5). Philadelphia.

Wentworth, C. K. 1933. Fundamental limits to the sizes of clastic grains. *Science* 77: 633–34.

Wetherington, Ronald, ed. 1978. *The ceramics of Kaminaljuyu.* Monograph Series on Kaminaljuyu. University Park: Pennsylvania State University Press.

Wheeler, Mortimer R. E. M. 1954. *Rome beyond the imperial frontiers.* London: Bell.

————; Gosh, A.; and Deva, K. 1946. Arikamedu, an Indo-Roman trading station on the east coast of India. *Bulletin of the Archaeological Survey of India* 2: 17–124.

Wilmsen, E. N. 1972. *Social exchange and interaction.* Museum of Anthropology, University of Michigan, Anthropological Papers, no. 46.

Winchell, A. N. 1957. *Elements of optical mineralogy.* New York: John Wiley and Sons.

Wright, G. A. 1974. *Archaeology and trade.* Reading, Massachusetts: Addison-Wesley.

19. Porosimetric Investigation of Roman Terra Sigillata Molds from Rheinzabern, Germany

ROBERT B. HEIMANN
[Institute for Materials Research
McMaster University]

Introduction

Between 1974 and 1979, an archaeometric working group of scientists and archaeologists at Freie Universität Berlin, West Germany, jointly investigated Roman terra sigillata of various origins within the scope of a project entitled Materials, Decoration, and Techniques of Production of Ancient Ceramics. This project dealt mainly with ceramic ware from Rheinzabern, Palatinate, West Germany (Fig. 1), which in Roman times was apparently one of the major centers of terra sigillata production north of the Alps. Sherds from other East Gaulish sites (Blickweiler, Chemery-Faulquemont) and South Gaulish sites (La Graufesenque) were also investigated for comparison purposes. The decision to choose Rheinzabern ware as a reference material was triggered mainly by the fact that there large amounts of sherds, literally millions of them, were excavated during several campaigns. The finds cover a period between the first century B.C. and the second century A.D. The ancient clay sources are still present, and served a prosperous brick industry in the first decades of our century.

The author took charge of the investigation of ceramic textural properties, which included determination of mechanical strength (Heimann 1976a), firing temperatures (Heimann 1976b), and porosity (Heimann 1976c, 1978). During these investigations it became apparent that the terra sigillata found at the Rheinzabern site and the molds from the same site are almost indistinguishable in chemical composition and porosity parameters. These similarities are to be expected because both groups were made from the same clay.

A typical terra sigillata plate is depicted in Figure 2. It is characterized by its fine grained, homogeneously fired, uniform body, and by the high glossy coral red surface. This surface finish was obtained by dipping the plate in a slurry of very fine illite particles and subsequent firing of the object in an oxidizing atmosphere around 1000 °C. The figure shows a plate with a special decoration technique called barbotine. The flower motive was freely trailed on, using a slip of thick creamy consistency. The molds were frequently decorated by separate stamps. Figure 3 shows a relatively simple example, decorated by impression of a (somewhat off-centered) flower stamp and a stylus with circular cross section. These molds were mounted on a potter's wheel and clay pressed into them and smoothed on the inside by the thrower, who afterwards worked the rim of the bowl above the edge of the mold.

Attempts were made to find an analytical procedure to discriminate between these two groups and to

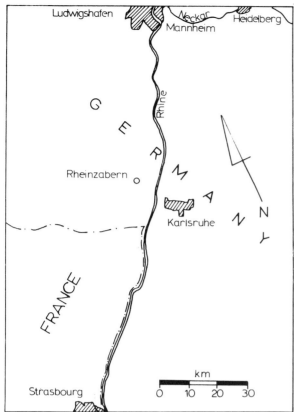

Figure 1. Sketch map of Rheinzabern, Palatinate, and surroundings.

Figure 2. Terra sigillata plate, Rheinzabern (S194). Courtesy H. Knoll, Research Group for Archaeometry, Freie Universität Berlin, West Germany.

Figure 3. Mold, Rheinzabern. Courtesy H. Knoll.

elucidate the peculiarities in technology which finally lead to understanding of the functional differences of ware and molds.

Chemical Analyses and Determination of Porosity Values

Eleven terra sigillata sherds and six mold sherds were chosen as a representative sample. Chemical analyses were carried out by X-ray fluorescence analysis (Schneider 1976) and porosity determinations were made by the simple water immersion method (for details, *see* Strunk-Lichtenberg 1976). The results are listed in Table 1, together with the values for reference samples from Blickweiler, Chemery-Faulquemont, and La Graufesenque. The relations between the porosity values are as follows:

(a) Apparent porosity $P_A = W + P_M = W \cdot R$
$\qquad$ (%)

(b) Total porosity $\quad P = P_A + P_c = (D-R)/D \times 100$ (%)

(c) Microporosity $\quad P_M = P_A - W = W(R-1)$
$\qquad$ (%)

(d) Closed porosity $\quad P_C = P - P_A$ (%)

[W = water absorbing capacity; R = raw density (volumetric density); D = powder density (= specific gravity)].

The water absorbing capacity W is the relative gain in weight measured after immersion of the sherd in water. The raw density R is determined from the volume of water displaced by immersion of the original sherd in a pycometer being the ratio of mass to (geometrical) volume, whereas the powder density refers to the displacement of water by the powdered sherd. In that way, R determines the density with pores, D the density of the pore-free material.

Figure 4 shows the composition of the Rheinzabern sherds and molds, as well as the other terra sigillata investigated, in the three-component system quartz-alumina-"flux." All samples are situated in the partial stability field diopside (wollastonite)-

210 $\qquad$ Robert B. Heimann

Table 1. Chemical analyses and porosity data of terra sigillata (W = water absorbing capacity, R = raw density, D = powder density, P_A = apparent porosity

P_C = closed porosity, P_M = microporosity and P = total porosity)

Sample No.	SiO_2	Al_2O_3	Fe_2O_3	CaO	MgO	K_2O	Na_2O	$W(\%)$	$R(g \cdot cm^{-3})$	$D(g \cdot cm^{-3})$	$P_A(\%)$	$P_M(\%)$	$P_C(\%)$	$P(\%)$	W/P	P_C/P
Rheinzabern (Rh)																
S 132	63.24	18.94	5.72	5.90	2.17	3.23	0.79	20.69	1.54	2.64	31.86	11.17	9.80	41.67	0.496	0.235
S 133	62.41	19.10	5.65	5.34	2.11	3.40	0.61	20.72	1.55	2.76	32.12	11.39	11.72	43.84	0.473	0.267
S 134	62.97	18.57	5.63	6.65	2.47	3.14	0.80	21.46	1.55	2.91	33.26	11.80	13.47	46.73	0.459	0.288
S 135	62.42	18.78	5.51	6.41	2.49	3.36	0.77	18.97	1.60	2.86	30.35	11.38	13.70	44.05	0.430	0.311
S 141	61.10	19.17	6.15	5.51	2.22	3.33	0.82	16.22	1.62	2.55	26.28	10.05	10.19	36.47	0.445	0.279
S 194	-	-	-	-	-	-	-	23.76	1.52	2.83	36.11	12.35	10.17	46.29	0.513	0.220
S 197	60.12	18.92	5.62	4.95	2.43	3.21	0.65	21.10	1.53	2.85	32.28	11.18	14.03	46.32	0.455	0.303
S 198	63.62	17.00	6.18	4.66	1.94	2.92	0.81	19.66	1.56	2.75	30.67	11.01	12.60	43.27	0.454	0.291
S 200	61.03	18.82	5.85	4.54	2.35	3.52	0.68	22.67	1.50	2.76	34.05	11.35	11.60	45.65	0.497	0.254
S 201	61.80	18.92	5.69	4.00	2.26	3.41	0.59	18.17	1.55	2.77	28.16	9.99	15.88	44.04	0.412	0.366
S 203	62.55	19.03	5.67	3.64	2.30	3.47	0.80	13.41	1.58	2.74	21.19	7.78	21.15	42.34	0.316	0.499
Molds (M)																
O 150	56.79	15.59	4.88	8.76	2.28	2.87	0.64	23.57	1.53	2.73	36.06	12.49	7.89	43.96	0.536	0.179
O 153	63.04	17.80	5.21	4.67	2.46	3.17	0.62	20.00	1.59	2.71	31.08	11.80	9.53	41.33	0.484	0.230
O 154	62.66	18.27	5.58	4.86	2.17	3.24	0.90	18.87	1.61	2.67	30.35	11.51	9.32	39.70	0.475	0.235
O 155	60.26	18.00	5.60	5.22	2.66	2.97	0.64	21.55	1.60	2.88	34.48	12.93	9.96	44.44	0.485	0.224
O 175	60.27	17.93	5.61	7.69	2.89	3.19	0.73	25.61	1.59	2.99	40.72	15.11	6.10	46.82	0.547	0.130
O 176	61.53	18.13	5.58	4.09	2.06	3.21	0.72	23.34	1.60	2.77	37.34	14.00	4.89	42.24	0.552	0.116
Blickweiler (B)																
S 142	54.58	20.49	7.15	4.80	4.50	5.83	0.45	17.45	1.58	2.54	27.57	10.12	10.22	37.79		
S 146	55.30	20.35	7.12	4.49	4.86	5.69	0.45	17.37	1.58	2.44	27.44	10.07	7.80	35.25		
S 147	55.07	19.81	6.77	5.88	6.13	5.36	0.39	17.05	1.67	2.44	28.47	11.42	3.08	31.56		
S 148	54.50	20.04	6.90	5.12	6.15	5.59	0.44	17.36	1.71	2.45	29.68	12.32	0.52	30.20		
Chemery (C)																
S 155	57.74	19.12	6.18	5.57	4.02	5.45	0.33	22.44	1.54	2.81	34.56	12.12	10.64	45.19		
S 152	62.49	19.27	6.20	2.57	3.31	5.50	0.38	13.11	1.60	2.85	20.97	7.87	22.88	43.86		
S 153	58.90	19.22	6.32	5.34	4.39	5.33	0.38	20.57	1.55	2.87	32.11	11.40	13.88	45.99		
S 158	60.79	19.46	6.50	3.40	3.94	5.32	0.35	14.47	1.55	2.77	22.43	7.96	21.61	44.04		
S 159	58.24	19.13	6.40	4.86	4.86	5.24	0.37	18.02	1.55	2.80	27.93	9.91	16.71	44.64		
La Graufesenque (G)																
S 171	53.38	22.32	5.00	9.87	1.54	3.50	0.40	20.28	1.64	2.63	33.26	12.98	4.38	37.64		
S 172	52.50	22.35	5.98	12.05	2.04	3.96	0.30	23.88	1.64	2.63	39.16	15.28	0.0	37.64		
S 173	54.72	22.75	5.89	10.18	1.71	3.59	0.37	20.01	1.65	2.59	33.02	13.00	3.28	36.24		
S 174	54.76	22.59	5.94	9.10	1.95	4.06	0.33	19.01	1.66	2.61	31.56	12.55	4.84	36.40		
S 175	54.88	22.23	6.01	9.81	1.78	3.62	0.36	20.37	1.66	2.56	33.81	13.44	1.34	35.16		
S 176	52.85	22.42	6.00	11.35	1.94	3.63	0.36	20.90	1.66	2.63	34.69	13.79	2.19	36.88		
S 177	54.15	22.42	5.85	9.91	1.71	3.66	0.35	20.54	1.62	2.70	33.27	12.74	6.72	40.00		
S 179	53.63	22.24	5.97	11.08	1.90	3.75	0.34	20.04	1.65	2.66	33.07	13.03	4.90	37.97		

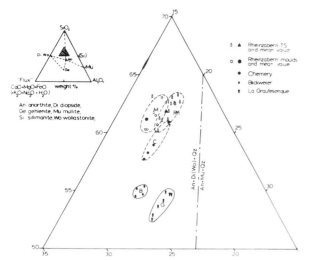

Figure 4. Representation of terra sigillata in the compositional plane diopside-anorthite-quartz of the three-component system quartz-alumina-"flux."

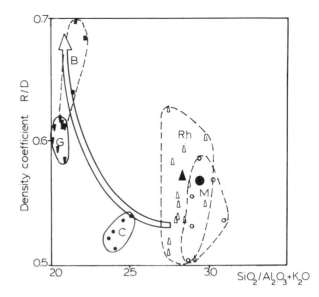

B **Blickweiler (East Gaulish),**

C **Chemery,**

G **Graufesenque (South Gaulish),**

Rh **Rheinzabern,**

M **Moulds (Rheinzabern).**

Figure 5. Density coefficient R/D against SiO_2/Al_2O_3 + K_2O ratio for East and South Gaulish terra sigillata.

anorthite-quartz. Therefore no mullite is to be expected during firing of these particular clays, and was never found in the X-ray diffractograms. The fields occupied by the Rheinzabern sherds and the molds overlap indicating once more the inherent compositional similarity of the two groups.

Figure 5 shows the density coefficient R (raw density)/D (powder density) against the ratio SiO_2/Al_2O_3 + K_2O. The latter is a rough measure for the clay content. The consolidation of a ceramic sherd increases exponentially with increasing clay content, i.e., decreasing the SiO_2/Al_2O_3 ratio as indicated by the arrow. The values for the Rheinzabern ware and the molds fall again in the same field obscuring any possible differences. However, the picture becomes somewhat clearer after considering the mineralogical composition of the clays recalculated from the chemical composition. This method is well known in petrology. It involves the calculation of the normative mineral content by distributing the elements found by chemical analysis amongst the mineral phases present as determined by X-ray diffractometry or thin section analysis. Table 2 shows the normative mineral content of the raw clays neglecting the phase changes and the dehydroxylation caused by the firing process. In some cases the sum of the minerals deviates from 100%. Here it ranges between 96% (O176) and 104% (S135). The total clay mineral content (illite + chlorite) amounts to about 33%, and the quartz content is about 40%. It should be noted that the total percentage of K_2O found was related to illite, and the total MgO content was attributed to chlorite; 20% of Fe_2O_3 was thought to be in-

corporated into chlorite, confirming X-ray results which point to iron-rich ferrochlorite (Heimann et al. 1980). The ratio quartz/sum of clay minerals permits a tentative differentiation between ware (F <1.2) and molds (F >1.2).

Relative Porosity Parameters (RPP)

To make the presentation of data more independent of random analytical errors, mean values and standard deviations were calculated. In addition, relative porosity parameters (RPP) were obtained by expressing the water absorbing capacity W, the microporosity P_M, and the closed porosity P_C as fractions of the total porosity P.

Thus,

$$\frac{W}{P} + \frac{P_M}{P} + \frac{P_C}{P} = 1$$

Table 3 lists the above values. Again, the density ratios R/D, and the total porosities P are almost identical. The difference in relative water absorbing capacity W/P amounts to 13%, those in relative micropo-

Robert B. Heimann

Table 2. Normative mineral content of the raw clays

Sample #	illite	chlorite	feldspar	quartz	hematite*	calcite	$F = \dfrac{qz}{illite + chlorite}$
S 132	27.5	6.35	19.3	40.18	4.57	5.05	1.18
133	28.9	6.37	18.3	39.20	4.52	4.15	1.11
134	26.7	7.46	13.65	42.39	4.50	9.77	1.24
135	28.6	7.52	12.29	41.54	4.41	9.05	1.15
141	28.3	6.71	13.40	40.15	4.92	7.05	1.15
197	27.3	7.34	13.95	39.18	4.49	5.37	1.13
198	24.8	5.95	12.53	44.91	4.94	5.35	(1.46)
200	29.9	7.10	10.60	40.44	4.68	6.02	1.09
201	29.0	6.83	12.12	41.06	4.55	3.90	1.14
203	29.5	6.95	11.77	41.69	4.53	3.20	1.14
							$\bar{x} = 1.15$
							$\sigma = .04$
O 150	24.4	6.89	8.69	39.59	3.90	17.52	1.26
153	26.9	7.43	11.33	43.38	4.17	5.91	1.26
154	27.5	6.55	12.34	42.60	4.46	5.95	1.25
155	25.2	8.04	13.65	40.16	4.48	6.20	1.21
175	27.1	8.73	10.73	45.32	4.49	8.83	1.26
176	27.3	6.22	12.39	41.65	4.46	4.00	1.24
							$\bar{x} = 1.25$
							$\sigma = .02$

* 20% iron compound in chlorite

Table 3. Mean values and standard deviations of porosity data, and relative porosity parameters (RPP)

	R	σ	D	σ	W(%)	σ	P_M(%)	σ	P_A(%)	σ	P_C(%)	σ	P(%)	σ
Rheinzabern TS	1.554	0.05	2.765	0.09	19.71	2.71	10.86	1.48	30.57	3.98	13.12	4.38	43.70	3.11
Rheinzabern molds	1.586	0.03	2.792	0.11	22.16	2.81	12.97	1.88	35.14	4.61	7.95	3.58	43.08	2.50

	W/P	P_M/P	P_A/P	P_C/P	R/D
Rheinzabern TS	0.45	0.25	0.70	0.30	0.562
Rheinzabern molds	0.51	0.30	0.81	0.19	0.568

214

Robert B. Heimann

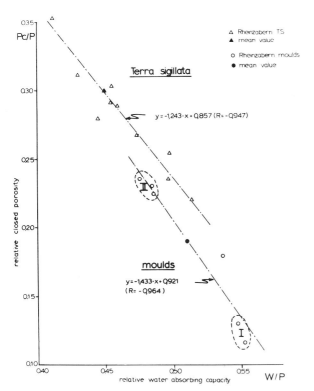

Figure 6. Correlation between relative closed porosity P_C/P and relative water absorbing capacity W/P.

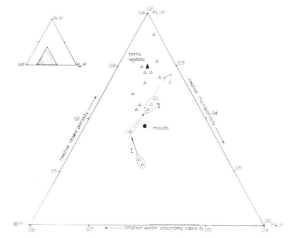

Figure 7. Representation of Rheinzabern terra sigillata and molds in the triangular diagram $W/P-P_C/P-P_M/P$.

rosity P_M/P and relative apparent porosity P_A/P to 20% and 16% respectively. A considerably greater difference is visible for the relative closed porosity (58%). The closed porosity is a measure for the degree of sintering of a ceramic sherd: it increases with increasing firing temperature by cutting off open pores due to progressive vitrification. Conversely, the macroporosity (= water absorbing capacity) decreases. Once a maximum is reached, the numbers of closed pores again decrease owing to the onset of strong vitrification which in turn leads to a collapse of the entire pore array. Therefore, high closed porosity is a rather reliable indicator for higher firing temperatures.

Figure 6 shows the linear dependence of relative closed porosity and relative water absorbing capacity. The values for the terra sigillata are distributed more or less uniformly along a straight line with negative correlation, whereas the molds form two clearly distinguishable groups.

Taking into account the relative microporosity, and plotting the data in a triangular diagram (Fig. 7), the grouping becomes even more pronounced. Group I has a mean relative water absorbing capacity of 0.55. This value decreases clearly for group II (0.48). Within group II, the samples show the same relative

microporosity (0.29). The solitary sample falling between the two groups (connected to the group clusters by thin arrows) belongs in terms of W/P to group I, in terms of P_M/P to group II. As outlined below, the relative microporosity is more indicative of the ceramics in question. Its connection to group II, as indicated by the wide arrow, raises an interesting question. The change of the relative water absorbing capacity could reflect different stages of use of the molds. Prolonged use of a mold leads to sealing of the coarser pores with salts (carbonates and sulfates, related to natural water hardness) or clay mineral particles, thus decreasing the ability of the porous sherd to take up water from the thrown-in wet clay lump.

Discriminant Analysis

As outlined above, the two ceramic object types with different functions were manufactured from the same clay. The different uses imply a conscious modification of the manufacturing process. The need, therefore, is to measure and evaluate the physical parameters that are characteristic for such modifications. Porosity and microporosity appear to be the most indicative properties.

The empirical procedures applied to the samples in order to evaluate discriminating parameters which could give information on different manufacturing techniques for both terra sigillata ware and molds are not always suited to the task. It is necessary to raise the question whether the discrimination is really as sharp as implied by Figure 6 and Figure 7. To test this contention, two statistical tests were employed.

A simple t-test (after Student) was applied to the two sets of data in Table 3.[a] The calculated t-values and the related error probabilities α for a degree of freedom f = 15 are listed in Table 4.

Table 4. Student t-test to discriminate between the two groups

Variable	t	α (%)
R	1.422	10–20
D	0.548	~50
W	1.759	10
P_M	2.559	~2
P_A	2.143	~5
P_C	2.466	2–5
P	0.418	60–70

Clearly, the raw and powder densities, and the values for the total porosity, do not permit a significant discrimination between the two groups in question. However, the microporosity P_M is the most reliable property to distinguish between terra sigillata and molds.

Statistical tests of this kind can easily be done when only a limited number of variables are to be taken into account. For more complex cases, a stepwise discriminant analysis might be applied. In the present case this treatment does not offer any advantage over the simple t-test. However, its usefulness as a powerful tool to handle difficult classification problems will be demonstrated below.

The program BMDPTM (U.C.L.A., 1977) uses classification functions to classify object taxonomical units (=OTU's) into groups based on the Mahalanobis D-square treatment.[b] The computer calculates an n-dimensional "face" which in an n+l-dimensional "space" separates the data points. For each data point the square of its distance from the boundary-"face" is calculated and compared to each other squared distance. According to their distances the points are grouped into clusters and a canonical function c(x) is calculated which describes the best fit of data. From the n+l-dimensional space, the function is projected onto a two-dimensional plane, thus giving a straight correlation line with only one (the most "critical") variable.

---

[a]This approach was suggested to me by Dr. Alan Franklin (NBS, Washington) to whom I am indebted for his interest.

[b]For computing the data, the author is indebted to Ms. Therese Stukel, Statistics Services, University of Toronto.

In this case the initial number of variables was six including one grouping variable (type, R/D, $SiO_2/Al_2O_3 + K_2O$, W/P, P_M/P, P_C/P). The system therefore is overdetermined because some of these variables are interrelated. The canonical variable was calculated to be

$$c(X) = -41.41 \cdot \frac{P_M}{P} + 11.07.$$

Its histogram is shown in Figure 8. The Rheinzabern terra sigillata (R) is defined by c(X) with values > -0.4 with a mean value: of approximately $+0.75$, the molds by values < -0.6 (mean value: approximately -1.40).

According to this treatment, the relative microporosity P_M/P is the only parameter which allows the discrimination between the two classes. This finding justifies the assignment of the solitary point in Figure 7 to the molds of group II.

However, the linear correlation between W/P and P_C/P (Fig. 6) is also true in the sense that an increase in the relative closed porosity ("relative sintering") at higher firing temperatures automatically causes a decrease in the relative water absorbing capacity.

Technological Interpretation

To summarize the experimental findings, the Rheinzabern molds have

(a) a higher quartz/clay ratio (difference 8%);

(b) a higher relative water absorbing capacity (difference 13%);

(c) a higher relative microporosity (difference 20%); and

(d) a lower relative closed porosity (difference 58%).

These differences can be explained by addition of extra quartz (sand) as temper material to the paste of the mold thus increasing the quartz/clay ratio, and also by application of a somewhat lower firing temperature which leads to a less sintered ceramic body. This accounts for a lower closed porosity, and likewise a higher relative microporosity.

The mold's technological purpose is an accelerated uptake of water. This is best obtained by introducing a large amount of macropores ($>10\mu m$), adding a larger amount of quartz grains and application of relatively low firing temperatures. The relative water-absorbing capacities measured represent only a lower limit because there is a likelihood that a certain amount of pores were sealed either by ancient use or by salt deposition due to migrating soil solutions. These pores are inaccessible by the porosity measurements applied (*see also* Rottländer 1976–77).

As can be seen from Table 3, the total porosities for both ceramic groups are equal. So a simple porosity determination as frequently applied to archaeo-

Robert B. Heimann

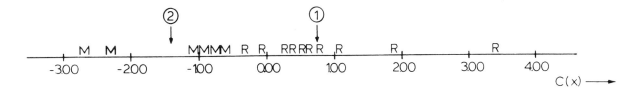

Histogram of canonical variable $C(x) = -41.41 \cdot \dfrac{P_M}{P} + 11.07$

Figure 8. One-dimensional histogram of canonical variable obtained by stepwise discriminant analysis. R = Rheinzabern TS, M = molds.

logical objects would have failed to make technological differences visible. Only the estimation of the newly introduced relative porosity parameters (RPP) gives some insight into the interrelation of ancient technologies.

A specific advantage of using relative porosity parameters is the possibility to plot porosity data regardless of their absolute values in a triangular diagram (Fig. 7). Thus, different ceramics can be compared easily.

Conclusions

(1) Terra sigillata sherds from Rheinzabern, West Germany, and molds made apparently from the same clay are grouped using relative porosity parameters $(W/P, P_M/P, P_C/P)$.

(2) A more detailed statistical discriminant analysis using the simple t-test (Student's test) and the stepwise Mahalanobis D-square treatment shows the microporosity P_M to be the only variable which can distinguish between the two groups.

(3) The differences between terra sigillata and molds in the quartz/clay ratio, relative water absorbing capacity, relative microporosity, and relative closed porosity are explainable by addition of more quartz (sand) to the paste and application of lower firing temperatures to the molds. Both factors contribute to higher values for the open porosity [open porosity (apparent porosity) = water absorbing capacity (macroporosity) + microporosity], thus leading to an increased uptake of water.

References

Heimann, Robert B. 1976a. Mikro-Härtemessungen an antiker Keramik (Terra sigillata). *Informationsbl. zu Nachbarwiss. Ur-und Frühgeschichte* 7.

_____. 1976b. Methoden zur Ermittlung der Original-Brenntemperatur von antiker Keramik. *Informationsbl. zu Nachbarwiss. Ur-und Frühgeschichte* 7.

_____. 1976c. Moderne Poren-und Gefügeuntersuchungen an Keramik. *Informationsbl. zu Nachbarwiss. Ur-und Frühgeschichte* 7.

_____. 1978. Korrelation von Porenkenngrössen und chemischer Zusammensetzung von provinzialrömischer Keramik. In: *Mineralische Rohstoffe als Kulturhist. Informationsquelle*, ed. H. W. Hennicke, Verlag Verein Dtsch. Emailfachl., Hagen, p. 234.

Heimann, R.; Maggetti, M.; and Einfalt, H. C. 1980. Zum Verhalten des Eisens beim Brennen eines kalkhaltigen illitischen Tones unter reduzierenden Bedingungen. *Ber. Dtsch. Keram. Ges* 6/8: 145–52.

Rottländer, R. C. A. 1976–77. Zur Standardisierung der Formschüsseln der Bildsigillata. *Acta Praehis. et Archaeol.* 7/8:53–63.

Schneider, G. 1976. Personal communication.

Strunk-Lichtenberg, G. 1976. Eine klassische Methode der Porositatsbestimmung von Keramik. *Informationsbl. zu Nachbarwiss. Ur-und Frühgeschichte* 7.

20. Indian Pottery from the Mississippi Valley: Coping with Bad Raw Materials

CAROLE STIMMELL
Department of Anthropology
University of Toronto,

ROBERT B. HEIMANN
[Institute for Materials Research
McMaster University],

and

R. G. V. HANCOCK
Slowpoke Reactor Facility
University of Toronto

Introduction

The modern archaeologist is becoming increasingly aware of the contribution that a ceramic technological investigation can make to the understanding of prehistoric culture. All too often, however, the thrust of such investigations is limited to identifying materials and locating their sources. Scientific techniques like neutron activation analysis, X-ray diffraction, and ceramic petrology can also be used to great advantage in the study of ceramic ecology, that interaction of resources, knowledge, and style which ultimately produces a viable pot.

One of the most interesting ceramic traditions of late prehistoric North America (800–1500 A.D.) is centered in the Mississippi Valley. Mississippian cultures differed from preceding and contemporary Woodland groups not only in the level of sociopolitical organization, subsistence strategy, and stylistic modes but also in technological adaptations. Some innovations in Mississippian pottery technology, especially the introduction and widespread use of shell tempering, are immediately apparent. Changes in firing temperatures, clay sources, and the use of fluxes are less obvious but just as important to an understanding of the ceramic system.

Mississippian pottery represents a significant advancement over Woodland wares. Mississippian ceramics are generally better constructed, with thinner walls, a greater variety of vessel shapes and uses, and decorated with more sophisticated techniques. This improvement occurs despite the reliance of Mississippian potters on inferior materials.

By late Mississippian times, shell had become the most common tempering material. While grit, limestone, and grog (sherd) tempers occur with some frequency in the south, in Upper Mississippian sites shell-tempered ware represents over 95% of all pottery excavated. Yet shell ($CaCO_3$) begins to decompose at temperatures well within the range of primitive, non-kiln firing techniques (600–900 °C) creating the risk of lime spalling or a gradual weakening of the matrix due to subsequent uptake of H_2O ($CaCO_3 \xrightarrow{>600\,°C} CaO + CO_2$). In general, Mississippian pottery shows no evidence of lime blowing and is often very well preserved.

Mineralogical analysis of alluvial materials from the Mississippi River and its major tributaries indicates that clays in the bottomland are high in montmorillonite (Holmes and Hearn 1942).

X-ray diffraction studies done on unfired Mississippian pots suggest that these clays were being used in the production of Mississippian ceramics (Carss 1962; Million 1975). Montmorillonite is not normally suitable for use in low fired, technically simple wares

Table 1. Analysis of Mississippian clays

	Kaolinite	Montmor-illonite	Illite
Mississippi River	5–15%	25–45%	40–60%
Western Tributaries: Milk, Yellowstone, Missouri, Platte, and Arkansas	10–20%	25–45%	40–60%
Eastern Tributaries: Ohio, Cumberland, Tennessee, Duck, and Clinch	10–20%	10–15%	67–75%

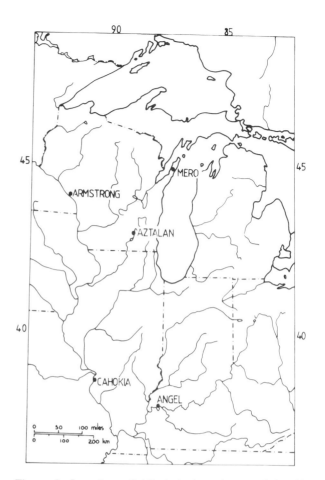

Figure 1. *Location of Mississippian sites used in this study.*

because its extreme plasticity and high shrink/swell ratio are difficult to overcome by the mechanical expedient of adding temper. Even a small amount of montmorillonite will significantly alter the workability of a clay body (Grim 1968).

In montmorillonite, parts of the octahedrally coordinated aluminum are replaced by magnesium, thus producing an over-all negative charge of the three-layer arrangement. This surplus charge is balanced by alkali or alkali earth ions loosely bonded between the layer stacks. They are susceptible to intercalation of large amounts of water which tends to separate the three-layer stacks as well as the particles. During drying and firing, the water is expelled causing profound shrinkage and frequent spalling of the ceramic object. In order to counteract this, it is necessary to add sufficient amounts of tempering material.

James Porter (1964) was one of the first archaeologists to seriously investigate the technical aspects of Mississippian ceramics. When he tried to replicate Mississippian pots using local Mississippi River clays, he reported that attempts to fire test tiles tempered with shell caused the tiles to explode. Million (1975) has also done extensive work on reproducing Mississippian ceramics. He noted a most interesting phenomenon. The addition of burnt shell to "gumbo" clays high in montmorillonite from Arkansas increased the clay's workability, almost within minutes.

The CaO created by burning the shell acts in two ways: first, it takes up water from the paste very quickly, making it more workable. Second, the $Ca(OH)_2$ formed provides calcium ions which cause a flocculation, further enhancing the workability.

The negatively charged clay particles of montmorillonite are electrically balanced by absorbed or intercalated alkali (Na^+, K^+) or alkaline earth (Mg^{2+}, Ca^{2+}) ions. Water molecules are then attached to the neutral particles by weak dipole interaction forces, forming "micelles" that act in the same way as electrical condensers which exhibit concentric charged shells. These shells give rise to an electric potential called the "zeta" potential. High zeta values, as in Na-bearing clay-water suspensions, cause the repulsion of particles, thus separating the clay platelets (deflocculation). Small zeta values are related to strongly absorbed Ca^{2+} or Mg^{2+} ions which in turn tend to form flocs (flocculation).

There is an apparent contradiction between inferior raw materials and superior pottery. This has not, however, attracted much other interest among archaeologists, undoubtedly because of a lack of the knowledge necessary to understand the implications properly. Those archaeologists aware of the problems of carbonate reactions have often assumed that firing temperatures did not exceed 600 °C.

Examination of Data and Interpretation of Artifacts

The present study was begun in an attempt to explain

C. Stimmell, R. B. Heimann, R. G. V. Hancock

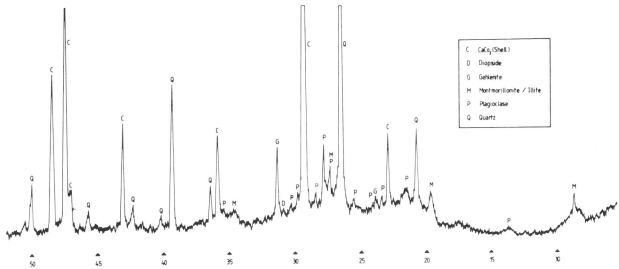

Figure 2. Representative X-ray diffraction pattern of Mississippian shell-tempered pottery.

not only the role of shell tempering, but also why such an innovation was so widely accepted. Material from five Mississippian sites spread over the Upper Mississippi Valley was studied. Special emphasis was placed on samples from Aztalan, containing a mixed Middle Mississippian/Late Woodland component (Fig. 1). Specimens from each site were subject to testing by neutron activation analysis, X-ray diffraction, scanning electron microscopy, and petrological examination. A considerable number of sherds were examined under a binocular microscope, roughly classified as to color (Munsell), hardness (Mohs), and macroporosity. Macroporosity was determined by first measuring dry weight and then reweighing the samples after immersion in distilled water for 24 hours.

Table 2. Macroporosity of shell-tempered Mississippian sherds

	Total Macroporosity	Standard Deviation
Aztalan	9.8%	1.7
Cahokia	12.3%	3.5
Mero	9.3%	1.9
Armstrong	10.6%	4.6
Angel	11.4%	.3
	10.7%	

This low porosity suggests a relatively dense and high fired ware.

Petrological examination of ceramic thin sections revealed additional evidence of a relatively high firing temperature. Well-rounded quartz grains, probably detrital to the clays, sometimes show glassy reaction rims and areas of vitrification can be identified. Except for a fair amount of quartz sand, thin sections show few other minerals present.

What is surprising is the amount of shell tempering. In many sherds, shell constituted up to 30% of the volume. A few samples contained as little as 10% shell, but even grog-tempered sherds often abound in shell-tempered grog.

The shell temper is generally well preserved, with the exception of the Armstrong site, where acidic soil conditions have helped to leach the exposed surfaces of sherds. The shell ranges from a fine powder to almost a centimeter in length, with 2–5 millimeters the most common size. The larger shell pieces are often elongated and aligned, probably owing to construction processes, parallel to the vessel walls.

In thin sections, particularly in areas where the samples are ground extra thin, the shell appears cryptocrystalline, sometimes with new structures superimposed over the original shell structure. Traces of mineral neoformation (gehlenite, albite) can occasionally be seen along the margins of shell pieces.

X-ray diffraction studies confirm the mineral content of the sherds. The X-ray diffraction results from all five sites were very similar despite their separation by hundreds of miles (Fig. 2). Quartz and $CaCO_3$ generated the strongest peaks. A plagioclase of undetermined composition appears in most of the Mississippian X-ray diffraction diagrams, but again in very small quantities. Traces of diopside are also visible.

The mineral gehlenite, a calcium aluminum silicate, is found in all shell-tempered sherds tested. There would seem to be direct correlation between amounts of $CaCO_3$ and gehlenite (Fig. 3). The plot

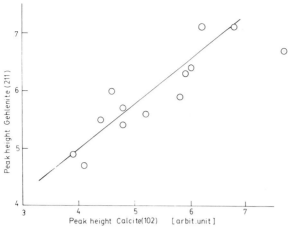

Figure 3. Relative X-ray diffraction peak heights of gehlenite (211) interference plotted against calcite (102) interference.

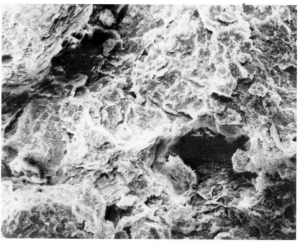

Figure 4. SEM photo of the exterior of a Mississippian sherd from Aztalan.

shows the relative peak heights of the gehlenite (211) interference at 2.85 Å against the calcite (102) interference at 3.86 Å. The correlation coefficient is 0.79. However, even if no shell temper is present, some gehlenite is still formed from the calcium in the matrix (1-2% CaO). Gehlenite will form at temperatures above 800°C from $CaCO_3$, quartz, and clay (Heimann and Maggetti 1980).

The occurrence of gehlenite suggests that firing temperatures must have exceeded 800°C. The higher the firing temperature, the shorter the firing time needed to complete this reaction. However, gehlenite converts to anorthite at temperatures above 950°C defining an upper temperature limit (Peters and Jenni 1973).

Another confirmation of a firing temperature range between 800° and 900°C is provided by the X-ray diffraction pattern of montmorillonite. When heated above 640°C, the crystal lattice of montmorillonite partially collapses. This causes a shift in the spacing of the (001) interference peak from 15 Å (montmorillonite in dehydrated state) to 9.8 Å at 760°C (Greene-Kelly 1957). The position of this peak alters slightly as the temperature rises until it disappears around 900°C. X-ray diffraction diagrams of Mississippian sherds indicate that montmorillonite was heated high enough to produce such a shift (Fig. 2).

Scanning electron microscope photographs show that the original arrangement of clay mineral platelets remains essentially unaltered (Fig. 4). This, again, places the firing temperature below 900-1000°C.

This evidence implies that firing temperatures were high enough to cause some deleterious effects due to the decomposition of $CaCO_3$ but not high enough to

cause the formation of a liquid phase. Since Mississippian pots show no ill effects from the presence of shell and at least some sintering has occurred, an explanation is needed.

Laird and Worcester's (1956) work on limestone impurities in brick manufacture indicate that the addition of as little as .5% NaCl will inhibit lime spalling. Salt acts as a flux either by promoting a reaction between $CaCO_3$ and iron which then forms stable compounds at temperatures below 900-1000°C (Butterworth 1956); or by lowering the onset of vitrification, so that the $CaCO_3$ is sealed off from contact with water vapor (Tite and Maniatis 1975); or, more importantly, by increasing the pore size of calcium carbonates (Shearer et al. 1978).

Figure 5 shows how the addition of rock salt, even in small amounts, alters the pore distribution curves of calcite. A liquid film of eutectic composition is formed around the decomposed calcite grains, and this in turn leads to an uptake of more calcia when the reaction proceeds. Accordingly, large pores form at the expense of small ones, shifting the mean pore diameter towards larger values. As evident from Figure 6, in the ternary system $CaCO_3$-NaCl-Na_2CO_3, the eutectic temperature is as low as 690°C for the NaCl-$CaCO_3$-$Na_2Ca(CO_3)_2$ (double carbonate) partial system and 640°C for the NaCl-$Na_2Ca(CO_3)_2$-$(Na_2,Ca)CO_3$ (solid solution) partial system. The Na_2CO_3 necessary may be provided by the ionic exchange reactions of the reciprocal salt pairs $CaCO_3$-NaCl and $CaCl_2$-Na_2CO_3 (Fig. 7). The larger pores produced by this mechanism counteract the volume effect caused by the reassimilation of H_2O by creating room for expansion.

The use of salt in $CaCO_3$-tempered pottery has also been reported in the ethnographic literature. Rye

C. Stimmell, R. B. Heimann, R. G. V. Hancock

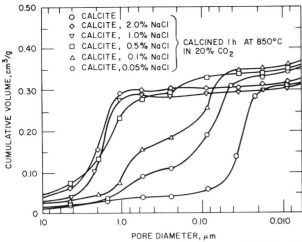

Figure 5. Porosity curve for calcite spar calcined with NaCl one hour at 850°C in 20% CO₂ (Shearer et al. 1978: 9).

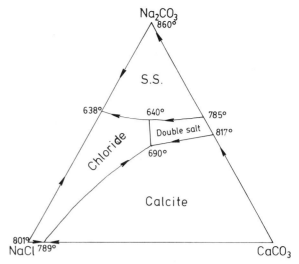

Figure 6. Ternary system phase diagram of CaCO₃–NaCl–Na₂CO₃ (Niggli 1919).

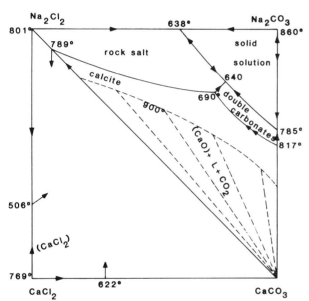

Figure 7. Reciprocal salt pairs CaCO₃–NaCl and CaCl₂–Na₂CO₃ (Niggli 1919).

(1976) proved that the use of seawater to wet clay allowed Melanesian pottery, tempered with beach sand high in shell content, to be fired at temperatures up to 1000°C without damage. Pottery made with fresh water failed when fired over 700°C. Rye was surprised that the addition of salt did not significantly decrease the workability of local clays. The introduction of small amounts of Na does not appear to act as a deflocculant in such a Ca-rich system. Arnold (1971) discovered that Yucatan potters who used temper containing a combination of calcite, dolomite, and attapulgite tasted clays to determine which

were "good" to use. "Good" clays tasted salty. A silver nitrate test confirmed that they contained a chloride salt.

The possibility that salt might be a factor in the successful manufacture of Mississippian shell-tempered pottery is intriguing because it appears that salt from the Mississippi Valley was first intensively exploited during the Mississippian period (Keslin 1964). Special vessels, long shallow basins called "salt pans," were used to facilitate evaporation of salt from saline springs located in the central Mississippi and Ohio River valleys. Early explorers to the area reported an extensive trade in salt spreading over much of the Southeast.

Rye (1976) suggests that salt additions to ceramics will appear as cubic pits visible on exterior surfaces or as cubic voids with yellowish reaction rims in thin section. Since the exterior surfaces of many Mississippian sherds are often altered by soil conditions, no conclusion was drawn from a macroscopic examination. A number of square voids, some with quite distinct reaction rims, were discovered in thin sections of Mississippian sherds (Fig. 8). However, such voids could be the result of "plucking out" of other cubic minerals in the process of making the thin sections.

The typical yellow reaction rims are caused by the melting of NaCl. Above 800°C the interaction of sodium chloride and montmorillonite in the presence of water leads to a quantitative removal of the chlorine in the form of HCl which is then vaporized (Puchelt 1979). The HCl reacts with iron-bearing compounds like hematite or magnetite forming volatile FeCl₃ which dissolves to a certain extent in the siliceous glass surrounding the original salt crystal.

During the NaCl/clay reaction at temperatures

Table 3. Composition of Mississippian shell-tempered sherds. Samples 1–11 are from Aztalan, 12 and 19 from Armstrong, 13 and 14 from Mero, 15 and 20 from Angel, 16–18 and 25 from Cahokia, 22 from Durst; 21, 23, and 24 are shell samples.

	1	2	3	4	5	6	7	8	9	10	11	12	13
Na	3050.00	3980.00	4290.00	4370.00	2380.00	4020.00	4200.00	3040.00	4050.00	4060.00	4160.00	3680.00	3180.00
Mg	.76	.91	.78	.92	.47	.67	.74	1.01	1.00	.75	.89	.78	.52
Al	4.60	5.94	5.53	5.90	4.53	6.13	5.33	5.34	5.44	5.44	6.81	5.21	4.85
K	1.80	2.48	2.14	2.12	.95	1.69	2.09	2.16	2.10	2.10	1.72	1.63	1.28
Ca	10.30	6.84	9.38	6.17	20.60	11.10	7.83	13.20	8.52	8.03	8.83	10.60	15.40
Sc	9.41	11.80	10.70	11.10	7.36	9.22	10.60	9.03	9.92	10.70	11.70	10.70	7.76
Ti	2600.00	3650.00	3100.00	3100.00	1800.00	3060.00	3080.00	2920.00	3410.00	3200.00	3680.00	2740.00	2820.00
V	65.00	110.00	83.00	84.00	89.00	112.00	83.00	89.00	76.00	92.00	139.00	77.00	85.00
Cr	61.00	74.00	69.00	68.00	51.00	66.00	65.00	58.00	63.00	67.00	83.00	70.00	54.00
Mn	649.00	750.00	639.00	708.00	830.00	835.00	644.00	733.00	632.00	835.00	461.00	482.00	327.00
Fe	3.20	4.11	3.50	3.60	2.37	2.92	3.47	3.22	3.44	3.59	3.84	3.99	2.33
Co	11.60	14.60	11.70	10.70	9.10	7.80	10.70	11.00	11.70	12.00	9.70	12.50	5.50
As	6.80	12.10	10.20	17.40	5.30	8.90	6.00	6.90	12.30	10.20	7.20	6.90	6.80
Rb	65.00	100.00	76.00	63.00	63.00	73.00	60.00	68.00	72.00	82.00	82.00	87.00	69.00
Sb	.27	.51	.49	.50	.62	.61	.66	.38	.37	.46	.51	.49	.74
Cs	2.38	3.83	2.90	2.38	4.10	3.89	2.14	2.58	2.48	2.31	4.06	3.24	4.28
Ba	1420.00	570.00	1060.00	1350.00	730.00	2090.00	1270.00	1180.00	990.00	1290.00	1760.00	1990.00	650.00
Ce	61.90	77.70	71.90	72.70	49.50	63.90	73.10	62.50	65.60	77.00	62.90	67.30	53.60
Sm	4.54	5.81	5.34	6.20	3.05	4.22	3.50	4.66	5.11	6.40	3.83	3.94	3.94
Eu	1.14	1.56	1.51	1.64	.74	1.00	1.46	1.14	1.25	1.60	.87	.94	.83
Hf	4.70	5.70	5.88	5.69	2.45	4.48	5.88	3.58	5.22	5.77	5.24	5.74	4.03
Ta	.74	.73	.66	.70	.46	.79	.34	.54	.66	.76	.87	.81	.47
Th	6.77	8.62	7.37	7.48	6.34	8.26	7.41	6.51	6.87	7.67	9.27	9.54	5.89
U	2.74	3.40	2.86	3.69	2.95	2.69	2.77	2.74	2.33	2.83	3.40	2.46	6.38

C. Stimmell, R. B. Heimann, R. G. V. Hancock

	14	15	16	17	18	19	20	21	22	23	24	25
Na	3800.00	3150.00	3030.00	2950.00	2910.00	1370.00	2780.00	1890.00	5150.00	30.00	1130.00	3910.00
Mg	.91	.50	.48	.59	.66	.62	.73	.85	.37	.97	.31	.60
Al	5.42	5.82	4.88	6.04	6.79	2.00	5.51	.33	5.96	.45	.34	3.77
K	2.56	1.64	1.38	1.63	1.43	.80	1.45	.10	3.00	.06	.92	1.01
Ca	4.92	9.09	15.40	11.20	12.10	28.90	9.58	40.90	6.33	39.80	35.00	19.90
Sc	8.66	9.96	8.33	10.10	9.63	4.38	10.10	.04	11.00	.80	.14	7.10
Ti	3150.00	3840.00	3090.00	2890.00	3360.00	1480.00	3980.00	1000.00	3900.00	900.00	1000.00	2320.00
V	65.00	80.00	94.00	114.00	124.00	27.00	71.00	18.00	102.00	17.00	19.00	67.00
Cr	55.00	64.00	56.00	70.00	66.00	29.00	63.00	2.00	82.00	6.00	2.00	51.00
Mn	531.00	363.00	1010.00	557.00	601.00	400.00	350.00	630.00	950.00	389.00	548.00	780.00
Fe	2.99	3.76	2.57	3.03	2.92	1.26	3.44	.02	4.04	.27	.07	2.20
Co	10.50	7.80	8.20	6.50	6.60	4.90	7.80	.23	14.30	1.30	.19	5.90
As	4.10	15.40	5.10	7.00	4.00	2.00	11.10	.50	4.60	.61	.91	4.80
Rb	96.00	74.00	76.00	77.00	68.00	29.00	68.00	5.00	109.00	5.00	5.00	68.00
Sb	.36	.37	.59	.79	.64	.24	.42	.07	.44	.07	.12	.34
Cs	2.60	2.87	3.95	5.50	3.47	1.50	3.50	.30	2.70	.24	.20	3.10
Ba	1210.00	1230.00	1560.00	1770.00	3520.00	470.00	1190.00	170.00	2130.00	190.00	160.00	500.00
Ce	71.80	77.20	54.10	55.00	55.80	42.80	76.50	2.00	85.90	9.60	2.80	49.80
Sm	4.48	5.23	3.77	3.99	3.79	2.69	5.35	.11	5.74	.44	.06	3.45
Eu	1.11	1.13	.93	1.05	.89	.74	1.48	.14	1.70	.21	.15	.89
Hf	5.59	6.19	3.20	3.82	3.42	2.69	6.38	.13	5.97	.31	.13	4.61
Ta	.45	1.12	.67	.70	.84	.35	1.00	.14	.65	.15	.15	.67
Th	7.92	8.42	7.02	8.42	7.77	3.45	8.54	.09	8.86	.72	.09	6.52
U	2.91	4.32	2.58	3.59	3.46	2.64	4.91	1.30	2.54	1.20	1.10	3.76

NOTE: The data given in this table were generated by a computer program that calculates to two decimal places. They have not been revised to include only the significant figures.

The elements Mg, Al, K, Ca, Fe are given in percentages, all other elements in parts-per-million (ppm).

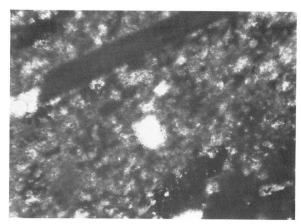

Figure 8. *Thin section (plain light) of Mississippian shell-tempered sherd from Aztalan with square void (400x).*

Figure 9. *SEM photo of newly formed albite in Mississippian sherd from Aztalan (4750x).*

above 800 °C, new minerals such as albite might be formed. Indeed, the plagioclase noted from the X-ray diffraction diagrams matches that of albite. However, it is not possible to distinguish albite from other forms of plagioclase on the basis of these X-ray diffraction patterns. Figure 9 shows a tiny crystal of newly formed albite in a Mississippian sherd from Aztalan taken by SEM and confirmed by EDAX analysis. It is probable that some plagioclase is also detrital in the clay.

Neutron activation analysis was conducted on 25 shell and Mississippian shell-tempered pottery samples (Table 3). Twenty-four elements were individually correlated against Ca, Na, Al, K, Sc, and Ti (Table 4). Only Mg and Mn failed to correlate reasonably in all cases, Mg probably because of poor analytical precision of measurement and Mn probably because of the Mn enrichment in the shell. The degree of correlation between other pairs of elements appears to be influenced by analytical precisions, i.e., precisely determined elements correlated well and imprecisely determined elements correlated less well.

All elements correlated negatively with Ca. This is an example of the calcium dilution effect (Figs. 10 and 11) (Hancock 1979). Apart from Ca, all elements correlated positively with each other. This implies not only that they are all predominantly associated with the clay from which the ceramics were made, but also that the clay itself was relatively free from other mineral additions. This data further confirms the very similar composition of pottery collected from widely scattered areas of the Mississippi Valley.

Part of the reason the neutron activation analysis (NAA) was undertaken was to test the hypothesis that the addition of NaCl might leave the pottery sodium enriched. From the correlation coefficients, it was established that most of the elements are very highly correlated. In this respect, the sodium does not appear to behave differently from the other elements. So no information has thus far been obtained from NAA to confirm a sodium enrichment. However, since the addition of only .5% NaCl is required to produce the optimum effect, the total Na contribution is so small as to be almost undetectable without comparison with original clay compositions. As seen in Figure 10, the high amounts of shell temper decrease the relative concentration of sodium. Clay sources are unknown for most Mississippian sites. Further NAA work is planned using experimentally produced ceramics made from clays obtained near Cahokia.

Summary

Mineralogical and textural evidence indicates that Mississippian pottery was fired to a temperature somewhere between 800° and 900°C. Shell-tempered pottery heated this high should experience lime spalling and little or no vitrification. Mississippian pottery does not appear to have reacted in the expected way. It was hypothesized that the addition of NaCl could account for these discrepancies. NaCl lowers the onset of sintering and acts as a catalyst during the calcination of $CaCO_3$. Ethnographic and archaeological data lends credence to this idea. The presence of cubic voids surrounded by yellow reaction rims and the appearance of newly formed albite crystals support this hypothesis. While present neutron activation analysis proved inconclusive, further work involving replication studies is ongoing.

If our assumptions prove true, they have important implications for the understanding of Mississippian cultural development. Peoples in central North

C. Stimmell, R. B. Heimann, R. G. V. Hancock

Table 4. Correlation coefficients for Ca, Na Al, K, Sc, and Ti

Elements	Ca	Na	Al	K	Sc	Ti
Ca						
Na	−.895					
Al	−.945	.802				
K	−.888	.838	.767			
Sc	−.968	.844	.961	.817		
Ti	−.921	.794	.918	.798	.911	
Mg	−.138	.101	.104	.142	.160	.094
V	−.771	.699	.915	.607	.836	.782
Cr	−.948	.855	.968	.800	.987	.906
Mn	−.210	.431	.214	.347	.221	.138
Fe	−.961	.841	.929	.845	.985	.914
Co	−.864	.806	.769	.882	.876	.744
As	−.697	.580	.649	.543	.707	.689
Rb	−.912	.843	.892	.838	.905	.866
Sb	−.644	.538	.766	.423	.692	.576
Cs	−.645	.500	.782	.380	.707	.628
Ba	−.595	.473	.722	.449	.613	.605
Ce	−.957	.831	.894	.858	.951	.908
Sm	−.914	.796	.849	.831	.908	.872
Hf	−.926	.844	.826	.803	.912	.884
Ta	−.739	.564	.796	.474	.786	.821
Th	−.940	.805	.957	.752	.966	.899
U	−.508	.350	.560	.230	.517	.563
Eu	−.877	.809	.770	.863	.871	.823

Correlation
coefficients (R) = 0.444 (95% confidence)
= 0.561 (99% confidence)

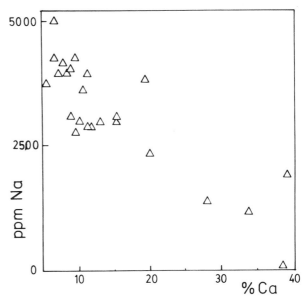

Figure 10. Neutron activation analysis correlation of amounts of Na/Ca in Mississippian sherds.

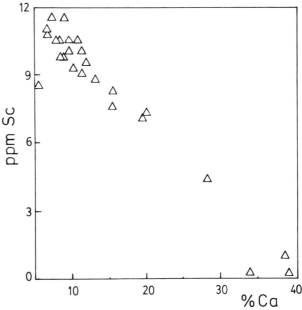

Figure 11. Neutron activation analysis correlation of amount of Sc/Ca in Mississippian sherds.

America began a shift to more intensive forms of agriculture in the late prehistoric period. Sites became more commonly located on or near fertile bottomlands in major river valleys. The clay of these regions was high in montmorillonite and presented problems for the primitive craftsman. The addition of $CaCO_3$, in the form of either limestone or shells, solved the problem of clay workability but created another. The addition of salt, abundant in the central Mississippi Valley, became the answer but created a technological need for salt in areas in which it did not naturally occur. A trade system resulted with salt as an important commodity, stimulating development of trade and cultural centers such as Cahokia and Angel which were located close to the northern margins of this raw material resource (Fig. 12).

Prehistoric peoples were able to cope successfully with a series of difficult challenges when the need arose. During the process of experimentation, they extended the boundaries of their craft, enabling them to do more with less. Undoubtedly, had other clay resources been available, potters would not have expended the necessary time, energy, and resources needed for such a breakthrough. Archaeologists and physical scientists alike must be made aware that major alterations in technology are probably not due

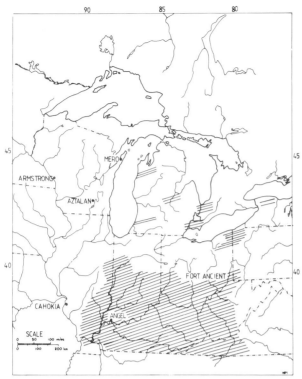

Figure 12. Location of primary salt (NaCl) occurrences in the central Mississippi Valley.

to such commonly invoked factors as diffusion, conquest, or whim alone. Such change requires the right combination of natural environment (raw materials), intellectual environment (knowledge), and cultural environment (needs) mixed with a little luck to produce the technological pot of gold.

Acknowledgments: The authors gratefully acknowledge Dr. M. Maggetti, Professor of Mineralogy, Fribourg, Switzerland, for his assistance to this research.

References

Arnold, D. E. 1971. Ethnomineralogy of Ticul, Yucatan: Etic and Emics. *American Antiquity* 36: 20–40.

Butterworth, B. 1956. Lime blowing: some notes on the literature. *Transactions of British Ceramic Society* 55: 532–44.

Carss, Brian. 1962. Progress report on the clay mineral analysis of pottery and soils recovered from the American Bottoms. In Fowler, M. L., ed., *First Annual Report: American Bottoms Archaeology, July 1, 1961–June 30, 1962.* Urbana: Illinois Archaeological Survey, University of Illinois.

Greene-Kelly, R. 1957. Montmorillonite. In MacKenzie, Robert, ed., *The Differential Thermal Investigation of Clays.* London: Mineralogical Society.

Grim, R. E. 1968. *Clay mineralogy.* 2d ed. New York: McGraw-Hill.

Hancock, R. G. V. 1979. Some aspects of the analysis of ancient artifacts by neutron activation. *Journal of International Institute of Conservation–Canadian Group* 3: 21–27.

Heimann, R., and Maggetti, M. 1980. Experiments on simulated burial of calcareous terra sigillata (mineralogical change). *British Museum Occasional Papers* 19, 163–77.

Holmes, R. S., and Hearn, W. E. 1942. Chemical and physical properties of some of the important alluvial soils of the Mississippi drainage basin. *U.S. Dept. of Agriculture, Technical Bulletin*, no. 833.

Keslin, Richard. 1964. Archaeological implications on the role of salt as an element of cultural diffusion. *Missouri Archaeologist* 26.

Laird, R. T., and Worcester, W. 1956. The inhibiting of lime blowing. *Transactions of the British Ceramic Society* 55: 545–63.

Million, Michael. 1975. Ceramic technology of the Nodena Phase Peoples. *Southeastern Archaeological Conference Bulletin* 18: 201–208.

Niggli, Paul. 1919. Untersuchungen an Karbonat- und Chloridschmelzen. *Zeitschrift für Anorganische und Allgemeine Chemie* 106: 135, 140.

Peters, T., and Jenni, F. P. 1973. Mineralogische Untersuchungen über das Brennverhalten von Ziegeltonen. *Beitr. Geol. Schweiz. Geotechn. Serie* 50. Bern: Kümmerly & Frey.

Porter, James. 1964. Thin section descriptions of some shell-tempered prehistoric ceramics from the American Bottoms. *Southern Illinois Univ. Museum Lithic Laboratory Research Paper*, no. 7.

Puchelt, H. 1979. University of Karlsruhe, Germany, private communication.

Rye, O. S. 1976. Keeping your temper under control: materials and the manufacture of Papuan pottery. *Archaeology and Physical Anthropology in Oceania* 11: 106–137.

Shearer, John A.; Johnson, Irving; and Turner, Clarence. 1978. The effect of sodium chloride on the reaction of SO_2/O_2 mixtures with limestones and dolomites. *ANL/CEN/FE-78-8 Argonne National Laboratory*, Argonne, Illinois.

Tite, M. S., and Maniatis, Y. 1975. Scanning electron microscopy of fired calcareous clays. *Transactions of British Ceramic Society* 74: 19–22.

Archaeological Examples
C. Ceramics in Metallurgy: Crucibles and Slags

21. Metallurgical Crucibles and Crucible Slags

R. F. TYLECOTE
Institute of Archaeology, London

NOTE: Citations for this chapter are signaled in the text, the tables, and the illustration captions by superior numbers that refer to the combined listing of *References and Notes* at the end of the chapter.

Crucible Types

The earliest known crucibles come from the Eastern Mediterranean[1] and are typified by those found by J. L. Caskey at Kea[2] which are dated to the Late Bronze Age (ca. 1200 B.C.) — (Fig. 1). We know from Egyptian tomb drawings of a slightly earlier period[3] that a rather shallow and open type of crucible was probably being used in the reign of Tuthmosis III (ca. 1500 B.C.), although the similarity of drawings in tombs separated by hundreds of years makes it possible that this was a much earlier type (Fig. 2).

The Kea crucible not only is the most common — even if confined to only two sites — but it presents many important characteristics. The first is its overall shape with an outlet at one side. This, as Savage and his colleagues have shown,[4] can be plugged during melting so that slag and dross are confined to the space above (Fig. 3). The metal that is poured through the hole is clean because the "bar" across the hole holds back the dross.

Some of these crucibles have grooves on the underside which seem to be connected with pouring. It is unlikely that such a large crucible holding up to 6 kgs would be lifted to pour the metal. It was more likely rocked with the aid of the groove, or pushed and pulled with a suitable tool[5] (Fig. 4).

The Egyptian crucible is open but is small enough to hold with withies (Fig. 5). What is shown in the drawings must have been a very rapid series of events since the wide and shallow crucible loses heat very rapidly. It was certainly heated from above (Fig. 6), and the wide-open character would be good for heat absorption and bad for heat loss. Many crucibles show external vitrification due to wood ash and it is clear that they were put at the bottom of a fire in contact with the wood ash. The metal would protect the inside from slagging with wood ash but cause other degradation problems, as we shall see.

In Britain, the typical crucible of the EIA (600 B.C. to the Roman period) was the triangular type (*see* Fig. 7).[6] This was comparatively wide and shallow and the corners provided three pouring lips which must have been its main advantage. By this time iron tongs were available and the lifting problems were not as great as in earlier periods (Fig. 8).[7]

By the Roman period the types of crucibles in use in the Roman world had multiplied. We have D-shaped (*see* Fig. 7), conical, and hemispherical crucibles and some with side holes from Nidda-Hedernheim[8] and Corbridge (Fig. 9) which show that this style had not died out with the LBA. The bigger crucibles are all round-bottomed; only the very small ones are flat. The reason for this is that they stood on or in charcoal like Neolithic pots; flat bottoms were

Figure 1. Eastern Mediterranean type crucible from Sinai. Maximum breadth 19 cm; capacity, 7.6 kg copper. (From Petrie and Currelly, Researches in Sinai[1].)

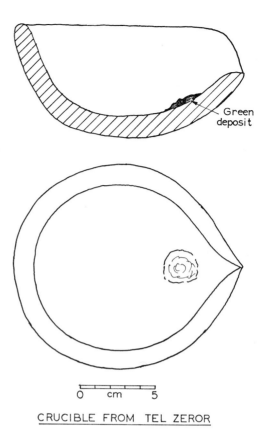

Green deposit

CRUCIBLE FROM TEL ZEROR

Figure 2. Shallow type of LBA crucible from Tel Zeror, Israel.

Figure 3. Function of "bar" in pouring Eastern Mediterranean crucible. (Courtesy R. Savage and S. R. Whittall, Cheltenham.)

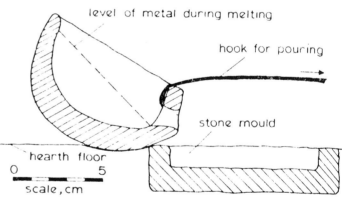

level of metal during melting

hook for pouring

stone mould

hearth floor

scale, cm

Figure 4. Normal method of pouring Eastern Mediterranean crucible.

R. F. Tylecote

Figure 5. Use of withies for pouring shallow crucibles (from tomb of Rek-me-Re, Thebes).

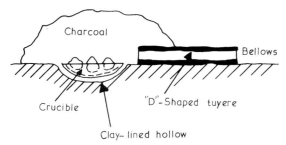

Figure 6. Heating crucible from above; tuyere and crucible from Ambelikou, Cyprus.

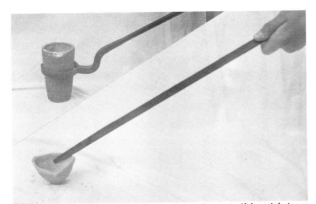

Figure 8. Method of holding triangular crucible with iron tongs, and round crucible with ring shanks.

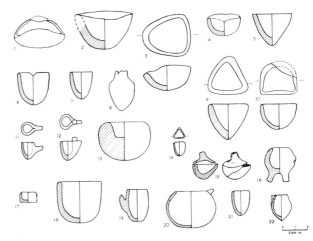

Figure 7. Various types of crucibles from the United Kingdom.

Figure 9. Side-hole crucible from Nidda-Hedernheim.

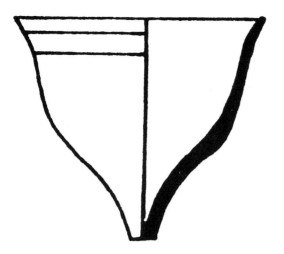

Figure 10. Chinese tapered crucible; no scale. (After Barnard⁹.)

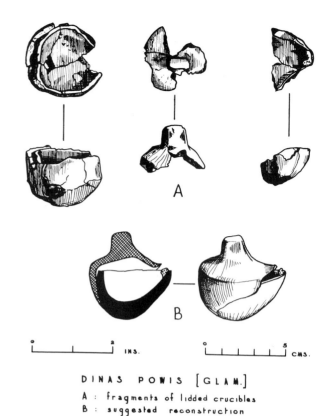

DINAS POWIS [GLAM.]
A : fragments of lidded crucibles
B : suggested reconstruction

Figure 11. Integral lidded crucibles from Dinas Powis. (Courtesy Professor L. Alcock.)

Figure 12. Bag-shaped and other types of crucibles from Corbridge, Northumberland.

quite superfluous, and probably difficult to place in the charcoal. The Chinese seemed to have preferred the tapered crucibles shown by Barnard⁹ (Fig. 10).

After the Roman period, in western Europe particularly, we see odd shapes, all with lugs to make handling easier (*see* in Fig. 7). These are clearly jeweler's crucibles for noble metals since most of them would not hold more metal than is needed for a ring or pendant. Some have legs reminiscent of some Trojan crucibles shown by Schliemann. The legs make heating under the crucible, as with a three-legged cauldron, a possibility. But it is doubtful whether much continuous heat could easily be produced in this position. Small pieces of charcoal would have to be pushed between the legs continuously.

One way of keeping heat in a crucible is to provide a lid. But the viscous nature of the slag and vitrified fuel ash make the removal of such a lid a risky business. If it gets stuck, the metal and crucible will go cold, accentuating the difficulty. So we do not find many crucible lids.

Still, in the immediate post-Roman period there is a tendency to produce an integral lidded crucible in which the lid was formed by the outer layer of a double-walled crucible (Fig. 11); this had the disadvantage of leaving a very small hole for putting in the solid metal to be melted. Apart from the additional difficulty of having to cut up the metal finely, this was a good type as the heat was kept in longer during pouring. Even so, when Dr. K. Lamm made her own Viking-type crucibles and heated them, filled with metal, in one of her hearths at Helgö, she had to be very quick in pouring it before the metal inside the crucible became solid.¹⁰ About 2–5 seconds were all

that could be allowed for the pouring operation. This was mainly because the fabric was so poor, that the crucible would slump if the normal amount of superheat (100–200 °C) was given to the melt.

The Saxon crucible was bag-shaped (Fig. 12) and we have no idea how it was lifted — perhaps with ring tongs round the rim? There was much variety in the medieval period and this is when the flat-bottomed crucible was being utilized. Agricola¹¹ shows it

234

in his book of 1540, and so does Biringuccio.[12] By this period, we have, of course, more permanent hearths and furnaces. Not surprisingly, the triangular (Hessian) crucible makes a comeback, and this type lasted until the end of the nineteenth century A.D., together with various types of round crucibles, mostly with flat bottoms. The flat-bottom types were suitable with muffle furnaces for assay work and small melts, but for charcoal or coke-fired furnaces, the round-bottom types were preferred. These were used for the melting of brass and later for the melting of steel. About halfway through the eighteenth century, the clay-graphite or plumbago pot came into use in England but it was used earlier on the Continent; this and the refractory clay crucible were to be the common types of the nineteenth and twentieth centuries until the advent of the silicon carbide crucible of today.

Crucible Materials

One normally assumes the Neolithic pottery-using peoples came before the advent of metallurgy. But if we accept the possibility that native metals were melted before the making of pottery, then some sort of crucible was used before pottery was introduced. Early pottery was fired at lower temperatures than the melting point of gold (1060°C) and copper (1084°C), so the technology used for the making of pots may not have been of much use to the maker of crucibles.

Some stones are sufficiently fire-resisting to serve as crucibles (steatite?) and stone crucibles are known from the Irish Early Christian period. But little work has been done on them to find out what they could stand in the way of heat.

Clearly the making of clay crucibles that could stand a temperature of 1100°C was something of a problem. The first approach was to make them thick. The weak pottery clays would then be adequate — the Kea crucibles seem to be examples of this — and heating from above would obviate the need for heat transmission through the fabric. The weight of clay involved would retain heat while pouring (not lifting but rocking perhaps). It is quite possible that the outside never reached the temperature of the inside.

Heat transfer through the walls of a crucible can be reduced by increasing porosity by using some carbonaceous material that burns out during firing. This is not easy as it needs long firing times and high temperatures if the fabric is otherwise dense. Straw temper usually gives rise to a weak fabric. But highly porous cokelike fabrics are known.

So far, little work has been done on crucible fabrics. This is partly because the metallurgist is not necessarily a ceramicist although the study of metallurgical bricks is normally part of an extractive metallurgy course. The archaeo-metallurgist hopes that the more recent scientific study of pottery will have some spinoff in this direction. While he continues to concern himself with the slags and metals, the examination of the fabric could best be the province of the pottery specialist. But, of course, there are other subjects of interest to the archaeo-metallurgist and these are molds and furnace linings. Perhaps these — and crucibles — will one day become the subject of an archaeo-metallurgical ceramicist.

The techniques required have recently been applied by Professor Kingery[13] (MIT) and Professor Reuss[14] (Tufts University) to archaeological materials from Israel, Egypt, and Sardinia. This involves heating in stages and noting physical changes with the aid of a scanning electron microscope (SEM). Grains of quartz, etc., partially dissolve in the matrix and become rounded at higher temperature and the clays become vitrified (slagged). The composition may be studied by the normal thin section mineralogical technique supplemented with XRF and XRD. On the whole, these techniques seem to be more time-consuming than chemical analysis and metallography, but the need is there — and more work must and will be done on this subject. Meanwhile, the archaeo-metallurgist studies the furnace linings as though they were slags, which they often are. But he is more interested in finding out what the furnace was used for, rather than the composition and provenance of its lining.

One of the most important sites recently excavated in southern Britain is the EIA hillfort of Gussage All Saints. This site was excavated by Dr. G. Wainwright in 1972[15,16] and produced evidence of an extensive industry for the production of bronze harness fittings using the lost-wax process. This is the first *solid* evidence for the use of this process in Britain. The metal was melted in triangular crucibles of the normal EIA type found at Glastonbury and elsewhere.[17]

Two crucibles were examined by EPMA. They were dark gray in color with a thin coating of vitreous material (slag) on both internal and external surfaces near the rim. The fabric contained many coarse grains of quartz and was relatively poor in aluminosilicate.[18] Fragments of these crucibles have been recently examined by Hilary Howard[19] and she found that she could recognize two main fabric groups amongst the one hundred crucible fragments that she examined from a single pit. All samples contained evidence of high-temperature firing with partial and often complete vitrification visible along the upper edges, especially around the pouring lip. Color suggested that the same white firing clay had been used.

Table 1. Statistical analysis of quartz inclusions in Gussage crucibles (after Howard[19])

Section No.	Mean size MzØ	S.D. O$_I$	Skewness SK$_I$	Kurtosis K$_G$	V	
267	2.793	1.412	0.140	0.682	50.54	Fabric 1
237	2.756	1.4603	0.0987	0.780	52.98	
5071	2.710	1.5578	0.187	0.539	57.45	
229	2.763	1.0979	0.034	1.102	39.73	
466	3.320	0.900	−1.4908	0.81063	27.12	Fabric 2
5B	3.440	1.119	−0.1473	3.708	32.52	

The technique used is that suggested by D.P.S. Peacock (Petrography of coarse pottery, in *Excavations at Fishbourne, 1961–69*, ed. B. Cunliffe, London: 1971).
V = Coefficient of variation; Mz = $-\log_2 Ø$ (mm).

It was found that gray to black reduction zones refired to white at 1200 °C in an oxidizing atmosphere. The first group had a crumbly texture due to large-size quartz grains, a sparse matrix, and high porosity. The second group had a high content of fine quartz and was denser and less porous.

The friable character made impregnation necessary for petrological analysis. All the sherds were found to contain a high density of fairly well-sorted grains of angular and subangular quartz in a sparse clay matrix. Almost all the larger grains (>0.25 mm) showed signs of extensive cracking resulting from stresses set up during heating to, and a rapid cooling from, 1200 °C. A particle size analysis was performed which showed that the first group consisted of predominantly fine grains (0.14 mm) with a tail of very fine grains. It was possible to say that all sherds from this group emanated from one source (Table 1). The heavy mineral residue was found to consist of 63% tourmaline with small amounts of zircon, rutile, and kyanite. This tends to indicate the tertiary sands of the Wareham-Poole area as the origin of raw material supply. These sands occur within the Bagshot beds and are associated with a good quality white firing clay. This is the closest source to the Gussage site.

Graphite-containing pottery has been found at Manching in Germany and in the surrounding area.[20] The graphite content of La Teñe and Roman pottery from Manching varies from 5% to 40%. Some other sites have even higher levels (83%). It is suggested that wares with less than 10% graphite be termed "graphite-containing" while those with more than 10% be called "graphited clays." Such mixtures have

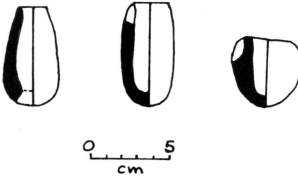

Figure 13. Graphited clay crucible from southern Germany. (After I. Kappel[20].)

been used for crucibles. Graphited clay crucibles are rarely found on La Teñe sites but at least three graphited clay crucibles are known with slag contamination (Fig. 13). Triangular graphited crucibles are also known from La Teñe and Roman contexts. There is little doubt that the sources of graphite were local, either from around Passau or from southern Bohemia.

The LBA crucible fragments from Dalkey Island, Co. Dublin,[21] varied from 12 mm to 17 mm in wall thickness. These differ from the coarse domestic pottery of the period having no coarse grits. Several show definite layers of internal slip (usually multiple). In one case there were three distinct layers, separated from the original crucible and from each other by layers of slag. These added 5 mm to the initial thickness. The crucible wall contained quartz and oligoclase with mica or illite. The slip coats were similar in composition but the quartz was finer and slightly greater in quantity. The inner surface had been hotter than the outside. No mullite was present and there are no indications of a very high temperature. The Early Christian fabric from the same site was quite different, cindery and cellular and typical of EC fabric in Ireland.

At Helgö, Dr. Lamm examined the constitution of the molds and crucibles in order to be able to reproduce them.[22] She also found that the local (Malar) clay material had been tempered with fine-grained quartz which had probably been artificially crushed and sifted. The percentage was variable, 30–60% SiO$_2$ being obtained. Analyzed fragments of molds showed the addition of fine pulverized charcoal and it is possible that this had been added to the crucible fabric and burnt out. It was found that the firing temperature of the crucibles exceeded 900–1000 °C. It was also found that with more than 60% quartz the crucible crumbled to pieces, while with small amounts the crucible was not sufficiently refractory;

R. F. Tylecote

Table 2. Chemical analyses of crucible fabric (%)

	Meare[23] (Som) (EIA)	York[24] (Rom-Med)	Wootz[25]
SiO_2	76.7	62.6	52.10
Fe_2O_3	2.7 (FeO)	2.6	5.67
Al_2O_3	13.1	30.6	22.13
CaO	1.5	1.2	1.06
MgO	1.5	0.1	0.78
$Na_2O + K_2O$	3.2	—	—
TiO_2	1.0	—	—
Carbon	—	—	11.25

50-55% of quartz was best. The strength could be increased by the further addition of 5-10% chamotte in the form of fine-ground, used crucibles. Another way to increase the strength was to roll the crucible at the last moment after drying in ground quartz. Such a crucible can stand 1600°C. This was probably the technique used at Helgö. Dr. Lamm used clay that had been completely dried, crushed it, and then put it into water. After 10 minutes the supernatant water was poured off and 50% fine pulverized quartz was added. After the clay had been worked to a pliable consistency the lidded crucible was molded with a handle and an outer layer of more fluid clay was painted on, but the amount of quartz was the same. It is clear that the need for special refractory fireclays was realized in Britain by the pre-Roman period, from about 600 B.C. at least, and workers in settlements carrying out metallurgical operations were able to use deposits of suitable clays — in the case of Gussage — some 30 miles away. We do not know how this sort of thing was organized. Most likely the clay was traded just like salt and other necessary commodities.

Development of crucible materials, until the reuse of graphite in the eighteenth century, was slow. We see that, chemically, medieval crucible materials were high alumina clays (Table 2). Theophilus[26] does not have much to say on this subject apart from the use of clay-lined iron plate crucibles for bell metal. It is odd that with all the wealth of bell foundries now excavated in Britain, we have not been able to find a substantial number of crucibles. Theophilus was certainly a believer in additions of chamotte (grog). Ground white clay was added to crushed old crucibles or, if these were not available, white earthenware pots. Two-thirds of white clay was mixed with one-third burned pots and warm water. The crucibles were then formed by molding over a piece of wood.

Biringuccio[27] refers to "Valencia" and "Treguanda" clay but also suggests Vienna as a good source (Passau graphite?), but clearly he knows little about the matter as he recommends the addition of iron hammer scale. Agricola[28] has a little more to say on the subject. He also uses chamotte and clay to make his triangular assay crucibles. In the seventeenth century we know that charcoal dust was used for furnace linings.[29] By the eighteenth century Cornish clays were not considered good enough for tin assay crucibles and good clay had to be brought from long distances such as Stourbridge (Midlands).[30] By the time we arrive at the eighteenth century, crucibles become a specialists' item and the specialist knew where to get the right materials even if it meant international trade. Cornish crucibles today consist of 50% ball (white) clay and 50% sand. Hessian (triangular German) crucibles, 2 parts clay and 4-5 parts sand. Huntsman's (1740) crucibles — for his crucible cast steel process — were presumably based on brass founders' crucibles. The making of these crucibles has been described by Brearley and others and almost became folklore.[31,32] But the melting point of steel, with 1% carbon in it, is 1470°C and one has to allow 20-40°C superheat above this to get a cast. So the necessary temperature for this purpose had to be above 1500°C, a rise of 300°C above previous needs. This required careful preparation of the clay by "treading," sometimes mixing old pots with new Stourbridge clay, a little local (Stannington) clay, and some China clay (kaolin). The dry ingredients were usually mixed together, and water was added and left to be absorbed by the clay mix. In England, very little carbon was added as it affected the carbon content of the steel[33] (Table 3). For some reason the Sheffield steel makers (Table 4) found that they could manage with a minimum of carbon, while foreign competitors, who could not get the right clays, had to turn to graphite pots with their tendency to in-

Table 3. Clays used for Sheffield steel crucibles (1895-1898) (after Barraclough[33])

Quality	1	2	3	4
Clay %	Research	Normal	Normal (preferred)	Casting pot
Stourbridge	45	40	20	Nil
Derby	21	17	39	20
Stannington	21	17	14	30
China clay	10	20	20	35
Coke dust	3	6	6	15

Table 4. Chemical composition of clays used by Sheffield steelmakers (after Searle[34])

%	China clay	Stour- bridge clay	Derby clay	Stanning- ton clay
SiO$_2$	46.3	63.3	52.0	47.6
Al$_2$O$_3$	39.9	23.3	36.0	25.4
FeO	0.3	1.8	1.8	3.5
CaO	0.4	0.5	0.8	1.0
MgO	0.4	—	0.5	1.1
H$_2$O + ign. loss	12.7	11.1	8.9	21.4

Table 5. Composition of graphitic crucibles (after Percy[38])

	I	II	III
SiO$_2$	51.4	45.10	50.00
Al$_2$O$_3$	22.0	16.65	20.00
Fe$_2$O$_3$	3.5	0.95	1.50
Graphite	20.00	34.50	25.50
CaO	0.20	0.00	0.50
H$_2$O + loss	2.90	2.80	3.50

(*Compt. Rendu,* 1867, 64: 1093)

crease the carbon content of the melt.[35]

It is clear that in 1766, black-lead (clay and graphite) crucibles were being made in England as well as the more usual clay ones.[36] It would seem likely that some of these were being made at Truro. Certainly black-lead pots were produced at Calenick (*see* note 30, above) in 1815, as there was an advertisement in the *West Briton* referring to the difficulty in obtaining satisfactory black-lead (graphite). From this date (2.3.1815), Calenick was able to supply black-lead melting pots of all sizes and of best quality, as well as the normal (clay) copper assaying crucibles.

It is well known that there was at least one English source of graphite, that from Borrowdale near Keswick in Cumbria.[37] But the quality of this source, no doubt like others such as that from Passau in Bavaria, was variable and sometimes contained large amounts of iron oxides. However, Percy[38] gives analyses from various sources, including Keswick and Passau, from which we see that the Borrowdale graphite had an ash content of 7–16%, the iron oxide content of which was 7.5–12.0%. On the other hand, the ash content of the graphite from Passau could be as high as 65%; but the iron oxide content of ash was in the range 0.5–12.6%. It would appear that a good grade of Bavarian graphite might be superior to the best English graphite.

According to Percy, in 1865 Cornish clay crucibles were then made in two sizes which fitted into each other. The larger were 7.6 cm external diameter at the top and 8.9 cm high. They were coarse in grain and grayish-white on the surface. The ware was pitted with iron inclusions; their external surface was reddish-brown and they were "kiln-burnt," which seems to mean that they could be plunged into a hot furnace without cracking, but they softened at a white heat. The well-known makers of these were Juleff of Redruth and Michell of Truro. Both types

were rapidly corroded by PbO but Michell's more so than Juleff's. They were made on a potter's wheel. It seems that the clays came from Bovey Tracey (Devon), Poole (Dorset), St. Agnes and St. Austell (Cornwall), but clay from the latter was only added to the less refractory types. Black-lead crucibles made from a mixture of graphite and clay were made for tin assaying by Juleff, and Morgan of Battersea. Percy gives three compositions for black-lead crucibles (Table 5). He also mentions that specimens from crucibles made by Morgan of Battersea were found to contain 48.34% graphite, so it is clear that there was at least one other grade with a higher graphite content. According to Boon (*see* note 37, above), graphite was imported into Britain from Passau but it is unlikely that in 1766 this was of crucible grade, as the export of such quality had been prohibited from 1613 to 1805. It is therefore likely that the graphite used in 1815 in Cornwall could have been German and that the release of this quality in 1805 was the reason for the start of black-lead crucible manufacture there.

Some sherds of thick graphite crucibles were found at Calenick in Cornwall. These sherds represented two types: a fine black shiny ware and a dull coarse brown-black ware. Small samples were removed and subjected to thermogravimetric analysis. The results are shown below:

Calenick graphitic crucibles — TGA results

Type A Black, shiny Weight loss (600–900 °C) 52%
Residue: pure white clay

Type B Brown-black, dull Weight loss (700–900 °C) 19%
Residue: red-brown clayey material (iron oxides)

R. F. Tylecote

These clearly represent the lowest grade (I in Table 5), and the best. Type A has been made with a white clay, while Type B has been made with a clay containing appreciable amounts of iron.

In the Indian subcontinent and probably in other parts of Asia, steel was made by the "Wootz" crucible process. This process was described in 1807 A.D. and must have been operated several hundred years earlier at least.[39] Recently several investigations have been made into the process and its products. Rao et al. (see note 25, above) have sectioned some crucibles, both used and unused, and found that the clay contained about 11% carbon (Table 2). Some at least of this carbon was absorbed by the contents resulting in their partial carburization. The crucible fabric consisted of clay and free quartz. After use it was found to be porous but the condition of the silica showed that it had been heated to over 1400°C. Unburnt carbon was still present. In China this process was used with coal for the making of cast iron with larger crucibles in the nineteenth century.[40]

Crucible Slags

This is the aspect which is most familiar to the archaeo-metallurgist. Smythe carried out some early chemical analyses on slags and crucible fabrics (see note 23, above), while Moss analyzed many Irish crucible slags[45] (Table 6). A crucible slag is formed by the release on melting of slags already in the metal, by the absorption of fuel ash, and by the reaction of either or both of these with the crucible fabric. Alloying metals, their oxides, and impurities may also be present (Fig. 14). Smelting slags are usually high in iron and these are the main reason for the iron content of crucible slags. But another is the iron from the raw copper being melted which can often be as high as several percent.[46] The fuel ash contribution is mainly one of lime and alkalis such as sodium and potassium, and the contribution from this source should not be underestimated. The smelting slag itself may well have 10% CaO in it with corresponding amounts of alkalis. Some analyses of wood ash are given in Table 7.[47]

The contribution from the crucible fabric can be minimized by using a lining containing a high proportion of charcoal dust but this does not seem to have been understood until the sixteenth or seventeenth century A.D. Before this crucibles were relined several times during their life with refractory clay. As examples of the various types of crucible slags we have, first, ore believed to be from the melting of native copper in Niger, West Africa (see note 41, above), in the second millennium B.C. (see Table 6, col. A). This is low in iron because the metal was not smelted, so no ferruginous flux or iron impurity

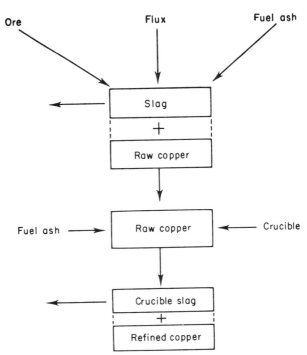

Figure 14. *Flow sheet showing sequence of copper extraction metallurgy and crucible melting.*

was involved. In addition, the MgO and CaO contents are high because the metal was found in a cupriferous dolomite and pieces of this mineral were fluxed with the aid of the alkaline fuel ash.

Another example comes from the fourth millennium site of Abu Matar in the Negev near Beersheba, Israel (see note 42, above). This was derived from a ferruginous copper metal and slag and has a fairly normal composition when compared with other slags (see Table 6; cf. col. B with cols. J, O, P). The Irish slags show quite high sulphur contents. This element tends to favor the copper rather than the smelting slag and, like the iron, appears as an impurity removed by remelting in the crucible. Naturally, small amounts of Ni, Sb, etc., give a clue to the origin of the metal. Ni tends to go with the copper, while As and Sb tend to be gradually lost under oxidizing conditions in the melting of the copper.[48] The correct technique for crucible melting is to oxidize out the impurities by melting under oxidizing conditions, i.e., by blowing the melt with a blast of air or adding copper oxide. These products should be skimmed off and the melt reduced by stirring with a piece of charcoal or wood (poling). Then, and only then, should the tin be added to make a bronze, and lead also if desired.

Conclusions and Recommendations

Clearly, the specific raw materials were carefully se-

Table 6. Composition of crucible slags

%	A Afounfoun Niger (ca. 800 B.C.) Crucible (F14)	B Abu Matar Israel (4th Mill.) Am 485	C Dalkey Is Ireland (BA)	D Dalkey Is Ireland (BA)	E Gussage, UK (EIA) Red slag	F Gussage, UK (EIA) Orange	G Gussage, UK Slag nodule; metal	H Gussage, UK Slag nodule; matrix
Ref. No.	41	42	21	21	18	18	18	18
SiO_2	43.0	48.22	21–32	4–8	56–61	43–61	—	45
Al_2O_3	7.9	8.08	2–4	—	5–10	5–9	—	4.5
Fe_2O_3	—	—	0.7	pres.	2.5	2	—	23
FeO	2.1	7.47	—	—	—	—	—	—
CaO	27.0	11.08	3–4	0.7	4–10	3	—	11
MgO	10.0	2.57	2	—	—	—	—	—
K_2O	0.9	—	—	—	5–8	1	—	2
Na_2O	2.6	—	!	—	—	—	—	—
TiO_2	nd	—	—	—	—	—	—	—
Cu_2O	(Cu)1.2	(Cu)8.31	(Cu)5–10	—	4–9	34–39	(Cu)86	1
SnO_2	—	nil	(Sn)3–5	0.01	3	3	(Sn)13	12
NiO	—	—	—	—	—	—	—	—
ZnO	—	<0.1	—	—	—	—	—	—
P_2O_5	—	0.52	4–10	2.0	nd	nd	nd	nd
Pb	—	nil	0.5	0.04	—	—	—	—
SO_3	—	—	—	—	—	—	—	—
As_2O_3	—	—	—	—	—	—	—	—
MnO	—	—	—	—	—	—	—	—

nd = not detected   — = not sought

Table 7. Composition of wood and peat ash (after Evans and Tylecote[47])

	Wood Ash (not vitrified)	Wood Ash (vitrified)	Ash Tree Leaf Ash	Peat Ash
SiO_2	1.5–6.5	4.5	5.5	3–30
Fe_2O_3	0–7	tr	0.1	10–20
Al_2O_3	0–2	—	tr	0–5
Mn_2O_3	0–30	—	0.1	0–1
CaO	14–60	60.0	49.6	24–30
MgO	1–25	0.27	10.6	1–7
K_2O	10–20	5.6	19.0	0–1
Na_2O		0.93	1.2	0–2
P_2O_5	4–18	—	7.07	0–3
S	0–1.5	—	2.0	5–10
CO_2	rest	rest	rest	—

— = not determined

lected and the less refractory pottery clays discarded. Probably this started by trial and error, a process that one sees in a more recent period going on in the evolution of the Sheffield steel crucible. There seems to be no evidence for the transport of finished crucibles, except by the itinerant smith. They would be too delicate. There seem to be two early types of crucibles: a clay-sand variety and a porous coke-like crucible. So far the only petrological work has been done on the former and we eagerly await work on the latter. Crucibles must have adequate refractoriness, adequate density to avoid leakage and resist dissolution by the melt, and the thermal shock resistance. This seems to require a high concentration of quartz sand and/or the mixing in of previously used crucibles as "grog" or chamotte. Some sand is often present in the raw clay and this may be removed and additional quartz of controlled size added after washing the clay, or the correct amount of each grade obtained by

R. F. Tylecote

Table 6. Composition of crucible slags

23	43	44	24	45	45	45	45	31
J Meare, UK (EIA) Slag glaze	K Craigywarren, UK (EIA) External slag	L Wilderspool, UK (Roman) Slag	M York, UK (R. or Med.) Slag	N Antrim, UK (E. Christ.) Slag	O Cavan Ireland (EC) Slag	P Dunshaughlin Ireland (EC) Slag	Q Irish No. 158 Slag	R Sheffield steel (18th cent.) Slag
66.8	46.2	41.3	57.1	46.2	45.0	43.9	43.2	44.36
14.5	10.6	—	19.6	10.6	2.2	—	18.2	18.05
—	—	9.4 (inc alk)	8.6	—	—	—	—	3.66
7.3	11.2	—	—	11.2	7.7	8.7	15.2	4.41
6.2	12.8	—	3.0	12.8	1.0	3.7	4.9	7.74
2.0	6.5	—	1.73	6.5	0.5	0.8	0.5	} 4.41
nd	} 8.8	—	—	4.7	—	—	1.2	}
nd		—	—	4.1	—	—	1.0	—
tr	tr	—	—	tr	—	—	—	—
2.0	1.0	(CuO)43.7	(CuO)2.0	1.0	(Cu)23.4	(Cu)28.2	—	—
—	—	(SnO) 4.9	(SnO)6.7	—	—	—	—	—
—	—	—	tr	—	—	—	—	—
—	—	0.75	nil	—	—	—	—	—
—	1.2	—	—	1.2	tr	—	0.5	—
tr	0.2	—	—	0.2	—	0.3	—	—
(S)0.3	0.4	—	—	0.4	—	(S)2.6	—	—
—	0.5	—	—	0.5	—	—	0.9	—
—	—	—	—	—	—	—	—	17.43

nd = not detected   — = not sought

blending the right raw clays as with the Sheffield steel crucibles. At Gussage (*see* note 19, above), the average proportion of sand to matrix was 79.18% sand to 20.82% clay and voids. This exceptionally high proportion of quartz sand may have resulted in the failure of some of the crucibles. This seems to be a characteristic of EIA crucibles, as the composition of the Somerset (Meare) crucible shown in Table 6 suggests much the same proportion. On the other hand, the York and Sheffield crucibles seem to have a higher clay content.

Excessive quartz can be deleterious because of the volume changes connected with the alpha-beta transformation at 573 °C and its corresponding inversion during the cooling process. On the other hand, too great a proportion of clays of low refractoriness containing iron and alkalis will reduce the temperature of use and allow the crucible to "slump." Additions of graphite or carbon as charcoal dust reduce the tendency of the melt to dissolve the crucible; this tendency is well shown by the Al_2O_3 contents of the crucible slags (Table 6). These slags tell us something about the quality of the crucibles, but much more about the metals and alloys melted.

We lack information on the chemical composition of the crucible fabric and we lack petrographic data on crushed crucibles which would have told us something about the provenance of the crucible materials; and we lack similar data on heated crucibles which would tell us more about the temperatures achieved. Both these aims can be achieved by the use of well-established techniques for the examination of refractories. Whether this should be done by the metallurgist or the archaeological ceramicist is a matter for discussion. I feel that the subject divides into two sections: slags and furnace linings to be examined by the metallurgist; molds and crucibles to be the province of the archaeological ceramicist.

References and Notes

1. Sir Flinders Petrie and C. J. Currelly. *Researches in Sinai*. New York: 1906.

2. Seen and measured at Aya Irini, Kea, Greece [by courtesy of J. L. Caskey].

3. From the tomb of Rek-me-Re; No. 100 at Western Thebes, Egypt.

4. Experiment conducted by R. Savage and P. Wagner on behalf of BBC Television. [*See* C. J. Evans, *Tin and its uses*, 1976 (107), 14–15.]

5. R. F. Tylecote. *A history of metallurgy*. London: 1976. 18, Fig. 9.

6. R. F. Tylecote. *Metallurgy in archaeology*. London: 1962. Fig. 31.

7. R. F. Tylecote. *Metallurgy in archaeology*. London: 1962. Plate IX.

8. H.-G. Bachmann. Crucibles from a Roman settlement in Germany. *J. Hist. Met. Soc.* 1976. 10: 34–35.

9. N. Barnard. *Bronze casting and bronze alloys in China*. Canberra: 1961. Fig. 13.

10. K. Lamm. The manufacture of jewellery during the Migration period at Helgö in Sweden. *Bull. Hist. Met. Group*. 1973. 7: 1–7.

11. G. Agricola. *De re metallica* (trans. H. and L. Hoover). Dover Publ.: 1950.

12. V. Biringuccio. *Pyrotechnia* (ed. and trans. C. S. Smith and M. T. Gnudi). New York: 1942.

13. W. D. Kingery and W. H. Gourdin. Examination of furnace linings. M.I.T. Report; W. H. Gourdin and W. D. Kingery. *J.F. Arch.* 1975. 2: 133–50.

14. Donna Rizzone, personal communication from Professor R. Reuss of Tufts University.

15. G. J. Wainwright and M. Spratling. The Iron Age settlement of Gussage All Saints. *Antiquity*. 1973. 47: 109–30.

16. G. J. Wainwright et al. Gussage All Saints: an Iron Age settlement in Dorset. London: HMSO, 1979.

17. A. Bulleid and H. St. G. Gray. *The Glastonbury Lake Village*. 1911. Vol. I, pp. 303–304.

18. C. M. Wilson. *Electron microprobe analysis of Iron Age crucibles*. Sheffield University, 15 March 1976.

19. Hilary Howard. Preliminary petrological report on the Gussage All Saints crucibles. *Aspects of early metallurgy* (ed. W. A. Oddy). 2d ed. British Museum Occas. Paper, no. 17. 1980.

20. Werner Krämer and Franz Schubert, eds. *Die Ausgrabungen in Manching, 1955–1961*. [7 vols. 1969–74, Wiesbaden: Steiner.] Vol 2, I. Kappel, *Die Graphittonkeramik*, 1969, pp. 19, 49.

21. D. Liversage. Excavations at Dalkey Island, Co. Dublin, 1956–1959. *Proc. Irish Acad.* 1967. 66: 53–234 (p. 150).

22. K. Lamm (note 10, above), p. 45.

23. H. St. G. Gray and A. Bulleid. Meare Lake Village. Taunton: 1948. Vol 1.

24. J. Dyer and P. Wenham. Excavations and discoveries in Feasgate, York. 1956. *Yorks. Arch. Soc.* 1958. 39: 419–26.

25. K.N.P. Rao et al. Some observations on the structure of ancient steel from South India and its mode of production. *Bull. H.M.G.* 1970. 4 (1): 12–17.

26. Theophilus. *De diversis artibus* (ed. and trans. J. G. Hawthorn and C. S. Smith). Chicago: 1963. 171–2: 96.

27. V. Biringuccio (note 12, above), p. 128.

28. G. Agricola (note 11, above), p. 230.

29. Notabilia, in Essays of Oars and Metals. C. S. Smith and B. Walraff. *J. Hist. Met. Soc.* 1974. 8 (2): 75–87.

30. R. F. Tylecote. Calenick: A Cornish tin smelter, 1702–1891. *J. Hist. Met. Soc.* 1980. 14 (1): 1–16.

31. K. C. Barraclough. The cementation and crucible steelmaking processes. *Bull. Hist. Met. Group*. 1967. 1 (8):24–34.

32. H. Brearley. *Steelmakers* (cited in Barraclough, note 33, below).

33. K. C. Barraclough. A crucible steel melter's log book. *JHMS*. 1978. 12 (2): 98–101.

34. A. B. Searle. *Refractory materials*. 1941.

35. K. C. Barraclough, personal communication, 1980.

36. W. Pryce. *Mineralogia Cornubiensis*. Barton, Truro: 1972. 32, 269.

37. G. Boon. An early Tudor coiner's mould and the working of Borrowdale graphite. *Trans. Cumb. and West Antiq. Arch. Soc.* 1976. 76: 97–132.

38. J. Percy. *Metallurgy: refractories etc*. London: 1875. 312.

39. F. Buchanan. *A journey from Madras . . .* 3 vols. London: 1807.

40. W. H. Shockley. Notes on the coal- and iron-fields of S. E. Shansi. *Trans. Amer. Inst. Min. Met. Eng.* 1904. 34: 841.

41. R. F. Tylecote, forthcoming.

42. R. F. Tylecote; Beno Rothenberg; and A. Lupu. An examination of metallurgical material from Abu Matar, Israel. *JHMS*. 1974. 8 (1): 32–34.

43. G. Coffey. Excavations at Craigywarren crannog Co. Antrim. *PRIA*. 1906-7. 26: 109–118.

44. T. May. Britain's earliest iron furnances. *Iron and Coal Trades Review*. 1905. 71: 427 *et seq*.

45. R. J. Moss. A chemical examination of the crucibles in the collection of Irish Antiquities of the Royal Irish Academy. *Proc. Roy. Irish Acad.* 1924–27. 37/C, 175–93.

R. F. Tylecote

46. H. Otto and W. Witter. *Handbuch der ältesten vorgeschlichlichen Metallurgie in Mitteleuropa*. Leipzig: 1952.

47. R. T. Evans and R. F. Tylecote. Some vitrified products. *Bull. Hist. Met. Group*. 1967. 1 (9): 22–23.

48. R. F. Tylecote; H. A. Ghaznavi; and P. Boydell. Partitioning of trace elements . . . during the smelting of copper. *J. Arch. Sci*. 1977. 4: 305–33.

22. Analysis of Nonmetallic Phases in Metallic Artifacts: The Development of the Japanese Mokume Technique

MICHAEL R. NOTIS
Department of Metallurgy and Materials Engineering
Lehigh University

Introduction

A number of years ago, the energy-dispersive X-ray fluorescence analyzer was described as the museum curator's dream instrument (Hanson 1970). Since that time developments in electron optics and X-ray analytical techniques have far surpassed initial predictions — and in all likelihood there are many developments yet to come. Today, a wide variety of methods exist, such as X-ray fluorescence analysis (XRF), X-ray analysis in the scanning electron microscope (SEM) or in the electron microprobe (EMP), and most recently, X-ray analysis of thin foil specimens in a scanning transmission electron microscope (AEM) (Bender, Williams, and Notis 1980; Notis, Bender, and Williams 1981). These X-ray and electron optic analytical techniques have been used increasingly over the past few years, first for qualitative analysis (Hall 1961; Hornblower 1962; Condamin and Picon 1964, 1965; Ogilvie 1967) and then for quantitative chemical analysis and for the examination of structures (Whitmore and Young 1970; Ogilvie 1970). However, electron optics and X-ray analytical techniques have not yet reached their full potential, for examination of archaeological artifacts and for museum provenance, as problem-solving tools that combine their quantitative ability for chemical analysis with the microstructural interpretive capability of materials science.

The wide variety of analytical techniques now available to the archaeologist makes the proper choice of technique a difficult one. In many cases there is a conflict between the ability to obtain quantitative chemical information and the ability to maintain high spatial resolution; the ideal is true quantitative microchemistry. The area of analysis in XRF is large, and this coupled with the large depths of analysis ($>2\mu$m) makes XRF impractical for many studies. The desire for increased spatial resolution (at the micron level) has accounted for the growth of SEM and EMP, and (at the submicron level) foretells the increased application of AEM in the near future. In common practice, in SEM and AEM, X-ray detection is accomplished through the use of X-ray sensitive semiconductor diode detectors which are used to collect energy dispersive spectra (EDS); in the EMP, crystal detectors are used to collect wavelength dispersive spectra (WDS). The order of magnitude increased sensitivity of WDS over EDS allows for the detection of elements at the trace level. The thin foil specimen used in AEM provides for a significant (order of magnitude) increase in spatial resolution over SEM and EMP, but the small specimen volume sampled by the electron beam limits the mass detectability. However, in general, all of these methods offer good microchemical analytical capability.

The electron microprobe has been used for quantitative studies of gold-silver-copper alloys found in Greece (Darling and Healy 1971), and to examine the bonding techniques used for silver coating of copper artifacts (Charles 1968). The capability of EMP for performing quantitative chemical analysis combined with spatial resolution has been used to obtain diffusion profiles in Japanese nonferrous layered alloys (mokume, or "woodgrain"); analysis of these profiles has made possible the determination of the fabrication temperature used for the manufacture of the artifact involved (Notis 1969). While all of the above analyses involve the investigation of composition and composition variation in metallic phases, one particularly significant aspect of microchemical techniques is the ability to perform analysis of nonmetallic inclusions in metallic artifacts.

Nometallic inclusions are extremely useful features of the microstructure. In ancient ferrous artifacts, whose metallic phases consist predominantly of iron and carbon, inclusions contain the vast majority of chemical and structural information relating to sources and processing. As pointed out by Charles (1979), inclusions can provide an indication of forging temperature, since viscous flow of these nonmetallics is such as to give stringers only above the glass transition temperature for the slag; in certain circumstances the inclusions may be used to determine the directions and extent of forging if relative plasticity of slag and matrix are known. When a number of pieces have been forged together, internal variations of both metallic and nonmetallic components may be used to interpret fabrication history.

Although thermodynamic properties and phase equilibria have been studied for many of the binary, ternary, and some quaternary systems of interest for slag studies, very few investigations have been performed that are concerned with the relationship between microstructure, kinetics, and chemistry (Allmand 1962; Insley and Frechette 1955; Kiessling and Lange 1979; Konig and Ernst 1970; Sims 1959; Trojer 1963). Microstructural studies in the wustite (FeO)-fayalite ($2FeO \cdot SiO_2$) system, of particular interest in the present study, have been well documented (Baldwin 1954; Morton and Wingrove 1969, 1972; Wingrove 1970), and a number of studies have been made relating slag microstructure to furnace processing and ore sources (Avery and Schmidt 1979; Schmidt and Avery 1978; Todd 1979; Todd and Charles 1977, 1978). On the other hand, it is known that slag microstructures can be greatly modified by only small additions of other components, but only very few studies have examined this problem; one exception is the addition of titanium to furnace slags (Pickering 1955; Sommerville and Bell 1980).

In many cases, examination of slag microstructure and knowledge of metal/oxygen stoichiometry in the slag can give important information on the extent of oxidizing or reducing conditions present in the furnace. Perhaps of most significance (Charles 1979), inclusions present in iron produced in the solid state may provide information concerning provenance by indicating the ore type from which the iron was made. If chemical contributions from fuel ash are taken into consideration, over-all analysis of the non-metallic inclusions provides information about the general proportions of the major components such as SiO_2, Al_2O_3, etc. In recent work using EMP analysis of slag inclusions in early iron currency bars found in southern England (Hedges and Salter 1979), a systematic study has been suggested which considers the presence of slag chemical constituents first as originating from ore sources, then as originating from materials added during smelting (i.e., flux additions, furnace lining, fuels), and finally as originating from smithing or fabrication processes. It has previously been shown (Tylecote 1962) that high alkali content (K, Na) would indicate wood or charcoal as fuel source as opposed to coke. The presence of specific impurities, e.g., V_2O_3, Cr_2O_3, TiO_2, can in certain cases be used to identify ore sources with unique local characteristics, as will be shown in the present paper.

Point X-ray analysis (electron beam held on a specific spot) is able to provide information concerning the composition of an individual phase within a multiphase slag. Over-all composition of a multiphase slag may sometimes be estimated from an X-ray area scan (Todd and Charles 1977, 1978) that includes all slag phases in a representative manner. However, there is an inherent error in this method as the corrections for X-ray absorption and fluorescence that must be made are dependent upon the composition of each separate phase. Also, the presence of porosity and local fractured areas within the slag can contribute to significant error. The most appropriate method to obtain the over-all slag composition would be to combine quantitative image analysis (to obtain the area fraction of each phase) with point X-ray analysis (for the composition of each phase separately). This latter approach may also be inaccurate if significant inhomogeneity exists in any of the phases present. In any event, a number of investigators (Morton and Wingrove 1969, 1972; Todd and Charles 1977, 1978) have used microprobe analysis for over-all bulk slag compositions and have determined the operating temperature range in a furnace by matching these compositions against previously determined isotherms on a ternary phase diagram. The same approach can be used to obtain

Michael R. Notis

pertinent information from nonmetallic slag inclusions in a metallic artifact.

As an example of the applicability of these analytical techniques, we have studied a number of fabricated iron Japanese swordguards (tsuba) having a characteristic "woodgrain" (mokume) appearance. Electron optical examination and X-ray microanalysis have been performed in order to compare the structure and chemistry of a number of differently dated pieces as part of a study of the development of this specific metalworking technology. This paper first describes the development of the mokume metallurgical technique and then demonstrates how this technique is used as the basis for the development of an artistic style.

Development of the Mokume Technique

The mokume technique is a method developed to produce a woodgrain surface texture from thin laminated layers of heterogeneous materials (Fox 1974). The layers are first joined together by forge welding, then deformed out-of-plane, and then made to intersect the surface by finally cutting the surface flat (Smith 1967; Savage and Smith 1979). The piece is then etched and patinated to bring out the textural effect. The technique appears first to have developed with ferrous materials, and then to have been applied to other metal and lacquer systems (Savage and Smith 1979; Notis 1979); only ferrous mokume will be discussed here.

Three early examples (fourteenth to seventeenth century) are shown in Figures 1 through 3. Although these are not dated pieces, they are all thought to have been fabricated by early swordsmiths and are arranged here in increasing order of estimated dating. In Figure 1, it appears that the laminates have been rolled, as one would roll a newspaper log, and then discs cut perpendicular to the cylinder axis. In Figure 2, the laminated layers appear to be completely parallel to the plane of the disc, and the layered structure is apparent only in the edge view of the rim. In Figure 3, the first appearance of a woodgrain texture may be seen on the disc surface along the edge.

All of the artifacts examined in the present study were produced in the Tatara furnace. The Tatara ("bellows") process has been described in a number of publications (Tanimura 1980; Kubota 1973; Horikawa 1970; Kozuka 1968; Matsushita 1971). It is basically a charcoal fired, bellows driven, rectangular blast furnace. The process is capable of producing a wide variety of ferrous materials ranging from wrought iron to crude steel to liquid, high carbon iron depending upon time into the run and position in the furnace. Since the tuyeres are positioned near

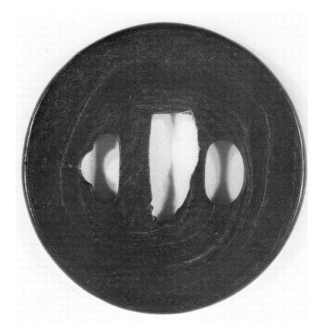

Figure 1. Mokume iron tsuba fabricated from transverse-cut round stock.

Figure 2. Mokume iron tsuba fabricated from laminates in the plane of the disc. Lower figure shows edge view (2x).

Figure 3. Mokume iron tsuba fabricated from laminates hammered out-of-plane (2x).

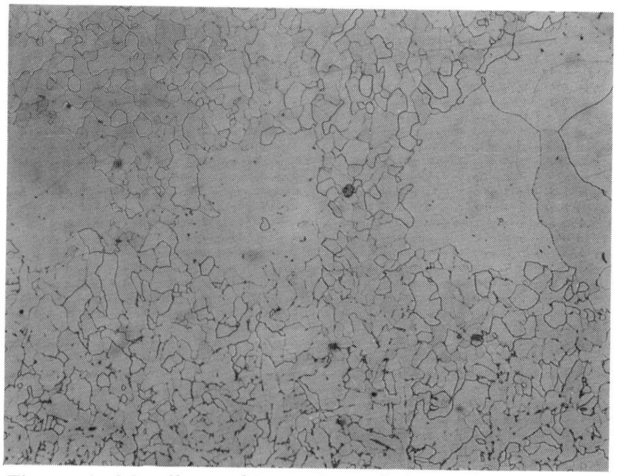

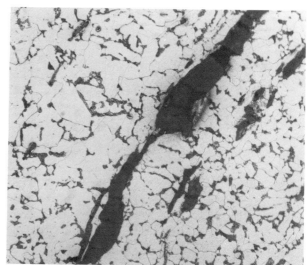

Figure 4. Metallographic section of the tsuba shown in Figure 1 (50x); 1% nital etch.

the bottom of the furnace, depending on operating conditions, the air blast could be directed to the molten high carbon iron in order to provide an oxidizing and decarburizing environment. This situation, combined with an ore feed into this zone from above, could lower the carbon content and raise the melting point until the mass resolidifies; this action is somewhat similar to the operation of the Bessemer converter. The product from the Tatara process was therefore highly variable and demanded further processing by some homogenization process in order to produce a product with uniform properties.

The ore source for the Tatara process was almost always a titaniferous iron sand of quite high purity produced from the weathering zones of granite or diorite, or in coastal regions obtained from beach sands. These iron sands are all of extremely high purity, but the titanium composition is highly variable from one regional district to another (.5–15%), and studies are available which document the composition of ore sources by small local regions (Kozuka 1968; Kubota 1970, 1971; Matsushita 1971). The products of the Tatara process therefore offer the opportunity to determine ore source through the analysis of slag inclusions (Hedges and Salter 1979).

A metallographic section of the tsuba in Figure 1 is shown in Figure 4. Regions of both coarse and fine grained ferrite (low carbon iron) may be seen in the middle and upper portions of the figure; higher carbon material consisting of ferrite plus pearlite (a reaction product of fine alternating lamella of iron and iron carbide) is shown in the lower portion of this figure and at higher magnification in Figure 5. The layers of low and high carbon material have been joined together so that the interface between them is

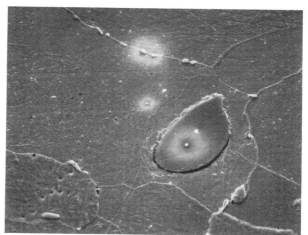

Figure 5. Higher carbon region of the tsuba shown in Figures 1 and 4 (250x); 1% nital etch.

Figure 6. SEM picture of slag inclusion found in ferritic region of the section shown in Figure 4 (1300x); 1% nital etch.

Michael R. Notis

Table 1. Electron microprobe analysis of slag inclusions

	Tsuba, Figure 1			Tsuba, Figure 2					Tsuba, Figure 3					
	A	B		A		B		C	A		B		C	
	W	W	F	W	F	W	F	W	W	F	W	F	W	F
Fe	I	I	II	I	I	I	I	I	II	I	I	I	I	I
Si		II	I	II	II		II				II		II	II
Ti			VI		VI				I	III	II			III
K		IV	V	III	IV		V			IV		III	IV	
Al		V	IV	V	V		III		III		III			
Ca		III	III	IV	III		IV		IV			III	III	
P		VI												IV
S														
V	II													

A = Low Carbon Region
B = Higher Carbon Pearlite/Ferrite
C = Interfacial Slag
W = Wustite
F = Fayalite

Compositions are shown in relative amounts for each phase ranging from I (highest) to VI (lowest).

not an optimum condition for the development of an etched texture appearance, as may be seen from the crude pattern visible in Figure 1.

Slag inclusions present in the coarse grain ferrite regions of this piece (Fig. 6) are almost pure single phase wustite (FeO) and have not been extensively elongated; a small amount of vanadium was detected as the only impurity present. Composition analysis for both regions of this tsuba, as well as for the other tsuba analyzed, are given in Table 1. Slag inclusions present in the higher carbon region (Fig. 7) are typically elongated and are two-phase wustite/fayalite. The slag inclusions present in this region are found to be rich in Ti and K as well as the more usual components Fe, Si, Al, Ca, and P. The significant difference in composition between slag inclusions present in high carbon and low carbon regions of the laminate indicates that the different layers could come from different sources of material; the absence of inclusions at the interfacial regions and the uniform blending of high and low carbon regions indicate good control of the forging operation.

A metallographic section of the tsuba shown in Figure 2 is presented in Figure 8. While there is some inhomogeneity of the microstructure, it is not as apparent in the first tsuba; Figure 9 shows a "lower" carbon region, while Figure 10 is taken from a "higher" carbon region. Microprobe analysis (Figs.

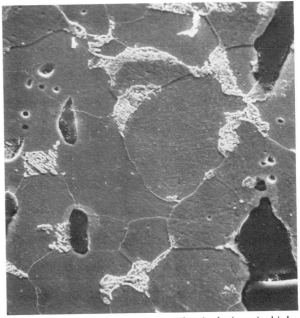

Figure 7. SEM picture showing slag inclusions in higher carbon region of the section in Figure 4 (1200x); 1% nital etch.

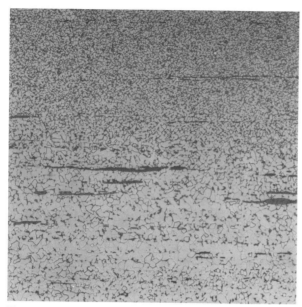

Figure 8. Metallographic section of the tsuba shown in Figure 2 (10x); 1% nital etch.

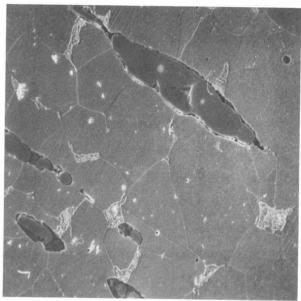

Figure 9. Lower carbon region of the tsuba shown in Figures 2 and 8 (SEM, 680x); 1% nital etch.

8 and 9, and Table 1) indicates very similar compositions for the slag inclusions found in both regions and it appears that the laminates are all of the same material folded on itself. The large inclusions present at the interface (Figs. 8 and 11, and Table 1) are of very different composition, i.e., almost pure FeO, and appear to have been purposely added in order to maintain separation of the laminates during forging. It is interesting to note the elongated nature of the slag inclusions present in Figure 9, and the internal cracks present in the slag inclusion of Figure 11. Both of these give indication of limited plasticity during forming.

The shape and microstructure of slag inclusions in a forged object are strongly influenced by the plasticity of the slag. In the fluid condition at high temperatures, silicate inclusions will elongate into stringers; at lower temperature the inclusions become rigid and voids are produced at both sides of the inclusion in the line of flow (Charles 1980a, 1980b; Salter and Pickering 1968). The addition of iron to silica dramatically increases its plasticity, and the addition of glass formers such as K_2O and Na_2O to the Fe-silicate phase provides both decreased melting point and decreased viscosity (Charles and Uchiyama 1968).

A measure of the refractory nature of the slag is the ratio of Al_2O_3 to $(CaO + SiO_2)$; the higher the ratio, the more refractory the slag. On the other hand the desulfurizing ability of the slag generally increases with the ratio of basic components $(CaO + MgO)$ to acidic components $(SiO_2 + Al_2O_3)$; the desulfurizing ability of a slag and its fluidity are

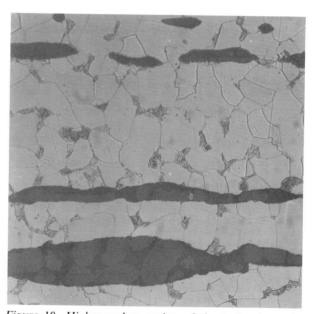

Figure 10. Higher carbon region of the tsuba shown in Figures 2 and 8 (500x); 1% nital etch.

both enhanced if the Al_2O_3 content is kept low. The relative basicity of the slag also influences the crystallinity of the slag, i.e., more acidic slags are more likely to crystallize and provide high viscosity. Alkali oxides (K_2O, Na_2O) are the best desulfurizing agents, and thus contribute to both low sulfur levels and good fluidity (White 1980).

It therefore appears that the tsuba shown in Figure 2 was forged at a fairly low temperature where slag plasticity was poor, and that slag inclusions were pur-

Michael R. Notis

Figure 11. Slag inclusion present at interfacial region between layers of the tsuba shown in Figures 2 and 8 (SEM, 680x); 1% nital etch.

Figure 12. Metallographic section of the tsuba shown in Figure 3 (20x); 1% nital etch.

Figure 13. SEM picture showing alternating high and low carbon regions in the tsuba of Figures 3 and 12 (320x); 1% nital etch. Microhardness indentations are shown for reference.

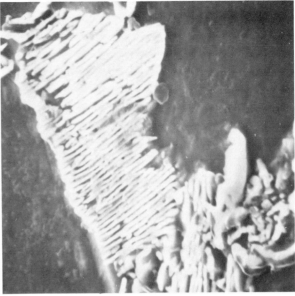

Figure 14. High magnification view of pearlitic structure present in higher carbon regions of Figure 13 (8000x); 1% nital etch. Note the fine detail of alternating Fe and Fe_3C lamella.

posely added at the interface to emphasize the layered structure during subsequent etching.

A metallographic section of the tsuba shown in Figure 3 is presented in Figure 12; the contrast between low and high carbon regions is now quite obvious, as is the presence of large elongated interfacial inclusions. A higher magnification picture taken in the SEM and showing these alternating regions is presented in Figure 13. The microhardness indentations give an indication of the relative hardness of the low and high carbon regions. Figure 14 is a high magnification photograph of the pearlite regions found in the higher carbon layers and demonstrates the lamellar structure of alternating Fe and Fe_3C layers within this phase. Figures 15, 16, and 17 respectively show slag inclusions typical of the ferrite layer, the high carbon layer, and the interface regions; compositions for each of these slag inclusions are again given in Table 1. The titanium level present in the low carbon region is extremely high; sulfur is found to be present only in the interfacial inclusions, but no aluminum. It appears that the smith who fabricated the tsuba has taken advantage of two factors which contribute to the development of the mokume effect: first, the use of laminated layers of exteme difference in carbon content, and second, the use of inclusions at the interface. This piece seems to combine the fabrication effects observed in the two earlier pieces.

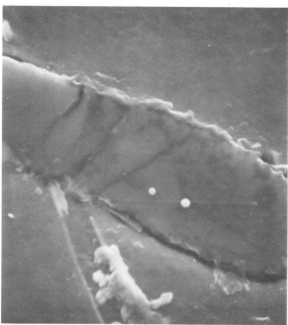

Figure 15. *SEM picture of slag inclusion found in ferrite region of the section shown in Figure 12 (4000x); 1% nital etch.*

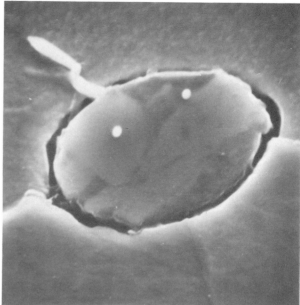

Figure 16. *SEM picture of slag inclusion found in higher carbon region of the section shown in Figure 12 (8000x); 1% nital etch.*

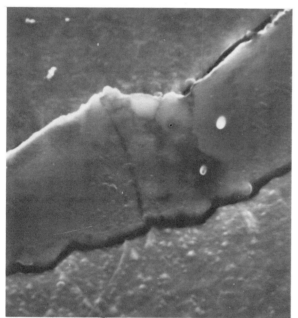

Figure 17. *SEM picture of slag inclusion found at interface region between layers of the tsuba shown in Figures 3, 12, and 13 (8000x); 1% nital etch.*

Development of the Mokume Art Style

The swordguard (tsuba), in addition to the central wedge-shaped opening through which the tang of the swordblade is passed, commonly possesses two smaller and usually semicircular holes meant to accommodate the placement of a small knife (kozuka) and a skewerlike implement (kogai). If these accoutrements are not present, or if the tsuba is meant to be used as an artistic piece rather than for mounting on a sword, these holes may be either plugged with a patinated or gilt copper-gold alloy (shakudo) or they may be completely absent.

Early swordguards were made by swordsmiths, commonly from scraps of material remaining from the swordblade forging process (Smith 1967). The blade itself is, in part, made from laminated iron forged and folded on itself many times. When the blade surface is polished, the laminated structure often appears visible as the layers intersect the blade surface. In a number of art-swords made by certain smiths, e.g., Sadamune Hosho Goro (early fourteenth century) and Gwassan Sadayoshi (mid-nineteenth century) (Smith 1967), this pattern is heavily emphasized. It is therefore not unexpected that a similar laminated and folded, or "wood-grain," appearance (mokume) was sometimes emphasized as an artistic and decorative technique used in conjunction with the swordguard (or vice versa). As metalworking techniques developed, and as the sword and its decorations became esteemed

Michael R. Notis

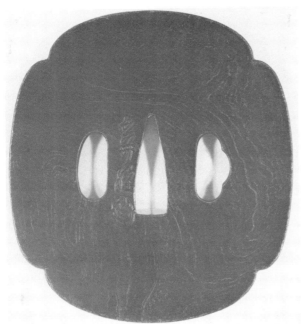

Figure 18. Iron mokume tsuba, mokko form; signed Sankei with kakihan.

Figure 19. Iron mokume tsuba, signed Suiju ju Miochin Yoshihisa.

heirlooms and art objects, the craft techniques associated with sword manufacture became more specialized, and separate smiths were used for the fabrication of the sword and as craftsmen for the manufacture of the sword decorations. Between the fifteenth century (e.g., Goto school) and the seventeenth century (e.g., Nara school), the variety of techniques and materials flourished, and during this period highly skilled artisans worked under the sponsorship of a number of lords and princely families (Robinson 1970).

Three examples, all based on the iron mokume technique, may be used to demonstrate the growth of the tsuba as an art form. An obvious and early development is the change from a plain circular shape or oval shape to a simple geometric form with obvious rotational symmetry. This may be seen in the first example (Fig. 18) which pictures a quadrifoil (mokko) shape made from a flat piece of heavily etched mokume iron. This piece is signed with both the craftsman's name (first two characters), and his personal artistic seal or trademark symbol (kakihan, lower character). A problem often found in provenance of an object such as this was encountered with this piece in that the Japanese characters may be read in a number of ways. For example, the piece shown may be read Ueda (family name) Chuzaimon (given name) Sankyo (later name chosen by the craftsman) (Wakayama and Shibata 1974). But the kakihan for this reading seems incorrect. A second possible read-

ing given to the same piece is Kisai Kyosai, an eighteenth-century craftsman (Seattle Art Museum 1960). The best reading, however, appears to be Sankei, of Kii Province, near Tokyo, whose mokume work is in the style of Masahide (Joly 1963).

The second example (Fig. 19), also noncircular in form, has a most graceful continuously curved but four-sided shape. The holes for kozuka and kogai are plugged, and a simple design in negative silhouette (kosukashi) consisting of an ax-like cutting implement (ono) and droplets (mizutama) have been added. Most significant, the cross section of this piece is not of uniform thickness, but rather is thinned out towards the center in order to reduce weight but maintain rigidity and strength. The guard is signed Suiju ju Miochin Yoshihisa, indicating the piece to have been made by a member of the Miochin family, a famous group of armorers, swordsmiths, and iron craftsmen. Yoshihisa is probably the smith who was active in Horikawa, Ichijo, Kyoto, between 1469 and 1486 (Gilbertson 1977).

The swordguard shown in Figure 20 is signed Mito ju Setuai (also read Mito ju Tokichika). Setuai (or Tokichika of the Sugiyama family) worked in the town of Mito in Hitachi province about 1790 during the Meiji era. This tsuba maker belonged to the school of Tokinobu; other pieces by the same artisan appear in the Museum of Fine Arts, Boston (No. 11.11858-178a) and the Victoria and Albert Museum (M1285-1931). It is usual for the "front" (?) of the

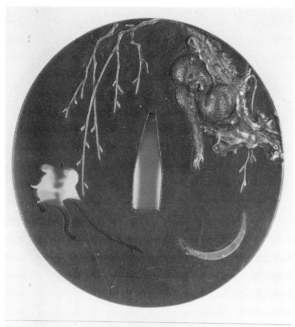

Figure 20. Iron mokume tsuba, signed Mito ju Setuai.

that this guard was never intended for use on a sword, but rather only as a work of art, as mentioned previously. The three fine-cut lines (itosukashi) at the bottom, giving the impression of a water level, are made by piercing a small hole and then moving an impregnated wire back and forth in order to cut the line. Finally, the mokume background gives the appearance of ripples in water.

A number of art forms or themes, generated by the Zen influence, are apparent in the tsuba shown here (Fig. 20). Negative silhouette is commonly found in much of the twelfth to fourteenth century art work and is intended to suggest the presence of an object by its absence — a Koan exercise in the reason of unreason. Similar expression is seen in the suggestion of a butterfly made by the extremely large kozuka and kogai holes of the tsuba shown in Figure 2, and also in Figure 19.

By the eighteenth century, art was heavily influenced by a long period in which thought, literature, and art had been steeped in Zen Buddhism. Sung painting was the criterion of all that was desirable in art. Paintings by the Chinese Zen masters Liang K'ai and Mu Ch'i were treasured as among Japan's very great masterpieces. In the tsuba showing a monkey's straining to snatch a mere reflection of the moon, we are given a sermon on the futility and emptiness of much of humanity's strivings. This is compounded with the monkey's reflection shown in negative silhouette in the water, also reaching for the same object, and possibly meant to question the concept of reality.

Summary

In plain carbon iron materials such as those studied here, information gained from examination of slag inclusion microstructure and chemistry is unobtainable from the metallic matrix phase constituents. The over-all chemistry, the microstructure, and the apparent plasticity of the slag all provide significant information relating to the fabrication and processing history. Study of key impurities can lead to the identification of ore sources or fuel types used during smelting.

Electron optical analysis of slag inclusions found in the mokume tsuba described in the present work appear to indicate increasing sophistication of fabrication technology with time. It is interesting to note that in the twenty or so years since the introduction of electron analytical techniques, our ability has grown enormously to perform quantitative chemical analysis and structural studies on an extremely fine spatial scale. To a significant degree this provides a measure of the growth of our own technology as well as an indication of technology in the past.

swordguard to be signed, and also to be the most decorated. However, in the guard shown here, the signature is on one side and the overlaid image is on the reverse. It is therefore possible that the original guard was a simple plain iron piece with only a negative silhouette and an inlaid silver moon, as shown on the signed side, and that the overlaid monkey and tree limb were added at a later date.

Other unusual aspects of this guard are that there are no side holes near the central cut-out, indicating

254

Michael R. Notis

Acknowledgments: The author wishes to express his gratitude to the Mellon Foundation and Lehigh University for their support of this work. Most of the metallographic work included in this paper was performed by Ms. Nicola Stenton, an undergraduate student from the University of Manchester, while on a summer research program at Lehigh.

References

Allmand, T. R. 1962. *Microscopic identification of inclusions in steel.* London: British Iron & Steel Research Association.

Avery, Donald H., and Schmidt, Peter. 1979. A metallurgical study of the iron bloomery, particularly as practiced in Buhaya. *Journal of Metals* 31 [10]: 14–20.

Baldwin, B. G. 1954. Formation and decomposition of fayalite. *Journal of the Iron & Steel Institute* (London) 180:312–16.

Bender, B. A.; Williams, D. B.; and Notis, M. R. 1980a. Absorption effects in STEM microanalysis of ceramic oxides. *Journal of the American Ceramic Society* 63:149–51.

_____. 1980b. Investigation of grain boundary segregation in ceramic oxides by analytical scanning transmission analysis. *Journal of the American Ceramic Society* 63:542–46.

Charles, J. A. 1968. The first Sheffield plate. *Antiquity* 42:278–85.

_____. 1979. From copper to iron — the origin of metallic materials. *Journal of Metals* 31[7]:8–13.

_____. 1980a. Hot processability and the optimization of hot-worked properties. In *Hot working and forming processes*, pp. 87–98. London: Iron & Steel Institute Special Report, no. 264.

_____. 1980b. Discussion concerning mechanisms of enhanced ferrite nucleation from deformed austenite in microalloyed steels. In *Hot working and forming processes*, p. 43. London: Iron & Steel Institute Special Report, no. 264.

Charles, J. A., and Uchiyama, I. 1968. Behavior of silicate inclusions in iron during hot rolling. *Journal of the Iron and Steel Institute* (London) 207:979–83.

Condamin, J., and Picon, M. 1964. Influence of corrosion and diffusion on the percent silver in Roman denarii. *Archaeometry* 7:98–105.

_____. 1965. Notes on diffusion in ancient alloys. *Archaeometry* 8:110–14.

Darling, A. S., and Healy, J. F. 1971. Microprobe analysis and study of Greek gold-silver-copper alloys. *Nature* 231:443–44.

Fox, Abraham S. 1974. Composite micro-laminated structures. *Metals and Materials*: 230–32.

Gilbertson, E. 1977. The genealogy of the Miochin family — armourers, swordsmiths and artisans in iron: twelfth to eighteenth century. In Hickman, B., ed., *Japanese crafts, materials, and their applications,* pp. 305–327. London: Fine Books Ltd.

Hall, E. T. 1961. Surface enrichment of buried metals. *Archaeometry* 4:62–66.

Hanson, Victor F. 1970. A curator's dream instrument. In *Application of science in examination of works of art*, pp. 18–30. Boston: Museum of Fine Arts.

Hedges, R. E. M., and Salter, C. J. 1979. Source determination of iron currency bars through analysis of the slag inclusions. *Archaeometry* 21:161–75.

Horikawa, Kazuo. 1970. *Tatara restoration project (Tatara Seitetsu No Fukugen to Kera)* Special Report, no. 9. Iron and Steel Institute of Japan.

Hornblower, A. P. 1962. Archaeological applications of the electron microprobe analyzer. *Archaeometry* 5:108–112.

Insley, H., and Frechette, V. D. 1955. Slags. Chap. 14, pp. 245–57, in *Microscopy of ceramics and cements*. New York: Academic Press.

Joly, H. L. 1963. *List of names and kakihan.* London: Holland Press.

Kiessling, R., and Lange, N. 1979. *Nonmetallic inclusions in steel.* London: Metals Society.

Konig, G., and Ernst, T. 1970. Determination of the composition and origin of oxide inclusions in steel (Part II). *British Iron & Steel Industries Translation,* no. BISI8584.

Kozuka, Jukichi. 1968. Tatara process: a pig iron and steel making process transmitted from ancient times in Japan. *Transactions of the Iron & Steel Institute of Japan* 8:36–47.

Kubota, Kurao. 1970. Japanese original steel making and its development under the influence of foreign techniques. Paper presented at International Meeting on the History of Technology Pont-a-Mousson, France.

_____.1971. *Steelmaking in ancient Japan.* Japan Iron and Steel Federation.

_____.1973. *Japan's original steelmaking and its development under the influence of foreign techniques (Tetsu no Kokogaku).* Tokyo: Yuzan Kaku.

Matsushita, Y. 1971. Restoration of the Tatara iron making process. Proceedings ICSTIS, Section I, *Supplement to Transactions of Iron & Steel Institute of Japan* 11:212–18.

Morton, G. R., and Wingrove, J. 1969. Constitution of Roman bloomery slags. London: *Journal of the Iron & Steel Institute* 207:1554–64.

_____.1972. Constitution of medieval bloomery slags. London: *Journal of the Iron & Steel Institute* 210:478–88.

Notis, M. R. 1979. Study of Japanese mokume techniques by electron microprobe analysis. *MASCA Journal* 1:67–69.

Notis, M. R.; Bender, B. A.; and Williams, D. B. 1981. STEM analysis of segregation and precipitation in impurity doped nickel oxide. *Advances in Ceramics*, vol. 1, forthcoming.

Ogilvie, Robert E. 1967. Electron microanalysis of paint samples from the Bersheh sarcophagus. In *Application of science in examination of works of art (I)*, pp. 223–29. Boston: Museum of Fine Arts.

_____.1970. Applications of the solid state X-ray detector to the study of art objects. In *Application of science in examination of works of art (II)*, pp. 84–87. Boston: Museum of Fine Arts.

Pickering, F. B. 1955. A microscopical examination of samples of iron containing iron bearing inclusions. London: *Journal of the Iron & Steel Institute* 181:147–49.

Robinson, B. W. 1970. *The arts of the Japanese sword.* London: Faber and Faber.

Salter, W. J. M., and Pickering, F. B. 1968. Composition and constitution of non-metallic inclusions in 1% C–Cr steels. London: *Journal of the Iron & Steel Institute* 207:992–1002.

Savage, Elaine I., and Smith, Cyril Stanley. 1979. The technique of the Japanese tsuba-maker. *Ars Orientalis* XI:291–328.

Schmidt, Peter, and Avery, Donald H. 1978. Complex iron smelting and prehistoric culture in Tanzania. *Science* 201:1085–89.

Seattle Art Museum. 1960. *Japanese art in the Seattle Art Museum.*

Sims, C. E. 1959. The nonmetallic constituents of steel. *Transactions AIME* 215:367–93.

Smith, Cyril Stanley. 1957. A metallographic examination of some Japanese sword blades. In *La Technica di Fabbricazione Delle Lame di Acciaio Presso gli Antichi:Quaderno II del Centro per la Storia della Metallurgia*, pp. 42–68. Milan.

_____.1967. Sectioned textures in the decorative arts. In Elias, Hans, ed., *Stereology.* New York: Springer-Verlag.

Sommerville, I. D., and Bell, H. B. 1980. Behavior of titania in metallurgical slags. Paper presented at International Symposium on Metallurgical Slags, Nova Scotia.

Tanimura, Hiromu. 1980. Development of the Japanese sword. *Journal of Metals* 32[2]:63–73.

Todd, Judith A. 1979. Studies of the African Iron Age. *Journal of Metals* 31[11]:39–45.

Todd, Judith A., and Charles, J. A. 1977. The analysis of non-metallic inclusions in ancient iron. *PACT (Council of Europe)* 1: 204–220.

_____.1978. Ethiopian bloomery iron and the significance of inclusion analysis in iron studies. *Journal of Historical Metallurgy* 12:63–87.

Trojer, F. 1963. *The oxidic crystal phases of inorganic industrial products.* Stuttgart: E. Schweizerbart'sche Verlagsbuchandlung.

Tylecote, R. F. 1962. *Metallurgy in archaeology,* p. 348. London: Arnold.

Wakayama, Homatsu. 1974. *Kinko Tsuba Ko Mei To Kakaku.*

White, John R. 1980. Historic blast furnace slags: archaeological and metallurgical analysis. *Journal of Historical Metallurgy* 14:55–64.

Whitmore, Florence E., and Young, William J. 1970. Applications of the laser microprobe and electron microprobe in the analysis of platiniridium inclusions in gold. In *Applications of science on examination of works of art (II)*, pp. 88–95. Boston: Museum of Fine Arts.

Wingrove, Joyce. 1970. Identification of iron oxides. London: *Journal of the Iron & Steel Institute* 208:258–64.